Law and the State

NEW HORIZONS IN LAW AND ECONOMICS

Series editors: Gerrit De Geest, *University of Ghent and University of Antwerp, Belgium and University of Utrecht, The Netherlands*; Roger Van den Bergh, *University of Rotterdam and University of Utrecht, The Netherlands*; and Thomas S. Ulen, *University of Illinois at Urbana-Champaign, USA*.

The application of economic ideas and theories to the law and the explanation of markets and public economics from a legal point of view is recognised as one of the most exciting developments in both economics and the law. This important series is designed to make a significant contribution to the development of law and economics.

The main emphasis is on the development and application of new ideas. The series provides a forum for original research in areas such as criminal law, civil law, labour law, corporate law, family law, regulation and privatization, tax, risk and insurance and competition law. International in its approach it includes some of the best theoretical and empirical work from both well-established researchers and the new generation of scholars.

Titles in the series include:

The Economics of Harmonizing European Law
Edited by Alain Marciano and Jean-Michel Josselin

Post-Chicago Developments in Antitrust Law
Edited by Antonio Cucinotta, Robert Pardolesi and Roger Van den Berg

From Economic to Legal Competition
New Perspectives on Law and Institutions in Europe
Edited by Alain Marciano and Jean-Michel Josselin

New Perspectives on Economic Crime
Edited by Hans Sjögren and Göran Skogh

Law, Economics and Cyberspace
The Effects of Cyberspace on the Economic Analysis of Law
Niva Elkin-Koren and Eli M. Salzberger

Games and Public Administration
The Law and Economics of Regulation and Licensing
George von Wangenheim

Law and the State
A Political Economy Approach
Edited by Alain Marciano and Jean-Michel Josselin

Law and the State
A Political Economy Approach

Edited by

Alain Marciano

University of Reims Champagne Ardenne (OMI-EDJ), GREQAM- CNRS and Institut d'Economie Publique (IDEP), France

Jean-Michel Josselin

University of Rennes 1 and CREM-CNRS, France

NEW HORIZONS IN LAW AND ECONOMICS

Edward Elgar
Cheltenham, UK • Northampton, MA, USA

© Alain Marciano and Jean-Michel Josselin 2005

All rights reserved. No part of this publication may be reproduced, stored in a retrieval system or transmitted in any form or by any means, electronic, mechanical or photocopying, recording, or otherwise without the prior permission of the publisher.

Published by
Edward Elgar Publishing Limited
Glensanda House
Montpellier Parade
Cheltenham
Glos GL50 1UA
UK

Edward Elgar Publishing, Inc.
136 West Street
Suite 202
Northampton
Massachusetts 01060
USA

A catalogue record for this book
is available from the British Library

ISBN 1 84376 800 3

Printed and bound in Great Britain by MPG Books Ltd, Bodmin, Cornwall

Contents

List of contributors   vii
Acknowledgements   ix

1 Introduction   Making sense of the state: a political economy approach   1
Jean-Michel Josselin and Alain Marciano

PART I   HOW TO SHAPE A DEMOCRATIC STATE: THE INFORMATIONAL CONSTRAINT

2 Schumpeterian political economy and Downsian public choice: alternative economic theories of democracy   21
Michael Wohlgemuth

3 The effects of cyberspace on the economic theory of the state   58
Eli M. Salzberger and Niva Elkin-Koren

4 Explaining the great divergence: medium and message on the Eurasian land mass, 1700–1850   100
Leonard Dudley

5 George Orwell and his cold wars: truth and politics   121
Manfred J. Holler

6 Measuring terrorism   142
Bruno S. Frey and Simon Luechinger

PART II   HOW TO CONTROL A DEMOCRATIC STATE: THE LEGAL CONSTRAINT

7 Rule of law, finance and economic development: cross-country evidence   185
Stefan van Hemmen and Frank H. Stephen

8 Judicial independence as a necessary component of the rule of law: preliminary insights and economic consequences   242
Stefan Voigt

9 Democracy, citizens and judicial power: do judges contribute to democracy? 269
   Sophie Harnay

10 Law, justice and republic: the French republican model of judicial regulation 283
   Christian Barrère

11 Should non-expert courts control expert administrations? 310
   Georg von Wangenheim

PART III THE STATE AT WORK: REGULATION AND PUBLIC POLICIES UNDER INFORMATIONAL AND LEGAL CONSTRAINTS

12 *Pelle sub agnina latitat mens saepe lupina:* copyright in the marketplace 335
   Giovanni B. Ramello

13 Competition in banking: switching costs and the limits of antitrust enforcement 358
   Donatella Porrini and Giovanni B. Ramello

14 Old Master paintings: price formation and public policy implications 381
   Paolo Figini and Laura Onofri

15 Living it off or living it down: the economics of disinvestments 399
   Jürgen Backhaus

Index 405

Contributors

Jürgen Backhaus University of Erfurt, Germany.

Christian Barrère University of Reims Champagne Ardenne, France.

Leonard Dudley University of Montreal, Canada.

Niva Elkin-Koren University of Haifa, Israel.

Paolo Figini University of Bologna, Italy.

Bruno S. Frey University of Zurich, Switzerland.

Sophie Harnay University of Reims Champagne Ardenne, France.

Manfred J. Holler University of Hamburg, Germany.

Jean-Michel Josselin University of Rennes 1, France.

Simon Luechinger University of Zurich, Switzerland.

Alain Marciano University of Reims Champagne Ardenne, France.

Laura Onofri University of Bologna, Italy.

Donatella Porrini University of Studi di Milano, Italy.

Giovanni B. Ramello University of Cattenao, Italy.

Eli M. Salzberger University of Haifa, Israel.

Frank H. Stephen University of Strathclyde, United Kingdom.

Stefan Voigt University of Kassel, Germany.

Georg von Wangenheim Max-Planck-Institute for Research into Economic Systems, Evolutionary Economics Unit, Germany.

Michael Wohlgemuth Walter Eucken Institute, Germany.

Acknowledgements

This book evolved out of two Corsica Law and Economics Workshops, respectively held in Marseilles (May 2003) and in Reims (May 2004). Scholars invited to give papers were given *carte blanche*, but were asked to revise their contributions after the conference discussions. Here we present a selection of those papers. The chapters reflect current research on the subject, unified by the same concern, namely understanding the law and economics dimension of European integration. They also show a diversity of opinions that we did not try to smooth. Underlying many contributions are strong preferences as to what the *jus commune* will be or should be in the future. This gives a wide-ranging approach to a most important subject.

The 4th and 5th Corsica Law and Economics Workshops were sponsored by the Institut d'Economie Publique and the University of Reims Champagne Ardenne (OMI-EDJ). We thank the local organizers and, in particular Maryse Boulay, Danièle Durieu and Monique Demarne for their help.

1. Introduction   Making sense of the state: a political economy approach

Jean-Michel Josselin and Alain Marciano

1   INTRODUCTION

Even if mainly devoted to private law, the law and economics literature has certainly not neglected constitutional issues. In particular, the intricate relation between law and the state has been frequently analysed, either from a positive point of view or for normative purposes. Thus, vexed questions were raised as to the necessity to ground the legitimacy of the state on rules of law or, reciprocally, as to the need to justify law in the state. To provide tentative and partial answers to these questions, the different chapters that constitute this book employ the specific tools of a political economy approach. These will of course relate to the standard programme of constrained maximization, but in which 'institutions matter'. The first step is then the objective function. When organizing the seminars leading to this book, we manifestly did not have to be specific about an attachment to a democratic state as an objective. Strikingly, the contributors dealing with this foundational concern (how to shape a democratic state) all focused on the constraint which delineates the democratic state, namely the informational constraint. Publicity of law and of decisions, transmission, manipulation and creation of information are some of the many facets that contribute to the delicate balance between democracy as freedom and democracy as order (Part I). In this respect, law and lawfulness prove to be media as strong as they are to be handled carefully. Indeed, legal rules play a similar role as information, being in the same way the key to the foundation of a democratic state. However, the role of law and the institutional position of judges, crucially depend on how the democratic state is organized. In other words, the way democracy is defined influences the role that legal rules play (or have to play). All the contributions of the book that are dedicated to this question converge towards this necessary condition (Part II). Building on these pillars, the state can then make incursions into the markets. The control over the institutions governing competition requires a fine tuning of legal regulations. Public policies are to be interpreted here in the light of the first two parts of the book. The state can put forward and implement regulations in order to improve the circulation of relevant information on markets. It must do that under constraints meant to prevent incursions from becoming invasions. These usually self-imposed constraints on the domain of state intervention will have to serve Pareto improvements to the economy (Part III).

2 HOW TO SHAPE A DEMOCRATIC STATE: THE INFORMATIONAL CONSTRAINT

'Good' information can certainly enhance democratic virtues. 'Bad' information obviously impedes political competition. How do law, and more generally institutions, convey this informational constraint? What is the contribution of political economy to the definition of what is good or bad in this respect?

2.1 Enhancing Democracy through Competitive Information

To build and shape a democracy demands that constitutional and post-constitutional safeguards be carefully devised. In this respect, the status of information is of the utmost importance. Let us first take the example of a basic action in a democracy: voting is indeed a founding decision for individuals participating in a forum of collective action. In Chapter 2, Michael Wohlgemuth demonstrates how even at this stage the informational constraint does matter. There may have been a fallacy in considering Schumpeter as one of the founders of 'public choice'. The latter mostly rests on the Downsian spatial voting model, where citizens' preferences are given on the ideological space. Politicians adapt to it and, beyond rent-seeking and bureaucratic deviations, they more or less carry the will of the representative voter: 'However, by attaching high standards of rationality to political actors, by treating political issues and preferences as given and by modelling political competition as a state of affairs in which politicians passively adapt to a given majority will, much of public choice remains ironically close to rationalistic and idealistic traditions' (Wohlgemuth, this volume). This Hobbesian view of the likely Pareto improvement associated with a democratic state is dramatically challenged by the two hypotheses of the Schumpeterian theory. Here, political leadership replaces the search for the optimal location on the ideological space: 'democracy is competition for leadership and not for given voter distributions' (Wohlgemuth, this volume). The role of political leadership is all the more important that, as far as individual behaviours are concerned, Schumpeter departs from one of the core assumptions in 'standard' public choice theory, thereby anticipating recent developments in psychology, in assuming that the level of rationality typically drops when citizens enter the political field. To use a game-theoretic analogy, let us suggest that the Downsian message is carried out under assumptions of *perfect* information (the vote-maximizing politician is a 'position taker' as he/she would be a price taker on usual markets) or *imperfect* information (probabilistic voting being an example). On the contrary, the Schumpeterian vision of politics could be one of *incomplete* information where the types of voter are unknown. Political entrepreneurship then not only consists in discovering them, but also affects the formation of the individuals' political opinions. In other words, by creating political issues, entrepreneurs endogenize types of voters.

From this perspective, democracy is no longer viewed as a means to reach an equilibrium but has rather to be considered as a process in which individuals learn from others. As a consequence, truth emerges from and evolves through the confrontation of individual opinions; it thus will not be easily circumscribed (we shall come back to this later). On the other hand, the plasticity of individual beliefs (amounting to irrationality?) allows a politician to shape and select political preferences best suited for his/her own purposes. Much attention is thus paid to possible manipulation of information (Wohlgemuth 2002).

This view not only challenges the standard public choice approach, it is also provocative to our Cartesian minds! Nevertheless, the gap between the two visions may be bridged by recalling that the rationalistic and idealistic tradition can also account for endogenous types of voters. Although Chapter 3, by Eli Salzberger and Niva Elkin-Koren mainly aims at understanding the influence of the cyberspace information revolution on the theory of the state, it also provides a valuable reminder of a quite neglected aspect of the rational theory of the state. Thomas Hobbes, John Locke and John Rawls have taken on most of the theoretical landscape, leaving Rousseau ([1762] 1992) largely outside the economic interpretation of the state. This lapse is unfortunate since it could provide a track of reconciliation between the Austrian and Downsian views: 'Economic analysis à la Rousseau assumes that individual preferences are not exogenous, but endogenous to the political process. In other words, the difference between the General Will and the sum of the wills of the individuals can be presented as the result of changes of preferences, from self-regarding towards more cooperative, other-regarding and less conflicting preferences' (Salzberger and Elkin-Koren, this volume). Of course, as Salzberger and Elkin-Koren admit, the economic analysis of Rousseau still has to be carried out. Let us add that it may have significant consequences for constitutional economics.

What will remain of national constitutional law if cyberspace develops in non-territorial collective entities? Will the principle of personality supplant the principle of territoriality? Communication technology provides a means to easier consensus and enhances political participation. Cyberspace as a medium of information may 'compensate for the shift from unanimity to majoritarianism and from direct democracy to representative democracy' (Salzberger and Elkin-Koren, this volume). The relaxed informational constraint puts the deliberating process to the forefront; institutions and preferences would then be outputs of political participation. Quite strikingly, we are not very far from the French revolutionary debates on the relationship between democracy and participative education (Baczcko 1982).[1] Individual preferences are once again endogenous to the political process, but in a Cartesian and not Schumpeterian framework.

As demonstrated by Salzberger and Elkin-Koren, the relationship between information technology and democracy is of utmost importance if one wishes to understand the evolution of institutions, and in particular constitutional law. It remains to further interrogate the interplay between values, information technology and the law. Salzberger and Elkin-Koren leave this to others, and Leonard Dudley takes on the task in Chapter 4. The idea is to get a long-term view on the spatial pattern of innovations. Stylized facts are quite impressive. The concentration of scientific discoveries between 1700 and 1850 in a handful of European countries (plus the United States) questions the role of geography and institutions. It can also be illuminated, and this is the heart of Dudley's thesis, by the container and the content of information. What is at stake is the explanation of the striking development gap between the different regions of Eurasia over the period. Communication technology is envisaged here as a combination of a medium (vernacular languages at that time, cyberspace dialect now?) and of a message (ideas competing as a result of political entrepreneurship *à la* Schumpeter or as the consequence of educative democracy *à la* Rousseau). If we go back to the problem of values, communication technology in its two dimensions produces constitutional systems which either help innovations thrive or smother them inexorably. We leave it to the reader to discover the extent to which differentiated development can be explained by the intertwined influences of medium and message. Lessons from the previous two chapters may hint at the benefits of standardized ways of communication. This is reinforced by the views of Hobbes and Rawls as far as the publicity of law is concerned (Josselin and Marciano 1995). However, this common or shared knowledge through the medium should not arise at the expense of the message. Competition on the market for ideas provides fertile soil for innovations to flourish. Standardization should not suppress the competitive qualities of free communication. Cyberspace must remain under close scrutiny to ensure that competing messages still circulate.

In game-theoretic terms, Dudley shows that having the relevant information technology helps us both to avoid falling into chicken or prisoner's dilemma games and to reach a framework of an assurance game. This is also consistent with Rousseau's stag-hunt game, in which coordination of information as well as confidence in other players are sufficient conditions for Pareto improvements (Rousseau [1754] 1990). Freedom of speech thus seems to be a most important individual prerogative that may even have to be guaranteed by constitutional safeguards (Josselin and Marciano 2002a). But should we systematically take its value for granted?

2.2 Endangering Democracy through Strategic Information

When discussing the Schumpeterian message, we mentioned that the status of truth in politics is far from straightforward. This is the object of inquiry of Chapter 5, by Manfred Holler. Truth-telling, personal opinion, secrets, personal integrity in the face of public opinion, we are here again facing the dilemma of democracy as freedom and democracy as order. Holler builds on the dramatic history of George Orwell and his Cold War reverses. Game theory offers operational tools that help understand how individual reputation can be shaped by public opinion makers. All this would not be very interesting if the citizen involved – here Orwell and his collaboration with the Foreign Office's Information Research Department – were a standard player in a game of complete information. We pointed out before that politics is about incomplete information where the types of voter are unknown. When judging Orwell, public opinion makers also run their strategies in a world of incomplete information. The term 'judging' is intendedly ambiguous since '[t]he evaluation of public figures expresses social values and gives orientation to society and for this reason many legal systems contain, on the one hand, rules designed to protect the reputation of such personalities, but on the other permit the public dissemination of information about them and their private life' (Holler, this volume). The real Orwell may remain hidden but public opinion is provided with a revealed type consistent with collective beliefs.

The game-theoretic approach emphasizes the strategic nature of information, more precisely the strategic nature of its construction. If democracy is to build on discussion and debate, on progressively shared knowledge, then the strategic nature of truth may endanger it. If we add to the picture some propaganda combined with preference falsification (Kuran 1995), for instance, one may soon end up with a messy political landscape which stresses the pitfalls associated with endogenous locations of individuals in the ideological space. Political entrepreneurs and opinion makers may obviously get some profit by exploiting 'primitive' citizens (Schumpeter, quoted by Wohlgemuth, this volume). This positive account of the political arena is quite frightening, and the ensuing gloom may explain why on the normative side of the problem, one may wish to stick to the idealistic and rationalistic tradition of public choice. Holler's analysis nevertheless shows, in positive terms, how accurate the strategic approach is.

Leaving the Cold War behind us, information and opinion are again at stake in the case of what Bruno Frey and Simon Luechinger, in Chapter 6, label the curse of our times, namely terrorism. And if we leave history to study current events, we nevertheless face problems similar in many respects. Information in a framework of terrorism has many related dimensions: first of all, information about what terrorism is, what it costs to whom, and what its impact on individual utilities can be. To this must be added information about the consequences it has on the formation of opinion, both in the media and in the political arena. Hence the attempts at measurement that would help us understand in the most objective terms what the costs and benefits (if any) or losses of terrorism are. 'In any case, government policy against terrorism involves costs. It is therefore necessary to know the costs imposed on the people by terrorist activities. Only then can government decide what resources should be mustered to deal with terrorism. If the utility loss is underestimated, the government tends to undertake too little, and if it is overestimated, the government tends to overreact and activate too many resources' (Frey and Luechinger, this volume).

In the face of likely strategic behaviours with regard to the construction of information (exemplified in Holler's chapter), the question of measurement is all the more important in that it may help reduce informational biases, say between government and citizens. A straightforward instance would be the case of a political leader overestimating a threat in order to shift the attention of voters from problems other than terrorism (for example, unemployment or public deficits). Frey and Luechinger survey the various methods (contingent valuation, happiness functions and so on) offered by economic theory and they assess how they are or could be applied. Whatever their merits and drawbacks, those methods remain unconnected with the political arena, hence the proposition to put more emphasis on directly democratic procedures, like referenda, whenever fighting terrorism is involved. In many countries, this would require constitutional reform, and a shift of value from representative government to collective decision making in the political forum. As an innovative medium of communication, cyberspace may help to achieve this. It nevertheless remains to assess whether the message maintains its competitive properties and does not fall into the hands of political entrepreneurs or public opinion makers who could possibly display strategic behaviours.[2]

The informational constraint obviously shapes and delineates state prerogatives. Whenever information displays competitive properties, it enhances the goal and scope of democratic institutions; if it covers or allows strategic behaviours, then the 'true' purpose of democracy is somewhat blurred. In both cases, the question of control is relevant. This is manifest in the second case but no less necessary in the first one. Delegating power means entrusting part of individual natural rights to the sovereign. That the latter may be democratically elected does not change the nature of the 'delegation dilemma', as we may label it, although it may affect its magnitude. Let us see how the dilemma relates to democracy and legal rules.

3 HOW TO CONTROL A DEMOCRATIC STATE: THE LEGAL CONSTRAINT

Delegating power from the citizens to the state cannot be conceived without constraints that will help both develop and contain public prerogatives in reasonable limits. To reach this goal, to delineate the scope of government, legal rules are an undisputable theoretical prerequisite, but how are they worked out in practice? How do judges, experts and administrators contribute to the enhancement of democracy? Now, the legal system is part of a larger institutional framework. Therefore, as the developments of this part show, the practical answers envisaged and proposed to these questions depend on the institutions within which they are raised.

3.1 Independence versus Discretion: Constitutional Regimes versus Monist Democracies

Any individual endowed with the right and capacity to exercise power also benefits from the possibility to promote, or to utilize, rules to favour private interests. This is the delegation dilemma. The problem thus defined characterizes the paradoxical nature of power rather than reveals the flaws of a specific institutional structure. However, institutions are not without influence on the practical solutions that can be offered to solve the dilemma. From this perspective, it is important to keep in mind a usual distinction, recalled by Sophie Harnay in Chapter 9, between 'monist' and 'dualist' (or constitutional) democracies.[3] The former type of democracy, thus named because of the uniqueness of the source of power, focuses on the legitimacy of public decisions. It is thus assumed that power has to rest, ultimately, in the hands of the citizens or in those of their direct representatives, the elected politicians. In this respect, judges, being non-elected agents and thus having received no prerogatives from the citizens, have to remain under the control of the elected politicians. Thus, the political review of judicial decisions is viewed as possible and also as desirable. But, and this is stressed as an important limit to monist democratic states, the increase in legitimacy of the decisions could be compensated by possible abuse of power. The delegation dilemma indeed seems particularly difficult to avoid when power rests in the hands of agents that no one appears to be in a position to control.

An alternative to monist democracies, dualist democracies or constitutional regimes insist on the necessity of controlling elected agents. 'Dualism' is thus used to designate regimes in which power, although having a unique source, is none the less separated and divided among different institutions. Separation and division of power ensure institutional competition but also guarantees that the same rules equally bind citizens and the government. A constitutional regime is thus based on the rule of law. It is then assumed that, under this condition, the arbitrary use of power by elected politicians cannot but be restricted. Then, dualism, as noted by Ackerman, views 'the courts as an essential part of a well-ordered democratic regime . . . the courts serve democracy by protecting the hard-won principles of a mobilized citizenry against erosion by political elites who have failed to gain broad and deep popular support for their innovations' (1998, p. 10). In other words, a constitutional regime crucially depends on the possible judicial review of political choices. That judges are non-elected agents, and thus able to escape the control of the citizens, may generate losses in terms of legitimacy which are compensated by the gains that result from the containment of the delegation dilemma.

The possible gains due to an efficient control of the state are not only organizational but can also be evaluated in economic terms. From this perspective, in Chapter 7, Stefan van Hemmen and Frank Stephen survey the literature measuring the impact of legal rules and institutions on economic development. The evidence they provide is important since it sheds light on the importance of measurement when assessing the positive properties of alternative theories of the state and its organization. In this respect, their chapter is a matching piece to the analysis by Frey and Luechinger (the same remark can be applied to the chapter by Voigt, as will be seen later). Van Hemmen and Stephen analyse how financial laws and enforcement mechanisms both influence the development of financial markets, which in turn influences economic growth. Among the elements put forward in their presentation, one can mention the independence of courts and the weakness of state power. Therefore, an independent judiciary seems to be a decisive condition for economic development.

A similar argument as to the economic role of an independent judiciary is at the basis of Stefan Voigt's analysis in Chapter 7. In fact, in the first place, Voigt clearly, although implicitly, places his analysis within the framework of a constitutional regime. Then, building on authors such as Immanuel Kant or Friedrich Hayek, he argues that the rule of law is the basic condition for a just and efficient democratic – by which he means a *dualist* democratic – system. Judicial independence then appears as a practical institutional provision matching the theoretical prerequisite of a rule of law. Therefore, judicial independence has to be assessed and measured as precisely as possible in order to understand how it influences economic growth. However, the task is as important as it is difficult. Noting the discontent as to the standard criteria used to evaluate judicial independence, Voigt then suggests making the relationship between judicial independence and the rule of law empirically accessible by introducing two indicators. He proposes to distinguish between *de jure* independence, acknowledged by the constitutional documents, and an effectively respected *de facto* independence. The empirical studies, of which he presents the results, show that while *de jure* judicial independence does not have an impact on economic growth, *de facto* judicial independence positively influences real GDP growth per capita. To sum up Voigt's argument, judicial independence is a source of economic growth because it ensures that everyone will be bounded by the same legal rules. This argument confirms what is put forward by van Hemmen and Stephen in their analysis: the role of informal institutions is as important as the role of formal institutions even if 'more effort is needed to identify which formal (structure of the judicial system) and informal (levels of trust in the society) factors produce high enforcement' (van Hemmen and Stephen, this volume).

Nevertheless, a rule of law regime may suffer from certain flaws. Indeed, such regimes function correctly under the explicit condition that no one is in a monopolist position, providing him/her with the possibility of controlling the provision of law; that is, if and only if judges do not replace politicians as monopolists. This is acceptable from the perspective of the bottom-up logic of a legal system in which judges are not considered as the creators of legal rules. The role of judges then consists in clarifying imprecise and ambiguous rules in order to improve coordination among individuals. Within such legal systems, judges are assumed to act only as arbitrators whose task is to discover the rules resulting from the repeated interactions that take place between individuals. As arbitrators, judges therefore do not stand in the position of a monopolist, a central authority benefiting from coercive powers in the provision of law. They rather act *on behalf* of all the society members. As we have shown elsewhere (Josselin and Marciano 1995, forthcoming), the judge is the agent of the impartial spectator of the common law, in the sense given by Adam Smith and David Hume. Ormrod expresses a similar view when he notes the English predilection for the 'fantasy of the judge as a detached observer, reaching inevitably right conclusions by processes of impeccable logic, in conformity with the decisions of others' (1987, p. 125). This quotation gives a perfect summary of the virtues of a system based on the rule of law: being in the hands of 'detached observers', the rules are impersonal, general and are applied regardless of any specific circumstances. They are thus devoid of any arbitrary character. Now, there are many circumstances in which judicial decision making not only amounts to choosing a point from a set of given alternatives. There are indeed many circumstances in which, being in an 'open area' (to use Richard Posner's terms), judges are obliged to create rules because there is no rule to discover and no legal material to help them in rendering their decision. In other words, it seems impossible to envisage a legal system complete enough to avoid the manipulation of legal rules by the individuals effectively granted with the right to create them. This does not mean that judges – like elected politicians – are malevolent but they cannot be considered only as the impartial spectators of the common law (see also Josselin and Marciano 1997). This observation implies three different and complementary conclusions.

First, the fantasy of a system in which judges are only 'detached observers' is rather optimistic and cannot but be, as Voigt notes, an ideal difficult to actually reach. Second, even a regime based on the rule of law must envisage institutional provisions to control the behaviour of judges. Thus, as Voigt comments, beyond judicial independence, other criteria have to be respected: 'laws need to be general, abstract, and certain . . . procedural safeguards such as the prohibition of retroactive legislation, habeas corpus, proportionality and the like need to be in place. If all this is not the case, even a factually independent judiciary will not turn an arbitrary regime into one belonging to the family of rule of law regimes' (Voigt, this volume). Third, the vulnerability of a constitutional regime to the manipulation of rules by independent judges legitimates the comparison with a monist regime: are regimes in which political review of judicial choices is possible so vulnerable to delegation dilemmas? This question is at the core of Sophie Harnay's chapter.

Using the theoretical reference of Hans Kelsen, rather than that of Kant or Friedrich von Hayek, Harnay develops her analysis within the framework of a monist democracy. She thus assumes that a legal decision can always be replaced by a political choice because the norms produced by (democratically) elected politicians are higher than any other, in particular legal, norm. Therefore, *de jure* judicial independence is not guaranteed. Harnay develops an analysis which parallels Voigt's argument. Using a game-theoretic model, she demonstrates that discretionary power, that is *de facto* independence, is possible even in a regime which like, monist democracies, does not guarantee *de jure* independence. In fact, judges benefit from a discretionary power which is induced by the institutional structure.[4] The practical consequence of this situation is that judges utilize their discretionary power to protect the interests of the citizens. An illustration is then provided showing how French administrative judges, a particularly good example of dependent judges, systematically tend to favour citizens. Interestingly, a system in which judges remain structurally dependent from political decision makers has the same virtues as a dualist, constitutional regime. This is certainly one of the reasons explaining the not so bad ranking of France in Voigt's evaluations.

3.2 The Political Role of Administrations, Experts and Judicial Power

The models of democracy discussed in the two preceding chapters relate to contrasted modes of social regulation. Rule of law regimes are associated with spontaneous social orders and regulation is assumed to depend on market criteria: The customary foundation of rules is assumed to avoid the arbitrary and discretionary use of power by politicians. By contrast, monist democracies build upon the tenets of social contract and trust the criteria of political regulation. Thus, as said earlier and described in Harnay's chapter, the promoters of monist democracies state that, in spite of the hierarchy which exists between political and legal norms, judges none the less utilize their discretionary power to control politicians and defend the citizens' rights. This particular form of social regulation, based on a mix of legal and political rules, is part of a heritage typical of the French institutional structure. These characteristics have been incorporated in the French democratic state through a progressive accumulation of legal and political reforms, the most important of which was the creation of the Civil Code at the beginning of the eighteenth century (see Josselin and Marciano 2002b) or the reform of the Council of State at the end of the nineteenth century (Harnay and Marciano 2001). In Chapter 10, Christian Barrère interprets this model of regulation with regard to the principles of the French Revolution and the social contract theories. In a normative analysis which complements the positive developments made by Voigt or Harnay, Barrère not only stresses the role that judges have to play in social regulation, he also states that the criteria which guide judicial organization ought to be different from and larger than those used by market regulation. To some extent, Barrère goes beyond the usual distinction between constitutional regimes and monist democracies. Indeed, while he explicitly rejects market-based regulation, he implicitly refuses the pre-eminence of political criteria over those of judges. Judicial regulation would lie beyond market and political regulation. Then, we are left with a crucial question: where does the legitimacy of judicial choices come from? Barrère argues that judges must to be trusted as 'wise persons, deciding in the name of the French people' (this volume). Thus, *wisdom* legitimates judicial decision making. Although the argumentation developed by Barrère does not make reference to that literature, it is certainly possible to refer to wisdom as a kind of intrinsic motivation upon which one can rely to justify judicial choices. It none the less remains that no one can ascertain the rightness and the efficiency of these decisions since wisdom conveys self-justification. Let us then focus on efficiency.

Wisdom may not mean expertise. Judges may well contribute to democracy and promote order by improving social regulation, but their decisions may not be efficient for all that. Are judges able to separate welfare-improving from welfare-reducing projects? Or, to put the question in more precise terms: is the possible judicial control of the decisions made by public administration economically valuable for the society? This is the issue analysed by Georg von Wangenheim in Chapter 10. This, once again, is related to the delegation of decision making in a democracy. Indeed, in von Wangenheim's chapter, the question amounts to the economic legitimacy to authorize the substitution of decisions made by non-elected experts with choices of democratically elected non-experts. The model thus proposed leads to the conclusion that, even if courts have less expertise than public administrations and even if courts are more likely to approve welfare-reducing projects and to reject welfare-enhancing projects, the judicial control of administrative decisions may be welfare improving. Two reasons can be mentioned as explanations for this result. First, the lack of expertise of judges may be compensated by the information they infer from the appeal process. Second, potential judicial review plays the role of an incentive mechanism on administrators, thus inducing them to choose a better project in the first place. Even if they are not 'detached observers', judges promote more efficient public decisions, *ex ante* through incentives towards public administration and *ex post* through information revealed during the process of judgment.

In market-based economies, revelation of information rests on (imperfectly) competitive patterns of interactions. These interactions involve individuals as well as judicial and governmental institutions. Whether the political market works at equilibrium (the public choice approach) or as a search process (the Schumpeterian approach) does not fundamentally change the imperfect but competitive nature of the norms upon which law is organized.

In a planned economy, the legal constraint would be easily endogenized by the power in place. The latter will use it to serve its own purposes. In market-based economies, however, the legal framework remains a constraint instead of becoming an instrument. The democratic state must then build on 'good' information and on the rule of law to serve the purposes of the citizens.

4 THE STATE AT WORK: REGULATION AND PUBLIC POLICIES UNDER INFORMATIONAL AND LEGAL CONSTRAINTS

State intervention on markets can take many forms and obey various motives, from Pareto improvements to the promotion of private interests. Part III focuses on regulation and public policies for which informational and legal constraints are 'binding'.

4.1 Incursion into or Invasion of Markets: Fine Tuning Public Regulation

As shown by the preceding discussion, most of the contributions to this volume consider 'information' as a key element for a democracy. Therefore, unsurprisingly, misused information may shake the foundations of a democratic state. The necessity of avoiding a strategic and opportunistic use of information then provides a first justification for public intervention. Besides a correct *use* of information, the proper functioning of a democracy also requires a correct (not to say optimal) *amount* of information. For instance, economic development, as Dudley showed in Chapter 4, depends on an efficient informational technology. Moreover, the capacity of judges to promote just ('wise', in Barrère's terms) and welfare-improving projects depends on the information they have, as is stressed in von Wangenheim's chapter. If one adds the frequent statement that information is a public good, there may be another point in favour of state intervention, in order to guarantee an optimal provision of information. Hence, the not so unusual arguments among economists that the provision of information *per se* should be submitted to public regulation.[5]

Among the rules aimed at organizing the provision of information, copyright laws are usually put forward – in particular by lawyer economists – as necessary. The argument is that in the absence of property rights on ideas or information, individuals are denied the basic incentives they need to innovate. In other words, public regulation should be justified as a means to promote competition in the provision of information. Although correct, this statement also seems partial. Indeed, and this is the argumentation developed by Giovanni Ramello in Chapter 12, copyright legislation gives birth to many unexpected and overlooked side-effects. Thus, Ramello questions the standard analysis about the economic legitimacy of copyright laws in showing that these laws tend to negatively affect the functioning of the two sides of the market, limiting the demand and promoting the concentration of information in the hands of a limited number of individuals. Hence, the seemingly justified though radical conclusion: 'copyright today does not seem able to pursue the public goals that justify its existence, although it certainly does succeed in serving private interests. The former are, at best, manipulated in order to achieve the latter' (Ramello, this volume). Therefore, in contrast to what is usually assumed, copyright law would not promote competition and economic efficiency. One could envisage a second type of justification to possible control on the provision of information, namely organizational efficiency or the stability of social order. From this perspective, legal scholars as well as many economists have insisted upon the necessary regulation of information in order to avoid a possible decrease in the quality of information and the subsequent threats to social order. Hence there is a possible trade-off between two seemingly contradictory aspects of regulation, stability and competition: rules that promote stability are frequently detrimental to competition.

Public regulation in the banking sector faces a similar problem. This is the issue discussed by Donatella Porrini and Giovanni Ramello in Chapter 13. Their analysis starts from the particularly vivid tension which exists in the regulation policy in the banking sector between the promotion of stability and that of competition. Historically, *antitrust* rules in the banking sector have been shaped in order to obey the demands of stability, 'relegating competition to second place' (Porrini and Ramello, this volume). Therefore, 'the banking market becomes extremely rigid on the supply side and structurally not equipped for a competitive orientation, and banks come to occupy a privileged position *vis-à-vis* governments that – to a greater or lesser extent, depending on the countries and the situations – enables them to sidestep the antitrust authorities' (ibid.). Therefore, according to the authors, it seems impossible to reconcile stability and competition under the heading of standard antitrust banking legislation. Their argument is that regulation of banking activities from the perspective of the supply side must not be abandoned but has to be completed by rules which could favour competition through the demand side of the market, by enhancing consumer mobility. Porrini and Ramello then suggest that this objective could be reached by reducing the switching costs that currently restrict the mobility of consumers between different banks.

Regulation of information is thus at the heart of market regulation. Public policies nevertheless must make sure that such interventions do not generate strategic rather than competitive information. This responsibility must be borne not only for current and immediate situations, but also across generations, which we shall consider now.

4.2 Art and Heritage: The Social Contrivance of State Intervention

We have already made a number of incursions into history but without really taking into account the simple fact that 'each and every today is followed by a tomorrow'. In other words, we have not yet taken into account the generational and hence intergenerational nature of a number of public policies. The previous quotation is from Samuelson (1958, p. 482) and it works as a preamble to his now standard result according to which the first theorem of welfare economics does not hold in overlapping generations models. Money or the social contract are thus ways of ensuring 'collective collusion' in order to guarantee that a minimal link does exist from one generation to another. As is clear from the last two chapters of this book, preservation of patrimonial resources appear to sometimes require public intervention (Chapter 14 by Paolo Figini and Laura Onofri) or avoid it (Chapter 15 by Jürgen Backhaus) in order to transmit our heritage to the next generations.

Figini and Onofri examine the market for Old Master paintings. Using the hedonistic methodology, they identify the shadow prices of the characteristic of these art objects and further consider the role of the policy maker in the regulation of such a specific market. Faced with an instant demand that in some occasions will not hesitate to use illegal means (and take advantage of a flexible budget constraint), the regulator may be tempted to use law in order to pre-empt art objects. Purchase (legal or illegal) by private amateurs would indeed deprive future generations of the public good properties of art. The legislator may then use the social contrivance of legal rules (the authors consider here the Italian case, which can easily be extended to other countries). For instance, private collectors are submitted to strict rules of notification. As is too often the case with public incursions into markets, the good intention paves the way to hidden information and black markets. The recommendation to open official markets to more competition and less regulation would indeed serve instant efficiency but may at the same time threaten intergenerational equity. The chapter thus illustrates the ambiguous role of information that was stressed previously in this volume. It also points to the fact that the provision of intergenerational public goods such as works of art requires the conception of a legal constraint which can at the same time be coercive and not lead to the withholding of information from official channels of circulation.

The inability of governments to preserve intergenerational public goods reflects the standard failure of competitive markets emphasized by Samuelson. The bitter irony conveyed by the last chapter of this volume serves as a reminder that the imperfection of competition should not lead us too far in condemning it. Backhaus indeed shows how a government can avowedly decide not to provide intergenerational public goods in order to reshape public opinion. In a way, this brings us back to a drastic extension of Holler's chapter. Backhaus takes the example of the extensive disinvestment in the former communist countries. The decay in historical heritage and historical sites should not be attributed to a sheer neglect in upkeep. The intended destruction of such public goods (and of all the shared knowledge they convey) has the purpose of 'uprooting' people, in order to make them 'fungible' in state socialist society. Once again, the informational (through propaganda) and legal (through nationalization) constraints can be as many weapons in the hands of governments whose goals are not necessarily those of the people they represent.

5 CONCLUSION

This volume demonstrates that the relationship between law and the state has two fundamental dimensions. The first one relates to the making of the information of both citizens and government. The second one deals with the legal structure that will help both develop and contain public prerogatives. The contributions to this book have given sometimes contrasted views on these two points. In many respects, however, they all point to the same requirement: that the ongoing making of democracy must retain information and legal structures as endogenous variables in the political process. As long as these variables are present in the collective forum, one may hope that the balance will be kept between democracy as order and democracy as freedom.

NOTES

1. Jean-Michel Josselin would like to thank Max Leguem for pointing out how the French revolutionary debates helped shape the reflection on the links (through education) between citizenship and rational behaviour.
2. Rousseau ([1755/1758] 1990) has a strikingly similar credo when he writes 'La patrie ne peut subsister sans la liberté, ni la liberté sans la vertu, ni la vertu sans les citoyens; vous aurez tout si vous formez des citoyens' (pp. 77–8): The Homeland cannot survive without liberty, nor liberty without virtue, nor virtue without citizens; you will have the whole if you educate the citizens (our translation).
3. The terms 'monist' and 'dualist' are borrowed from Ackerman (1998). To be more precise, the advocates of dualist democracies prefer using the label 'constitutional regimes' to insist on the role of the constitution as a binding rule and also to make clear the difference from a monist democratic regime where the delegation dilemma is unavoidable. As Voigt notes in his chapter, 'Logically, a rule of law constitution does not imply that the political system be democratic' (Voigt, this volume).
4. Or 'structure-induced discretionary power' (see, among others, Steunenberg 1996; Schmidtchen and Steunenberg 2003).

5. Interestingly, as noted by Ronald Coase, economists, even when they are favourably disposed towards market competition, tend to defend the necessity to regulate the provision of ideas.

REFERENCES

Ackerman, Bruce (1998), *We the People, Vol. 1. Foundations*, Cambridge, MA: Belknap Press.

Baczko, Bronislaw (1982), *Une éducation pour la démocratie* [*An Education for Democracy*], Paris: Garnier.

Harnay, Sophie and Alain Marciano (2001), 'Independence and judicial discretion in a dualist regime: the case of the French administrative judiciary', in Bruno Deffains and Thierry Kirat (eds), *Law and Economics in Civil Law Countries*, Greenwich, CT: JAI Press, pp. 243–55.

Josselin, Jean-Michel and Alain Marciano (1995), 'Constitutionalism and common knowledge: assessment and application to a future European constitution', *Public Choice*, **85**: 173–88.

Josselin, Jean-Michel and Alain Marciano (1997), 'The paradox of Leviathan: how to develop and contain the future European state', *European Journal of Law and Economics*, **4**: 5–21.

Josselin, Jean-Michel and Alain Marciano (2002a), 'Freedom of speech in a constitutional political economy perspective', *Journal of Economic Studies*, **29**: 324–31.

Josselin, Jean-Michel and Alain Marciano (2002b), 'The making of the French Civil Code: an economic interpretation', *European Journal of Law and Economics*, **14**: 193–203.

Josselin, Jean-Michel and Alain Marciano (forthcoming), 'Administrative law and economics', in Jürgen G. Backhaus (ed.), *The Elgar Companion to Law and Economics* (second revised and enlarged edition), Cheltenham, UK and Northampton, MA, USA: Edward Elgar.

Kuran, Timor (1995), *Private Truth, Public Lies*, Cambridge, MA: Harvard University Press.

Ormrod, R. (1987), 'Judicial discretion', *Current Legal Problems*, **40**.

Rousseau, Jean-Jacques ([1754] 1990), *Discours sur l'origine et les fondements de l'inégalité parmi les hommes* (Discourse on the origin and foundations of inequality among men), Paris: Garnier-Flammarion.

Rousseau, Jean-Jacques ([1755/58] 1990), *Sur l'économie politique; considérations sur le gouvernement de Pologne; projet de constitution pour la Corse* [*Discourse on Political Economy; Considerations on the Government of Poland; Constitutional Project for Corsica*], Paris: Garnier-Flammarion.

Rousseau, Jean-Jacques ([1762] 1992), *Du contrat social* (A treatise on the social contract), Paris: Garnier-Flammarion.

Samuelson, Paul (1958), 'An exact consumption-loan model of interest with or without the social contrivance of money', *Journal of Political Economy*, **66**: 467–82.

Schmidtchen, Dieter and Bernard Steunenberg (2003), 'European policymaking: an agency-theoretic analysis', in Alain Marciano and Jean-Michel Josselin (eds), *From Economic to Legal Competition: New Perspectives on Law and Institutions in Europe*, Cheltenham, UK and Northampton, MA, USA: Edward Elgar, pp. 143–63.

Steunenberg, Bernard (1996), 'Agent discretion, regulatory policymaking, and different institutional arrangements', *Public Choice*, **86**: 309–39.

Wohlgemuth, Michael (2002), 'Democracy and opinion falsification. Towards a new Austrian political economy', *Constitutional Political Economy*, **13**: 223–46.

PART I

How to shape a democratic state: the informational constraint

2. Schumpeterian political economy and Downsian public choice: alternative economic theories of democracy

Michael Wohlgemuth[*]

1 INTRODUCTION

> No one ever knew quite what to make of this neat saturnine man with a taste for dramatic prose and theatrical gestures. He was undoubtedly brilliant – but he was perplexing. (Robert L. Heilbronner 1953, 302 about Schumpeter)

Joseph Schumpeter is often regarded a pioneer, if not the founder of 'public choice' or the economics of politics.[1] Looking back at the development of mainstream public choice and looking closely at Schumpeter's own writings on democracy (and on the limits of static equilibrium analysis), this seems rather odd. There may be a hidden irony in the history of ideas which only a few observers[2] have uncovered in its manifold aspects.

Usually Schumpeter is only *mentioned* as a precursor, but hardly ever quoted in his own words. Already Downs (1957) in probably the most influential book in its field is a telling case when he states: 'Schumpeter's profound analysis of democracy forms the inspiration and foundation of our whole thesis, and our debt and gratitude to him are great indeed' (ibid., 29, fn. 11). In the whole thesis, however, Schumpeter is mentioned only twice with the same quote describing his general approach which regards social functions of politics as incidental byproducts of the competitive struggle for power and office. Schumpeter's core assertions on irrationality in politics and the vital role of political leadership are neither mentioned nor accepted. Nevertheless, it has become 'common to talk about the "Schumpeter–Downs" theory of democracy' (Udehn 1996, 18). It may be even more puzzling to find Wittman (1995, 23, fn. 5) paying equally unqualified tribute to Schumpeter in his *Myth of Democratic Failure* – one of the most outspoken denials of Schumpeter's view published so far.

This chapter will show that there are fundamental differences between Schumpeter's theory of democracy and mainstream public choice. The main motivation is not just to 'get the history of ideas right' but to address methodological issues which are increasingly recognized as uneasy foundations of public choice (such as bounded rationality in low-cost decision environments) and themes which have been largely neglected by public choice (such as political leadership and opinion formation). The intention is neither to praise nor to bury Schumpeter. It is to point at political economy issues that a progressing paradigm will need to address anyway and that it might as well address in a more or less Schumpeterian spirit.

Section 2 will present Schumpeter's 'Another theory of democracy' (1942/87, ch. xxii). In Section 3, I argue that both elements that are so crucial and dominant in Schumpeter's account – citizens' irrationality and politicians' leadership – are turned to their almost complete opposites in Downs's *Economic Theory of Democracy* (1957) and the ensuing theories of spatial voting. I also show that Downs's model of 'rational ignorance', while at first glance Schumpeterian, is strikingly different from Schumpeter's understanding of human nature in politics. In Section 4, two major issues on a research agenda of political economy are presented which may in fact claim Schumpeter as a precursor: a (cognitive) economics of bounded rationality in politics, and an (evolutionary) economics of political opinion formation. Section 5 is a short outlook. Again: this is not a Schumpeterian critique of the whole public choice enterprise. It is a confrontation of two assessments of democracy: the Schumpeterian view and the spatial voting model.

2 DEMOCRACY: SCHUMPETER'S VIEW, THE CLASSICAL DOCTRINE AND THE NEOCLASSICAL MODEL

> [O]ur chief troubles about the classical theory centered in the proposition that 'the people' hold a definite and rational opinion about every individual question and that they give effect to this opinion – in a democracy – by choosing 'representatives' who will see to it that that opinion is carried out. (Joseph A. Schumpeter 1942/87, 269)

Schumpeter's discussion of democracy (1942/87, part IV) complements his predictions that capitalist civilization is doomed (part II) and that socialist planning is the wave of the future (part III). With the benefit of hindsight, both predictions have failed so far – thus also eliminating the opportunity to test his claimed incompatibility of socialism and democracy (for example, ibid., 284). This is not the place to discuss these perplexing ideas. Irrespective of Schumpeter's daring predictions based on an unconventional blend of romantic conservatism and Marxist historicism, his account of the dynamics of capitalist systems and his unromantic model of democracy are of lasting value for modern economics. The question remains: to what extent does modern economics and, in our case, modern public choice, have Schumpeterian roots?

There are two common roots. First, modern public choice and Schumpeter largely share the same antagonists: those who explicitly or tacitly assume (a) that people act for the common good once they enter democratic decision making, and (b) that democratic government will maximize welfare once it knows (or is told by enlightened economists) how to do so. Second, most public choice scholars would have no problem in endorsing Schumpeter's (1942/87, 269) definition of democracy as a method rather than an ideal: 'the democratic method is that institutional arrangement for arriving at political decisions in which individuals acquire the power to decide by means of a competitive struggle for the people's vote'.

Very different from a mainstream public choice perspective, however, this 'competitive struggle' is driven by political leadership instead of political deference to given voter distributions. Schumpeter (ibid., 270) makes this point right at the outset:

> the theory embodied in this definition leaves all the room we may wish to have for the proper recognition of the vital fact of leadership . . . collectives act almost exclusively by accepting leadership – this is the dominant mechanism of practically any collective action which is more than a reflex.

Schumpeter adds that the 'classical' theory of democracy 'attributed to the electorate an altogether unrealistic degree of initiative which practically amounted to ignoring leadership' (ibid.). And what about the neoclassical economics of democracy?

In some respects, it reinstates more elements of the classical concept than Schumpeter's 'other theory of democracy' would allow. To be sure, modern economics of democracy departs from classical idealism by *not* starting with idealistic assumptions about the *motives* of political behaviour. However, by attaching high standards of rationality to political actors, by treating political issues and preferences as given and by modelling political competition as a state of affairs in which politicians passively adapt to a given majority will, much of public choice remains ironically close to rationalistic and idealistic traditions which linked democracy to given expressions of a *volonté générale*. As a result, much of the eighteenth-century ideal of democracy is merely revamped in equilibrium terms. Schumpeter (ibid., 250) defined the classical doctrine as 'that institutional arrangement for arriving at political decisions which realizes the common good by making the people itself decide issues through the election of individuals who are to assemble in order to carry out its will'.

Clearly, politicians in the public choice perspective do not assemble with the *intention* of carrying out the people's will. But, in most demand-driven models of democracy, their intention to maximize votes usually produces the *outcome* that they are forced to carry out the will of the median voter. And more often than not these results are interpreted as 'Pareto efficient' – welfare economists' favourite expression of 'the common good'.

Hence, there are reasons to suspect mainstream economics of democracy of being much more 'classical' in spirit, but not in style – whereas Schumpeter's argumentation is classic (less 'economic', more 'prosaic') in style, but his departure from the classical spirit is much more radical in fact. Two major aspects distinguish Schumpeter's theory of democracy most clearly from the classical doctrine *and* from the neoclassical model: political leadership and irrationality in politics.

2.1 Political Leadership

In Downsian spatial voting models (but also Chicago-style efficient political markets, Arrowian social choice, or most of contractarian constitutional economics), collectives act almost exclusively through politicians who take citizens' preferences as given. Just as in the neoclassical model of 'perfect' competition, prices and homogeneous goods are given and not created in the competitive process, preference distributions and issues are 'given' in most economics of politics. In both cases, entrepreneurship and the introduction of 'new combinations' have no room. Strictly adhering to the neoclassical pure logic of choice, public choice is barred from recognizing the Schumpeterian view that politicians act as entrepreneurs who create and change voters' preferences and opinions, or introduce new political products and forms of organization. Voter preferences, according to Schumpeter (1942/87, 282f.), 'are not the ultimate data of the process that produces government'. The electorate's choice 'does not flow from its own initiative but is being shaped, and the shaping of it is an essential part of the democratic process'. Hence, the 'psycho-technics of party management and party advertising, slogans and marching tunes, are not accessories. They are of the essence of politics. So is the political boss'.

These essential elements of the democratic process are hardly accepted even as accessories in spatial voting models which are clearly dominated by the view of politicians as passive retailers of given voter preferences. Contrast this again with Schumpeter's view that political leadership has 'only a distant relation, if any, with "seeing that the will of the people is carried out". . . Precisely in the best instances, the people are presented with results they never thought of and would not have approved in advance' (ibid., 278). Precisely these instances, by their very nature, cannot be accounted for in demand-driven equilibrium theories of the economics of politics.

2.2 Political Irrationality

If ever there was a common 'hard core' of the entire public choice paradigm, it is the assumption of rational conduct of all actors involved. And if ever there was a 'revolutionary' claim of public choice, it is to break with the notion of 'bifurcated man' who, as soon as he enters the political field, would display standards of behaviour which differ from those employed in market transactions. After all, that's what the *economics* of politics is all about: the universal application of the basic behavioural assumptions of *homo oeconomicus* (for example, Downs 1957, 4ff.; Buchanan 1972; Mueller 1989a, 1).

Schumpeter in fact denies this. In sharp contrast to what would later become the hard core of modern public choice – *and* to what he identifies as the 'requirements of the classical doctrine' (1942/87, 261) – he allows for a great deal of utter irrationality as a consequence of human nature and permissive circumstances, for example, when he argues, 'the typical citizen drops to a lower level of mental performance as soon as he enters the political field. He argues and analyzes in a way he would readily recognize as infantile within the sphere of his real interests. He becomes a primitive again' (ibid., 262).

Lack of mental effort, of rational calculation and consistent reasoning not only describe Schumpeter's citizen-voter who, as a 'member of an unworkable committee, the committee of the whole nation' (ibid., 261), has no impact on collective decision making and who can thus take a free ride on others' decision making (and must take a forced ride on collective outcomes). Lower levels of mental performance and pathologies of crowd behaviour even characterize Schumpeter's professional politicians, only in a somewhat milder form (see ibid., 257).

Schumpeter not only rejects using mainstream rationality assumptions for his study of politics. He also does not apply the *same* rationality assumptions for explaining political and economic phenomena but insists that '(t)here is no such thing as a universal pattern of rationality' (ibid., 258, fn. 10). Whereas today's standard procedure of economics is to explain different behaviour only as a consequence of different cost–benefit ratios or different restraints to action, but never to change the rationality assumption in the process, Schumpeter feels no inhibitions in doing just that. As a consequence, he 'came "dangerously" close to treating people as having . . . "bifurcated minds"' (Mitchell 1984, 76). And it is fair to conclude that '(b)ecause of this near-bifurcation in the choice of basic axioms Schumpeter has not influenced public choice' (ibid.).

It may be *outré* to bestow upon Schumpeter the dubious title 'founder of irrational choice theory' (Prisching 1995). But with regard to his theory of democracy, irrationality is a crucial element which is unduly ignored when celebrating Schumpeter as founder of a rational choice-dominated economics of politics. The differences will become clear, if I now contrast Schumpeter's theory of democracy with one of the most influential early contributions to modern public choice.

3 SCHUMPETER VERSUS DOWNSIAN MEDIAN VOTER LOGIC

> What strikes me most of all and seems to me to be the core of the trouble is the fact that the sense of reality is so completely lost. Schumpeter (1942/87, 261)

As Holcombe (1989, 115) observed, economists' 'median voter model in the public sector has served in much the same role as the model of pure competition in the private sector'. And it can be exposed to much the same Schumpeterian critique. Schumpeter repeatedly made the point that social development which is driven by the process of creative destruction and entrepreneurial innovation is ruled out in the model of 'pure' or 'perfect' competition. Indeed, 'all the essential facts of that process are absent from the general schema of economic life that yields the traditional propositions about perfect competition' (1942/87, 104). Most importantly, the entrepreneur who introduces new combinations and thus creates disequilibrating forces 'has no function of a special kind here, he simply does not exist' (Schumpeter 1912/34, 76). The same is true for spatial competition models in the Downsian tradition.[3]

3.1 'Political Leadership' versus 'Spatial Voting'

It was Downs's aim and achievement to 'treat government as an endogenous variable in general equilibrium theory' (1957, 280). By combining vote-maximizing political competitors and utility-maximizing voters with given preferences within a given issue-space, election outcomes could be deduced as equilibria under varying structural assumptions. In its 'perfect' form of two-party competition along a one-dimensional issue-space with perfect knowledge and single-peaked preferences, election outcomes are completely determined by the identical programme of both parties taking the position of the median voter. Hence, the vote-maximizing politician finds him- or herself in the same position as the profit-maximizing supplier in the model of perfect competition: just as the latter is reduced to a passive price taker, the former is reduced to an impotent 'position taker' who has to take the median voter's preference as given and imperative.

But, in addition to recreating similar properties based on heroic assumptions, the political variant of perfect competition is haunted by internal tensions among its assumptions. While the assumption that citizens vote is necessary for having a median voter (theorem) and a democracy to speak of, it violates the assumption of voters' instrumental rationality. Both major reasons for rational abstention – indifference and alienation – are maximized under 'perfect' political rivalry for the median voter. Hence, in equilibrium not only have rivalling substitutes vanished; the very act of voting becomes meaningless.

Downs and his followers developed the basic model in many different directions by relaxing particular assumptions of the strict median voter model. This made it possible to adapt the model to various voting procedures, and optimal locations of more than two parties facing more than single-peaked preference distributions in a more than one-dimensional issue-space were determined as more or less stable equilibrium states.[4] The basic conditions of vote maximization based on given distributions of voters' given preferences along a given issue-space, however, remained largely unchanged.

The greatest efforts were invested in dealing with multidimensional issue-spaces since it was discovered that multiple unstable outcomes can emerge, which, in addition, may not be Pareto efficient (for example, Mueller 1989a, 197ff.). Candidates who know with certainty which policy will attract which voters ('deterministic voting'), can always top the offer made by their rivals along multiple issues and thus upset equilibrium. As a consequence, the median voter was long regarded as an 'artefact' of the assumption of the one-dimensional issue-space (Hinich 1977). But meanwhile, with subtle variations towards 'probabilistic voting', stable equilibrium states were defined which, in addition, have the agreeable property of being welfare maximizing.[5]

But as with other variations on the median voter theme, the state 'appears as simply a voting rule that transforms individual preferences into political outcomes' (Mueller 1989a, 344). Competitive equilibrium still presupposes the parties' passive adaptation to voters' preferences and their distribution within a given interval of possible positions, which are equally identified and scaled by all actors (see Rowley 1984, 113). Another limitation is that many political issues cannot be meaningfully scaled at all; they are 'valence issues' that voters value either positively or negatively but do not position in space (Stokes 1992). Already Schumpeter (1942/87, 255) argued that chances for elections to produce results which reflect 'fair compromise' are

> greatest with those issues which are quantitative in nature or admit of gradation, such as the question how much to is to be spent on unemployment relief provided everybody favors some expenditure for that purpose. But with qualitative issues, such as the question whether or not to persecute heretics or to enter upon a war, the result attained may well, though for different reasons, be equally distasteful to all people whereas the decision imposed by a non-democratic agency might prove much more acceptable to them.

Similar reasoning led Schumpeter (ibid., 291) to stress as a 'condition for the success of democracy' that 'the effective range of political decision . . . has to be subject to constitutional constraints'. His account of the irrationality and irresponsibility of mass behaviour and voter conduct provides some justification for this claim – whereas in a world of rationality and spatial voting the very idea of limiting the 'issue-space' and disenfranchising the median voter is quite inconceivable. This, again, may point at a communality of demand-driven spatial models of democracy and common will-driven ideals of the classical doctrine. But it may suffice here to note once more that the assumption of given voter preferences (be they deterministic or probabilistic) to which political entrepreneurs simply adapt, displayed a remarkable persistence in a paradigm that marched out against the idealism of the classical doctrine.

Downs himself was among the first to observe that the selfish utility-maximizing actors of his model produce results that are not very different from those that the naïve idealist doctrines took for granted: 'if our hypothesis is correct, the men in government achieve their own goals by carrying out those government actions which most please voters, just as entrepreneurs make profits by producing things people want' (Downs 1957, 292). Unlike many of his followers, however, Downs (ibid., 177ff.) denies welfare-optimizing, Pareto-optimal properties of his model – mainly as a result of having inquired deeper into the very characteristics of the production of political goods. Downs also regarded the presentation of his basic logic of voting in a general equilibrium framework as 'only preliminary to the later analysis of behavior when uncertainty prevails' (ibid., 13). And in this later analysis, he does address issues such as deliberately obscured platforms, ideological immobility, the emergence of new parties, and even the role of political persuasion. In these parts, Schumpeterian themes are addressed. But eschewing Schumpeterian notions of irrationality and leadership, Downs tries to vindicate his model in rather inconclusive ways.

An interesting case is Downs's finding that in two-party systems it is rational for both parties 'to be as equivocal as possible about their stands on each controversial issue' (ibid., 136). As a result, voters may be

> encouraged to make their decisions on some basis other than the issues, i.e., on the personalities of candidates, traditional family voting patterns, loyalty to past heroes etc. But only the parties' decisions on issues are relevant to voters' utility incomes from government, so making decisions on any other basis is irrational. (ibid., 137)

But for Downs, '(a)pparently the more rational political parties are the less rational voters must be, and vice versa' (ibid., 137). He offers rather eclectic 'defences against being forced into irrationality' (ibid., 138f.), such as legal limits on parties' exploitative power, a change to multiparty systems, the desire to preserve democracy or, very reluctantly, the concession that voting may be 'less than perfectly rational as a mechanism for selecting governments'.

When it comes to the 'leadership' issue, persuasion is allowed only by providing correct information, not by shaping preferences or providing false information (ibid., 84). Political entrepreneurs are first of all followers, 'for they mould their policies to suit voters so as to gain as many votes as possible. Having done this, they attempt to lead all voters to believe these policies are best for them' (ibid., 88). Also, new parties yield precedence to the given voter distribution: they only enter *after* voters kindly make room for them in the political space (ibid., 125). Downs's political men in power do not create political 'markets' and followers, they aim to please rather than to lead.

Hence, even where Downs points at Schumpeterian themes he finally retreats to the safe grounds of instrumental rationality and spatial voting logic. Most of his followers also refrained from exploring these wild territories. The pure logic of voting created enough logical puzzles and mathematical curiosities (such as cycling) to keep public choice scholars busy working out technical details and variations. In the same way as the logical consistency and theoretical possibility of the bloodless construct of perfect competition fascinated economists more than the question how prices or goods are actually created in the market process, the question how voter positions and issues emerge has been dominated by problems of proving the possibility of stable and unique spatial equilibria in an aseptic world (Rowley 1984, 105). Schumpeter's (1942/87, 77) early critique of the former may also be applied to the latter: 'in the process of being more correctly stated and proved, the proposition lost much of its content – it does emerge from the operation, to be sure, but it emerges emaciated, barely alive'.

Certainly, spatial voting models can be very useful. Even the simplistic median voter model may provide empirically meaningful explanations for outcomes of direct-democratic elections with one-dimensional, ordinally scaleable issues or with two parties competing mainly in terms of one easily accessible and quantifiable issue such as tax policy. It is no accident that empirical tests of the median voter model (for example, Holcombe 1980; Munley 1984) mostly look at referenda in which the issue-space is, indeed, one-dimensional and given, and in which the median income recipient may serve as a proxy for the median voter (for example, Inman 1978; Pommerehne 1978). But in his survey, Mueller (1989a, 193) concludes that the empirical evidence is 'hardly encouraging as to the potential for predicting the outcomes of representative government with a model that treats the median voter as if he were dictator'.

This is where Schumpeter drastically differs from demand-driven spatial voting models. For him, democracy is competition for leadership and not for given voter distributions. And even if median voter positions had nothing to do with utilitarian notions of the common good (or, for that matter, Paretian welfare conditions), one can argue with Schumpeter (1942/87, 253) that this 'still leaves us with plenty of difficulties on our hands'. These difficulties deserve being quoted at length, since they also apply to some underlying characteristics of the spatial voting model:

> In particular, we still remain under the practical necessity of attributing to the will of the individual an independence and a rational quality that are altogether unrealistic. If we are to argue that the will of the citizens per se is a political factor entitled to respect, it must first exist. That is to say, it must be something more than an indeterminate bundle of vague impulses loosely playing about given slogans and mistaken impressions. Everyone would have to know definitely what he wants to stand for. This definite will would have to be implemented by the ability to observe and interpret correctly the facts that are directly accessible to everyone and to sift critically the information about the facts that are not. Finally, from that definite will and from these ascertained facts a clear and prompt conclusion as to particular issues would have to be derived according to the rules of logical inference – with so high a degree of general efficiency moreover that one man's opinion could be held, without glaring absurdity, to be roughly as good as every other man's. And all this the modal citizen would have to perform for himself and independently of pressure groups and propaganda, for volitions and inferences that are imposed upon the electorate obviously do not qualify for ultimate data of the democratic process.

As will be shown in the next section, this sketch of a moderate classical doctrine's underlying assumptions comes very close to what Downs (and most of his followers more implicitly) assume – and to what Schumpeter is not ready to accept. His assumption that 'modal citizens' have no independent, clear and definite position on political issues, no independent power to put issues on the political agenda and no adequate means to voice their opinion (if they have one) leads Schumpeter to infer the vital role of political leadership. It consists as much in shaping a 'manufactured will' of the masses as in turning latent 'group-wise volitions' into political factors (ibid., 270), thus *creating* voter distributions instead of just following them and creating 'voice' instead of just listening to it.

In addition, political entrepreneurship is a managerial challenge. Political parties are not, as Downs (1957, 25f.) defined them, 'teams . . . whose members agree on all their goals'. Treating 'each party as though it were a single person' (ibid.) also eliminates party leadership which for Schumpeter is equally important. He (1942/87, 277) describes the political leader in a way some well-remembered (and re-elected) prime ministers or presidents have in fact acted: they 'lead party opinion creatively – shape it – and eventually rise toward a formative leadership of public opinion beyond the lines of party, toward national leadership that may to some extent become independent of mere party opinion'.

The reader might endorse my claim that political leadership is essential in Schumpeter's theory of democracy, whereas in spatial voting models it is not. But one may still doubt whether Schumpeter's description of the typical citizen is categorically different from the representative citizen as modelled in most of public choice. Has not public choice (following Downs) shown that rational voters are, for good reasons, vastly uninformed about political programmes and issues? It has. But that does not make it Schumpeterian. I leave aside the internal tension that 'rational ignorance' creates within the median voter logic. Suffice to mention that now the model implies that competing candidates are driven to take exactly the position of a (median) voter who knows neither where he/she stands nor what he/she wants! Instead, I want to show that rational ignorance, as presented by Downs (1957) and dominantly used by public choice is logically flawed in itself and based on clearly un-Schumpeterian arguments.

3.2 'Irrational Impulse' versus 'Rational Ignorance'

Throughout Downs's thesis (including his discussion of 'rational ignorance') and in spatial voting models quite generally, party differentials are 'the most important part of a voter's decision' (Downs 1957, 40). Downs defines the party differential as 'the difference between the utility income he actually received in period t and the one he would have received if the opposition had been in power' (ibid.) – a rather demanding calculation to start with.[6] But that is not all. In addition, the rational voter amends his/her current party differential with two future-orientated modifiers: a 'trend factor' (to account for recently improving or degenerating performances of the parties) and another performance rating – in case the current party differential is zero (ibid., 41f.). In multiparty systems, the rational voter is also 'predicting how other citizens will vote by estimating their preferences' (ibid., 48) since he/she has to know whether his/her preferred party has a chance of ending up in the winning coalition. Furthermore, the rational voter must balance each party's net position (the mean of its policies) against its spread (their variance) within the issue-space. 'In short, voters choose policy vectors rather than policy scalars, and each vector is really a frequency distribution of policies on the left-right scale' (ibid., 133).

Already these calculations (omitting further variables[7]) seem more demanding (and less entertaining) than those necessary for enjoying (and occasionally succeeding in) a game of bridge. This is said in order to restate Schumpeter's (1942/87, 261) claim that

> when we move . . . into those regions of national and international affairs that lack a direct and unmistakable link with . . . private concerns, individual volition, command of facts and method of inference soon cease to fulfil the requirements of the classical doctrine . . . the private citizen musing over national affairs . . . is a member of an unworkable committee, the committee of the whole nation, and this is why he expends less disciplined effort on mastering a political problem than he expends on a game of bridge.

Downsian 'rational ignorance' does not build on this simple consideration, but on the voter's calculation of his/her party-differential which is 'the basic return upon which subsequent calculations are built' (Downs 1957, 272). The latter also include the voter's calculations of the optimal amount of ignorance he/she decides to leave rationally unhealed, carefully procuring political information only if its expected pay-off exceeds its cost (ibid., 272). From a history of ideas perspective, it is noteworthy that Downs anticipated much of what Stigler (1961) or Arrow (1962/85) later introduced as the economics of information. But thanks to Downs's frank verbal exposition, fundamental problems of subjecting individual ignorance to marginalistic calculations are more accessible here than in more modern variants.

> Three factors determine the size of his planned information investment. The first is the value of making a correct decision as opposed to an incorrect one, i.e. the variation in utility incomes associated with the possible outcomes of his decision. The second is the relevance of the information to whatever decision is being made. Is acquisition of this particular bit of knowledge likely to influence the decision one way or another? If so, how likely? . . . This probability is then applied to the value of making the right choice (the vote value in our example), From this emerges the return from the bit of information being considered, i.e., the marginal return from investment in data on this particular margin. The third factor is the cost of data. The marginal cost of any bit of information consists

of the returns foregone in obtaining it. A comparison of the estimated marginal cost and estimated return of any bit determines whether this particular bit should be acquired. (Downs 1957, 215f.)

These calculations of 'the quantity of information it is rational to acquire' (ibid., 214) show that most properties of the investment good 'information' are already known and hence that the investment must already have been made. This is already true for the first factor: how are voters to know the value of making the right decision if they do not already know future 'utility incomes' created by the parties in question? Voters seem to already have the relevant information (before they 'acquire' it). The paradox becomes even more glaring with the second factor: how are voters to determine whether and how much a bit of information will be influencing their decision, if they do not already know its content? The problem of marginal optimization of rational ignorance is more than just marginal. The problem is that the 'worth of new knowledge cannot begin to be assessed until we have it. By then it is too late to decide how much to spend on breaching the walls to encourage its arrival' (Shackle 1972, 272f.).

Even the calculation of the third factor shows that Downs's knowledge-seeking citizen already knows what he/she cannot know before he/she invests in knowledge. As the opportunity costs of investing in political information, Downs dominantly uses 'the time used for assimilating data and weighing alternatives' (ibid., 209) – which remains a relevant cost factor for free political information. But also the returns forgone by spending time investing in political information are by no ways known *ex ante* (if they can ever be known at all, see Buchanan 1969).

The very concept of rational ignorance based on the equalization of marginal costs and benefits of investments in new knowledge is, therefore, no serious qualification of perfect rationality assumptions. It is rather their elevation to logically absurd levels of 'super-optimization' (Knudsen 1993, 143) or the omniscient determination of ignorance. Such naïve information economics can at best yield 'as-if' heuristics of the simple fact that with subjectively expected rising benefits of more information, more information is demanded, and with subjectively expected greater benefits of alternative uses of scarce resources, investment in information is reduced. But there is no way to rationally optimize one's ignorance, since no one knows what he/she misses by not investing in new knowledge.

As in other instances, Downs (1957) is well aware of some inner tensions facing his rationalistic framework,[8] which leads him to develop interesting amendments to the basic logic in order to rescue the model. This time, he retreats to probabilistic calculations building on 'subjective estimates based on whatever information he has already acquired' (ibid., 242). Our voter may already have estimated his/her party differential at 50 utility units (the 'estimated cost of being wrong . . . upon which subsequent calculations are built', ibid., 241) and is now 'confronted' by a single bit of information (ibid.). 'All a voter really knows about each bit before [!] acquiring it is (1) a list of its possible values, (2) the probability associated with each value, and (3) its cost'. Thus, in Downs's numerical example, voters know in advance that they will have to sacrifice 10 units (utility forgone by not spending time or money on other uses). Now, they expect with probability 0.5 that knowing the content of the information would increase their party differential by 100 units, with probability 0.4 that it will decrease it by 10 units and with probability 0.1 that it will decrease it by 100 units. The expected value of knowing more is thus 36 units of enlarged party differential. Which, as such, would make the information valueless for their voting decision, since they would not have voted differently had the time (or money) been spent on something else (ibid.).

The reason is that Downs's 'rational voter is interested only in information which might change his preliminary voting decision . . . only this information provides returns in terms of a better decision or increased confidence in the present one' (ibid., 241). This follows indeed from pure instrumental logic; but it fundamentally contradicts psychological intuition and empirical observation.[9] But the story goes on. Rational voters are not guided by the overall expected value of the information they are about to acquire; rationally the entire distribution of each bit is considered before a decision is made. And since there was a 0.1 chance that it will shift their position to favouring the other party by 50 units, they buy it in order to avoid a loss of 40 units (after deducting the 10 units for acquiring it)!

Downs's example not only illustrates the above-mentioned information paradox in even more lustrous detail. It also shows just how far the rational ignorance model ignores 'the chapter of social psychology which might be entitled Human Nature in Politics' (Schumpeter 1942/87, 256).[10] In fact, Downs's (1957, 7) initial claim that 'our homo politicus is the "average man" in the electorate . . . he will not be as much of a calculating-machine-brained character as was the utilitarians' economic man' is nowhere contradicted more clearly than in Downs's treatment of 'rational ignorance'.

Only after having elaborated all details of the above logic of rational ignorance, does Downs introduce the complication that party differentials will have to be discounted to account for the fact that a single vote has minimal impact on outcomes. Now the rational voter has to start his/her calculations with the 'vote value' which 'is compounded from his estimates of his party differential and of the probability that his vote will be decisive' (ibid., 244). Had Downs introduced the simple fact of a single voter's impotence earlier, most of his rational voting calculus would have been redundant, which from the beginning was orientated only towards selecting a government which yields the highest personal utility income. Downs's categorical instrumentalism was introduced on page 7: 'The political function of elections in a democracy, we assume, is to select a government. Therefore rational behavior in connection with elections is behavior oriented toward this goal and no other' (see also ibid., 136, 145). It breaks down on page 245, when we learn:

> A rational man may buy information because (1) he wishes to influence the government's policies, (2) his prediction of how other voters will act indicates that the probability is relatively high that his own vote will be decisive, or (3) he derives entertainment value or social prestige from such data. (ibid., 245)

As a consequence, voters in any large-scale elections which a theory of democracy should reasonably address, buy information either because they are ignorant of the fact that millions of other voters upset their instrumental purpose, or because they strive for aims which were so far labelled 'irrational', since they are not related to the social function of democracy! Similar reasoning applies to Downs's chapter on rational abstention (ibid., 260ff.). Again, instrumental rationality solely aimed at selecting the 'right' party which yields the highest utility income does not suffice (once reasonably discounted for the fact of large numbers) to give 'reason' to vote as soon as costs are involved. And again, factors previously discarded as 'irrational' have to do the job.

Here Downs comes dangerously close to introducing 'classical' motives, for example, when he argues that '(i)t is sometimes rational for a citizen to vote even when his short-run costs exceed his short-run returns, because social responsibility produces a long-run return' (ibid., 261). Even mainstream public choice, after considering the free-rider problems, found it hard to follow Downs in rationalising voting as a contribution to the public good called 'making democracy possible' (ibid.). Instead, one was forced to refer to one of the two alternative explanations: (a) intrinsic or extrinsic benefits derived from being (known to be) a voter who performs his/her civil duty ('ethical voter hypothesis', for example, Riker and Ordeshook 1968; Pennock 1989, 26f.) or (b) satisfaction of being able to simply express one's opinions ('expressive voter hypothesis', for example, Brennan and Buchanan 1984; Brennan and Hamlin 2000). Both hypotheses entail 'irrational' voter behaviour if Downs's yardstick of instrumental rationality holds; they claim that 'neither the act of voting nor the direction of the vote can be explained as a means to achieving a particular political outcome' (Brennan and Buchanan 1984, 187).

3.3 Back to Schumpeter? Consequences for Public Choice

The consequences – not only for Downs's reasoning, but for public choice at large – are rather uncomfortable. Voters are both 'rationally ignorant' and 'rationally absent' if rationality is aimed at achieving maximum utility incomes from electing political alternatives. But obviously, citizens do have some (if poor) information about politics, they hold political opinions and many, often most, of them vote. Either these voters are effectively irrational (lured in the absurd belief that an individual voting decision affects outcomes) or they vote and have political opinions for better reasons than those derived from Downsian instrumental rationality. These better reasons could be entertainment value, social prestige or even moral convictions.[11] Adding elements of 'mass behaviour', 'impulse' and 'affection', we would, after a long and tiresome detour with calculations of 'party differentials' and 'vote values' be back at the Schumpeterian vantage point. And we might indeed have found strong reasons to substitute a chapter on 'human nature in politics' for the voter as *homo oeconomicus*.

The same reasons can lead us to make more allowances for Schumpeter's stress on the vital fact of political leadership. If voters do not position themselves on the drill grounds of given issue-spaces after having gone through painstaking calculations of party differentials – if they are indeed driven by such malleable forces as entertainment value, social prestige or perceived demands of social duty – political leaders have much more leeway in pushing through their own agendas and creating their own electorate.

Along both lines, public choice may find its way back to Schumpeter; or rather: may be challenged to take up his issues of bounded rationality and political leadership and integrate them in a more advanced theory of the political process.

4   SCHUMPETERIAN POLITICAL ECONOMY: STILL ANOTHER THEORY OF DEMOCRACY

> If . . . the straightjacket of neoclassical public choice is left behind and a more open view of political economy is adopted, it becomes clear that Schumpeter's writings still have very much to offer. (Bruno S. Frey 1981, 140)

Parts of public choice have already embarked on this journey towards a more Schumpeterian political economy. First, non-*homo oeconomicus* determinants of voter behaviour have been endorsed by economists who accept bounded rationality (rather than super-optimizing rational ignorance), 'sociological' forces (rather than independently determined reasons to act) and even 'moral dimensions' as relevant for voting behaviour under the special conditions of low-cost decisions.[12] Second, non-adoptive behaviour of political entrepreneurs has also been recognized by a number of public choice scholars who discuss the art of political manipulation, opinion leadership, decision framing, political innovation and reform and other aspects of supply-side political activity.[13]

But the more general models of electoral competition still remain very much in the Downsian tradition of analysing voters as rational calculators of party differentials and parties as passive brokers of given (median) voter preferences in a given issue-space. In addition, there has been a remarkable renaissance of rationalism, tight prior equilibrium and political efficiency which defies any 'sociological', 'psychological' (or, for that matter, Schumpeterian) explanations: the new Chicago political economy (for example, Wittman 1995). This chapter focuses on two areas of research in which public choice is leaving behind the straitjacket of neoclassical pure logic of choice and in which a theory of democracy could be developed in a more or less Schumpeterian spirit: bounded political rationality and political opinion formation.

4.1 Towards a (Cognitive) Economics of Bounded Political Rationality

Downs (1957, 6) explicitly used a 'narrow concept of rationality'. Its narrowness lies not so much in his definition of rationality of conduct, but of connecting it with a rationality of ends. The first entails standard assumptions drawn from Arrow (1951) such as the individual's ability to rank all alternatives in an ordinal and transitive way, to always choose the alternative that ranks highest, and to always make the same decision when confronted with the same alternatives (ibid.). The second element claims that 'rational behavior in connection with elections is behavior oriented towards this end (the selection of a government) and no other' (ibid., 7). Downs insists on end-orientated, instrumental rationality, which leads politicians to select policies which procure the highest voting share, and voters to select politicians which procure the highest utility income.

As Downs himself has more or less inadvertently shown towards the end of his study, rationality of behaviour and his idea of rationality of ends may well be in conflict. In the face of voters' impotence or indifference, party differentials can hardly be assumed to take the form of elaborated preference rankings which would dominate other (even less scaleable) elements of voting behaviour. And even if party differentials were still assumed to dominate, rational calculations on their basis make no (rational) sense as soon as opportunity costs are involved. Theoretical and empirical research meanwhile provides ample material for questioning political rationality on both fronts: the instrumentality of voter behaviour and the rationality of behaviour as such.

Non-instrumentalistic elements in voting behaviour

I have argued that the very decision to vote must be primarily motivated by a sense of duty or by pleasure derived from the (inconsequential) expression of one's political preferences. Voting cannot reasonably be regarded as an instrumental act aimed at choosing higher 'utility incomes'. It is the act of voting as such that may yield benefits in terms of self-respect or respect of others – both at very low costs.

Similar reasons hold for the decision to invest in political information. With large numbers of the electorate, there is no instrumental link between a better-informed vote and higher returns of 'making the right decision' in Downsian terms of party differentials. Again, reasons must be found outside the 'basic logic of voting' (Hardin 1999, 8). One reason may be the entertainment value of political news, scandals and opinions. Another reason may be the reputational value of being regarded as a good entertainer or a knowledgeable person. Hirschman (1989) presents good reasons for having opinions as elements of individual well-being: 'not to have an opinion is tantamount to not having individuality, identity, character, self' (ibid., 75), and: 'vacillation, indifference, or weakly held opinions have long met with utmost contempt, while approval and admiration have been bestowed on firmness, fullness and articulateness of opinion' (ibid., 76).

But if individuals mainly strive for reputational utility in the sense of Kuran (1995),[14] they are even 'more dependent on society in political contexts than in the realm of ordinary consumption' (ibid., 162). This dependence, in turn, begs recognition that political opinions rest to a large extent 'on beliefs shaped by *public discourse*, which consists of the suppositions, facts, arguments, and the theories that are communicated publicly' (ibid., 18). As will be shown in Section 4.2, it is exactly under these premises that the meaning of democracy as an opinion-forming process can be established, in which political entrepreneurship has an important role.

Different reasons *why* political opinions are formed and expressed also explain *how* citizens become informed – again differing sharply from Downs's assumptions of instrumental rationality. Remember that Downs's 'rational voter is interested only in information which might change his preliminary voting decision' (1957, 241); information that confirms the voter's established view has no instrumental value. But after discounting the instrumental value of political information to next to zero, a substantially different (and much more realistic) behavioural pattern emerges. This pattern can be built around (a combination of) psychological and economic-sociological theories. As an example of the first category, the theory of 'cognitive dissonance' suggests itself. This was developed by Festinger (1957) and interpreted for economists by Akerlof and Dickens (1982). The latter summarize the results of cognitive-psychological research:

> First, persons not only have preferences over states of the world, but also over their beliefs about the state of the world. Second, persons have some control over their beliefs . . . they can also manipulate their own beliefs by selecting sources of information likely to confirm 'desired' beliefs. Third . . . beliefs once chosen persist over time. (ibid., 307)

Applications of these propositions to a theory of political behaviour should prove most promising for a Schumpeterian theory of democracy in which the manipulation of beliefs would be a prominent feature (Brady et al. 1995). Whereas Schumpeter stressed the fact that voter-citizens are objects to be manipulated by political leaders, the (conscious or unconscious) attempts of individuals to 'manipulate' *themselves* by selecting confirming and comforting information also deserves recognition in a 'chapter of social psychology'. Selective perception and storage of information in accordance with established preconceptions or perception filters is a pattern persistently found by psychological research (Rosenberg 1991; Rabin 1998). As Kuran (1995, 173) summarizes: 'our beliefs govern what we notice in the first place. We perceive selectively, noticing facts consistent with our beliefs more readily. This bias imparts resistance to our beliefs by shielding them from counterevidence'.

The desire to verify and not falsify one's preconceived opinions is not only 'all-too-human' in general, it is also 'all-too-cheap' in politics. Ignoring alternative information and opinions and thus being led into self-assuring delusions must be expected to be particularly pronounced in areas of 'cheap talk' instead of consequential individual decisions (Kirchgässner and Pommerehne 1993; Caplan 2001). While such behaviour would be costly on the economic marketplace, on the 'marketplace of ideas' it is not. It may even be rather rewarding since it reduces the 'psychological costs' of dissonance (Weissberg 1996, 113) and the 'reputational costs' of disagreement (Kuran 1995).

The fact that political knowledge for most citizens is an instrument not so much to attain private returns from voting but to secure personal comfort and social approval, creates self-reinforcing and self-justifying tendencies of public opinion formation. Citizens exchange opinions and political information most likely with people who already share their political preferences (Huckfeldt and Sprague 1995). And they tend to *express* opinions which they expect to be generally accepted within the group in which they find themselves – even if they may secretly hold different opinions ('preference falsification', Kuran 1995; see also Section 4.2).

Finally, it should come as no surprise that serious deviations from Downsian instrumental rationality are also found in empirical analyses of the voting decision itself. If the participation at elections, the information selected, and the opinions expressed before the election were already based on such elements as social demands, moral impulse or the aim to please, the decision what to vote for should not be motivated much differently. Certainly, cunning voters may, in the anonymity of the voting booth, 'vote their pocket book' or party differential, even if in public they may pretend to be driven by more socially rewarding motives. But even this cleverness would be inconsistent. It may cause more inner strain than pleasure to live a political Jekyll-and-Hyde life; and it will certainly fail to produce different political results. If the individual vote makes no difference, voting for the most respected party in one's group of peers, or voting for the most likely winner does no harm. And if it produces any good feelings (be that 'inner peace' or 'outer peace'), such emotions should dominate the instrumental 'voting in my private interest' as prescribed by the *homo oeconomicus* model.

These considerations find support in empirical studies (see Mueller 1989a, 367ff.; Nannestad and Paldam 1994, 223ff.; Udehn 1996, 78ff. for overviews). In referenda, expenditures that benefit specific groups are also supported by members of groups who know that they would have to pay the bill; voters are more responsive to general economic conditions than to their personal economic situation ('sociotropic voting', Kinder and Kriewiet 1981). In addition, many voters seem to be more strongly affected by 'symbolic politics', traditional voting patterns, ideologies, moral convictions and socialization than by regards to their economic self-interest (Sears et al. 1980). A strong support for the influence of communication communities (neighbourhoods, families, churches) is also found in many studies (Butler and Stokes 1974; Huckfeldt and Sprague 1995).

It remains problematic to interpret this evidence. An 'ethical voter interpretation' could produce, by non-Downsian means, a rather Downsian result. In terms of modern contractarianism it can be argued that the factual 'veil of insignificance' (Kliemt 1986) of voter behaviour achieves much of what a hypothetical 'veil of ignorance' might be able to produce. The latter presupposes that citizens not knowing their social position in a future society will vote for generally fair rules (since these rules might apply to themselves). The former may work even if people know what their personal interests are; but the insignificance of their personal vote would make them more inclined to vote for a 'common good'. As a consequence, public choice may once again come dangerously near to the basic presumptions of the classical doctrine (see Mueller 1989b, 86).

Another interpretation, however, arrives at a very different valuation of the same facts. Much in a Schumpeterian spirit, Brennan and Lomasky (1989) argue that voters can afford to indulge in most short-sighted, irresponsible, ideological expressions of romantic or malicious ideas. In the aggregate they may make costly decisions, but individual voters face no costs as a consequence of their single decision. Anonymous voters can act in ways they would never dare to take if they were accountable for their decisions. Schumpeter (1942/87, 262) makes the same point when he expects that the voter, due to 'the absence of effective logical control over the results he arrives at . . . will relax his usual moral standards . . . and occasionally give in to dark urges which the conditions in private life help him to repress'. But 'it will be just as bad if he gives in to a burst of generous indignation', since this 'will make it still more difficult for him to see things in their correct proportions or even see more than one aspect of one thing at a time' (ibid.).

Already at this stage – without having to introduce 'policy failure' arguments from rent seeking or bureaucracy theory – Brennan and Lomasky (1989) arrive at a strong denial of the rationality of the democratic process. As a consequence of high arbitrariness of voting motivations, 'what emerges through democratic procedures may not be the will of the majority, and may not have been desired by a single voter' (ibid., 44). Thus having effectively destroyed *instrumental* rationality of both voter behaviour and the democratic process, Brennan and Lomasky still maintain that voters are at least 'not predominantly irrational' – even if 'they vote as they do for reasons that have little to do with an intention to affect outcomes'. Others, such as Caplan (2001) or Akerlof (1989) argue that individual irrationality, illusions and systematically biased beliefs are just what an economic opportunity cost reasoning would lead one to expect, since democracy sets the private cost of socially costly irrationality at zero. The next subsection will address the rationality issue as such.

Non-rationalistic elements in voting behaviour
Usually economists do not, as Downs did, extend their concept of rationality beyond the realm of means applied to achieve whatever ends. Individual ends pursued can be of any kind; *de gustibus non est disputandum*. But it is assumed that these ends (whatever they may be) are pursued rationally, that is, by choosing those alternatives which rank highest on a given preference scale and can be achieved under given constraints of scarce resources. This limitation of the rationality postulate is very reasonable in itself, since it avoids making presumptuous or paternalistic judgements about people's aims and values. However, it also brings the analysis closer to truistic statements: if any end is allowed, it is hard to identify

means that are not 'rationally chosen' in view of these ends as long as the latter are not known or at least postulated.[15]

I shall not go deeper into these methodological matters. Instead, I want to show that even if rationality is bound to a choice of means for achieving a wider range of ends, this does not create bounded rationality. Anomalies and 'irrationalities' remain even if one drops the determination of rational ends. Cognitive science and experimental psychology meanwhile substantiated much of what Schumpeter took for granted when he, for example, suspected that the voter's 'power of observation and interpretation of facts, and his ability to draw, clearly and promptly, rational inferences' are very limited, that his 'thinking becomes associative and affective' and would 'tend to yield to extrarational or irrational prejudice and impulse' (1942/87, 256 and 262). I cannot here discuss the manifold details of the experimental evidence and their often controversial interpretations.[16] But the overall evidence contradicting Bayesian (or for that matter Arrowian and Downsian) standards of rational behaviour and learning is impressive.

Much of the evidence can be explained in terms of Simon's model of bounded rationality. Due to limited cognitive capacities of the mind, individuals rely on rather simple behavioural heuristics and 'rules of thumb' which generally 'satisfice' learned levels of aspiration, instead of engaging in case-by-case optimization based on a comprehensive consultation of data and alternative modes of behaviour (Simon 1957, 1978, 1986).[17] More striking evidence of decision anomalies, biases and mistakes may be explained by 'prospect theory' (Kahnemann and Tversky 1984) which claims, among other things, that individuals choose schemata of arranging the outside world which at the moment are most available rather than most 'rational', 'objective' or 'effective'. Such conditions can be exploited by others who manipulate individual decisions by way of 'framing' the context of a decision and thus producing biased results in the framers' interest (see Quattrone and Tversky 1988).

It has rightly been observed that one has to be careful when drawing inferences from observing anonymous decisions of often isolated individuals playing experimental games in which errors are more or less costless (for example, Smith 1985; Wittman 1995, 41). Such objections carry much weight when, for example, financial investment decisions are put to laypeople in experiments that fail to recreate elementary characteristics of such markets – such as the monetary stakes, the professional division of labour, or competitive pressures which help avoid or creatively destroy at least some anomalies (for example, Thaler 1987). But peculiarities of *voter* decisions are very well reproduced by experiments with costless errors, anonymous decisions, lack of competitive selection and of a division of labour which would allocate property rights (voting rights) to those who are more specialized, experienced and knowledgeable and who may thus be less vulnerable to anomal behaviour.

This is exactly what Schumpeter, who links weaker mental performance with weaker incentives and weaker market forces, would have expected. Also the 'framing' issue is, of course, just another way to express the major element of Schumpeter's theory of democracy which links 'the weaker . . . logical element in the process of the public mind' with greater 'opportunities for groups with an ax to grind' (1942/87, 263). These groups of political entrepreneurs 'are able to fashion, and, within very wide limits, even to create the will of the people' (ibid.). In modern language: if individuals in situations such as those produced by experiments and general elections are susceptible to anomalies, framing and manipulations of contexts, there will be political (mis-) leaders who know the 'art of manipulation' (Riker 1986) and use it.

But not all political leadership needs to be manipulative. Much of it will be formative in rather innocent ways. An important case where political 'leadership' and 'framing' in a neutral meaning are active and, in fact, indispensable, is the formation of public opinion.

4.2 Towards an (Austrian) Economics of Political Opinion Formation

'Public opinion' is a non-issue in public choice theory. There are good reasons for this. Public opinion is one of the 'most controversial, ambiguous, and nontransparent concepts in the social sciences' (Splichal 1999, 1). To make things worse, what most definitions of public opinion do, after all, have in common, contradicts the Downsian or spatial politics perspective more than once: public opinion is *not* (i) an additive aggregation of (ii) isolated individuals' given preferences on (iii) given issues. I shall now present these elements of public opinion in order to highlight some aspects which would be essential for a Schumpeterian theory of democracy, but cannot be dealt with in a spatial politics framework (see Wohlgemuth 2002a and 2002b for more comprehensive accounts).

Qualitative and cognitive components of public opinion

Private opinions are more than the private preferences which usually serve as data of economic equilibrium models. As Vanberg and Buchanan (1989, 50) point out, preferences consist of a combination of evaluative and cognitive components. They depend on interest in results (what one wants) as well as on theories about the effects of certain actions (what one expects). The combination of idiosyncratic, subjective penchants and interests (evaluative component) with equally subjective, but fallible and possibly erroneous conceptions, expectations or theories (cognitive component), describes economic as well as political preferences.

In some respects, political preferences rely even more strongly on cognitive components. Preferences for daily consumption goods can mostly be a matter of taste, thus being unreflective and not affording any justification (*de gustibus* . . .). The formation of political preferences, however, cannot dispense with 'speculative or explanatory views which people have formed about . . . society or the economic system, capitalism or imperialism, and other such collective entities, which the social scientist must regard as no more than provisional theories' (Hayek 1952/79, 64). The citizen who wishes to express an opinion does this with reference to some conjectures about cause and effect (however inappropriate they are in the eyes of 'expert' observers).

In other words, the 'value image' or the 'ordering on the scale of better or worse' of given alternatives (Boulding 1956, 47), which in most of economics of politics exclusively motivates political actors, is only a part of the image that guides human action. And it is not a part that can be properly isolated from other aspects of the image, such as, most of all, the 'relational image' (that is, the subjective hypotheses on causal systems and regularities in the outside world, ibid. 48). This is most important when the static view of democracy as an aggregation of given preferences or pure value orderings is abandoned in favour of a dynamic view of democracy as a process that helps create and change opinions or value images combined with relational images.[18]

Even after combining individual preferences, interests or tastes with hypotheses, theories and (mis-) conceptions to private opinions, public opinion is not their mere aggregation. As Lowell (1913, ch. I) has already pointed out in his classical treatment, the impact of individual opinions on public opinion depends on qualitative rather than quantitative criteria. Whereas in elections votes are counted but not weighed, contributions to public opinion also depend on the intensity with which preferences are felt, the verve with which they are expressed and the thrust with which the theoretical part of opinions is presented. Thus minorities can override less interested, less active, less convinced or less convincing majorities in the process of public opinion formation and articulation.

Public opinion as a result of 'opinion falsification'

Kuran (1995) describes public opinion as the result of social interaction or, more precisely, social pressure. Public opinion is not the aggregation of private preferences, but the 'distribution of public preferences' (ibid., 17), that is, of publicly articulated views that can differ significantly from what individuals' preferences would be in the absence of social pressures. Most individuals appraise their opinion articulation by reference to their estimate of opinions held by those with whom they communicate. As a result, they engage in what Kuran calls 'preference falsification': preferences are opportunistically 'falsified' by those who carry their true preferences as their inner secret. This notion of 'falsification' relates to 'truth' in the sense of their public *expression* being honest ('true') or dishonest ('false').

But public discourse helps shape private preferences *and* private knowledge. And knowledge as embedded in a person's 'relational image' is subject to a different kind of falsification. Unlike values or tastes, theories about the world can be right or wrong. Individual experience and intersubjective exchanges of arguments and evidence can lead to the 'falsification' of previously held views in the sense of learning about flaws or sheer errors of beliefs formerly held to be 'true' or at least 'satisfying'. A wider concept of 'opinion falsification' (Wohlgemuth 2002b) embraces both: the disguise of true feelings ('preference falsification') and the discovery of false beliefs ('theory falsification'). It is, therefore, not only the fear of social isolation and the longing for social prestige, but also the exposure of the embedded theories to falsification by arguments and experience that lets public opinion 'rule' within socially interacting groups.

Certainly, the claim that communication leads to the reconsideration of personal beliefs remains a far cry from Popperian ideals of falsificationalism. Especially when it comes to political opinions, cognitive dissonance, selective perceptions and the innate tendency towards self-assuring delusions must be expected to be especially pronounced, since they form the background of 'cheap talk' rather than individual decisions. Nevertheless, parts of the market analogy can be applied to political opinion formation: when exchanging political opinions, citizens (and politicians) anticipate the social terms of trade and wish to 'sell' their view. This can induce them to (a) pick 'buyers' who most probably support the same basic views, (b) adjust their own views to those found in a given 'market' of opinions or (c) improve the quality of their 'product' by backing an opinion with more convincing evidence or logic. The fear of reputational losses, like a seller's fear of pecuniary losses, urges individuals to constantly check which opinions and modes of behaviour are approved and which are disapproved of in their environment (Noelle-Neumann 1993, 37ff.; Kuran 1995, 27). This, in turn, leads to self-reinforcing 'frequency-dependency-effects' as major propagation mechanisms of public opinion (Huckfeldt and Sprague 1995; Witt 1996).

Such theories about the interrelatedness of private and public opinion may be an integral part of a 'neo-Schumpeterian' economics of democracy. They may replace Gustave Le Bon's 'psychology of the crowds', which Schumpeter (1942/87, 256ff.) used to illustrate 'Human Nature in Politics' – well aware of its 'vulnerable points' such as its 'narrowness of the factual basis' (ibid., 257). Instead, interactive processes of 'image reformulation'

(Boulding 1956) or 'preference falsification' and the 'hidden complexities of social evolution' (Kuran 1995, ch. 17) triggered by these processes can be valuable contributions to a Schumpeterian agenda.[19]

A more obvious Schumpeterian contribution to a 'public choice of public opinion' follows from a third difference to standard assumptions of public choice: political leadership.

Political entrepreneurs and the creation of issues

Just as goods (the objects of interactive price formation) are not given in a market process, political issues (the objects of interactive opinion formation) are not given in the political process. Issues have to be discovered or created and then pushed on the agenda. This activity entails costs and affords skills since the public's attention is fundamentally scarce and ephemeral; it cannot deal with many issues at a time. Like competition on open markets, competition of ideas and opinions is driven by entrepreneurs.

As Sunstein (1996) shows, many political movements owe the attention to their cause, often associated with a surprisingly strong and sudden change of attitudes of the general public to 'norm entrepreneurs' or opinion leaders who deliberately aim at inducing a swing in opinions and values. In Kuran's theory, a similar role is attributed to 'activists' with 'extraordinarily great expressive needs' (Kuran 1995, 49) who dare formulate dissenting views and introduce new issues even in the face of an apparently hostile or indifferent public. In Boulding's (1956) chapter on the sociology of knowledge, changes in private and public images come about 'through the impact on society of unusually creative, charismatic, or prophetic individuals' (ibid., 75) as 'bearers of viable mutant images' – they are 'the true entrepreneurs of society' (ibid., 76).

Political entrepreneurs take advantage of the fact that on many issues no strong and articulated opinions (preferences and theories) exist in the first place. The stock of views and knowledge about some issues is devaluated in the course of time and new problems arise, which cannot be assessed by referring to established knowledge and ideological shortcuts. With the increasing complexity of political activities and environments the number of issues increases for which there is no public opinion ready at hand, no 'issue-space' exists and citizens have no idea where to position themselves. As a consequence, public opinion must become increasingly selective. The German sociologist Niklas Luhmann (1970/75, 16) concludes that the political system is more effectively shaped by attention rules than by decision rules.

With Luhmann (ibid., 18f.) one may describe the evolution of public opinions much in terms of product life cycles. An issue's 'career' usually starts with a latent phase, during which only a chosen few affected by, or intrinsically interested in, a specific political problem know and discuss the issue. At that point it cannot yet be assumed that politicians, the media and least of all 'the man on the street' are willing or able to 'take issue'. Some of the latent issues, however, do attract attention after political entrepreneurs (professional politicians or private agitators) have successfully invested in time, resources and personal contacts. With a bit of luck and a certain amount of skill, these entrepreneurs ensure that the matter is taken up by larger 'retailers' who are used to dealing with changing issues in the process of transforming them into political demands and, at the end, into laws and regulations. At this stage the issue becomes part of 'normal politics': an 'issue space' is created; the media and citizens can take a position, discuss the issue, and expect others to be familiar with the major positions of the contending camps. Often, but not always, the discussion produces a generally accepted point of view, a public opinion that is characterized by a sufficiently large overlap of individuals' images. Only now public opinion 'rules' within large groups by means of fear of isolation, preference falsification and knowledge consolidation. And now is the time for adherents of the current common understanding to transform it into party platforms, laws, regulations, or prescriptions of 'political correctness'. If the issue does not reach this stage, it may well lose momentum and either disappear into oblivion or end up having only ceremonial value as an inconsequential expression of common sense.

Among the 'issue entrepreneurs' and 'retailers' in this process, parties, interest groups and the media are the most prominent. And very much like their counterparts in capitalist society, they perform an entrepreneurial function, which is to overcome the resistance of those who cherish 'the routine tasks which everybody understands' (Schumpeter 1942/87, 132) by pushing through new issues on the limited agenda that public opinion is able to cope with. And, not unlike competition for consumers of most other goods, competition among issue entrepreneurs allows at best *temporary* 'pioneer' profits to be cashed in by creators of new issues. Profits from a monopoly of issue presentation and interpretation tend to disappear with the entry of other opinion makers. Thus, I argue, in the field of political leadership and issue entrepreneurship much of Schumpeter's analysis of the capitalist process can also be applied to a more comprehensive analysis of competition for leadership.[20]

5 OUTLOOK

Most of the creations of the intellect or fancy pass away for good after a time that varies between an after-dinner hour and a generation. Some, however, do not. They suffer eclipses but they come back again, and they come back not as

unrecognizable elements of a cultural inheritance, but in their individual garb
and with their personal scars which people may see and touch. (Schumpeter
1942/87, 3)

Mainly by ignoring the 'vital fact of leadership' and by not accepting voters
as 'primitives' (ibid., 270 and 262), the modern economics of politics left
both crucial elements of Schumpeter's 'other theory of democracy' largely
unexplored. In particular, today's economics of political competition,
which is still dominated by spatial voting models in the median voter tradition, cannot claim to have Schumpeter as a precursor. On the contrary, we
have even found occasions in which modern public choice, in terms of fundamental assumptions or of equilibrium results, looks strikingly similar to
the classical doctrine against which Schumpeter's whole thesis was directed.

Hence it is time to stop referring to a 'Schumpeter–Downs theory of
democracy' or celebrating Schumpeter as a pioneer of today's public choice.
But is it time for today's pioneers to start developing a neo-Schumpeterian
political economy instead? A radical break with public choice and a new
start with an old book by Schumpeter would be a fatal enterprise – its
costs being certainly high and its benefits highly uncertain. As Mitchell
(1984, 77) argued:

> Whatever Schumpeter's contributions to the study of politics, they assume the
> form not of positive theory in any strict sense, but a 'vision' . . . a sort of 'conceptual framework' profusely illustrated by historical examples and emotively-inspired generalizations about humans . . . Schumpeter did not set forth
> anything resembling a systematic, modern positivist theory of democracy.

This is not the best recommendation for academic entrepreneurs who set
out to succeed in the present world of economics. But new combinations of
modern (more or less 'mainstream economic') theories of democracy and
some of Schumpeter's visions and conceptual frameworks may be able to
succeed and, in fact, to help public choice out of a sterility and stagnation
which some critics are beginning to observe.[21]

Perhaps the most urgent and at the same time most difficult task remaining for public choice is to make sense of voter behaviour. Instrumental
rationality based on calculations of 'utility incomes' derived from 'party
differentials' leads to inner contradictions and provides a poor basis for
explanation and prediction. Instead, it seems imperative to take on board
cognitive psychology and communication theory in order to get more convincing explanations of why and how citizens vote, why and how they create
and communicate their political opinions. In the realm of low-cost decisions, *homo oeconomicus* finds not enough reasons to act as he should and
the economist finds not enough reasons to expect the same results 'as if' his

homo oeconomicus was still out there. If the defences, which still hold rather strongly in the economics of market transactions, break down in the economics of politics, then public choice is in trouble. But instead of giving up the field, it seems advisable to seek allies, for example, from theories of bounded rationality, cognitive dissonance, prospect theory, belief formation or preference falsification. These theories are much in line with Schumpeter's 'vision', but they provide 'conceptual frameworks' which are more robust and more easily reconcilable with economic analysis than Schumpeter's classic-style generalizations.

The second major topic on the Schumpeterian agenda, political leadership, seems less difficult to introduce into the overall research programme of public choice. However, mainstream neoclassical theory's problems of integrating entrepreneurship and innovation into its conceptual frameworks hardly inspire optimism that political entrepreneurs may soon be accorded a vital role in public choice. Here, above all the assumptions of given preferences and given 'issue-spaces', together with the view that democracy is a static aggregation method, oust the political leader. However, other economic paradigms such as evolutionary and Austrian economics, but also institutional economics and industrial organization have provided a large stock of theories that may (with some caution) also be applied to the political field (see Wohlgemuth 2000, 2002a).

The difficult choices that 'neo-Schumpeterian' new combinations in public choice would face are, again, best described in Schumpeter's own words quoted from a letter written only a few months before he died[22]: 'The main difficulty in the case of economics is to give full scope to the socio-psychological and sociological view without sacrificing at the same time the purely analytic filiation of scientific ideas, which asserts itself all the same'.

NOTES

* I wish to thank Israel Kirzner, Dennis Mueller, Mario Rizzo and Ronald Wintrobe for valuable criticism and suggestions. The usual disclaimer applies.
1. See, for example, Becker (1958, 105; 1985, 120ff.), Buchanan and Tullock (1962, 335), Buchanan (1987/88, 131; 1999, 20), Coe and Wilber (1985, 28), Mueller (1989a, 2; 1997, 6), Reisman (1990, 8, 300), Almond (1991), Rose and McAllister (1992, 117), Stolper (1994, 209), McNutt (1996, 2), Kinnear (1999, 932), or Bernholz (2000, 4, 7).
2. See Frey (1981), Mitchell (1984), Swedberg (1991), or Prisching (1995).
3. The model was first introduced by Hotelling's (1929) work carrying the characteristic title 'Stability in competition'. Black (1948) achieved its first full formulation for direct-democratic group decision making. But it was Downs (1957) who worked out the behavioural assumptions and structural conditions which allowed the theorem's application to more complex cases of representative democracy.
4. See Rowley (1984), Mueller (1989a), Enelow and Hinich (1990), Shepsle (1991) or Ordeshook (1997).

5. With 'probabilistic voting' parties do not, with the slightest move within the issue-space, lose or win clearly defined voters; they only affect the probability of winning or losing votes. Now, vote maximizing again drives both parties towards the same position within the given multidimensional probability space. The result equals that of a maximized Benthamite welfare function (Coughlin and Nitzan 1981; Ledyard 1984). The general validity of this potential reinstatement of democratic welfare functions is questioned on theoretical and empirical grounds by Kirchgässner (2000).
6. Modern versions apply various assumptions such as prospective or retrospective, deterministic or probabilistic voting. The demands on voters' rational calculation capacities, however, do not vary much.
7. The full calculation process would also include variables such as 'long-run participation values', 'the cost of voting' and 'preference for change'. For a full rendition of the logic, see Downs (1957, 271f.).
8. Downs (ibid., 241) notes that there is an infinite regress problem when starting with a party differential before investing in information. He cuts it short by assuming that there is a 'preliminary estimate' of the party differential 'derived without serious consideration of the cost and returns of making the estimate'.
9. As will be shown in more detail in Section 4.1, psychological and empirical research both strongly indicate that people's attitudes in selecting (sources of) information and opinion are fundamentally verificationist. Especially in politics, where such behaviour is 'cheap', it can loom large. But it has no place in Downs's world of pure instrumental rationality. Here, people are even advised to consult newspapers that are most likely to provide information that contradicts their ideological views (Downs 1957, 214).
10. Another consequence is that the more indifferent voters are (starting with low initial party differentials), the more willing they should be to invest in political information, whereas partisan voters would be most rationally ignorant, since it takes much more costly adverse information to change their mind – which remains the only rational reason for them to acquire it (ibid., 243). This inference is the exact opposite to empirical research in public opinion formation, as presented with overwhelming evidence, for example, in Zaller's (1992) *The Nature and Origins of Mass Opinion*.
11. Downs himself more recently criticized public choice for treating individual preferences and values as given, individual motivations as solely selfish and restrictions as solely external to the individual. He now stresses the functional qualities of shared moral values and informal conventions (see Downs 1991).
12. For example, Frank (1988), Brennan and Lomasky (1989), Kirchgässner and Pommerehne (1993), Brennan and Hamlin (2000).
13. For example, Frohlich and Oppenheimer (1978), McLean (1987), Buchanan and Vanberg (1989), Dunleavy (1991), Williamson and Haggard (1994), Johnson and Libecap (1999), Wohlgemuth (2000), Arce M. (2001), Sheingate (2001).
14. Kuran (1995, 24ff.) distinguishes three kinds of utility an individual can derive from publicly expressing an opinion: 'intrinsic utility' to be gained in terms of private benefits of collective decisions, 'reputational utility' derived from the social approval of others (which, if dominant, creates 'preference falsification', see below) and 'expressive utility' based on an individual's self-respect and self-assertion (which counteracts 'preference falsification'). While these utilities make a difference in *what* opinions are publicly articulated, they all provide reasons *why* political opinions are in fact entertained. As Kuran (ibid., 41) notes, standard economics tends to regard intrinsic utility as the sole driving force of individual action. Reputational and expressive utilities are rarely integrated in the rational choice model. This is fatal for the economic analysis of voter behaviour, as only these kinds of benefits are in fact attainable!
15. This is exactly Downs's position: 'Even though we cannot decide whether a decision-maker's ends are rational, we must know what they are before we can decide what behavior is rational for him. Furthermore, in designing these ends we must avoid the tautological conclusion that every man's behavior is always rational because (1) it is aimed at some end and (2) its returns must have outweighed its costs in his eyes or he would not have undertaken it' (1957, 6).

16. See Kahnemann and Tversky (1984), Lau and Sears (1986), Thaler (1987), Tversky and Kahnemann (1987), Quattrone and Tversky (1988), Frey and Eichenberger (1991), Rosenberg (1991), Wahlke (1991).
17. Different models of 'bounded', 'procedural' or 'rule-following' rationality have been proposed which share most of Simon's basic assertions. See, for example, Hayek (1968/78), Fiske and Taylor (1984), Selten (1990), Vanberg (1993) or Denzau and North (1994).
18. See Wohlgemuth (2002b) for a more detailed discussion of the differences between these two concepts of democracy. One defines democracy as a 'procedure for passing from a set of known individual tastes to a pattern of social decision making' (Arrow 1951, 2), the other as 'a process of forming opinion' (Hayek 1960, 108). In the Arrowian (or Downsian) understanding, democracy is a mechanism to aggregate given preferences in a given issue-space; and its task is to guarantee the logically consistent rule of a given will of the majority. In the Hayekian (or Popperian) understanding, democracy is a process of the formation and discovery of changing opinions on changing issues; and its task is the replacement of incompetent leaders, the creation of knowledge, and the contestability of majority opinions.
19. These models would not only substantiate important shortcomings of political discourse compared to the articulation and satisfaction of private preferences on competitive *markets* (see Wohlgemuth 2005) They can also help to formulate some modest virtues of democracy compared to other realistic methods of *political* decision making. After all, Schumpeter's theory of democracy also seeks 'to clarify the relation that subsists between democracy and individual freedom' (1942/87, 271). While Schumpeter (much like Hayek) claims no necessary relation between majority rule and personal liberties, he (again, like Hayek), acknowledges the value of the 'freedom of discussion for all', which quite naturally follows from the principle that 'everyone is free to compete for political leadership' (ibid., 271f.). Under these premises, it is possible to engage in comparative institutional analysis of political systems and argue in a rather Austrian spirit that democracy can be a 'discovery procedure' of such knowledge and opinions as, without resort to it, may not be known or at least not be utilized (see Wohlgemuth 1999).
20. Another application along these lines would be to draw on Schumpeter's discussion on 'plausible capitalism' (1942/87 ch. iv) and enter a similarly structured discussion of favourable conditions for 'plausible democracy'. Wohlgemuth (2000) discusses two political 'Schumpeter hypotheses' about relations between entry barriers in politics and the incentives and opportunities for political entrepreneurs to invest in long-term positive-sum reforms.
21. See many contributions to Rowley et al. (1993), to Monroe (1991), or the discussion of Green and Shapiro (1984) in the *Critical Review*, vol. 9 (1995). See also Udehn (1996).
22. Schumpeter (2000, 393; letter to William A. Weisskopf, dated 18 November 1949).

REFERENCES

Akerlof, George A. (1989), 'The economics of illusion', *Economics and Politics*, **1**, 1–15.

Akerlof, George A. and William T. Dickens (1982), 'The economic consequences of cognitive dissonance', *American Economic Review*, **72**, 307–19.

Almond, Gabriel A. (1991), 'Rational choice theory and the social sciences', in Kristen R. Monroe (ed.), *The Economic Approach to Politics: A Critical Reassessment of the Theory of Rational Action*, New York: Harper Collins, pp. 32–52.

Arce M. Daniel G. (2001), 'Leadership and the aggregation of international collective action', *Oxford Economic Papers*, **53**, 114–37.

Arrow, Kenneth J. (1951), *Social Choice and Individual Values*, New York: Wiley & Sons.

Arrow, Kenneth J. (1962/85), 'Economic welfare and the allocation of resources for invention', in Arrow (1985), *Collected Papers of Kenneth J. Arrow*, Vol. 5, Cambridge: Cambridge University Press, pp. 104–19.

Becker, Gary S. (1958), 'Competition and democracy', *Journal of Law and Economics*, **1**, 105–9.

Becker, Gary S. (1985), 'Pressure groups and political behavior', in Richard D. Coe and Charles K. Wilber (eds), *Capitalism and Democracy: Schumpeter Revisited*, Notre Dame, IN: University of Notre Dame Press, pp. 120–42.

Bernholz, Peter (2000), 'Democracy and capitalism: are they compatible in the long-run?', *Journal of Evolutionary Economics*, **10**, 3–16.

Black, Duncan (1948), 'On the rationale of group decision making', *Journal of Political Economy*, **56**, 23–34.

Boulding, Kenneth E. (1956), *The Image*, Ann Arbor, MI: University of Michigan Press.

Brady, Gordon L., J.R. Clark and William L. Davis (1995), 'The political economy of dissonance', *Public Choice*, **82**, 37–51.

Brennan, Geoffrey and James M. Buchanan (1984), 'Voter choice: evaluating political alternatives', *American Behavioral Scientist*, **28**, 185–201.

Brennan, Geoffrey and Alan Hamlin (2000), *Democratic Devices and Desires*, Cambridge: Cambridge University Press.

Brennan, Geoffrey and Loren E. Lomasky (1989), 'Large numbers, small costs: the uneasy foundation of democratic rule', in Brennan and Lomasky (eds), *Politics and Process: New Essays in Democratic Thought*, Cambridge: Cambridge University Press, pp. 42–59.

Buchanan, James M. (1969), *Cost and Choice: An Inquiry into Economic Theory*, Chicago: University of Chicago Press.

Buchanan, James M. (1972), 'Toward analysis of closed behavioral systems', in James M. Buchanan and Robert D. Tollison (eds), *Theory of Public Choice*, Ann Arbor, MI: University of Michigan Press, pp. 11–23.

Buchanan, James M. (1987/88), 'Justification of the compound republic: the calculus in retrospect', in James D. Gwartney and Richard E. Wagner (eds), *Public Choice and Constitutional Economics*, Greenwich, CT and London: JAI Press, pp. 103–14.

Buchanan, James M. (1999), 'Origins, experiences and ideas: a retrospective assessment', in James M. Buchanan and Richard A. Musgrave (eds), *Public Finance and Public Choice: Two Contrasting Visions of the State*, Cambridge, MA and London: MIT Press, pp. 11–28.

Buchanan, James M. and Gordon Tullock (1962), *The Calculus of Consent: Logical Foundations of Constitutional Democracy*, Ann Arbor, MI: University of Michigan Press.

Buchanan, James M. and Viktor Vanberg (1989), 'A theory of leadership and deference in constitutional construction', *Public Choice*, **61**, 15–27.

Butler, David and Donald Stokes (1974), *Political Change in Britain: The Evolution of Electoral Choice*, New York: St. Martin's.

Caplan, Bryan (2001), 'Rational ignorance versus rational irrationality', **54**, 3–26.

Coe, Richard D. and Charles K. Wilber (1985), 'Schumpeter revisited: an overview', in Coe and Wilber, *Capitalism and Democracy: Schumpeter Revisited*, Notre Dame, IN: University of Notre Dame Press, pp. 1–59.

Coughlin, Peter and Shmuel Nitzan (1981), 'Electoral outcomes with probabilistic voting and Nash welfare maxima', *Journal of Public Economics*, **15**, 113–21.
Denzau, Arthur T. and Douglass C. North (1994), 'Shared mental models: ideologies and institutions', *Kyklos*, **47**, 3–31.
Downs, Anthony (1957), *An Economic Theory of Democracy*, New York: Harper & Row.
Downs, Anthony (1991), 'Social values and democracy', in Kristen R. Monroe (ed.), *The Economic Approach to Politics: A Critical Reassessment of the Theory of Rational Action*, New York: Harper Collins, pp. 143–70.
Dunleavy, Partick (1991), *Democracy, Bureaucracy and Public Choice*, New York: Harvester Wheatsheaf.
Enelow, James and Melvin Hinich (eds) (1990), *Advances in the Spatial Theory of Voting*, Cambridge: Cambridge University Press.
Festinger, Leon (1957), *A Theory of Cognitive Dissonance*, Palo Alto, CA: Stanford University Press
Fiske, Susan T. and S.E. Taylor (1984), *Social Cognition*, New York: Random House.
Frank, Robert H. (1988), *Passions within Reason*, New York: Norton.
Frey, Bruno S. (1981), 'Schumpeter, political economist', in Helmut Frisch (ed.), *Schumpeterian Economics*, New York: Praeger, pp. 126–42.
Frey, Bruno S. and Reiner Eichenberger (1991), 'Anomalies in political economy', *Public Choice*, **68**, 71–89.
Frohlich, Norman and Joe A. Oppenheimer (1978), *Modern Political Economy*, Englewood Cliffs, NJ: Prentice-Hall.
Green, Donald P. and Ian Shapiro (1984), *Pathologies of Rational Choice Theory: A Critique of Applications in Political Science*, New Haven, CT: Yale University Press.
Hardin, Russell (1999), 'Street-level epistemology and political participation', Paper presented at the European Public Choice Society Meeting, Lisbon, April, mimeo.
Hayek, Friedrich A. von (1952/79), *The Counter-Revolution of Science: Studies on the Abuse of Reason*, 2nd edn, Indianapolis: Liberty Press.
Hayek, Friedrich A. von (1960), *The Constitution of Liberty*, Chicago: University of Chicago Press.
Hayek, Friedrich A. von (1968/78), 'The confusion of language in political thought', in Hayek (1978), *New Studies in Philosophy, Politics, Economics and the History of Ideas*, Chicago: University of Chicago Press, pp. 71–97.
Heilbronner, Robert L. (1953), *The Wordly Philosophers: The Lives, Times, and Ideas of the Great Economic Thinkers*, New York: Simon & Schuster.
Hinich, Melvin J. (1977), 'Equilibrium in spatial voting: the median voter result is an artifact', *Journal of Economic Theory*, **16**, 208–19.
Hirschman, Albert O. (1989), 'Having opinions: one of the elements of well-being?', *American Economic Review: Papers and Proceedings*, **79**, 75–9.
Holcombe, Randall G. (1980), 'An empirical test of the median voter model', *Economic Inquiry*, **18**, 260–74.
Holcombe, Randall G. (1989), 'The median voter model in public choice theory', *Public Choice*, **61**, 115–25.
Hotelling, Harold (1929), 'Stability in competition', *Economic Journal*, **39**, 41–57.
Huckfeldt, Robert and John Sprague (1995), *Citizens, Politics, and Social Communication: Information and Influence in an Election Campaign*, Cambridge: Cambridge University Press.

Inman, Robert P. (1978), 'Testing political economy's "as if" assumption: is the median income voter really decisive?', *Public Choice*, **33** (4), 45–65.
Johnson, Ronald N. and Gary Libecap (1999), 'Information distortion and competitive remedies in government transfer programs: the case of ethanol', Discussion Paper 07–99, Max-Planck-Institute for Research into Economic Systems, Jena.
Kahnemann, Daniel and Amos Tversky (1984), 'Choices, values, and frames', *American Psychologist*, **39**, 341–50.
Kinder, Donald R. and D. Roderick Kriewiet (1981), 'Sociotropic voting: the American case', *British Journal of Political Science*, **11**, 129–61.
Kinnear, Douglas (1999), 'Public choice theory', in Phillip O'Hara (ed.), *Encyclopedia of Political Economy*, London: Routledge, pp. 931–3.
Kirchgässner, Gebhard (2000), 'Probabilistic voting and equilibrium: an impossibility result', *Public Choice*, **103**, 35–48.
Kirchgässner, Gebhard and Werner W. Pommerehne (1993), 'Low-cost decisions as a challenge to public choice', *Public Choice*, **77**, 107–15.
Kliemt, Hartmut (1986), 'The veil of insignificance', *European Journal of Political Economy*, **2**, 333–44.
Knudsen, Christian (1993), 'Equilibrium, perfect rationality and the problem of self-reference in economics', in Uskali Mäki, Bo Gustafsson and Christian Knudsen (eds), *Rationality, Institutions and Economic Methodology*, London: Routledge, pp. 133–70.
Kuran, Timor (1995), *Private Truths, Public Lies: The Social Consequences of Preference Falsification*, Cambridge, MA: Harvard University Press.
Lau, Richard R. and David Sears (eds) (1986), *Political Cognition*, Hillsdale, NJ: Lawrence Erlbaum.
Ledyard, John O. (1984), 'The pure theory of large two-candidate elections', *Public Choice*, **44** (1), 7–41.
Lowell, A. Lawrence (1913), *Public Opinion and Popular Government*, New York: Longmans, Green, & Co.
Luhmann, Niklas (1970/75), 'Öffentliche Meinung' [*Public Opinion*], in Luhmann, *Politische Planung. Aufsätze zur Soziologie von Politik und Verwaltung [Political Planning Essays on the Sociology of Politics and Administration]*, 2nd edn 1975, Opladen: Westdeutscher Verlag, pp. 9–34.
McLean, Iain (1987), *Public Choice: An Introduction*, Oxford and New York: Basil Blackwell.
McNutt, Patrick A. (1996), *The Economics of Public Choice*, Cheltenham, UK and Northampton, MA, USA: Edward Elgar.
Mitchell, William C. (1984), 'Schumpeter and public choice, Part I: Precursor of public choice?', *Public Choice*, **42**, 73–88.
Monroe, Kristen R. (ed.) (1991), *The Economic Approach to Politics: A Critical Reassessment of the Theory of Rational Action*, New York: Harper Collins.
Mueller, Dennis C. (1989a), *Public Choice II: A Revised Edition of Public Choice*, Cambridge: Cambridge University Press.
Mueller, Dennis C. (1989b), 'Democracy: the public choice approach', in Geoffrey Brennan and Loren E. Lomasky (eds), *Politics and Process: New Essays in Democratic Thought*, Cambridge: Cambridge University Press, pp. 78–96.
Mueller, Dennis C. (1997), 'Public choice in perspective', in Mueller, *Perspectives on Public Choice: A Handbook*, Cambridge: Cambridge University Press, pp. 1–17.

Munley, Vincent G. (1984), 'Has the median voter found a ballot box he can control?', *Economic Inquiry*, **22**, 323–36.
Nannestad, Peter and Martin Paldam (1994), 'The VP-function: a survey of the literature on vote and popularity functions after 25 years', *Public Choice*, **79**, 213–45.
Noelle-Neumann, Elisabeth (1993), *The Spiral of Silence: Public Opinion – Our Social Skin*, 2nd edn, Chicago: University of Chicago Press.
Ordeshook, Peter C. (1997), 'The spatial analysis of elections and committees: four decades of research', in Dennis Mueller (ed.), *Perspectives on Public Choice*, Cambridge: Cambridge University Press, pp. 247–70.
Pennock, J. Roland (1989), 'The justification of democracy', in Geoffrey Brennan and Loren E. Lomasky (eds), *Politics and Process: New Essays in Democratic Thought*, Cambridge: Cambridge University Press, pp. 11–41.
Pommerehne, Werner (1978), 'Institutional approaches to public expenditure: empirical evidence from Swiss municipalities', *Journal of Public Economics*, **9**, 255–80.
Prisching, Manfred (1995), 'The limited rationality of democracy: Schumpeter as the founder of irrational choice theory', *Critical Review*, **9**, 301–24.
Quattrone, George A. and Amos Tversky (1988), 'Contrasting rational and psychological analysis of political choice', *American Political Science Review*, **82**, 719–36.
Rabin, Matthew (1998), 'Psychology and economics', *Journal of Economic Literature*, **36**, 11–46.
Reisman, David (1990), *Theories of Collective Action: Downs, Olson, and Hirsch*, New York,: St. Martin's.
Riker, William H. (1986), *The Art of Political Manipulation*, New Haven, CT: Yale University Press.
Riker, William H. and Peter Ordeshook (1968), 'A theory of the calculus of voting', *American Political Science Review*, **62**, 25–43.
Rose, Richard and Ian McAllister (1992), 'Expressive vs. instrumental voting', in Dennis Kavanagh (ed.), *Electoral Politics*, Oxford: Clarendon, pp. 114–40.
Rosenberg, Shawn W. (1991), 'Rationality, markets, and political analysis: a social psychological critique of neoclassical political economy', in Kristen R. Monroe (ed.), *The Economic Approach to Politics: A Critical Reassessment of the Theory of Rational Action*, New York: HarperCollins, pp. 386–404.
Rowley, Charles K. (1984), 'The relevance of the median voter theorem', *Zeitschrift für die gesamte Staatswissenschaft*, **140**, 104–26.
Rowley, Charles K., Friedrich Schneider and Robert D. Tollison (eds) (1993), 'The next twenty-five years of *Public Choice*', *Public Choice*, **77**, 1–7.
Schumpeter, Joseph A. (1912/34), *The Theory of Economic Development. An Inquiry into Profits, Capital, Credit, Interest Rates, and the Business Cycle*, Cambridge, MA: Harvard University Press.
Schumpeter, Joseph A. (1942/87), *Capitalism, Socialism and Democracy*, London 1987: Unwin Paperbacks.
Schumpeter, Joseph A. (2000), *Briefe/Letters – ausgewählt und herausgegeben von Ulrich Hedtke und Richard Swedberg* [*Letters, Selected and Edited by Ulrich Hedtke and Richard Swedberg*], Tübingen: Mohr Siebeck.
Sears, David O., Richard R. Lau, Tom Tyler and A.M. Allen Jr. (1980), 'Self-interest vs. symbolic politics in policy attitudes and presidential voting', *American Political Science Review*, **74**, 670–84.

Selten, Reinhard (1990), 'Bounded rationality', *Journal of Institutional and Theoretical Economics*, **146**, 649–58.
Shackle, George L.S. (1972), *Epistemics and Economics: A Critique of Economic Doctrines*, Cambridge: Cambridge University Press.
Sheingate, Adam (2001), 'Entrepreneurial innovation and institutional change', Johns Hopkins University, mimeo.
Shepsle, Kenneth A. (1991), *Models of Multiparty Competition*, Chur: Harwood Academic Publishers.
Simon, Herbert A. (1957), *Models of Man*, New York: Wiley.
Simon, Herbert A. (1978), 'Rationality as a process and as a product of thought', *American Economic Review*, **68**, 1–15.
Simon, Herbert A. (1986), 'Rationality in psychology and economics', *Journal of Business*, **59**, 209–24.
Smith, Vernon L. (1985), 'Experimental economics: Reply', *American Economic Review*, **75**, 265–72.
Splichal, Slavo (1999), *Public Opinion. Developments and Controversies in the Twentieth Century*, Lanham, MD: Rowman & Littlefield.
Stigler, George J. (1961), 'The economics of information', *Journal of Political Economy*, **69**, 213–25.
Stokes, Donald (1992), 'Valence politics', in Dennis Kavanagh (ed.), *Electoral Politics*, Oxford: Clarendon, pp. 141–64.
Stolper, Wolfgang (1994), *Joseph Alois Schumpeter: The Public Life of a Private Man*, Princeton, NJ: Princeton University Press.
Sunstein, Cass R. (1996), 'Social norms and social roles', *Columbia Law Review*, **96**, 903–68.
Swedberg, Richard (1991), *Schumpeter: A Biography*, Princeton, NJ: Princeton University Press.
Thaler, Richard (1987), 'The Psychology and Economics Conference Handbook: Comments on Simon, on Einhorn and Hogarth, and on Tversky and Kahnemann', in Robin M. Hogarth and Melvin W. Reder (eds), *Rational Choice*, Chicago: University of Chicago Press, pp. 95–100.
Tversky, Amos and Daniel Kahnemann (1987), 'Rational choice and the framing of decisions', in Robin M. Hogarth and Melvin W. Reder (eds), *Rational Choice*, Chicago: University of Chicago Press, pp. 67–94.
Udehn, Lars (1996), *The Limits of Public Choice: A Sociological Critique of the Economic Theory of Politics*, London and New York: Routledge.
Vanberg, Viktor (1993), 'Rational choice, rule-following and institutions: an evolutionary perspective', in Uskali Mäki, Bo Gustafsson and Christian Knudsen (eds), *Rationality, Institutions and Economic Methodology*, London: Routledge, pp. 171–200.
Vanberg, Viktor and James M. Buchanan (1989), 'Interests and theories in constitutional choice', *Journal of Theoretical Politics*, **1**, 49–63.
Wahlke, John C. (1991), 'Rational choice theory, voting behavior, and democracy', in Albert Somit and Rudolf Wildenmann (eds), *Hierarchy and Democracy*, Baden-Baden: Nomos, pp. 165–87.
Weissberg, Robert (1996), 'The real marketplace of ideas', *Critical Review*, **10**, 107–21.
Williamson, John and Stephan Haggard (1994), 'The political conditions for economic reform', in John Williamson (ed.), *The Political Economy of Policy Reform*, Washington, DC: Institute for International Economics, pp. 527–96.

Witt, Ulrich (1996), 'The political economy of mass media societies', Papers on Economics and Evolution no. 9601, Max-Planck-Institute for Research into Economic Systems, Jena.

Wittman, Donald A. (1995), *The Myth of Democratic Failure: Why Political Institutions are Efficient*, Chicago: University of Chicago Press.

Wohlgemuth, Michael (1999), 'Democracy as a discovery procedure: toward an Austrian economics of the political process', Discussion Paper 17–99, Max-Planck-Institute for Research into Economic Systems, Jena.

Wohlgemuth, Michael (2000), 'Political entrepreneurship and bidding for political monopoly', *Journal of Evolutionary Economics*, **10**, 273–95.

Wohlgemuth, Michael (2002a), 'Evolutionary approaches to politics', *Kyklos* **55** (2), 223–46.

Wohlgemuth, Michael (2002b), 'Democracy and opinion falsification: towards a new Austrian political economy', *Constitutional Political Economy*, **13** (3), 223–46.

Wohlgemuth, Michael (2005), 'The communicative character of capitalistic competition. A Hayekian response to the Habermasian challenge', *The Independent Review*, **10** (1), 83–115.

Zaller, John R. (1992), *The Nature and Origins of Mass Opinion*, Cambridge: Cambridge University Press.

3. The effects of cyberspace on the economic theory of the state*

Eli M. Salzberger and Niva Elkin-Koren

1 INTRODUCTION

The Western world celebrates two centuries of liberal democracy in theory and about one century of liberal democracy in practice. Concepts such as majority decision making, representative government, human rights, the rule of law and separation of powers have become self-evident. Our debates concerning the good state and good government take these concepts as presuppositions, which do not require additional justification or reasoning. Indeed, we live in the paradigm of liberalism.[1] The term 'paradigm' was used by Thomas Kuhn, when he put forward a theory of the development of natural science (1962). But his description of the evolution of science can be extended to the way we think about normative issues, about practical laws rather than merely theoretical ones.

The current political theory discourse is conducted within the boundaries of the liberal paradigm. The current debate is based on a set of presuppositions, which was left unchecked through the last 100 years. The paradigm of liberalism, which is the result of the Enlightenment, as well as technological breakthroughs of the modern era (such as the invention of the printing press), has been shaken by the technological revolution of the last decade. This chapter examines whether cyberspace requires a paradigmatic shift in our thinking about collective action, the public sphere and the state.

Cyberspace may affect the normative and positive economic analysis of the state and its main powers and governing tools. It may break the notion of states as independent identifiable entities; it changes the analysis of collective action and rule-making processes; it affects the concept of law. This chapter focuses on normative analysis – on the economic theory of the state and on possible effects of cyberspace on this theory. It is important to emphasize, however, that the normative argument regarding the state, its institutions and its collective decision-making process, is also contingent upon significant elements of positive analysis, which will not be discussed here.[2]

The chapter begins with a brief history of economic analysis of the theory of the state (Section 2), followed by mapping the normative sources of such theories (Section 3). The heart of the chapter constructs a fresh skeleton argument for a theory of the state, based on the consensus leading normative principle, and in light of the effects cyberspace may have on the various links in this argument (Section 4). The chapter concludes with the major two fundamental problems that cyberspace poses to the theory of the state (Section 5).

2 ECONOMIC ANALYSIS AND THE THEORY OF THE STATE

Ever since the eighteenth-century works of Borda (1781) and Condorcet ([1785] 1955) on majority decision making, the economic approach can be viewed as having a stake in analysing the 'state', its organs and its tools conducting and coordinating the activity in the public sphere. *Public choice* is the major branch of economics that focuses on these issues, as it is interested in economic analysis of non-market decision making, or in individual decision makers as participants in a complex interaction that generates collective decision making and political outcomes (Mercuro and Medema 1997, p. 84). Questions related to the theory of the state are also dealt with in the framework of *game theory* (Baird et al. 1994). Indeed, Hobbes's *Leviathan* ([1651] 1979) can be regarded as the first game theory-based explanation for the creation of modern states. Likewise, the main stream of *neoclassical* economics on its various branches, or the traditional *microeconomic* paradigm, in both normative and positive levels of analysis, is also employed as a methodological tool to discuss various questions related to the theory of the state.

The microeconomic analysis of the emergence of the state focuses on possible market failures, which justify central intervention in the market. Such central intervention requires the existence of a state and central government. More particularly, the market failure of public goods is often portrayed as the main rationale for the very establishment of the state (Buchanan 1975, pp. 35–52 – on the normative level of analysis; North 1981 – on the positive level). One of the major goals of such a creation is to enable economic markets to operate, thus establishing property rights and ensuring that they will not change hands, bypassing the markets. The ability to operate markets is itself a public good which needs a central pre-market intervention in the shape of a political entity such as the state. The creation of property rights is also one of the focal points of the contractarian view of the state (Skogh and Stuart 1982).

In recent years *neo-institutional* law and economics is engaged in projects in which the traditional market analysis – microeconomic or welfare economics – is incorporated into the public choice paradigm.[3] The new theoretical and methodological frameworks brought about an increasing interest of the economic approach in the analysis of the public sphere, as can be exemplified by the recent writings on constitutional law and economics (Mueller 1996; Cooter 1999; Voigt 1999).

On a positive level of analysis, the various economic methodologies aim to explain why institutions are structured the way they are and how these structures affect the outcomes of social or collective choices. On a normative level, different theories offer an ideal model for the structure of government, the division between constitutional and post-constitutional arrangements, the desirable form of separation of powers and related questions. Some of the differences between the normative models are the result of different starting points with regard to the leading moral principles, which ought to guide collective action. Thus, most Chicago school law and economics writings aim at wealth maximization as the ultimate normative goal, while most public choice literature is constructed upon the social contract tradition, or its economic equivalent – the Pareto principle. We shall elaborate on these different exogenous foundations in Section 3.

3 LOCATING AND MAPPING THE NORMATIVE SOURCES OF THE ECONOMIC THEORY OF THE STATE

Before delving into the details of the economic theory of the state, and the possible effects cyberspace may have on it, let us sketch a thick brush map of theories of the state, and try to locate the economic theory within this map.

The oldest and still most important debate within jurisprudence (the theory of law) is the debate between positivist theories of law and non-positivist theories, prominent among which are natural law theories. One can point at a parallel framework with regard to the theory of the state, a framework that goes back to the great Greek philosophers. Plato viewed the state, similarly to his view of the law, as a natural creation, while Aristotle viewed it as man-made. The economic theory of the state is naturally in the Aristotelian path. As the broader liberal paradigm, the economic approach originates from the eighteenth-century Enlightenment – an intellectual and cultural movement that emphasized reason, knowledge, human interaction and progress. Indeed, one of the most important foundations of the economic approach is the presupposition of rational individuals, who are the atoms of society. It views collective organization units, such as states and governments, as artificial and instrumental creations whose sole purpose is to enhance individuals' well-being.

The positivist approach to the state is also the intellectual setting for the emergence of the social contract theories, which are the bedrock of most modern theories of the state, among which, liberal democracy, as well as the economic theory of the state. Social contract theories view the emergence of the state as the result of a contract between its future citizens. The focal point in this view is the normative justification for collective organization, decision making and enforcement. The justification rests on the initial consent of all those who subject themselves to the state, and for the sake of this general framework it is less important to specify at this stage whether this consent is real, hypothetical, counterfactual and so on.[4]

What is important to emphasize is that the consensus principle of the social contract theories resembles very much the Pareto improvement criterion of microeconomic theory. Both justify a collective decision making only if it is supported by *all* individuals who are affected by it. Individuals would support a decision if it enhances their well-being or leaves them indifferent in comparison to their well-being prior to the decision. Hence, consensus will bring Pareto improvement or Pareto optimality (Coleman 1988, part IV). However, there is also a significant difference between the two. While the Pareto principle was offered as second best to utility maximization, the consensus principle is the leading normative principle of the social contract theories of the state, and the economic theory, which follows this tradition.

To understand better this important difference, we have to go back to the common cradle of both principles – the Enlightenment and its view of rational individuals as the centre of moral philosophy or political morality. From this common origin one can point at two parallel (chronologically and substance matter) developments. One is the birth of the neoclassical economic theory; the other is the framework for the public choice theory of the state.

Many regard Adam Smith's *Wealth of Nations* ([1776] 1961) as the birth of modern economic science. The invisible hand that brings free markets to equilibrium is still one of the bedrocks of microeconomic theory. This monumental work was published a few years after utilitarianism – Jeremy Bentham's ([1789] 1948) new moral theory – was launched.[5] Although Adam Smith was also a moral philosopher, and Bentham was also writing on economics, no direct connection was made between Smith's economic theory and Bentham's moral philosophy. This connection was made only a generation later by the neoclassical economists, who adopted for their market analysis the assumptions of utilitarianism, and advocated the market solutions as those that maximize total utility. The works of Harsanyi (1955 and 1977) can be regarded as a direct offspring of this heritage, applied to the analysis of the constitution. Under several postulates, constitutional choices, according to Harsanyi, should reflect maximization of expected individual utilities.

It is important to highlight the new paradigm within which utilitarianism and microeconomic theory were nurtured. This paradigm assumes that individuals are rational, that they opt for choices that maximize their happiness or utility or welfare, and that there is no value in society beyond the values individuals attribute to every decision or action. These presuppositions leave room only for a limited debate as to what is the best way to aggregate or balance between individuals' well-being or individual preferences, when a collective choice is needed, and what are the optimal collective institutions and procedures to achieve this aggregate. The utilitarian answer, which was adopted by neoclassic economic theory, was that maximization of the sum of individual utilities is the right normative criterion.

But economists faced a problem with the implementation of the maximization of utility as the leading normative principle. How can individual utility be measured, and how can it be compared across different individuals? When the market is fully competitive, argued the economists, there is no need for such measurement, as the invisible hand or the market powers through voluntary interactions will bring about the desirable equilibrium, which maximizes social utility. But markets are usually not fully competitive. In most markets there are market failures, which require central intervention, and then the application of the utility-maximization principle is problematic.[6]

The microeconomics theory of the early twentieth century found two solutions to the practical difficulties with utility measurement and comparison. One solution resorted to ordinal preferences – a weaker assumption that individuals can rank various options, but cannot attribute a precise utility measure to each. This solution is reflected by the Pareto principle. The other solution was put forward by welfare economics – substituting utility with wealth. Money units are measurable and comparable. It is important to emphasize that both paths view themselves as second best, while utility maximization is still the desirable ultimate normative goal. This is also the reason why Richard Posner's (1979) advocacy of wealth maximization as the leading normative principle is innovative and can be viewed as departing from traditional welfare economics, as it views wealth maximization as the leading normative principle rather than second best.

The social choice and public choice literature originates from different Enlightenment scholars who shared the same presupposition about human rationality. This tradition goes back in time to encompass the social contract philosophers – Thomas Hobbes ([1651] 1979) and John Locke ([1690] 1989). It passes through the works of Borda (1781), Condorcet ([1785] 1955) and Charles Dodgson (who was no other than Lewis Carroll). Their twentieth-century followers include Duncan Black (1948) Kenneth Arrow (1951) and James Buchanan (1975). The incorporation of the positive analysis of social choice theorists and the normative analysis of the social contract philosophers resulted in the works of Anthony Downs (1957), James Buchanan and Gordon Tullock (1962) and John Rawls (1971). The corresponding normative analysis of the latter direction was based on unanimity rather than maximization of utility (or, later, maximization of wealth).

The unanimity or consensual principle is neither teleological (consequential, like utilitarianism) nor deontological (governed by natural law). It belongs to a set of principles that judge desirability according to the decision-making process. Majority rule belongs to this group, but majority decision making does not have any coherent and integral internal normative justification. Unanimity, or consensus, does. Under the assumption that individuals are rational, no one will give his or her consent to a decision that harms him-/herself. Thus, every decision, based on unanimity, will benefit at least one person, without harming any other.

In a world of no transaction costs (or no market failures), the requirement of unanimity will also lead to utility maximization. If there were a decision that enhances the total utility, consensus would be achieved in adopting it, as it will be possible to compensate all those who are harmed by the decision and still those who gain will be better off; thus everyone will vote for the decision. This principle, therefore, guarantees individual rights (set by each and every person) and it is also efficient in the sense of the Pareto principle. However, in the real world, transaction costs are not zero and very few collective decisions can be reached by consensus. So, as will be elaborated below, unanimity is the base line, from which rational individuals will depart in order to enable society to handle its daily business.

As indicated above, the public choice–social choice theory of the state is structured upon the social contract theories and the consensus principle. There is, however a secondary, but not less significant debate within social contract theories, where Thomas Hobbes represents one pole and Jean Jacques Rousseau ([1762] 1998) represents the other. This debate was also the source for the major controversy of the American Founding Fathers: between pluralists and federalists, on one side, and republicans and antifederalists, on the other side. It is important also in the context of the economic theory of the state, which can be viewed as founded upon, or as a direct continuation of, Hobbes's social contract, rejecting the Rousseau analysis.

In modern economic terms, Hobbes views individuals as rational and self-interested, with a set of preferences that are exogenous to the collective decision-making process and institutions.[7] Thus, the collective sphere is principled on bringing about an improvement for some individuals without impinging on the well-being of others. Hobbes portrayed a minimal or very thin social contract, in which all people are prepared to deposit all their rights in the hands of the Leviathan in exchange for personal security. Locke had a broader view of the content of the contract, and modern legal philosophers of this tradition, for example, Rawls (1971), have yet a broader view of the content of the social contract. This view contrasts natural law approaches, which hold that the good is divine or precedes human conception of it, but also contrasts 'communitarian' social contract approaches, which assume that there is a value in society beyond the values reflected by the preferences of its individuals. Such is Rousseau's theory, which views the 'general will' (or the general good) as distinct or separate from some kind of summing of all individuals' wills.

We are unaware of any attempt to present Rousseau's work in the framework of an economic analysis and we are not sure that he himself would have been happy with such a presentation. Yet, we think that such an attempt is worth exploring, especially in the context of cyberspace and its effect on the theory of the state. From an economic analysis perspective, one can present Rousseau's theory as differing from Hobbes and his tradition in one important assumption or presupposition. Economic analysis *à la* Rousseau assumes that individual preferences are not exogenous, but endogenous to the political process. In other words, the difference between the general will and the sum of the wills of all individuals can be presented as the result of changes of preferences, from self-regarding towards more cooperative, other-regarding and less-conflicting preferences. This change of preferences is the result of collective endeavours, such as deliberation and participation. We shall return to this important theme later.

Let us examine now how, on the basis of the unanimity normative principle, a theory of the state can be derived, and how cyberspace may affect the traditional liberal democratic notion of the state.

4 THE ECONOMIC THEORY OF THE STATE – THE SKELETON ARGUMENT

In the previous section we laid down the possible leading normative principles for a theory of the state. We shall continue by adopting the consensus as this leading principle, setting aside deontological theories, on the one hand, and utility or wealth maximization, on the other, although we shall refer to those normative guidelines as well. What follows are several links in a chain construction of a theory of the state based on the consensus principle, alongside analyses of the effects of cyberspace on each link of the argument.

4.1 The Justifications for the Creation of States

The common theme of most positivist theories (as opposed to natural law theories) that discuss the creation of the state is that the establishment of the collective entity called 'state' can benefit the individuals who are to become its future citizens. The meaning of 'benefit' is, of course, contingent upon the substantive–normative foundations adopted by each theory. But these foundations are not limited to a consequential (teleological) or procedural sort of morality, such as utilitarianism, wealth maximization or Pareto optimality or consent. They are broader than the common foundations of the economic approach. This idea of transformation from a state of anarchy to a centrally governed society was put forward by Thomas Hobbes in *Leviathan* ([1651] 1979). Indeed, Hobbes can be viewed as both the founder of the social contract theory of the state and the founder of the economic theory of the state. His ideas were rephrased in economic language in the second half of the twentieth century, by, among others, Downs (1957), Buchanan and Tullock (1962), Buchanan (1975), North (1986) and Mueller (1996, pp. 51–4).

There are different contemporary variations of this idea. Some theorists emphasize that the establishment of the state, or any political society, is a response to the market failure of public goods. Those goods will not be produced (or will be underproduced) in the absence of a central collective organization. Thus, the state is created, according to this rationale, because it enables the production and consumption of public goods, which are not produced or supplied in the state of nature (Buchanan 1975, pp. 35–52). Defence and justice are two of the most significant examples of such goods (the former is the sole justification for the establishment of the state according to Hobbes). The mere ability to operate markets founded on private property and voluntary transactions is another such good (John Locke justified the state as a common mechanism to protect private property).

Other theorists view the emergence of the state in a way similar to Coase's (1937) description of the emergence of the firm – a result of vertical integration. This is caused by transaction and information costs associated with contracting within markets, which force production and exchange out of the markets and into organizations such as the firm or the state (Silver 1977; Macey 1989). A related view portrays the state as a framework for providing alternative institutional arrangements to contracts in the free market, which cannot be negotiated due to high transaction costs (Tullock 1982).

These rationales focus on market failures as the justification for the creation of the state. But one must keep in mind that even in a perfect market with no failures whatsoever, a collective organization will be required to ensure that the market will not be bypassed. Markets cannot operate without the concept of private property (Easterbrook 1996, pp. 212–14), and a collective organization is required to create and protect private property. The state is also required to ensure that market transactions are followed by the parties to the transaction and by third parties. This applies even in a perfect world where there are no internal market failures impeding the conclusion of efficient transactions.

Cyberspace may have an effect on all of these rationales. For instance, it can remedy some public goods failures by enabling exclusion through the usage of sophisticated technological means, thus turning some goods that were public in the non-virtual world into private goods (Elkin-Koren and Salzberger 1999, pp. 559–61; 2004, ch. 5). This is true for some public goods, which can be distributed by, or through, cyberspace, such as education or information (these goods can easily be excluded and commodified in the online environment). It is also applicable to other goods traditionally provided by governments, such as the provision of tools of enforcement, for example of contracts or of intellectual property rights. Indeed, powerful technologies allow individuals to rely on self-help means for executing and enforcing their contracts, thereby reducing (though not diminishing) their reliance on the state's enforcement services. It is not true for other public goods such as defence and health. Having said that, since cyberspace may also break the territorial notion of political communities, it may abridge the need for traditional defence methods, diminishing the demands for such services, while creating new security needs across territorial borders. We shall touch upon this point below.

Cyberspace also reduces transaction costs (Elkin-Koren and Salzberger 1999, pp. 567–71), which may also have some implications on the traditional roles of the state. Thus, if we apply the Calabresi–Melamed (1972) model of private law to cyberspace and especially the terms it set of using liability rules versus property rules we will conclude that much more than in the non-virtual world property rules ought to be preferred to liability rules. Since property rules to protect entitlement do not require central government for their enforcement in cyberspace, another rationale for the emergence of the state is seriously impaired (Elkin-Koren and Salzberger 2004, ch. 8).

As noted above, cyberspace also challenges the territorial notion of communities and thus of the state as a collective organization that resides within specific geographical borders (ibid., ch. 9). The traditional social contract literature, as well as the economic theory of the state, assumed that the only sensible way of organizing communities is along territorial units, thus viewing the state as reflecting a distinct geographical unit. Montesquieu ([1748] 1977) even argued that differences in political cultures are the result of climate and geography. Indeed, the borders between existing political units are heavily influenced by geography. All this is significantly altered by cyberspace. Geography does not play the same central role in the creation of commercial, cultural, social or political communities in cyberspace, and cyberian citizens face similar climatically and geographical conditions – they sit facing the computer screen in a closed room. There is no significance whatsoever to mountains and oceans, which separate physical locations. In fact, communication between two next-door neighbours can pass through several continents in the same way as communication between geographically distant individuals.

Be that as it may, these changes may affect the compass of the state, its territorial nature and the division between the public sphere and the private one. But as long as the cyberian citizens have to walk out of their computer room to the nearby grocery, as long as they may be threatened by non-virtual burglars, these developments would not abrogate altogether the justification of the state or a similar collective entity altogether.

4.2 The Foundation of the State

Following the consensus leading normative principle, the establishment of the state is viewed by the economic approach as the result of a contract, to which all individuals who are its future citizens are parties. In political or legal terms, this contract is dubbed 'constitution'. This consensual agreement is portrayed by some scholars (for example, Rawls 1971; Posner 1979) as a hypothetical consent, and indeed, we can hardly find historical examples for full consensus as to the content and wording of the constitution.

However, the drafters of constitutions who set the terms for their ratification in many cases make a serious attempt to obtain very wide support for the document as a condition for its adoption. This can characterize the process in which the United States Constitution was ratified (a unanimous vote of the constituent assembly and ratification by all future states' legislatures), as well as the more recent process of adopting new constitutions in the countries of East and Central Europe, which have undergone a transition from communism to democracy (Salzberger and Voigt 2002). In the majority of these countries the constitution was the result of an agreement in roundtable talks including representatives of all political groups followed by a referendum. The consensual mode or justification for a constitution ensured that many constitutional documents reflected numerous compromises and additions of various articles in order to obtain general consent.

Conventional constitutional making is perceived as possible only through the work of agents – members of constitutional assemblies – rather than a product of the general consent of all future citizens of the emerging entity. In many cases, however, the constitution-making process was conditional upon approval by general referendum. The reason for the need of agents is high decision-making costs. In the physical world, these costs might be so high that it will be impossible to obtain consensus. In cyberspace, these costs are significantly lower. Information technologies enable not merely cheap and widespread communication of individual preferences, but the employment of software that can aggregate preferences, negotiate bargains across different issues and identify resolutions and packages that enjoy consensual support. In addition, the weakening of the strict correspondence between territories and political entities, combined with the cheap exit option, enable the formation of communities or states based on real wall-to-wall consensus. These entities comprise various individuals around the globe who have common or similar preferences, enabling better outcomes of collective action in terms of satisfying individual profiles. Online communities increasingly emerge instantly, organized *ad hoc*, to serve an immediate, often limited, agenda.

Even if territorial entities are still needed to produce certain goods or services, which are territorial in their nature, such as defence, the role of such entities diminishes, as they co-exist alongside non-territorial collective entities. The development of worldwide threats to personal security, in the form of global terrorism, often indifferent to geographical borders, can be analysed in the same context. The idea of governments without territorial monopoly was put forward, without special attention to cyberspace, by Bruno Frey (2001, 2003). The ability to conduct collective debates and voting through the Net contributes to this breakdown of the territory-dominated collective organization and to the proliferation of collective entities, as it also weakens the role of intermediaries in the process of establishing collective organizations.

What should be emphasized here is that from a pure normative point of view, formation of collective entities, such as the state, can be justified only by the consent of all the members to the general framework and basic rules of these entities. Cyberspace enables us to get closer to this utopist idea, a fact that should cause us to re-think the current conventions with regard to constitution-making processes.

Thus far, we have outlined the justifications for a collective decision-making mechanism, which might interfere with the private sphere. According to the leading normative principle, however, this collective mechanism ought to be founded on the basis of the contractual or consensual principle. We also saw that the new world of cyberspace weakens this rationale and the scope for justifiable collective actions, but it does not discard it altogether. It seems that we still need a collective organization based on a social contract of individuals living in the same geographical proximity. However, this agreement can exist side by side with other social contracts of individuals who do not live in the same geographical areas. In this sense, cyberspace has an important role of breaking the monopoly of the traditional state and creating alliances across territorial borders.

4.3 The Rise of Central Government

The contract, or the constitution, should lay down the basic principles guiding the interactions of individuals – the protective role of the state – and the basic principles dealing with collective action, its productive role (Buchanan 1975, pp. 68–9). In its protective role the state serves merely as an enforcement mechanism of the various clauses in the social contract, making no 'choices' in the strict meaning of the term. In its productive role the state serves as an agency through which individuals provide themselves with – produce and allocate – 'public goods' (Gwartney and Wagner 1988).

In the old, pre-cyberian, world, the rationale for the establishment of the state, in fact, merges into the rationale for the rise of central government, as Mueller (1996, p. 57) puts it:

> The constitutional perspective towards government sees its normative foundation as resting on the unanimous agreement of the community in the constitutional contract that creates the government, a unanimous agreement that arises because the institutions defined in the constitutional contract are designed to advance the interests of all citizens.

The unique features of cyberspace, especially regarding enforcement, may lead to interesting insights on these two functions of the state – its protective role and its productive one. We shall also examine whether the combined rationale for the establishment of the state and the emergence of central government also exists in cyberspace.

The argument of the economic theory of the state justifying the construction of central government goes like this: the initial contract, obviously, cannot foresee every potential problem in both domains – the protective and productive roles of the state, especially where the constitution is designed to be in force for a very long term. According to the unanimity rationale, the solution for a new public issue would have been to gather everyone whenever a new problem arises, and to decide upon it unanimously. But such a solution would involve immense decision-making costs, or 'internal costs', in the language of Buchanan and Tullock (1962, pp. 63–84). This is the major justification, given by most scholars, for the need to have a central government in which the powers to protect and produce are deposited, or, rather, entrusted. It is intended to represent the will of the people. In contractual terminology, the establishment of central government and other state institutions is the result of uncertainties that exist in each individual's mind about the future of the society in which one lives and about the future behaviour of other members of that society (Mueller 1996, p. 61).

The two solutions offered by modern democratic theory to the immense costs of maintaining unanimous decision making in the public sphere are representative democracy and majority decision making. Indeed, the Athenians' resort to majority rule and to the appointment of government personnel by lottery was intended to overcome the difficulties of consensual decision making (although the latter remained the ultimate goal); so does the modern developments of representative democracy and the tools, such as the separation of powers, designed to overcome its fallacies.

Representative government
Representatives acting on behalf of their constituents save the costs of frequently measuring public preferences on each and every issue and the prohibitively high costs of coordinating massive numbers of people. Cyberspace significantly reduces the costs of communicating and processing individuals' preferences. It makes it possible to efficiently collect information from individuals by asking them to click their preferences directly onto the screen. It reduces transaction costs involved in collecting information about preferences.

Cyberspace also facilitates fast and cost-effective information processing that allows real-time feedback on public preferences and choices. This, in turn, lessens the need for agencies and for their scope of functions. The reduced costs of coordination and communication diminish the extent of collective action problems. If transaction costs involved in coordination are low or non-existent, there is no need for representatives – intermediaries – to reflect the aggregated will of their constituents. Individuals may directly communicate their preferences on each and every matter.

Imagine that every morning we were asked to vote on several policy issues, and the various motions could pass only by consensual support or by a super-majority (super-majority as opposed to unanimity will diminish the ability of a handful of individuals to have excessive veto power). This sounds like a remote dream in the non-virtual world, but it becomes increasingly feasible in the virtual world. Policy makers may efficiently collect public comments on bills posted on the Internet. The low cost of communication and information processing enable government not only to consult the public but also to delegate to the public the actual decision-making powers. Not only can this vote be carried out swiftly and cheaply, but technology can offer automated negotiation tools that facilitate the ability to reach compromises on various issues, so that a consensus or near consensus can be reached. Information technologies may provide tools for diverse stakeholders to actively participate in policy making. Automated simulations, for instance, may support deliberation and debate on various public issues such as urban planning, education, environmental concerns and budget allocation.

In addition, low transaction costs allow individuals, who were unable to get organized in the non-virtual world (Olson 1965), to become organized. Connectivity, interactivity and search tools reduce the cost of identifying relevant parties, communicating, acting together, and spreading information that concerns all. The ability to collaborate with individuals outside the territorial boundaries of the state may create new interest groups that were unable to get organized in the past due to high transaction costs. This can lead to increased democratization and decentralization of rule-making processes, in whose various stages cyberspace allows groups and individuals to participate.

From the perspective of economic theory, two important problematic phenomena, which exist in representative democracy, ought to be mentioned, as they are toned down significantly in cyberspace. The first is agency costs, which are associated with representative government. These costs are the result of ineffective monitoring of representatives by their voters and the ability of the former to act in a self-interested manner without being penalized by voters (or where the costs of the penalties are smaller than the political or personal gains). Cyberspace allows citizens to take a more active part in governance, and to effectively monitor government actions. The easy and relatively cheap access to information and the lower costs of collective deliberation and action in cyberspace are likely to increase the effective monitoring level and thus reduce these agency costs.

The second phenomenon of representative democracy is the power of interest groups to seek rents at the expense of the general public, and make gains through pressure on the representatives. Interest groups are able to succeed in their actions because of the costs of collective action. These costs allow only small groups to organize – groups whose potential gain from collective action is higher than the costs of organization (Olson 1965; in the legal context, see Farber and Frickey 1991, pp. 12–37). Cyberspace, as indicated above, tends to lower the costs of collective action, which in turn enables broader interest groups to organize, bringing more equality to the political markets and diffusing the impact of narrow interest groups.

A separate economic rationale for central government in general and representatives, in particular, comes from the theory of specialization. Traditional economics assumes that specialization can contribute to total welfare. Applied to the theory of government, this rationale can imply that better collective decisions would be reached if those decisions are reached by specialized bodies – administrators or politicians, who devote their time to studying carefully the issues and possible courses of actions. Cyberspace may affect this line of argument as well. An experiment conducted by the American National Aeronautics and Space Administration can serve a good example.

NASA launched a challenge to Internet users to volunteer in mapping the planet of Mars. Clickworkers in this experimental project were invited to assist in mapping small portions of the Mars landscape by performing tasks such as marking craters on maps of Mars or classifying marked craters. The project was designed in such a way that the volunteers were given small overlapping segments, and the accumulation of the findings corrected for possible discrepancies and mistakes. The project resulted in mapping equivalent to the work of several full-time paid scientists working for a year, and yielding the same qualitative results. The Mars project proves that lower transaction costs can shift complicated work conducted by several professionals within the hierarchy of an organization to the masses operating voluntarily, on the same basis of contractual relations in the open market. One of the interesting findings from the experiment was that the accumulated effort of many individuals was found equivalent (in quality as well as quantity) to the year-long work of several specialists. This finding stands in conflict with the specialization rationale, and one can induce that if this is true with regard to scientific projects, it may well be applicable to decision making, which involves value judgement and scientific or professional components.

It is unrealistic to assume that had we been asked to take part in every public decision making, we would have researched and mastered every question we are dealing with. However, the individual decision of which areas to study and in which vote to take part, signal the intensity of our preferences in this area. A regular dichotomous vote does not reveal the intensity of preferences and this is one of the deficiencies of majority decision making, in the light of the consensus normative principle (and for this matter, also in the light of utilitarian morality). The participation of everyone in every decision, which is made possible in the new technological environment, will also assist in revealing intensity of preferences. This, in turn, might enable departure from a strict unanimity rule towards some qualified majority.

Parliaments in many countries are currently engaged in various projects to delegate more decision-making powers to the public at large or to incorporate the general public in the decision-making process. However, from the theoretical and normative perspective of liberalism, it is the public at large that delegates powers to representatives. The rationales for such delegation, such as the immense decision-making costs of the public at large, are seriously impaired by the technology provided by the Internet. In other words, when legislators and other politicians talk today about more participation of the general public in their work, they talk within the current democratic paradigm, in which representative government and majority decision making are taken as given normative truths. Yet, the opportunities for collective action in cyberspace call for re-examination of the existing paradigm. We ought to rethink whether representative government, and indeed central government, is needed at all, and if so, whether it should be guided by majority decision making. We turn now to this second pillar of the current liberal democracy paradigm.

Majority rule
So far we have touched upon one pillar of the existing liberal paradigm of the state – representative government. We now turn to the other pillar – majoritarianism. Regardless of the question of who should operate the state – its citizens in a form of direct democracy or a central government representing the public at large (according to pluralists) or guiding it (according to republicans) – there is a no less important issue of the desirable daily decision-making rule. The economic reasoning for the shift from consensus to majority rule is best represented by the model of collective decision making, set by Buchanan and Tullock's *Calculus of Consent* (1962). This model can be considered as one of the classical presentations of a normative analysis of collective decision making in the framework of the consensus principle. It is a good reference point for the analysis of collective action in cyberspace.

Buchanan and Tullock distinguish between external costs of collective decision making and internal costs. The former is the total costs to individuals negatively affected by the collective decision. These costs diminish, as the majority that is required for reaching a decision is larger. In unanimous decision making the external costs are reduced to zero, as rational individuals will not grant their consent to decisions that harm them. A super-majority decision-making rule will, on average, impose less external cost than a simple majority. A dictator's rule (one dictator has the power to make the decisions) inflicts the highest external costs on the members of his or her community. The internal cost function reflects the costs involved in the decision-making process itself. It is shaped in an opposite way to the external cost function: dictatorial rule is the least expensive to operate. As the majority required for passing a decision is greater, so are the costs involved in the decision-making process. Consensual rule is the most expensive to operate.

The optimal decision-making rule, according to Buchanan and Tullock, is the one that minimizes the sum of the two types of cost. Buchanan and Tullock show that in most areas this optimal rule is a simple majority, but there might be special types of decisions in which the optimal decision-making rule is a qualified majority (for example, decisions which touch upon basic human rights). These latter types of decisions are usually characterized by asymmetry between the external costs and benefits inflicted on the members of the community, for example, decisions that touch upon basic human rights, for which the costs to the members whose rights are violated are far greater than the benefits to the others. The Buchanan–Tullock model is one of the few modern justifications for majority rule.

The application of this analysis to cyberspace is interesting. Its results depend on the definition of the cyberian community. If we regard the whole of cyberspace as the unit of analysis, it seems that the external cost function will not change notably in comparison with the non-virtual world (subject to the assumption that individual preferences are exogenous to the political process), while the internal cost function – the decision-making costs – will decrease significantly. Collective decisions, as we have already discussed, are cheaper to arrive at because of lower information costs, negotiation costs and communication costs. If the marginal cost function of decision making as related to the majority required for deciding is more moderately sloped, we can expect the optimal decision-making rule to be greater than a simple majority. Hence, the democratization in cyberspace is reflected not only by weakening the dependency on representative structure and the agency costs it is associated with, but also by shifting the decision-making rule from simple majority towards unanimity, all within the framework of consensus as the leading normative principle for collective action. This can increase the total well-being of the members of the community.

So far we have referred to cyberspace as one community. If, however, we view it as a conglomerate of communities, a change will also occur with regard to the external cost function. This is because of the exit option, which is much easier to opt for in virtual communities. The availability of this option is likely to decrease the external cost function in addition to the internal cost function. This might not change our conclusion regarding the optimal decision-making rule, as this conclusion is contingent upon the marginal functions of both types of cost. But this assumption will lead us to an even greater total advantage from collective action, as for every decision-making rule, the total costs – decision making and the reduction in one's utility – will be lower than the equivalent decision-making rule in the non-virtual world.

To summarize, the new technological frontiers enabled by cyberspace ought to make us re-think two fundamental ingredients in the current liberal democracy paradigm – the need for a central and representative government and the resort to majority decision making. In the traditional economic theory of the state, both are the result of immense costs that will be incurred when operating a state by direct democracy based on unanimous decision making. We have tried to show here that the new technological frontier of cyberspace might weaken the justification for central government and majority decision making. It may, however, not discard these two foundations altogether, but fresh thinking is needed as to the functions, decision-making process and scope of operation of central government, as well as to its structure. But before delving into the structure of government let us discuss briefly the republican view of central government *vis-à-vis* the economic approach.

4.4 The Republican View of Central Government and the Economic Approach

The challenge to the justification of representative government is highly significant from a republican point of view. Some republican theorists of the state, in contrast to liberal theorists, emphasize that central government is not only needed to reflect the preferences of the general public in a more efficient or cheaper way, but that it should lead the community towards civic virtues and 'better' preferences. This idea was phrased sharply by Edmund Burke in his famous *Address to the Electors of Bristol* (1774). He said: 'Your representative owes you, not his industry only, but his judgment; and he betrays, instead of serving you, if he sacrifices it to your opinion'. Other republican theorists emphasize the need of the desirable political community to have not only technical mechanisms of preference aggregation through representatives, but also a more substantive content to the public sphere, which will enable real deliberation and participation by all individuals.

The republican view rejects the notion that the democratic scene is a competitive marketplace of ideas that must be kept free so it can best reflect the aggregated choice of citizens. Political institutions, according to the republican view, shape public discourse, and thereby affect preferences. Preferences are considered a byproduct of a political process that takes place in the public sphere and are shaped by deliberation or sometimes by the inability to deliberate. The way public discourse is structured affects the way individuals develop their ideas, shape their positions, identify their interests, and set their priorities. Preferences do not exist prior to the deliberating process, but are rather the output of political processes. Institutions and processes, which are based on individual participation and responsibilities, it is argued, are likely to shift self-centred individual preferences into more public-regarding preferences. This latter republican idea is reflected by Rousseau's distinction between the general will and the sum of individual wills or preferences.

One of the major arguments of the republican perspective of the state (as it was, for example, put forward by the anti-Madisonian or anti-federalist camp among the American founding fathers) is that civic virtues can be developed by the participation of citizens in government, their exposure to different and conflicting views and the deliberation of these views (Sunstein 1988). Participation in the public sphere is likely to enhance the element of public-regarding in the individual utility function (Sen 1987). Civic virtue describes an *other-regarding* rather than a purely *self-interest* approach – a willingness to give priority to the communal interest. Civic virtue thus enables participants in their capacity as citizens to undertake responsible decisions that are informed by, and respectful of, the claims of other groups and individuals. This may also enhance the well-being of individuals by creating a sense of communal belonging and social solidarity.

We indicated above that there are hardly any attempts to incorporate republican thinking into the economic approach.[8] In fact, one can reconcile the two, or phrase some of the republican claims in economic terms. In economic terminology, Republicans view individuals' preferences as endogenous, rather than exogenous, to the political process. They believe that deliberation and participation may change individual preferences to be more other-regarding, thus enabling a higher sum of utilities in collective actions or an ability to reach a superior point on the Pareto frontier. This is the reason why the American republican Founding Fathers (or anti-federalists) opposed a strong federal structure for the United States, in which, according to them, individual involvement in the public sphere would be minimal, the preferences of individuals more self-regarding, and thus, the outcome of collective action would be worse.[9]

From a republican perspective, cyberspace might change the conditions for achieving desirable participation and deliberation. On the one hand, the ability to deliberate and participate in cyberspace is much less dependent upon the number of participants, and especially on their geographic distance from the major collective institutions of central government. The picture of Mr. Smith from the Midwest, who is so remote from the power centre in Washington that he loses interest in the public sphere, is no longer true for cyberspace. The ideal Athenian city-square can be achieved in cyberspace with many more participants who do not gather physically, but virtually. The Swiss cantons' excuse not to grant women voting rights because there is no physical place where they can join the general assemblies in the main square cannot be sustained.

From the republican perspective, the way information markets are structured is of great importance for shaping preferences since preferences are not prior and exogenous to the political process, but rather an output of that process. Processes in the *public sphere* should be given a broad understanding to include all discursive will formation processes that take place in our cultural life (Elkin-Koren 1996). Cyberspace facilitates more opportunities for individuals to undertake an active part in the public sphere. While public discourse in the pre-cyberspace age was facilitated exclusively by the mass media, online exchange allows more individuals to directly communicate with each other. The low cost of communication provides individuals with more affordable access to news, large databases and cultural artifacts.

Digital networks further affect the quality of participation in the public sphere, enabling interactivity and facilitating more active involvement. Participation is no longer limited to passively consuming television shows and editorials of major newspapers. There are increasing opportunities to speak out and actively take part in online debates, by using talkbacks, posting one's own position and analyses in online forums, and challenging the views of others. The low cost of producing and distributing informational goods (Elkin-Koren and Salzberger 2004, chs 5 and 6), and the interactive nature of digital representation, allow individuals to participate in creating their own cultural artifacts, publish on their own Web pages, adopt fictional characters to reflect their own meaning or political agenda, participate in collaborative writing of online stories or report news to a newsgroup. Online discourse, therefore, opens up opportunities for transforming the structure of public discourse from the mass media scheme of one-to-many, to a more decentralized, and more democratic structure of many-to-many.

Cass Sunstein in his recent book, *Republic.com* (2001), expresses an opposing view. Sunstein argues that the architecture of cyberspace can encourage people to shut themselves up in homogeneous communities or enclaves, immune from diverse views, thus, in danger of being part of cybercascades. This, according to Sunstein, will eliminate shared national experiences and the real deliberative nature of democracy will be lost. In economic terminology, Sunstein argues that cyberspace may make people more egocentric in their preferences and less other-regarding. Thus, from the point of view of collective decision making, the result will be worse for everyone.[10]

These arguments, however, are made in the framework of the old paradigm of representative democracy and in the context of the traditional territorial conception of society. They are also made under the assumption of a lack of regulative intervention in cyberspace or against specific content of regulation. They are not made against the new technological frontiers or the development of cyberspace as a provider of new opportunities for forming, expressing and negotiating preferences and for forming new a-territorial communities. In other words, Sunstein's argument is made in the context of the debate regarding whether cyberspace should be regulated, and if so, how, and not in the context of examining how cyberspace might affect our basic philosophy of the state.

We may agree with Sunstein in his conclusions as to the question of whether cyberspace should be regulated. But this question is a false one anyway, as the architecture of cyberspace is itself a form of such regulation (Lessig 1999), and there is no real option, therefore, of abstaining from its regulation. The only question is how to govern it (Salzberger 2002), or what is the substance of such regulation. Be that as it may, we do not share Sunstein's concerns regarding the loss of social cohesion, the alienation and shutting oneself up in homogeneous cyberian communities. This may be true in an interim stage, although we have doubts that even at this point, people are exposed, more than in the non-virtual world, to differing views. In the long run, however, we can expect a process in which all preferences will be endogenized and even homogenized.

The republican perspective expands the traditional reasons for establishing a central government beyond a good (and cost-saving) representation of the public preferences, focusing on its role in shaping individual preferences. Many republicans focus on political participation of citizens in government as a process that can produce civic virtue. From this perspective cyberspace offers more opportunities for participation, potentially bringing participating individuals towards more cooperative and responsible preferences and choices. This, in turn, can diminish the need for central government even in republicans' eyes. Cyberian communities managing their own affairs with no central government, it can be argued, will bring the participating individuals towards more cooperative and responsible preferences and choices.

To sum up, from both perspectives of collective action – liberal and republican – cyberspace enhances opportunities for participation of individuals in setting the rules, thus facilitating decentralization and democratization of rule-making processes. Rules may be increasingly created in a bottom-up fashion, and therefore, in the absence of the failures discussed above, reflect more diversified social and economic interests by increasingly complex societies. A legal regime in which individuals are able to directly communicate their preferences has several advantages over a legislative process exercised by elected representatives. Individuals are able to reflect their preferences directly, hence more accurately. This reduces the chances of mistaken assessment of public preferences and therefore inaccurate setting of the rules. This factor should be viewed as an advantage from both republican and pluralist–liberal vantage points.

4.5 The Organization of Government – Separation of Powers

The next link in a skeleton argument for the economic theory of the state concerns the structure of central government. This desirable structure ought to be derived from the list of functions assigned to the state. The list of these functions is embodied in the rationale for central government itself. Here we want to relate to their specification and organization. The doctrine of separation of powers is the major structural principle of the economic theory of government. Separation of powers can be viewed as comprising several components: separation of functions, separation of agencies, separation of persons and a form of relation between the powers. In the following subsections, we shall elaborate on each of these components in turn, and examine the effects that cyberspace may have on their traditional analysis.

Separation of functions
There are two types of separation of functions; one of them is usually overlooked. We have distinguished between the protective function of the state and its productive function. The protective function is connected mainly, but not exclusively, to the constitutional stage and the binding force it exercises upon post-constitutional collective processes. The productive function is related mainly to the post-constitutional stage (Buchanan 1975, pp. 68–70). From a theory of a state point of view, this distinction should be considered as the more important ground for separation of functions.

A second functional division of central government is between rule making, rule application and rule adjudication, or, as they are more commonly called, legislation, administration and adjudication. History reveals that this functional division has always existed, regardless of the era (or at least long before the doctrine of separation of powers was under discussion) or the type of regime (Montesquieu [1748] 1977, Book I, Section 3). This phenomenon also has an 'economic' logic: governing according to rules, their application and their enforcement, rather than making each decision individually and independently, is more efficient. It minimizes transaction costs from the point of view of the government or of the decision makers, as it is cheaper to apply a rule than to deliberate every question from initial principles. It also minimizes agency costs from the viewpoint of the citizens, namely the exercise of individual control over the government, by providing certainty and predictability (Brennan and Buchanan 1985, chs 7–9).

Cyberspace may alter both divisions of functions. The primary division – between the protective and the productive functions – is a direct consequence of the shift from consensus in the constitutional stage to majority rule in the post-constitutional stage. If such a shift is not needed, as described in the previous section, then this division loses its magnitude. In other words, if post-constitutional collective decisions can be reached through direct votes (rather than votes of representatives) using unanimity or super-majorities, then the distinction between constitutional and post-constitutional spheres loses its viability.

The secondary division (between rule making, rule application and rule adjudication) is also blurred by cyberspace. First, cyberspace can provide technological means for enforcement that can replace some of the existing human institutions (Elkin-Koren and Salzberger 2004, ch. 9). Thus the need for enforcement apparatus as a separate governmental function diminishes. Second, the regime of norms in cyberspace is less hierarchical than in the non-virtual world. In contrast to the conventional pyramid of norms, in cyberspace we are likely to see overlapping and contradicting norms. Individuals could have greater freedom to subject themselves to certain norms and not to others. This phenomenon blurs the distinction between general and individual norms, or between rules and their execution. This point adds to obfuscating the boundaries between the three traditional functions of central government.

Separation of agencies – between constitutional and post-constitutional organs

There is a long way, both historically and conceptually, between mere separation of functions and the separation of agencies. The latter principle has a significant effect on the structure of government, because, according to it, not only do the three functions – legislative, executive and judicial – exist, but also they should be carried out by separate institutions or branches of government. Before discussing this type of separation of agencies, however, we shall spare a few words on the separation of agencies aspect of the earlier distinction between the protective and productive functions of the state.

A careful look at the role definition of the protective and the productive functions will result in the conclusion that a corresponding separation of agencies is necessary due to the conflict that arises between the two functions. While the protective state is aimed at enforcing the initial contract – the constitution – the productive state is engaged in activities involving production of public goods for which the costs are shared by the individuals, and hence involve reallocation of resources. There are, naturally, conflicting desires within the productive state, but in the non-virtual world their resolution cannot be based on unanimity (as was explained, the optimal decision-making rule, which takes into account the excessive costs of the decision-making process, will depart from unanimity). Conflicts between the outcomes of the productive state and the initial social contract are, therefore, to be expected.

The productive state will tend to overstep the boundaries of the initial contract, aiming to reach its 'technical productive frontier' (North 1986; Eggertsson 1990, pp. 319–28). This may be worsened by principal–agent problems between the government and the people, interest-group politics and rent-seeking activities (Gwartney and Wagner 1988, pp. 17–23; Eggertsson 1990, pp. 350–53). The protective state will not take into account the benefits of any one alternative against its opportunity costs, and its outcomes will not necessarily be the set of results which best represent some balance of opposing interests (Buchanan 1975, pp. 68–70). Even if the productive state were to be guided by utility maximization or wealth maximization, it will not compensate those who become worse off from the decisions, because their votes will not be needed to pass decisions (unlike the case where unanimity is required for passing a decision). For these reasons it is desirable to separate the agencies assigned to fulfil the protective and the productive functions.

Parliaments in the physical world are the main institutions of the productive state. Separating between the protective and productive agencies means that parliaments should not be given constitutional-making powers. The constitution is aimed at limiting the powers of the parliament, and it will not perform its tasks if it is drafted and approved or amended only by parliament.

In the post-constitutional stage, the protective function is of a judicial nature, and in most common law countries it is indeed assigned to the judiciary; but it is distinguishable from the role of the judiciary within the productive state. Indeed, in many civil law countries, the protective function is assigned to a body such as a constitutional court, which is not perceived to be part of the ordinary judiciary. This distinction between the regular court system and the constitutional court makes sense *vis-à-vis* the rationales for separating agencies of the productive and protective states. The constitutional court has to be independent from the post-constitutional organs of the state, but accountable to the people. The regular courts, whose main task is to adjudicate disputes between individuals, must be independent from the public, but less so from the post-constitutional organs of government.

Cyberspace, as specified above, blurs the distinction between the productive and protective states, and this should also have a bearing on the need for separate agencies. Furthermore, even under the assumption that some sort of separation of functions is needed, the necessity for separating agencies diminishes. The problems with the productive state in the non-virtual world are toned down in cyberspace, as (i) rent-seeking problems decrease, due to the low costs of collective organization and (ii) agency costs are lower due to the improved technological methods of principals to monitor their agents. To this, one has to add the ability in cyberspace to shift the decision-making rule of the productive function from simple majority towards unanimity, as well as the low exit costs of shifting from one normative regime to another.

Indeed, if one looks at the norms created in cyberspace, the typical Kelsenian pyramid of norms, and especially the pyramid of institutions cannot be easily traced. Cyberspace permits a plurality of rules. It allows the development of diversified regimes that will be shaped indirectly by way of interaction between sysops defining the terms of use, and users making choices regarding their preferred system and services (Post and Johnson 1997). Internet service providers, list moderators, or website owners will adapt their rules to the wishes of users, and users who disagree with such rules will be able to leave and find an alternative regime that better serves their interests and values. The advantage of cyberspace is that it can facilitate the coexistence of different regimes. Rules and norms may thus be generated by the 'invisible hand' or by 'market of rules'. Under such vision of idealized democracy, users of cyberspace may choose the laws that apply to them (Post and Johnson 1996), and there is, thus, no need to separate protective and productive agencies.

Separation of agencies – legislature, executive, judiciary

Let us return to the more familiar separation of agencies between the legislature, executive and judiciary, which can be seen as a division of powers within the productive state. The productive state can be perceived, from a microeconomics perspective, as a micro-decision unit (like a firm) or perhaps as a set of micro-decision units (like an industry), producing primarily public goods. In this context, separation of agencies is connected to the monopoly problem (Silver 1977; North 1986; Whynes and Bowles 1981). The concentration of all governing powers in the grasp of one authority creates a vertically integrated state, which has monopoly powers, or even discriminating monopoly powers. Monopolies cause inefficiency and a distorted division of wealth between the producers and the consumers, that is, in the case of the state between the government and the citizens.

There are several possible ways to promote competition in the case of the state as a monopoly: the existence of other states, to which it would be possible to emigrate, namely the 'exit' option (Hirschman 1970), a federal structure (Tullock 1969; Posner 1987; Mueller 1996), and the separation of agencies. These forms of promoting competition can be regarded as substitute measures. Thus, a more accessible exit option can soften the need for separation of powers. Likewise, a federal state weakens the need for a rigid separation of powers. We noted above that cyberspace increases the possibility of using the exit option, at least with regard to some sort of public goods (for example, education, culture, community services). This means that in the cyberian era, the necessity of a strict separation of agencies might be weaker than in the traditional world.

It is important to note that the rationales for separation of functions and for separation of agencies are different. Theoretically, one could devise a structure of government in which separated agencies are performing similar functions. It can be argued, however, that in the non-virtual world, de-monopolization through separation of agencies assigned to carry out the various functions (every agency performing a different function), or a vertical disintegration of the state, would be efficient, as derived from a basic rule of economics – the rule of specialization and trade. But separation of powers can also increase the production costs due to a combination of higher communication costs and reduced costs of non-optimal operation (Posner 1987, pp. 11–14).

The efficacy of separation of agencies and its correspondence to the separation of functions, therefore, will also depend on the size of the society or jurisdiction (Silver 1977). It can be argued, for example, that American-style separation of powers does not suit smaller countries. This may be one explanatory factor for differences in government structures across the world. This constraint disappears when we talk about possible future cyberian political entities. Geography does not have any importance in cyberspace, and the number of citizens in a cyberian community can be worked out to the optimal number more easily than in the traditional world.

In the non-virtual world, separation of agencies, when vertical (within the central government), rather than horizontal (federalism), can, in fact, increase the monopolistic powers of the government *vis-à-vis* the general public, by diminishing the quantity of public goods produced (Brennan and Hamlin 2000). In other words, when a monopoly is broken up into several firms, each producing a different ingredient of the final product, the monopolistic exploitation of the consumers rises. Only competition in the production of the same ingredients achieves desirable results. Thus, separation of agencies itself does not guarantee desirable results from the point of view of the public well-being. Only certain kinds of separation – in which the separated organs are fulfilling together some overlapping functions – will achieve the desirable results. This component will be analysed in the last point of this skeleton argument.

Lower transaction costs in cyberspace abolish the need for a federative structure or horizontal separation of powers, as was observed by Dennis Mueller (1996, pp. 77–8), writing to justify federalism:

> In a world of zero-transaction (decision-making) costs, and in which unanimity rule in the national (highest) legislative level, no other level of government would be necessary. All collective decisions for all citizens could be made in a single legislative body formed of representatives from across the entire country.

Mueller's insight should be extended to vertical separation of powers. Unanimity and zero transaction costs diminish the rationale for separation of agencies. Therefore, to the extent that transaction costs in cyberspace are lower, the justification for separation of agencies is reduced.

There is another important rationale for separation of agencies – diminishing agency costs. As we have seen above, the democratic system is a kind of a compromise or a second-best option, which is the result of the need to transfer powers from the people to a central government, and at the same time place the government under the control of the people in a way that would not be too costly. In this sense it was probably appropriate to describe democracy as the least bad system of government. The main problem of the transmission of powers to a central government, leaving only periodical control, is agency costs, which are caused by the differences between the incentives of the agents – the politicians – and the incentives of the principals – the citizens.

There are three typical categories of costs involved in a principal–agent relationship: bonding costs, monitoring costs and residual loss (Jensen and Meckling 1976). In the case of central government (agent) and citizens (principals), the residual loss is the dominant element. This loss is created by the mere fact that the rulers–politicians seek to maximize their own utility by gaining more powers (or materializing their private ideologies), instead of maximizing the population's well-being (Michelman 1980; Backhaus 1979). One way to reduce these agency costs is to divide the agency into separate sub-agencies, creating different incentives for each. In that way, while legislators act to maximize their political powers and chances of re-election, administrators and judges have different incentives, as a result of different institutional arrangements. If this is the case, the reduction of agency costs would be more significant if the division of powers were not only by separation of agencies but also by assigning each agency a different governing function (Macey 1988). Here we are getting closer to the classical idea of separation of powers.

The economic history explanation (for example, North 1981) to the political changes in seventeenth- and eighteenth-century Europe, among them the emergence of separation of powers, is a particular example related to the theoretical explanation above. In a nutshell, this explanation focuses on the financial crises of the early nation states, which brought the rulers (the monarchs) to seek loans from the public. One of the methods of gaining the confidence of the lenders in the government's commitment to honour its credit was the creation of other governmental agencies, including an independent judiciary, which were assigned to enforce these contracts in an impartial manner. The emergence of representative government is also associated with this explanation.

This rationale may hold when we consider relations between different cyberian entities. In other words, some separation of agencies to credibly commit a cyberian community might be beneficial and thus desirable. One sort of such separation can be separation between bodies whose major aim is economic profits and bodies who are not geared primarily to maximize profits. The regulation or government of cyberspace through the code or its architecture is one of the bold examples for this insight. Cyberspace, much more than physical political forums, is regulated by its architecture, or by the code. This code was originally designed by the US army with the goal of decentralization and by university professors whose aim was to create an egalitarian, democratic, open and deliberative forum. Today, cyberspace is captured more and more by economic powers whose interests are very different. Since the code is a very significant source for the government of cyberspace, it can be argued that there is a pressing need for some separation of agencies in the regulation and rule of cyberspace.

This conclusion is, on the one hand, in sharp contrast to the call for traditional governments to leave cyberspace alone to its own anarchic development. On the other hand, our conclusion does not necessarily endorse heavy regulation of the economic players in cyberspace and their prevention from regulating through the code and technological innovation. The separation of agencies approach endorses competition between the economic forces and non-economic governing forces (which in cyberspace, can be performed by the community of all users). Regulation should, therefore, focus on enhancing technological freedom, enabling competition among different technologies, and preventing anti-competitive economic and technological strategies.

Separation of persons
Separation of persons is the third fundamental element in the pure doctrine of separation of powers (together with separation of functions and of agencies), and the most dramatic characteristic of it (Marshall 1971, pp. 97–100). In fact, this element has already been incorporated into our analysis of separation of agencies, because economic analysis is based on

individuals and their rational-personal choice. This choice (or the utility function) is crucially dependent upon exogenous circumstances. Thus, choices made by government personnel are dependent upon the branch of government in which they work. In other words, in the context of economic analysis there is no meaning to establishments and institutions without their human operators; likewise, there is no meaning to the analysis of individuals' behaviour without the examination of the institutional arrangements and incentive mechanisms to which they are subject. Thus, separation of agencies is meaningless unless separation of personnel is an integral component of it. This applies equally to the separation of persons in the context of separating the constitutional and post-constitutional agencies. Thus, there is no meaning for such a separation, from an economic analysis point of view, if the composition of the constituent assembly is identical to the composition of a parliament, or if parliament also functions as a constituent assembly.

This does not mean that only lawyers should be part of the judiciary and that only bureaucrats should work in the executive. There are legal systems (especially in continental Europe) in which a mixture of professionals in the different branches of government is encouraged, and from our perspective this may even be more efficient. Separation of persons merely means that no one should be part of more than one branch of government at the same time. This is not a trivial requirement, as it appears at first glance. In many countries, such separation of persons does not exist, when, for example, cabinet members can and in some systems must also serve as parliament members.[11]

We noted above that separation of agencies is likely to reduce agency costs, which are the result of the government–citizens (agent–principals) relationship. One way of achieving this is different representation structures for each of the branches, which can increase the people's control over the government and the interplay between particular and general issues on the public agenda and between short-, medium- and long-term interests. Without separation of persons, a significant share of these advantages would fade away. The desirability of separation of persons is further derived from the optimal relationships between the powers, as will be explained below. The American system, which uses the advantages of different representation structures, is also quite strict about this element of separation of persons. The vice president is the only top figure who is part of more than one branch of government (as he functions also as the Speaker of the Senate).

Since we concluded that in cyberspace the urge for separation of agencies of both types – constitutional versus post-constitutional, and legislature, executive and judiciary – is decreased because of the ability to maintain direct rule by consensus or near consensus, the need to separate persons correspondingly decreases too. In addition, when applying the argument for separation of persons to cyberspace, we have to bear in mind that cyberspace transforms not only the notion of collective communities, but also that of the individual, who is the basic unit for liberal philosophy of the state and for economic analysis. In the non-virtual world the basic unit of reference – the individual – is one physical person. In cyberspace the individual is a username with a password and an electronic address. There is no strict correlation between the cyberian individual and the non-virtual individual, as the same physical individual can appear in cyberspace as several entities, each with different identification features and a different character. Cyberspace allows multiple representations of the same physical individual, as well as a single virtual representation of several physical individuals. The separation of persons, which is central to the traditional theory of the state, is, therefore, significantly muted in cyberspace.

The relationships between the powers
The most controversial element of the desirable structure of government is the relationships between the separated powers or branches of government. There are at least two distinct, though interrelated, questions here: (i) to what degree is separation of powers advantageous (this question involves the issue of delegation of powers); and (ii) what is the degree of freedom or independence that we ought to assign each of the branches. The former question relates mainly to functional separation; the latter to institutional separation (separation of agencies). These questions are strongly interrelated in the sense that there could be a great deal of trade-off in different combined solutions to them.

Judicial review can serve as a good example. The conventional debate concerning judicial review is usually within the boundaries of the second question: should the legislature and the executive be controlled by the judiciary, and if so, to what extent? But this issue could also be raised in the framework of the first question. In this context we would first ask whether judicial review is part of the legislative or the judicial function. If it is seen as part of the legislative function, we have to ask whether the allocation or delegation (Salzberger 1993) of the powers to participate in rule making to the judiciary is desirable or legitimate (Salzberger and Voigt 2002).

The two extreme approaches to the second question are the independence approach or the pure doctrine of separation of powers, on the one hand, and the checks and balances approach, on the other (Vile 1967; Marshall 1971, pp. 100–103; Yassky 1989). Analytically these two approaches can refer to the functional level, which is directly related to the first question about sharing powers (or delegating powers), or to the institutional and personal levels, that is, the accountability of agents in each branch to those in the other branches, or to both levels.

It is possible, for example, to argue that an optimal structure of separation of powers would adopt the checks and balances doctrine with respect to the functional level, and the independence doctrine with regard to the personal level. This is the underlying idea behind the American form of separation of powers: on the one hand every collective decision of one of the branches of government is subject to approval or review by the other branches. On the other hand, it is very difficult for one branch of government to remove any of the agents in any of the other branches. Thus, in contrast to popular perception, the checks and balances approach is adopted in the United States only on the functional level, while independence (or pure separation) is adopted on the personal level. In contrast, in most European parliamentary democracies, there is no independence on the personal level. The members of the executive are accountable to the legislature and the prime minister has the power to dissolve parliament. Likewise, appointment and promotion of judges is under the power of the executive. However, there is relatively more independence on the functional level. For example, the legislature cannot review appointments within the executive, and legislation is not subject to a veto by the executive.[12]

The theoretical framework for analysing these questions is, again, transaction costs and decision-making costs on the one hand, and agency costs on the other. A smaller degree of independence is inclined to raise the former costs but reduce the latter ones, and the optimal level may depend on variables such as the size of the jurisdiction (Silver 1977), the representation structure of each branch, and so on. Cyberspace, as indicated before, is expected to decrease both transaction or decision-making costs and agency cost. Thus, on the one hand, the need for different branches of government to balance and monitor each other decrease. On the other, the costs involved in such a conduct also decrease. Since the rationale for monitoring and balancing weakens, and the increased decision-making costs are just a secondary result of the need in the non-virtual state to tackle agency costs and monopolistic costs, one may conclude that cyberspace should ease the need for a strict mechanism of checks and balances between the different branches of government.

As to the first question about the degree and rigour of the desirable separation, the solution might be a result of a cost–benefit analysis, or, more accurately, a comparison of costs analysis. This analysis is the second stage in a theoretical hierarchical decision-making model. Let us take, for example, the function of rule making. In the first stage of this model we have to decide on the merits of a substantive issue – whether a certain decision is desirable at all. In the second stage we have to decide which of the three branches of government can make the decision most cheaply. The costs include both transaction costs (the costs of the decision-making process) and agency costs (Aranson et al. 1982, pp. 17–21). In making general rules, we would expect the legislature to be the most expensive with respect to transaction costs, but the least expensive regarding agency costs. This might not be the case with minor, secondary or more particular rules, and if it is, one can conclude that separation of powers (or, rather, separation of functions) should not be absolute. Cyberspace enables new mechanisms for creating rules and it blurs the distinction between rules and particular decisions. Hence, again, its effect on a theory of the state level points towards a less rigid separation of powers.

Another factor connected to the transaction costs of decision making as well as to agency costs, which should be considered when deciding the degree of separation or the degree of functional independence, is the theory of collective decision making. The theory of social choice taught us that majority rule, which is usually employed by legislatures in the non-virtual world, might bear the grim results of cycling or arbitrariness. One method for ameliorating this situation is to allow additional bodies to take part in the decision making, bodies that have different decision-making processes, incentives and representation structures. The legislative veto and judicial review in the American system can be seen as performing this task (Tullock 1981; Aranson et al. 1982; Mayton 1986; Moe 1990; Salzberger 1993), and indeed some scholars argue that they were designed for this purpose.

The conclusion drawn from this consideration is, again, the rejection of the 'pure' doctrine of separation of powers, in favour of some degree of power-sharing and functional dependency. It is important that the institutional structure and division of powers would be specified in the constitution; otherwise they would be subject to the same problems of cycling and arbitrariness and thus unstable. A constitution ought to reflect unanimous decisions, and therefore is not subject to the problems of majority rule (Eggertsson 1990, pp. 70–74). But if in the new cyberian world we can also change the dominant decision-making rule in the post-constitutional stage from simple majority towards unanimity, the rationale for separation of powers is moot and the crucial debate in the traditional world with regard to the desirable relations between the powers is much less significant.

A sharp analysis of the relation between the powers of government was offered by Brennan and Hamlin (2000). They show how 'strategic' separation of powers (pure separation) leads to exactly the opposite results from the point of view of the population's welfare from 'competitive' (checks and balances) separation of powers. While the former will reduce the quantity of the public goods supplied to increase government gains, strengthening the monopolistic powers of government and exploitation of the public, the latter will increase competition and will improve the public welfare.

The interrelations between the branches of government can digress from the protective function to the productive function of the state. It is possible to advocate, for example, as some do, checks and balances within the protective state or with regard to 'ultimate power', and independence or pure separation within the productive state, or with regard to 'operational power'. In other words, the checks and balances model could be employed to enforce the initial contract, but within this contract each power would be given full autonomy. Again, since cyberspace is likely to blur the boundaries between the protective state and the productive state, the need for coexistence of different types of separation of powers is diminished.

To summarize, separation of powers is the major tool of liberal democracies to compensate for the shift from unanimity to majoritarianism and from direct democracy to representative democracy. Cyberspace enables us to operate more direct democracy and more consensual or super-majoritarian decision-making and rule-making processes. This, in turn, invalidates some of the rationales for separation of powers and diminishes the magnitude of others. As the structurally crafted and structured separation of powers in the physical world and, especially, the establishment of mechanisms of checks and balances are themselves costly, the bottom line is that the cyberian state will need less structured separation and checks and balances mechanisms. Those will evolve naturally from the decentralized and the somehow anarchic nature of the new cyberworld.

5 CONCLUDING REMARKS: THE MOST FUNDAMENTAL PROBLEMS CYBERSPACE POSES TO THE THEORY OF THE STATE

So far, we have gone along with the traditional argument of the economic approach towards the state and examined how cyberspace may affect its different links. To conclude, we would like to highlight the two major factors that can be viewed as the cornerstones of the traditional liberal–economic theory of the state and are seriously shaken by the new virtual universe: the territorial concept of collective action and the concept of individuals who are the atoms of any collective organization.

5.1 Geography, Markets and States

The models of the economic approach assume that individuals not only will engage in individual actions (within or bypassing markets) but also will benefit from collective actions. The economic approach, as in the liberal theories from Hobbes to Rawls, views the state as the most important collective organization or institution, and presupposes that markets correspond to states, which are basically territorial units. A social contract, or other form of collective action, is carried out by citizens of a specific territorial unit, which becomes a state or other form of a national unit.

Central government, its organs, and structure are analysed in a territorial context. This is true even for the broad approach of neo-institutional law and economics. Thus, in his recent book, Barzel (2002, p. 4), for example, writes:

> The state consists of (I) a set of individuals who are subject to a single ultimate third party who uses violence for enforcement and (II) a territory where these individuals reside, demarcated by the reach of the enforcer's power.

One of the most interesting features of cyberspace is the bankruptcy of this territorial conception of community and, by derivation, of law, thus threatening the traditional concept of the state.

Cyberspace breaks the territorial units from several perspectives. First, markets in cyberspace are global. A user sitting physically in North America can do business with another user located in Asia. For that matter, no differences exist between this transaction and a virtual transaction he or she might conduct with a user just across the street. Second, not only business, but also community activities – discussion groups, political groups, common culture and entertainment activities, cross geographical borders, developing new common and distinct cultural and social norms that are a-territorial. In fact, cyberians can simultaneously find themselves members of several communities that are very different from one other.

Third, virtual activity, when translated to actual electronic bits that are transferred from one user to another, may cross many borders. Communication between two neighbours may pass through several other countries. Cyberspace users cannot even know through which jurisdiction their activity is directed (Burk 1996). This has a significant effect on the traditional concepts of sovereignty and jurisdiction. Finally, not only do market and communal activities break territorial borders, but the ability to bypass markets and inflict externalities does the same (Post and Johnson 1997). While in the physical world externalities were phenomena attributed mainly to geographic neighbours, 'pollution' in cyberspace can be inflicted by remote players, where violation of privacy and pornographic sites are just two examples.

The implication of the borderless nature of cyberspace on economic analysis is highly significant. One can no longer take the state as the relevant framework for market activities, for decision-making calculus or for institutional analysis. This change is significant in both the normative and positive domains. Thus, while traditional normative law and economics analysis take the state as the basic maximization unit, which has implications for the definition of externalities and the analysis of other market failures, this cannot be the case in the networked information environment. Likewise, positive economic analysis is trickier, again because the identification of markets is less straightforward than in the old world.

This crucial feature of cyberspace ought to affect the theory of the state in two directions. First, if we relate to cyberian entities as substitutes to the traditional state, important components in a normative argument about the creation of states and their central government ought to be altered. The traditional doctrines of the state rely on presuppositions, such as the correspondence of geography, markets and communities, which no longer hold in the cyberian entities. Second, even if we remain more realistic, predicting that the traditional states are here to stay (we cannot be fed in cyberspace or by cyberian entities), they will stay alongside the new emerging cyberian market and communities. They enable the sophistication of traditional liberal democracies by more participation, more direct democracy, shifting decision-making rules from simple majority towards unanimity and abilities to save on some overlapping traditional powers.

5.2 Individuals as the Atoms of Society

As previously noted, cyberspace transforms not only the notion of collective communities, but also the notion of the individual person as the basic unit in the liberal philosophy of state and in economic analysis.

Most traditional economic analysis models assume that the players have preferences that are exogenous to their contractual and collective public activity; they also assume that perfect information will enhance rational choices by players that will meet their individual preferences. One of the important features of cyberspace is that it provides almost unlimited information. In fact, lack of information can no longer be held as affecting irrational behaviour. But perhaps the contrary is true. There is so much information that a need for processing tools for information arises. In the non-virtual world there are significant gaps in information, and on the other hand there is diversity within society and between societies that create different sets of information that are affected by given preferences – political, cultural, linguistic. By contrast, cyberspace is characterized by uniformity. The whole world becomes a small, global village, with a common language and cultural identities. Ironically, this combination of endless information and homogeneity might affect the independence of individuals in general and their preferences in particular.

In other words, while conventional economic thinking perceives individual preferences in the non-virtual world as exogenous to the political process and to the economic markets, cyberspace requires us to internalize even the analysis of individual preferences. Conventional economic analysis assumes that our basic identity, which can be framed in terms of various sets of preferences, is the result of distinguished historical, cultural, linguistic and even climatically different backgrounds. Those background factors are pre-given and predate any formation of markets and collective action organizations, such as states or other national units. The definitions of state boundaries, however, are very much influenced by these ancient groupings of preferences. Even if preferences change as the result of market interactions, such as successful marketing and advertising, they are initially founded upon these ancient differences, some of which are, presumably, almost permanent.

Cyberspace can be viewed as threatening this perception, because the new world of cyberspace blurs historical, cultural, national and even climatic boundaries. An Indian teenager who spends 10 hours a day in front of her computer has more in common with her German cyber-counterpart, than with an Indian her age 25 years ago. The decline of some of the more physical attributes of online users is accompanied by the pervasive effect of information technologies on processes such as individuation and will-formation. The online information environment constitutes the human condition of our time. People spend a large chunk of their time using the Internet for entertainment, business, social relationships and political activities. For an increasing number of people, some real-world activities are becoming and will become marginal. Rather than going to schools and universities, paying a visit to the public library or the museum, people view art, obtain knowledge and spend their leisure time in cyberspace. Instead of driving to the supermarket, the bank, or the social welfare borough, people click several buttons on their computer to do business, communicate with government agencies, or settle their finances.

The comprehensive character of the online environment makes individuals more vulnerable to external effects that shape their preferences. The emergence of media, communications and software multinational conglomerates, and the rise of new monopolies (Elkin-Koren and Salzberger 2004, chs 4 and 6), not only affect economic competition in the market for ordinary goods, but also affect individual autonomy. As phrased by Barber (2000):

> The new monopolies are particularly insidious because while monopolies of the nineteenth century were in durable goods and natural resources, and exercised

control over the goods of the body, new information-age monopolies of the twenty-first century are over news, entertainment, and knowledge, and exercise control over the goods of the mind and spirit.

Power exercised by private economic agents is also relevant for the formation of preferences in the public sphere. Powerful market players that control the means of producing informational goods are better positioned to express their own agendas and thereby marginalize diversity. When power accumulated in the market is used in the public sphere, it tends to distort equal participation and reduce fair access to participation means. Informational goods, such as news and data, but also photo images, music, novels, comics, or computer programs reflect an ideology, and may shape one's identity and presence. Informational products affect their own demand. Consequently, centralized power in such a marketplace could be very powerful in shaping preferences and agendas, reducing plurality as well as social and political diversity.

Individuals in the online environment are therefore cut off from their historical, cultural and geographical context, on the one hand, and widely exposed to a relatively homogeneous information environment, which affects their preferences, on the other. Indeed, a globalized market for goods could benefit from a relatively homogenized body of consumers, consuming goods under fairly standard interoperable settings.

We are in an interim stage of cyber-revolution, while in the future cyberspace may cause the disappearance of diversity, which in the non-virtual world fosters the definition of the unique self, leaving us with a brave new homogeneous human being. Thus, economic analysis has to internalize one of its basic foundations – the existence of atoms – individuals – whose basic features are given. A fresh way of thinking, if not a fresh paradigm of economic analysis have to emerge in which these basic presuppositions with regard to individual preferences will be internalized. Such a thinking would help us to assess whether cyberspace is a forum that creates much more free choice or a tool for suppressing independence – in fact limiting freedom of choice; whether technology sets new horizons for individual and collective well-being, or patterns our individual character, our self, by the same universal agents for all; whether it enhances communication of diversities, or the disappearance of diversity.

The last point will not sound alien to Jean Jacques Rousseau or those republicans who are not familiar with the economic approach. Perhaps cyberspace should be a trigger for broadening the economic theory of the state, to incorporate such views. This, however, requires fresh economic thinking and modelling, which is beyond the horizons of this chapter.

5.3 Conclusion

We still live under the governance of the liberal democracy paradigm. Netanel (2000, p. 407), summarizing the literature, defines liberal democracy as:

> a political system with representative government elected by popular majority, the rule of law enshrined to protect individuals and minorities, and a significant sector of economic, associational and communicative activity that is largely autonomous from government control. It rests upon the principles of individual liberty, civic equality, popular sovereignty and government by the consent of the governed.

In this chapter we questioned this paradigmatic view. We examined the sources for majority decision making and representative government, and argued that on the bases of the new technological frontiers the same normative foundations may lead to a different concept of the state. Using Netanel's framework, we examined whether the principles of individual liberty, civic equality, popular sovereignty and government by the consent of the governed, should direct us to a political system with representative government elected by popular majority. We argued that in the new world of cyberspace the answer ought to be negative, and that based on the same normative foundations, we must re-think the conventions of the existing concepts of the state.

The analysis and conclusions of this chapter can be seen as the result of the interplay among values, technology and the law. The scientific methodology was that of viewing values as fixed or pre-given, and examining, in the light of these value foundations, how the changing technology affects the basic institutional arrangements regarding the state. It is important to note that we ignored the opposite effect of the law (and values) on technology. We also ignored the effects of technology on values. These are fascinating topics for future study.

NOTES

* This chapter is part of a wider project on law, economics and cyberspace. The wider context and conclusions can be found in Elkin-Koren and Salzberger (2004).
1. We refer here to 'Liberalism' in its widest definition, which incorporates libertarianism, on the one hand, and social democracy, on the other. Indeed most normative debates of our times are within the range created by these two poles, whereas the concepts mentioned in the text – representative government and majority decision making – are pre-given.
2. For analysis of the effects of cyberspace on the positive analysis of the state, see Elkin-Koren and Salzberger (2004, Ch. 9).

3. The new political economics, the new institutional economics, positive political economics and the new economics of organization, can be viewed as some of the sub-branches, or related branches of the new institutional law and economics. See Mercuro and Medema (1997, Ch. 5).
4. See the interesting debate between Richard Posner (1979, 1980) and Ronald Dworkin (1980) with regard to this point.
5. Utilitarianism challenged the traditional natural law moral theory, which saw good and bad as pre-given and independent of individual human well-being. Utilitarianism sees good and bad only in the context of individual well-being, where the total utility of all individuals is the criterion for social or collective good.
6. There were other difficulties with utilitarianism on both moral and practical grounds. Who should be included in the utility calculus and what is the right time frame for such a calculus are some of these secondary considerations. However, most economists were not really bothered by these crucial questions.
7. The presupposition regarding the 'good' is linked to the rationality–self-interested assumption, but it ought to be emphasized that this assumption does not necessarily mean that individuals seek to maximize only wealth, as often some economic models assume with regard to the behaviour of 'ordinary' individuals. It also does not mean that individuals seek to maximize only political power as often is assumed with regard to the behaviour of politicians or other actors in the public arena. The rationality–self-maximization assumption requires only that individuals are able to rank various options facing them in every juncture of decision making, and that this ranking is complete and transitive.
8. Farber and Frickey (1991) incorporate republican thinking into their public choice and law analysis. However, they generally conclude (p. 45) that the two theories are in conflict, and they incorporate republican thinking into law and economics only on the positive level, showing why republican assumptions can explain, for example, the rare occurrence of collective decision-making problems, such as cycling. They do not go as far as implementing republican thinking to the basic assumptions of economic models with regard to the origin of preferences. See also Mashaw (1988).
9. This is, it should be emphasized, only one interpretation of republican thought. Whether the differences between Rousseau's general will and the sum of individual preferences can be attributed to the shift of preferences which is the result of collective organizations attempting to convince the general public as to the best course of action for society, is an open question. Some republicans would probably argue that this is not a fair and full view of the republican perception of the public sphere. We shall not elaborate on this interesting philosophical point here.
10. In the past, Sunstein (1995, p. 1783) argued that cyberspace, in contrast to the Madisonian vision of the state, enables large-scale substantive discussion, which brings us closer to the deliberative democracy or the republican vision of the state. This is somehow different from his more recent arguments in *Republic.com* (2001).
11. The most notable example of a lack of personal separation of powers is the post of the Lord Chancellor in Britain, which was abolished just recently. The Lord Chancellor was a member of all three branches of government – a judge of the highest judicial instance – the judicial committee of the House of Lords, a member of the House of Lords in its legislative capacity and a cabinet minister.
12. In most European countries legislation is subject to judicial review, but not by the regular judiciary. The reviewing body is a special constitutional court, which cannot be identified fully with the judicial branch of government.

REFERENCES

Aranson, P., E. Gellhorn and G. Robinson (1982), 'The theory of legislative delegation', *Cornell Law Review*, **68**, 1.

Arrow, K. (1951), *Social Choice and Individual Values*, New York: John Wiley.
Backhaus, J. (1979), 'Constitutional guarantees and the distribution of power and wealth', *Public Choice*, **33** (3), 45–65.
Baird, D., R. Gertner and R. Picker (1994), *Game Theory and the Law*, Cambridge, MA: Harvard University Press, Cambridge, UK: Cambridge University Press.
Barber, B.R. (2000), 'Globalizing democracy', *American Prospect*, **11** (20), http://www.prospect.org/print-friendly/print/V11/20/barber-b.html, 1 September 2003.
Barzel, Y. (2002), *A Theory of the State*, Cambridge: Cambridge University Press.
Bentham, J. (1789), *A Fragment on Government and an Introduction to the Principles of Morals and Legislation*, reprinted in Wilfrid Harrison (ed.) (1948), London: Basil Blackwell.
Black, D. (1948), 'On the rationale of group decision-making', *Journal of Political Economy*, **56**, 23–4.
Borda, J.C. (1781), 'Mémoire sur les élections au Scrutin', *Histoire de l'Académie Royale des Sciences*, Paris.
Brennan, G. and J. Buchanan (1985), 'The reason of rules: constitutional political economy', [Electronic version] in J. Buchanan, *Collected Works of James M. Buchanan*, Indianapolis, IN: Liberty Fund.
Brennan, G. and A. Hamlin (2000), *Democratic Devices and Desires*, Cambridge: Cambridge University Press.
Buchanan, J. (1975), *The Limits of Liberty: Between Anarchy and Leviathan*, Chicago: University of Chicago Press.
Buchanan, J. and G. Tullock (1962), *The Calculus of Consent: Logical Foundations of Constitutional Democracy*, Ann Arbor, MI: University of Michigan.
Burk, D. (1996), 'Federalism in cyberspace', *Connecticut Law Review*, **28**, 1095–137.
Burke, E. (1774), *Address to the Electors of Bristol*, 1095–137.
Calabresi, G. and D. Melamed (1972), 'Property rights, liability rules and inalienability: one view of the cathedral', *Harvard Law Review*, **85**, 1089–129.
Coase, R. (1937), 'The nature of the firm', *Economica*, **4**, 386–405.
Coleman, J.L. (1988), *Markets, Morals and the Law*, Cambridge: Cambridge University Press.
Condorcet, J.N.A. (1785), *Sketch for a Historical Picture of the Progress of the Human Mind*, reprinted in J. Barraclough (trans.) (1955), London: Weidenfeld & Nicholson.
Cooter, R.D. (1999), *The Strategic Constitution*, Princeton, NJ: Princeton University Press.
Downs, A. (1957), *An Economic Theory of Democracy*, New York: Harper.
Dworkin, R.M. (1980), 'Is wealth a value?', *Journal of Legal Studies*, **9**, 191–226.
Easterbrook, F. (1996), 'Cyberspace and the law of the horse', *University of Chicago Legal Forum*, **1996**, 207–16.
Eggertsson, T. (1990), *Economic Behavior and Institutions*, Cambridge: Cambridge University Press.
Elkin-Koren, N. (1996), 'Cyberlaw and social change: a democratic approach to copyright law in cyberspace', *Cardozo Arts and Entertainment Law Journal*, **14** (2), 215–95.
Elkin-Koren, N. and E. Salzberger (1999), 'Law and economics in cyberspace', *International Review of Law and Economics*, **19**, 553–81.
Elkin-Koren, N. and E. Salzberger (2004) *Law, Economics and Cyberspace: The Effects of Cyberspace on the Economic Analysis of Law*, Cheltenham, UK and Northampton, MA, USA: Edward Elgar, pp. 553–81.

Farber, D. and P. Frickey (1991), *Law and Public Choice: A Critical Introduction*, Chicago: University of Chicago Press.

Frey, B. (2001), 'A utopia? Government without territorial monopoly', *The Independent Review*, **6**, 99–113.

Frey, B. (2003), 'Flexible citizenship for a global society', *Politics, Philosophy and Economics*, **2**, 93–114.

Gwartney, J. and R. Wagner (eds) (1988), *Public Choice and Constitutional Economics*, Greenwich, CI: JAI Press.

Harsanyi, J.C. (1955), 'Cardinal welfare, individualistic ethics and interpersonal comparisons of utility', *Journal of Political Economy*, **63**, 309–21.

Harsanyi, J.C. (1977), *Rational Behavior and Bargaining Equilibrium in Games and Social Situations*, Cambridge: Cambridge University Press.

Hirschman, L. (1970), *Exit, Voice and Loyalty: Responses to Decline in Firms, Organizations and States*, Cambridge, MA: Harvard University Press.

Hobbes, T. (1651), *Leviathan*, reprinted in 1979, London: Dent.

Jensen, M. and W. Meckling (1976), 'Theory of the firm: managerial behavior, agency costs and ownership structure', *Journal of Financial Economics*, **3**, 305–60.

Kuhn, T. (1962), *The Structure of Scientific Revolution*, Chicago: University of Chicago Press.

Lessig, L. (1999), *Code and other Laws of Cyberspace*, New York: Basic Books.

Locke, J. (1690), *Two Treatises of Government*, reprinted 1989, P. Laslett (ed.), Cambridge: Cambridge University Press.

Macey, J. (1989), 'Public choice: the theory of the firm and the theory of market exchange', *Cornell Law Review*, **74**, 43–62.

Marshall, G. (1971), *Constitutional Theory*, Oxford: Clarendon.

Mashaw, J. (1988), 'As if republican interpretation', *Yale Law Journal*, **97**, 1685–1703.

Mayton, W. (1986), 'The possibilities of collective choice: Arrow's theorem, Article 1 and the delegation of legislative powers to administrative agencies', *Duke Law Journal*, **5**, 948–70.

Mercuro, N. and S. Medema (1997), *Economics and the Law: From Posner to Post-Modernism*, Princeton, NJ: Princeton University Press.

Michelman, F. (1980), 'Constitution, statutes and the theory of efficient adjudication', *Journal of Legal Studies*, **9**, 430–61.

Moe, T. (1990), 'Political institutions: the neglected side of the story', *Journal of Law, Economics and Organization*, **6**, 213–45.

Montesquieu, C. (1748), *The Spirit of the Laws*, Carrithers D.W. (ed. and trans.) (1977), Berkeley, CA: University of California Press.

Mueller, D.C. (1996), *Constitutional Democracy*, New York: Oxford University Press.

Netanel, N.W. (2000), 'Market hierarchy and copyright in our system of free expression', *Vanderbilt Law Review*, **53**, 1879–932.

Netauel, N.W. (2000), 'Cyberspace self-governance: a skeptical view from liberal Democratic Theory', *California Law Review*, **88**, 395–498.

North, D. (1981), *Structure and Change in Economic History*, New York: Norton.

North, D. (1986), 'Is it worth making sense of Marx?', in J. Elster (ed.), *Making Sense of Marx*, Cambridge: Cambridge University Press, pp. 57–63.

Olson, M. (1965), *The Logic of Collective Action*, Cambridge, MA: Harvard University Press.

Posner, R. (1979), 'Utilitarianism economics and the legal theory', *Journal of Legal Studies*, **8**, 103–40.

Posner, R. (1980), 'The ethical and political basis of the efficiency norm in common law adjudication', *Hofstra Law Review*, **8**, 487–507.
Posner, R. (1987), 'The law and economics movement', *American Economic Review*, **77** (2), 1–13.
Post, D. and D. Johnson (1996), 'Law and borders: the rise of law in cyberspace', *Stanford Law Review*, **48**, 1367–403.
Post, D. and D. Johnson (1997), 'And how shall the net be governed? A meditation on the relative virtues of decentralized, emergent law', in B. Kahin and J. Keller (eds), *Coordinating the Internet*, Cambridge, MA: MIT Press.
Rawls, J. (1971), *A Theory of Justice*, Cambridge, MA: Belknap/Harvard University Press.
Rousseau, J. (1762), *The Social Contract, or Principles of Political Right*, reprinted 1998, H.J. Tozer (trans.), Wordsworth.
Salzberger, E. (1993), 'On the normative facet of the economic approach towards law', *Mishpatim*, in Hebrew, **22** (1), 261–99.
Salzberger, E. (2002), 'Cyberspace, governance, and the new economy: how cyberspace regulates us and how should we regulate cyberspace', in H. Siebert (ed.), *Economic Policy Issues of the New Economy*, Berlin: Springer.
Salzberger, E. and S. Voigt (2002), 'On the delegation of powers: with special emphasis on central and eastern Europe', *Constitutional Political Economy*, **13** (25).
Sen, A. (1987), *On Ethics and Economics*, Oxford: Clarendon Press, New York: Norton.
Silver, M. (1977), 'Economic theory of the constitutional separation of powers', *Public Choice*, **29**, 95–103.
Skogh, G. and C. Stuart (1982), 'A contractarian theory of property rights and crime', *Scandinavian Journal of Economics*, **84** (1), 27–42.
Smith, A. (1776), *An Inquiry into the Nature and Causes of the Wealth of Nations*, reprinted 1961, C. Edwin (ed.), London: Methuen.
Sunstein, C. (1988), 'Beyond the republican revival', *Yale Law Journal*, **97**, 1539–90.
Sunstein, C. (1995), 'The first amendment in cyberspace', *Yale Law Journal*, **104**, 1757–1804.
Sunstein, C. (2001), *Republic.com*, Princeton, NJ: Princeton University Press.
Tullock, G. (1969), 'Federalism: problems of scale', *Public Choice*, **6**, 19–36.
Tullock, G. (1981), 'Why so much stability?', *Public Choice*, **37**, 189–213.
Tullock, G. (1982), 'Welfare and the law', *International Review of Law and Economics*, **2**, 151–63.
Vile, M. (1967), *Constitutionalism and the Separation of Powers*, Oxford: Liberty Fund.
Voigt, S. (1999), *Explaining Constitutional Change – A Positive Economic Analysis*, Cheltenham UK and Northampton, USA: Edward Elgar.
Whynes, D. and R. Bowles (1981), *The Economic Theory of the State*, New York: St. Martin's Press.
Yassky, D.A. (1989), 'Two tiered theory of constitution and separation of powers', *Yale Law Journal*, **99**, 431–52.

4. Explaining the great divergence: medium and message on the Eurasian land mass, 1700–1850

Leonard Dudley

1 INTRODUCTION

In 1712, an ironmonger named Thomas Newcomen and a plumber named John Calley installed a steam-powered engine to pump water from a coalmine near Dudley Castle in Staffordshire, about 200km northwest of London. Although to James Watt, some 50 years later, the technology of their atmospheric steam engine already appeared quite primitive, the machine was arguably the most important innovation of the past 500 years. It marked the first use of heat to generate mechanical power (Rolt and Allen 1977). The machine combined three ideas developed shortly before by physicists of different nationalities: first, a vacuum used to move a piston (Otto von Guericke, a German); second, condensed steam to generate a partial vacuum (Denis Papin, a Frenchman); and third, a separate boiler to generate steam (Thomas Savery, an Englishman). Yet the two inventors had no scientific training. Moreover, they had developed their invention in Dartmouth, a remote port on the southwest coast of England. Both were devout Baptists, members of a non-conformist religious sect who insisted that their children be able to read and write.

At the beginning of the eighteenth century, when Newcomen and Calley began their experiments, average income levels were quite similar across the Eurasian land mass. Estimates by Maddison (2001) suggest that in 1700, Europe had a per capita GDP of about 870 dollars at 1990 prices. Average incomes elsewhere at that time were 550 dollars in India, 600 dollars in China and 565 dollars in the rest of Eurasia. Yet barely a century and a half later, in 1870, European incomes were almost three times the level of the rest of Eurasia – a gap remarkably similar to that which exists today.

If one looks for possible explanations of the divergence between Europe and the rest of Eurasia that occurred over the century and a half after

1700, a good starting point is the example of Newcomen and Calley. Their invention, the atmospheric steam engine, was but one of roughly 115 important innovations developed in this interval that have been noted by historians of technology. All were developed in Europe, and their diffusion prior to 1850 was limited essentially to Europe and its offshoots (Dudley 2003). Why was this so? Why did China, which had contributed the most important innovations over the previous two millennia, stop innovating around 1300? Why did what Lal (1998) has called the 'closing of the Muslim mind' occur at about the same time? And why did India make no important contributions to technology after the first millennium AD?

An examination of the literature on economic progress written over the past half-century, reveals two types of answer to these questions. One group of authors has emphasized geography. McNeill (1963, 114) attributed the rise of the West to its resource base and to political competition that encouraged innovation. Jones (1987, 226; 2002) suggested that this competition is explained by the mountain chains and marshes of Europe, which formed barriers sufficient to prevent a single state from dominating the entire territory. Diamond (1997, 409–12) also emphasized the importance of geography, noting Europe's abundant rainfall and the favourable effects of its indented coastline and high mountains on political competition. For Landes (1998), Europe's temperate climate was important in allowing its residents to accumulate a surplus above the subsistence level. Pomeranz (2000) emphasized Europe's stocks of coal and its access to the resources of the Americas.

A second group of analysts has given precedence to institutions. North (1981, 17) argued that the structure of a society's political and economic institutions determines the performance of its economy and its rate of technical change. His argument is straightforward. Institutions determine the degree to which property rights are protected and contracts enforced, that is, the cost of transacting. The lower are transaction costs, the greater will be the degree of specialization and the division of labour (North 1990, 27). Josselin and Marciano (1997) suggested that in constraining the growth of the public sector, a country's legal system can have a considerable impact on its development. Comparing societies across Eurasia, Lal (1998, 173) attributed the success of the West to cultural factors: cosmological beliefs, political decentralization and 'the inquisitive Greek spirit'.

Which camp is right? There can be little doubt that favourable geographic conditions are a necessary condition for economic progress. A minimum of heat and water would appear indispensable, as a cursory examination of living standards in Siberia and the Sahara indicates. However, it is questionable whether geography's influence on inventiveness operates through its effects on the degree of political competition. China has a relatively short coastline and few important barriers to internal movement. In general, political power has been highly centralized. Yet as Mokyr (1990, 209–18) has shown, over the two millennia prior to the modern era, China had the highest rate of innovation of any society (hydraulic engineering, the iron plough, the seed drill, cast iron, the spinning wheel, the loom, the waterwheel, clocks, the compass, paper, printing and porcelain).

Regarding institutions, once again there would appear to be some minimal level of respect of property rights and enforcement of contracts that is essential for sustained innovation. However, it does not necessarily follow that societies run by merchants will be more inventive than societies run by bureaucrats. During the period from 1700 to 1850, the Netherlands, where property rights were strictly enforced, contributed not a single innovation of note, whereas France, with a spottier record in protecting commercial interests, developed a number of important innovations. Nevertheless, institutions do seem to matter. Mokyr (1990, 233–6) notes that in China, the state was favourable to innovation before 1400 but withdrew its support during the Ming and Qing periods.

This chapter argues that while both geography and institutions are important in determining a society's rate of innovation, there is a further set of phenomena intermediate between the two that is crucial. Following the path set out by Innis (1950, 1951), we shall look at the characteristics of a society's communication system. In particular, we shall inquire whether there is a relation between economic progress and the extent to which the written and spoken language (the *medium*) and its content (the *message*) are standardized. As Holler and Thisse (1996, 180) observe, little research has been done on the pure coordination problems involved in developing social standards. Here, it is shown that while geography plays an important role in determining the parameters by which people interact within a society, the social equilibrium of the resulting game is not necessarily unique. Accordingly, shocks from outside or within a society can jolt it from one equilibrium to another, thereby altering the rate of social innovation.

Section 2 sets out the facts to be explained, namely the unprecedented rate of innovation in Europe during the century and a half after 1700. Section 3 points out some remarkable differences in the systems of communication of the four main cultural regions of Eurasia at the beginning of this period. One dimension is the degree of standardization of the medium of communication while the other is the extent of standardization of the message that is transmitted. Each cultural region had chosen a distinct pattern, most likely for reasons of geography. Section 4 examines the consequence of these differences for the willingness to cooperate in developing innovations. The great divergence between East and West is explained by two developments in the early modern period that resulted from the introduction of movable type in Europe. The first was the emergence of standardized written versions of the vernacular languages that allowed information to be shared at low cost. The second was a series of revolutions, as rising literacy within European societies shifted them from a non-cooperative to a cooperative equilibrium. In the other regions of Eurasia, the introduction of movable type was less appropriate because of characteristics of the writing systems and was therefore delayed. Finally, Section 5 concludes.

2 THE STYLIZED FACTS OF INNOVATION, 1700–1850

This section sets out the facts to be explained: first, the divergence in per capita income levels across Eurasia during the century and a half after 1700; second, the unprecedented number of technological innovations during this period; and finally, the location of these innovations, confined essentially to three Western nations.

2.1 The Great Divergence

Table 4.1 displays the levels of per capita GDP between 1700 and 1870 across Eurasia, based on Maddison's (2001) estimates. Note that the figures for Europe include the United Kingdom, Ireland and the former USSR, while those for East Eurasia exclude Japan. As mentioned in the introduction, the initial gap in living standards was not very great. In 1700, the Eurasian income level was about two-thirds that of Europe, a gap that falls within the range of measurement error.[1] However, over the following century and a half, average incomes stagnated or fell in the major regions

Table 4.1   Per capita GDP in 1990 dollars

Region	1700	1870	1998
Europe	870	1 521	10 939
East Eurasia	571	543	2 936
China	600	530	3 117
India	550	533	1 746
Others	565	565	3 734
Eurasia	647	846	4 464

Source: Maddison (2001).

of Eurasia while rising sharply in the West. By 1870, Europe's per capita income was almost three times that of the rest of Eurasia. Although the size of this gap fluctuated over the following decades, by the end of the twentieth century, it was still roughly three to one.

2.2 Innovations, 1700–1849

If per capita incomes rose after 1700 in Europe while stagnating elsewhere in Eurasia, the principal reason was that Europeans learned before their East Eurasian counterparts how to increase systematically the level of production output per unit of labour input. Underlying these productivity increases was an unprecedented wave of technological innovation. Historians of technology have long been interested in the individual innovations and when they were developed. Table 4.2 brings together the research of four studies, each by an author of a different nationality, namely Cardwell (1991), Daumas (1979), Mokyr (1990) and Paulinyi (1989). If only those contributions to technology mentioned by two or more of these authors are counted, a list of 115 innovations is obtained.

2.3 The Location of Innovations, 1700–1849

It is interesting to note exactly when and where these innovations occurred. As Figure 4.1 indicates, for the first half-century after 1700, almost all of the innovations were from the regions that today comprise the United Kingdom. Over the following fifty years, while the pace of innovations in Britain accelerated, both France and the United States also began to produce significant numbers of innovations. This pattern continued over the half-century after 1800. In all, these three countries accounted for 91 per cent of the world's significant technological innovations during the full century and a half after 1700. The few remaining developments were scattered among Germany, Switzerland and northern Italy. It is remarkable that Scandinavia, southern and central Europe and the entire remainder of the Eurasian land mass played no role in these developments. Not a single innovation of note came from outside the core countries in northwestern Europe and North America.

When we look at how these new technologies diffused prior to 1850, we also find a limited number of participants. The Industrial Revolution that these innovations triggered spread first from Great Britain to France and Belgium, then to the United States, Germany, Switzerland and northern Italy. With the exception of Belgium, during the initial century and a half, no innovation also meant no industrialization.

3 THE IMPACT OF GEOGRAPHY ON MEDIUM AND MESSAGE

Let us examine communication systems across the Eurasian land mass in 1700. Our first concern will be to discover the extent to which the medium and the message were standardized. We shall compare four societies – the Middle East, India, China and Europe. We shall then explore whether geography's influence on these societies' destiny has been exerted through the development of their communication systems.

3.1 Medium and Message in 1700

The middle east
In 1700, states with a majority of Muslims stretched across the southern part of the Eurasian land mass from the Balkans to the Malaysian peninsula, interrupted only by the Indian subcontinent, where they nevertheless formed an important minority. If one looks at the medium of communication over this territory, one finds a wide variety of spoken languages, some Altaic (for example, Turkish) some Semitic (for example, Arabic) and some Indo-European (for example, Persian). Most of the spoken dialects had no written counterpart. For written communication, educated people used one of three vehicular languages, Arabic, Turkish or Persian. Writing was with the Arabic consonantal script, of which there were several important variants.[2] The diacritical notation used for the short vowels was not standardized and was generally omitted in ordinary books and private documents (Bauer 1996, 562). As a result, it was difficult for most people to learn to decode written messages accurately (Ibrahim 1988). Within the Ottoman Empire, there were no printing presses in Arabic before the nineteenth century.

What messages were transmitted across this territory? In the Ottoman and Persian states, there was tight control over what information was allowed to circulate. For the most part, censure came from the *ilmiye*, those learned in Islam. The Koran and the Hadith, the sayings attributed to the Prophet, had been standardized by the ninth century. Outside the sphere of religion, there was also little tolerance for dissent. The Ottoman state was a centralized autocracy in which both the officials (the *devshirme*) and the soldiers (janissaries) were slaves of the sultan.

India
Some 200 different languages were spoken on the Indian subcontinent. As in the Muslim world outside India, they belonged to several different

Table 4.2 Significant innovations, 1700–1849

Country	1700–1749	1750–1799	1800–1849
France	Loom coded with perforated paper (Bouchon, 1725) Loom coded with punched cards (Falcon, 1728)	Automatic loom (Vaucanson, 1775) Single-action press (Didot, 1781) Two-engine steamboat (Jouffroy d'Abbans, 1783) Hot-air balloon (Montgolfier, 1783) Parachute (Lenormand, 1783) Press for the blind (Haüy, 1784) Chlorine as bleaching agent (Berthollet, 1785) Sodium carbonate from salt (Leblanc, 1790) Visual telegraph (Chappe, 1793) Vacuum sealing (Appert, 1795) Illuminating gas from wood (Lebon, 1799)	Automatic loom with perforated cards (Jacquard, 1805) Wet spinning for flax (de Girard, 1815) Single-helix propeller (Sauvage, 1832) Three-colour textile printing machine (Perrot, 1832) Water turbine with adjustable vanes (Fourneyron, 1837) Photograpy (Daguerre, 1838) Multiple-phase combing machine (Heilmann, 1845) Measuring machine (Whitworth, 1845)
Germany		Lithography (Senefelder, 1796)	
Great Britain	Porcelain (Böttger, 1707) Seed drill (Tull, 1701) Iron smelting with coke (Darby, 1709) Atmospheric engine (Newcomen, 1712) Pottery made with flint (Astbury, 1720) Quadrant (Hadley, 1731)	Crucible steel (Huntsman, 1750) Rib knitting attachment (Strutt, 1755) Achromatic refracting telescope (Dollond, 1757) Breast wheel (Smeaton, 1759) Bimetallic strip chronometer (Harrison, 1760) Spinning jenny (Hargreaves, 1764) Creamware pottery (Wedgewood, 1765) Cast-iron railroad (Reynolds, 1768)	Machines for tackle block production (Brunel, 1800) Illuminating gas from coal (Murdock, 1802) Paper-making machine (Robert, 1803) Steam locomotive (Trevithick, 1804) Winding mechanism for loom (Radcliffe, 1805) Arc lamp (Davy, 1808) Food canning (Durand, 1810)

Hot blast furnace (Nielson, 1733)
Flying shuttle (Kay, 1733)
Glass-chamber process for sulphuric acid (Ward, 1736)
Spinning machine with rollers (Wyatt, 1738)
Stereotyping (Ged, 1739)
Lead-chamber process for sulphuric acid (Roebuck, 1746)

Engine using expansive steam operation (Watt, 1769)
Water frame (Arkwright, 1769)
Efficient atmospheric steam engine (Smeaton, 1772)
Dividing machine (Ramsden, 1773)
Cylinder boring machine (Wilkinson, 1775)
Carding machine (Arkwright, 1775)
Condensing chamber for steam engine (Watt, 1776)
Steam jacket for steam engine (Watt, 1776)
Spinning mule (Crompton, 1779)
Reciprocating compound steam engine (Hornblower, 1781)
Sun and planet gear (Watt, 1781)
Indicator of steam engine power (Watt, 1782)
Rolling mill (Cort, 1783)
Cylinder printing press for calicoes (Bell, 1783)
Jointed levers for parallel motion (Watt, 1784)
Puddling (Cort, 1784)
Power loom (Cartwright, 1785)
Speed governor (Watt, 1787)
Double-acting steam engine (Watt, 1787)
Threshing machine (Meikle, 1788)
Single-phase combing machine (Cartwright, 1789)

Compound steam engine (Woolf, 1811)
Rack locomotive (Blenkinson, 1811)
Mechanical printing press (Koenig, 1813)
Steam locomotive on flanged rails (Stephenson, 1814)
Safety lamp (Davy, 1816)
Circular knitting machine (M.I. Brunel, 1816)
Planing machine (Roberts, 1817)
Large metal lathe (Roberts, 1817)
Gas meter (Clegg, 1819)
Metal power loom (Roberts, 1822)
Rubber fabric (Hancock, 1823)
Horizontal water wheel (Burdin, 1824)
Electromagnet (Sturgeon, 1824)
Locomotive with fire-tube boiler (Stephenson, 1829)
Self-acting mule (Roberts, 1830)
Lathe with automatic cross-feed tool (Whitworth, 1835)
Planing machine with pivoting tool-rest (Whitworth, 1835)
Even-current electric cell (Daniell, 1836)
Electric telegraph (Cooke and Wheatstone, 1837)

Table 4.2 (continued)

Country	1700–1749	1750–1799	1800–1849
		Machines for lock production (Bramagh, 1790)	Riveting machine (Fairbairn, 1838)
		Single-action metal printing press (Stanhope, 1795)	Transatlantic steamer (I.K. Brunel, 1838)
		Hydraulic press (Bramah, 1796)	Assembly-line production (Bodmer, 1839)
		High-pressure steam engine (Trevithick, 1797)	Multiple-blade propeller (Smith, 1839)
		Slide lathe (Maudslay, 1799)	Steam hammer (Nasmyth, 1842)
			Iron, propellor-driven steamship (I.K. Brunel, 1844)
			Multiple-spindle drilling machine (Roberts, 1847)
Italy			Electric battery (Volta, 1800)
Switzerland		Massive platen printing press (Haas, 1772)	
		Stirring process for glass (Guinand, 1796)	
United States		Continuous-flow production (Evans, 1784)	Single-engine steamboat (Fulton, 1807)
		Cotton gin (Whitney, 1793)	Milling machine (Whitney, 1818)
		Machine to cut and head nails (Perkins, 1795)	Ring spinning machine (Thorp, 1828)
		Interchangeable parts (Whitney, 1797)	Grain reaper (McCormick, 1832)
			Binary-code telegraph (Morse, 1845)
			Sewing machine (Howe, 1846)
			Rotary printing press (Hoe, 1847)

Sources: Daumas (1979); Cardwell ([1972] 1991); Mokyr (1990); Paulinyi (1989).

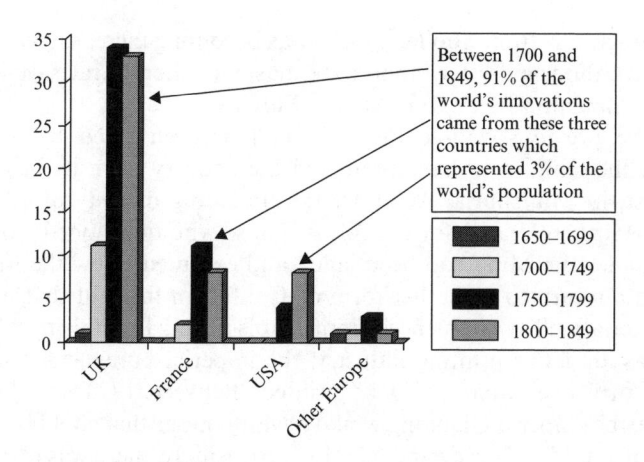

Figure 4.1   Innovations by country, 1650–1849

language families. The largest group was made up of those who spoke Indo-European languages. In 1700, Sanskrit was still in use as a vehicular language for religious texts and poetry. However, modern vernaculars such as Bengali and Hindi were beginning to develop their own literatures. Most languages that had writing systems used semi-phonetic alphabets, known as alphasyllabaries, which were descended from Aramaic, the ancestor of classical Arabic. Each consonant–vowel combination in a syllable was written as a unit consisting of a consonantal symbol plus a vowel diacritical.[3] In 1700, the printing press had still not been introduced into India. Consequently, literacy rates were low.

The Mughal Empire which controlled most of the Indian subcontinent in 1700 promoted the Muslim faith and used the Persian Arabic script for its own records. However, Muslims comprised only about 10 per cent of the total population, and the emperors showed considerable tolerance of other religions, notably, Hindu and Sikh.[4] As mentioned, in the modern period, the major Indian languages were developing their own literatures. Writers in Persian, Urdu and Hindi were all patronized by the Mughal court.[5]

China

By 1700, most Chinese spoke one of the mutually intelligible dialects of Mandarin. Although Mandarin and the six non-Mandarin dialects spoken in the southeast were not mutually understandable, all used the same logographic writing system consisting of thousands of ideograms. Indeed, since the symbols represented words rather than phonemes, they could easily be adapted to any spoken language, including Korean and Japanese. Printing using xylography from wooden blocks was becoming increasingly popular. Despite the thousands of symbols to be mastered, literacy rates were higher in China than anywhere else in eastern Eurasia.

For the previous half-century, China had been ruled by a foreign dynasty, the Qing, who had conquered the country from its base to the northeast, in Manchuria. As under the preceding dynasty of the Ming, there was little tolerance for new ideas. Those who questioned Confucian norms under the Ming had been jailed and executed. Now the Manchus favoured a return to an earlier form of Confucian thought that was considered untainted by influences from Daoism and Buddhism. Although there was an active printing industry, the imperial bureaucracy imposed tight control over what could be printed. Between 1774 and 1778, for example, the emperor Qianlong would have all books that could be deemed critical of the Manchus destroyed. Not surprisingly, there was little political debate. Intellectuals confined themselves for the most part with discussions of texts dating from the Han period which had ended some 1500 years earlier.

Europe
Like the Chinese, most Europeans in 1700 used a standardized writing system. However, unlike the systems of any of the other cultural regions in Eurasia, the Latin alphabet was fully phonetic, with separate symbols to represent vowels. As a result, it had been readily adapted to the dialects of the major printing centres that had by now become standardized national vernaculars. Equally important, the Latin alphabet was the only writing system in Eurasia that had been adapted to movable metallic type. With inexpensive reading matter using a compact set of phonetic characters available in the vernacular, Europe had been able to outdistance the rest of Eurasia in effective literacy rates. By 1700, in northern Europe, roughly half of the adult population was able to read and write (Graff 1991).

Unlike China and the Muslim world, but like India, there was considerable tolerance of religious diversity in many parts of Europe by 1700. Although France had expelled its Protestants after 1685, Great Britain had extended full rights to protest dissenters after the Glorious Revolution of 1688. Moreover, censorship was much less severe in Europe than in other parts of Eurasia. Great Britain had abolished censorship in 1688. Books and newspapers printed in French in the Netherlands circulated widely in France. Finally, Europe was the only area in Eurasia where multi-party political competition was to be found. The Glorious Revolution had introduced the principle of government responsible to an elected legislature in Great Britain. Over the course of the eighteenth century, first Britain's

American offshoot, the United States, and then France would also adopt this principle.

3.2 Geography and Standardization

Let us now try to generalize from this brief survey of communication systems across Eurasia. Our discussion suggests two dimensions of languages that should be considered. One dimension, shown on the vertical axis of Figure 4.2, is the degree of standardization of the *medium* of communication. We saw that the degree of medium standardization was relatively low both in India and in the Muslim territories of the Ottoman Empire and Iran. In each region, there were multiple non-phonetic scripts and distinct vehicular and vernacular languages. We also saw that in the two remaining regions, China and Europe, the degree of medium standardization was high. Both of these cultural areas had a uniform writing system accessible to people from their vernacular languages.

How might these differences in the degree of standardization of the communications medium be explained? India and the Middle East, the two regions of low standardization, are centrally located in Eurasia, with only low to moderate geographic obstacles to external invasion. Over the two millennia prior to 1700, the Middle East had experienced many successive waves of conquerors: the Persians, the Macedonians, the Romans, the Arabs, the Mongols and the Turks. India was somewhat better protected geographically but nevertheless its rich northern plains had been raided many times, from the Indo-European invasion in the middle of the second

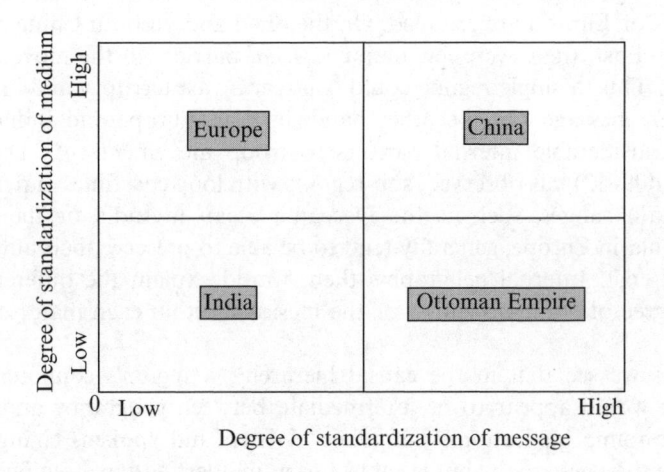

Figure 4.2   Medium and message in Eurasia, c. 1700

millennium BC to the Turko-Afghan conquest of the early sixteenth century. Since each set of conquerors had brought along its own language and writing system, the result was an accumulation of written and spoken languages.

As for Europe and China, their eccentric geographic positions sheltered them to a great extent from outside conquest. A millennium had now elapsed since the last successful invasion of western Europe from outside the region. Even that attack, by Muslims from North Africa in the eighth century, had been stopped at the Pyrenees. Parts of China had several times been conquered by peoples from beyond its northern borders. However, on each occasion, the invaders had either been assimilated or expelled without leaving any permanent cultural heritage. In addition, by 1700 both Europe and China had adapted printing to their vernacular languages. As a result, there were large sub-regions in Europe and China where a significant fraction of the population could communicate with one another easily using a common written and spoken medium.

A second dimension to be examined is the degree of standardization of the message that was transmitted over the media in a given region. This variable is measured on the horizontal axis in Figure 4.2. By this new criterion, the pairs of similar regions have changed. In 1700, China was similar to the Muslim world in that a strong central regime was able to monopolize the medium with a uniform cultural message. In the former, the Confucian system of thought prevailed, in the latter the Muslim religion. At the same time, by this new criterion, India resembled Europe in that in religion, literature and politics, there was considerable competition.

Once again, geography offers a possible explanation for the way the regions of Eurasia are grouped. On the one hand, in both China and the Middle East, there were few major *internal* barriers to the movement of troops. Thus a single regime could conquer a vast territory and impose a uniform message. On the other hand, in both Europe and India, there were considerable internal barriers to troop movements. As Diamond (1997, 409–12) has observed, sub-regions with long coastlines and internal mountain ranges, such as the Deccan plateau in India or the Italian peninsula in Europe, generally tend to be able to preserve their autonomy at low cost. Internal geography, then, would explain the differences in the degree of standardization of the message within each major cultural region.

Thus we see that in the causal hierarchy, a region's communication system would appear to be intermediate between geography and political–economic institutions. Language, written and spoken, changes less rapidly than geography but is subject to more inertia than a region's economic and political system.

4 THE INNOVATION GAME

Our discussion began in Section 2 by comparing of rates of innovation across the Eurasian land mass during the Industrial Revolution. It then turned in Section 3 to a description of the characteristics of communications systems in Eurasia's main regions in the year 1700, just before the wave of innovations that characterized the Industrial Revolution. The obvious question is whether there is any relationship between these two sets of phenomena. We begin this section by examining how innovations occur, noting that for the creation of new ideas it is essential to bring together hitherto unrelated units of information. We then turn to the question of cooperation, studying the conditions under which it will emerge. Finally, we bring together the characteristics of communication systems into the discussion to learn which societies were more likely to favour cooperation in the exchange of information and therefore to innovate in the years after 1700.

4.1 The Nature of Innovation

In *The Act of Creation*, Koestler (1964) argued that innovation occurs when existing ideas are combined in hitherto untried ways. Weitzman (1998) has formalized this process in a model of 'recombinant' growth. Innovation involves the successful crossing of old ideas to replace existing ways of doing things. If this approach is valid, then the rate of innovation in a society should be an increasing function of the frequency with which existing ideas are brought together for the first time. Now the greater the degree of standardization of the *medium*, the *more* likely it is that individuals with different sets of knowledge can successfully exchange ideas when they come together. In addition, the greater the degree of standardization of the *message*, the *less* likely it is that new crossings of existing knowledge will occur. Thus a society's rate of innovation will depend on the degree of standardization of *both* the medium and the message of its communication system, the former having a positive effect and the latter a negative effect.

4.2 Three Games

Consider a game between two randomly selected agents to develop a collective good, namely a technology. Think, for example, of a partnership made up of Newcomen and Calley to develop a pumping device based on steam. In essence, the technology is a club good as defined by Buchanan

(1965). Both players benefit whatever the contribution of each to the development costs. In addition, third parties may be excluded from at least a part of the benefits at moderate cost. Let Q be the quantity of output. Let n be the fraction of the two agents who contribute to production, where $0 \leq n \leq 1$, with K the cost to the individual of cooperating in this way. Each player can either defect or cooperate. If both players defect, then output will be zero. If one player defects while the other cooperates, then we shall assume that they succeed only in reproducing the existing technology. However, if both cooperate, combining their ideas, they will be able to produce a new technology that is superior to the present one.

The basic structure of this coordination problem has been studied by Heckathorn (1996). The new element here is to allow for both scale economies and network effects.[6] Let c be the fixed cost of production and let e represent a network effect. The production function is assumed to take the form:

$$Q = \frac{c+1-e}{c+1/n-en}. \tag{4.1}$$

It may be seen that if $n=0$, then $Q=0$, while if $n=1$, then $Q=1$. There are some interesting special cases. First, if there are neither scale economies nor network effects, that is, $c=e=0$, the production function is linear in n. Second, if $c>0$ while $e=0$, the function is concave in n. Finally, if $c=0$, while $e>0$, production is convex in n.

The implications of this function for the players may be seen from the following matrix of payoffs to player 1:

		Player 2's strategy	
		Cooperate	Defect
Player 1's strategy	Cooperate	Reward (R): $1-K$	Sucker (S): $\dfrac{c+1-e}{c+2-e/2} - K$
	Defect	Temptation (T): $\dfrac{c+1-e}{c+2-e/2}$	Penalty (P): 0

If neither player cooperates, then both players receive the Penalty (P) payoff of 0. If both players cooperate, then each receives the Reward payoff of $1-K$. If one player defects while the other cooperates, then the defecting player receives the Temptation payoff of:

$$T = \frac{c+1-e}{c+2-e/2}. \quad (4.2)$$

Meanwhile, in the latter case, the cooperating player receives the Sucker payoff of

$$S = \frac{c+1-e}{c+2-e/2} - K. \quad (4.3)$$

This coordination problem allows us to reinterpret the information concerning the degree of standardization of the communication systems across Eurasia in 1700. The characteristics of each society's information technology now determine the game that will be played by its citizens, as shown in Figure 4.3. Once again, consider the degree of standardization of the *medium* of communication. The greater the number of people who are able to read and write in the same language, the greater will be the network externalities within the society. Thus the vertical axis indicating standardization of the medium may be interpreted as measuring the importance of network effects, e.

Now turn once again to the degree of standardization of the *message*. We have suggested that low internal barriers to troop movements, as in China

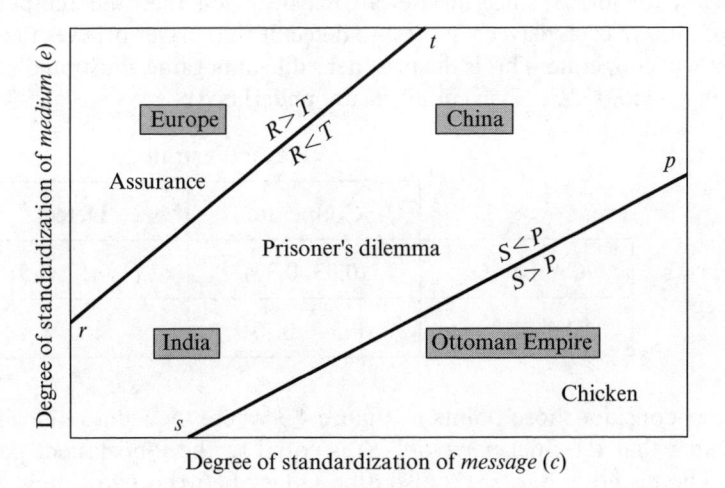

Figure 4.3. Coordination games in Eurasia, c. 1700

and the Middle East, will enable a single ruler to control an entire region. To maintain power, such a regime will tend to regulate the information that is transmitted, thereby standardizing the message. Once this system has been established, the fixed costs of entering with an alternative message become very high. Accordingly, in Figure 4.3, the horizontal axis indicating the degree of standardization of the message may be interpreted as measuring the fixed cost of processing information, c.

Consider those points in Figure 4.3 where the values of c and e are such that the Reward payoff (R) is equal to the Temptation payoff (T). For $K = 2/3$, the result is the line rt. Above this line, the Reward payoff is greater than the Temptation payoff. As a result, if each player is assured that the other will cooperate, there is no incentive for the players to defect. Thus, in the upper zone of the figure, we have the game of assurance, an example of which appears in the following matrix ($c = 0$; $e = 0.5$; $K = 2/3$, Nash equilibria are underlined):

		Player 2's strategy	
		Cooperate	Defect
Player 1's strategy	Cooperate	(<u>0.33, 0.33</u>)	(−0.38, 0.29)
	Defect	(0.29, −0.38)	(<u>0, 0</u>)

Below the line rt, since the Reward payoff is less than the Temptation payoff, it is in each player's interest to defect if that player believes that the other will cooperate. This is the prisoner's dilemma game, illustrated below ($c = 0$; $e = 0$; $K = 2/3$, Nash equilibria are underlined):

		Player 2's strategy	
		Cooperate	Defect
Player 1's strategy	Cooperate	(0.33, 0.33)	(−0.17, 0.5)
	Defect	(0.5, −0.17)	(<u>0, 0</u>)

Now consider those points in Figure 4.3 where the values of c and e are such that the Sucker payoff (S) is equal to the Punishment payoff (P). The resulting line, sp, is also a boundary between two games. This is the space of the prisoner's dilemma. Below the line, since the Sucker payoff is greater than the Punishment payoff, it is now in the interest of a player to cooperate if that player believes the other will defect. Accordingly, this area corresponds to the game of chicken, an example of which is presented below ($c = 2$; $e = 0$; $K = 2/3$, Nash equilibria are underlined):

Player 2's strategy

		Cooperate	Defect
Player 1's strategy	Cooperate	(0.33, 0.33)	<u>(0.08, 0.75)</u>
	Defect	<u>(0.75, 0.08)</u>	(0, 0)

4.3 Cooperation and Innovation

We have suggested that cooperation between economic agents, as in the example of Newcomen and Calley, is a prerequisite for successful innovation. Let us then re-examine the information systems of Figure 4.3 in order to determine which configurations are most likely to foster cooperation between agents. Consider first the lower zone marked 'Ottoman Empire'. As the example in the chicken matrix shows, joint cooperation is never a Nash equilibrium in this game. As a result, the rate of innovation should be extremely low in this region.

Next examine the region of the intermediate zone of Figure 4.3 that is close to the origin. We see that India falls into this region. In the one-shot game illustrated in the prisoner's dilemma matrix, the only Nash equilibrium is joint defection. Should people interact frequently, the threat of retaliation will tend to induce cooperation. However, since the degree of standardization of both medium and message is low, agents who interact frequently will be rare in such a society. There should therefore be a low rate of innovation.

The region of the prisoner's dilemma zone farther from the origin, where Chinese society is situated, would also seem at first glance to be unfavourable to innovation. However, the common medium will lead to more frequent interaction than in the case of India. If such a society is left undisturbed for long periods, it should be able to generate novelty. However, should foreign conquest disrupt patterns of social interaction, the rate of innovation would be expected to decline.

The final region in Eurasia, Europe, falls into the upper zone, which corresponds to the game of assurance. As the assurance matrix shows, there are two Nash equilibria in this game. Joint defection is one possibility, as in the prisoner's dilemma. However, a sufficiently strong shock could shift the society into the alternative equilibrium of joint cooperation. The political revolutions that occurred in England in 1642 and 1688, the American revolution of 1776 and the revolution in France that began in 1789 might be interpreted in this way. Conscious of their collective identity as a nation with sovereign power, the citizens of these countries were arguably more willing to cooperate with one another than previously when they had simply considered themselves as subjects of the same monarch.

5 CONCLUSION

This chapter has returned to the question posed by Kuznets (1966) in his pioneering compilation of the statistics of modern economic growth: why over certain periods have income levels risen more rapidly in some societies than in others? With the help of Maddison's (2001) recent extension of the Kuznets methodology, we were able to focus on a per capita income gap that opened up between Europe and the rest of Eurasia in the century and a half after 1700 and has persisted to this day. To explain this income divergence, it was suggested that we must understand why the unprecedented number of important technological innovations developed over the time interval from 1700 to 1849 were *all* invented in the West.

Since the data for the period under study do not allow us to test statistically a formal growth model, we have been obliged to confine ourselves to a search for historical patterns. We have focused on a typology of characteristics of a society's communication system. Allowing the degree of standardization of both the *medium* and the *message* to be either high or low, we saw that there were four possible types of society. We then examined the impact of the communication system on the outcome of a two-player coordination game. Only one of the four types of society was able to sustain high rates of cooperation, and then only if it was somehow able to reach the 'good' rather than the 'bad' equilibrium.

Our discussion suggests a possible explanation for the economic success of the West between 1700 and 1850. It was the only one of Eurasia's four main cultural regions to have both a *standardized medium* and a *non-standardized message*. As a result, once the shock of nationalism had jolted enough people out of their initial low willingness to cooperate with one another, they could combine existing ideas at low cost to generate novelty. The two cooperating Baptists, Newcomen and Calley, and their seminal innovation, the atmospheric engine, are but one example of over a hundred developments that transformed western society in the years before 1850.

NOTES

1. Pomeranz (2000) offered evidence that there was no gap at all in per capita income between Europe and China in 1750.
2. Note that three of the 28 symbols used for consonants in Arabic also double to represent long vowels (Bauer 1996, 561).
3. Bright (1996, 384).
4. Aurangzeb, who reigned from 1658 to 1707, was an exception to this general rule of Moghal tolerance, but the religious repression of his reign could not be maintained by his successors.
5. Again, Aurangzeb is an exception. It should be noted however, that after military defeat in 1739 by the Persians, the Mughal empire broke up into numerous autonomous kingdoms.
6. This same function is used to analyse political revolutions in Dudley (2000).

REFERENCES

Bauer, Thomas (1996), 'Arabic writing', in Peter T. Daniels and William Bright (eds), *The World's Writing Systems*, Oxford: Oxford University Press, pp. 559–64.
Bright, William (1996), 'The Devanagari script', in Peter T. Daniels and William Bright (eds), *The World's Writing Systems*, Oxford: Oxford University Press, pp. 384–90.
Buchanan, James M. (1965), 'An economic theory of clubs', *Economica*, 32, 1–14.
Cardwell, D.S.L. (1991), *Turning Points in Western Technology: A Study of Technology, Science and History*, Canton, MA: Science History Publications.
Daumas, Maurice (ed.) (1979), *A History of Technology and Invention, Volume III: The Expansion of Mechanization, 1725–1860*, New York: Crown Publishers.
Diamond, Jared (1997), *Guns, Germs and Steel: The Fates of Human Societies*, New York: Norton.
Dudley, Léonard (2000), 'The rationality of revolution', *Economics of Governance*, 1 (1), 77–103.
Dudley, Léonard and Ulrich Witt (2003), 'Innovation during the Industrial Revolution: where, when, why?', Economics Department, University of Montreal.
Graff, Harvey J. (1991), *The Legacies of Literacy: Continuities and Contradictions in Western Culture and Society*, Bloomington, IN: Indiana University Press.
Heckathorn, Douglas (1996), 'Dynamics and dilemmas of collective action', *American Sociological Review*, 61 (2), 250–77.
Holler, Manfred J. and Jacques-François Thisse (1996), 'The economics of standardization: introduction and overview', *European Journal of Political Economy*, 12, 177–82.
Ibrahim, Amr Helmy (1988), 'Questions posées par l'arabe à une théorie générale des systèmes d'écriture' ['Questions posed by Arabic for a general theory of writing systems'], in Nina Catach (ed.), *Pour une théorie de la langue écrite* [Towards a System of Written Language], Paris: Editions du CNRS, pp. 225–31.
Innis, Harold A. (1950), *Empire and Communications*, Oxford: Clarendon.
Innis, Harold A. (1951), *The Bias of Communication*, Toronto: University of Toronto Press.

Jones, Eric L. (1987), *The European Miracle: Environments Economics and Geopolitics in the History of Europe and Asia*, 2nd edn, Cambridge: Cambridge University Press.

Jones, Eric L. (2002), *The Record of Global Economic Development*, Cheltenham, UK and Northampton, MA, USA: Edward Elgar.

Josselin, Jean-Michel and Alain Marciano (1997), 'The paradox of Leviathan: how to develop and contain the future European state', *European Journal of Law and Economics*, **4**, 5–21.

Koestler, Arthur (1964), *The Act of Creation*, New York: Macmillan.

Kuznets, Simon (1966), *Modern Economic Growth: Rate, Structure, and Spread*, New Haven, CT: Yale University Press.

Lal, Deepak (1998), *Unintended Consequences: The Impact of Factor Endowments, Culture, and Politics on Long-Run Economic Performance*, Cambridge, MA: MIT Press.

Landes, David S. (1998), *The Wealth and Poverty of Nations: Why Some Are So Rich and Some So Poor*, New York: Norton.

Maddison, Angus (2001), *The World Economy*, Paris: OECD.

McNeill, William H. (1963), *The Rise of the West*, Chicago: University of Chicago Press.

Mokyr, Joel (1990), *The Lever of Riches: Technological Creativity and Economic Progress*, Oxford and New York: Oxford University Press.

North, Douglass C. (1981), *Structure and Change in Economic History*, New York: Norton.

North, Douglass C. (1990), *Institutions, Institutional Change and Economic Performance*, Cambridge: Cambridge University Press.

Paulinyi, Akos (1989), *Industrielle Revolution: Vom Ursprung der modernen Technik* (The Industrial Revolution: on the Source of Modern Technology), Reinbek bei Hamburg: Rowohlt.

Pomeranz, Kenneth (2000), *The Great Divergence: Europe, China, and the Making of the Modern World Economy*, Princeton, NJ: Princeton University Press.

Rolt, L.T.C. and J.S. Allen (1977), *The Steam Engine of Thomas Newcomen*, Hartington, UK: Moorland Publishing.

Weitzman, Martin (1998), 'Recombinant growth', *Quarterly Journal of Economics*, **113** (2), 331–60.

5. George Orwell and his cold wars: truth and politics
Manfred J. Holler[*]

1 INTRODUCTION

This chapter is about truth-telling, personal opinions, secrets, and the matter of personal integrity and its protection. What follows is not research about George Orwell as a writer and social activist or a philosophical work on truth. Rather, Orwell is taken as an important paradigmatic case in identifying the problems of telling the truth as a writer and cultural figure concerned with politics. Moreover, because Orwell was not only a paradigmatic case but also a public figure, the evaluation of his behaviour has an impact on our social behaviour and our contemporary opinion about what is taken to be good and bad in politics and everyday life. The evaluation of public figures expresses social values and gives orientation to society and for this reason many legal systems contain, on the one hand, rules designed to protect the reputation of such personalities, but on the other permit the public dissemination of information about them and their private life.

In the case of Orwell, the public evaluation of his character is of special importance because truth was one of his major concerns throughout his writing. For many, he was an icon of truth and personal integrity. Yet, more than half a century after his death, there is an ongoing and often rather controversial discussion about Orwell's work and character. Was he a sincere, but perhaps ruthless, Cold War Warrior or was he corrupted by the 'circumstances' of his day? There are not only contradictions in his work, but also in the interpretation of his work and political life.

In this chapter, Orwell will serve as a model of a left-wing Cold War intellectual. We shall reduce him to a silhouette figure, but one that is alive enough to stir awareness of the truth problem in politics. Although one might well believe that truth is not an operational concept in politics – particularly because of the role of the mass media – its personification in terms of the reputation and personal integrity of public figures does in fact make it a relevant concept in the political arena. Thus the legal rules governing the protection of privacy can have a strong impact on how this issue is tackled.

This chapter will not deal with Orwell's fight against his own Englishness or against the British hypocrisy over British-India, Burma, and the other colonies.[1] Undoubtedly, Orwell 'came to see the exploitation of the colonies as the dirty secret of the whole enlightened British establishment, both political and cultural' (Hitchens 2002a, p. 6). It is unavoidable, however, that we will have to consider both issues inasmuch as they are reflected in Orwell's work and the interpretation of its political message. As Timothy Garton Ash (1998, p. 10) says: 'No one wrote better about the English character than Orwell, and he was himself a walking anthology of Englishness'.

In an overture, in Section 2, some internal and external truth problems of Orwell's *Nineteen Eighty-Four* will be illustrated. Section 3 discusses Orwell's 'List' and his cooperation at the beginning of the Cold War with the Foreign Office's Information Research Department. When this fact became public it was taken by many to be a body blow to a left-wing icon. In Section 4, we look briefly at Arthur Koestler, another outstanding cultural icon of the Cold War period, who recently suffered the posthumous destruction of his reputation. Here, Koestler serves as an anti-communist model with a communist past. His life sheds some light on the relationship of political activism and moral integrity, and its reflection in the press. A brief outline of selected stylized features of political propaganda in the Cold War period, presented in Section 5, adds to the interpretation of the attitudes and actions of Orwell and Koestler and sets the stage for a more formal treatment of the truth-telling problem. Section 6 discusses a standard game-theoretic model that analyses sincere and strategic truth-telling in the light of public opinion makers (that is, the press). The afterword in Section 7 points out some rather peculiar contemporary cases of the relationship between politics and truth-telling. I shall try not to quote the 'read my lips' story.

2 PRELUDE

In 1966, a series of articles was published in the *New York Times* on the CIA's covert operations. Amidst reports on political assassinations and ruthless political intervention, came details about the support which the CIA gave to the cultural sector. The consequence was that the moral authority which the intellectuals enjoyed during the height of the Cold War was 'seriously undermined and frequently mocked' (Saunders 2000, p. 6). Was this intended? What if the CIA had staged the discussion of its role in the Cold War cultural policy in order to tell the world how politically enlightened and sophisticated its leadership was, and perhaps still is, and how much it contributed to today's culture?

It is not always easy for a secret agency to bring the truth about its merits to the light. To some extent it is paradoxical because of its self-reference. In Orwell's *Nineteen Eighty-Four* we learn about truth from a book in the book, supposedly authored by the dissident hero Emmanuel Goldstein. Only towards the end of the book when Winston Smith is tortured in the Ministry of Love is he told by O'Brien, an officer of the thought police, that he, O'Brien, collaborated in writing the Goldstein book. That is where truth breaks down in Orwell's book and the attentive reader is left with crumbs of a society which contradicts itself in values and action.

Most likely, Orwell was not aware of the logical dilemma into which his book ran when he made the Goldstein book a possible thought police product.[2] To some extent, he himself became a victim of the 'strange loop' related to a posthumous interpretation of the story of the book. Orwell died in 1950. Before he died, he gave the specific instruction that *Nineteen Eighty-Four* should not be altered in any way. There was, however, a film of *Nineteen Eighty-Four* that was ready for distribution in 1956. Frances Stoner Saunders (2000, pp. 295–8) reports that Sol Stein, executive director of the American Committee for Cultural Freedom, helped producer Peter Rathvon to provide a Cold War version of *Nineteen Eighty-Four*. This needed a substantial reinterpretation of the book since Orwell's text is generally read as a protest against all lies, especially against all tricks played by government, and as an expression of distrust against mass culture. The book ends with Winston Smith's spirit broken: he loved Big Brother. Needless to say, this ending was not acceptable. In fact, the film was given two different endings, one for the American audience and one for the British public, and neither represented the ending of the book itself. In the British version, Winston Smith is shot down after crying 'Down with Big Brother!' – and so is Julia. Unfortunately, I have no specific information about the deviating US version so far.

The example demonstrates how detailed the interventions of a secret agency could be. However, perhaps we owe this very information to the agency itself and the argument circles in an Orwellian loop. Karl Jaspers claims that 'truth also needs propaganda' (quoted in Saunders 2000, p. 97), but there is the danger that truth becomes an impossibility.

History shows that the logical problem with *Nineteen Eighty-Four* was largely ignored by both parties: on one side were those who wanted to learn from it the truth about the socio-politico system in which they lived, while the other side tried to suppress the distribution of the book. *Nineteen Eighty-Four* became the equivalent to the Goldstein book in the reality of communist regimes. For instance, the Polish poet and essayist Czeslaw

Milosz observed in his book, *The Captive Mind*, written in 1951–52 and published in the West in 1953:

> A few have become acquainted with Orwell's *1984*; because it is both difficult to obtain and dangerous to possess, it is known only to certain members of the Inner Party. Orwell fascinates them through his insight into details they know well, and through his use of Swiftian satire. Such a form of writing is forbidden by the New Faith because allegory, by nature manifold in meaning, would trespass beyond the prescriptions of socialist realism and the demands of the censor. Even those who know Orwell by hearsay are amazed that a writer who never lived in Russia should have so keen a perception into its life. (Quoted in Hitchens 2002a, pp. 55f.)

A Ukranian edition of *Animal Farm* also reached a certain number of readers, however, Hitchens (ibid., p. 92) reports that 'most of the copies were seized and impounded by the American military authorities in Germany who turned them over to the Red Army for destruction'. He concludes: 'It was not only the British Ministry of Information which regarded Stalin's *amour-propre* as the chief object of propitiation in those days'.

Orwell himself and his writings are very useful objects to study the problems of truth and politics. More than 40 years after his death, he was accused of having handed a list of names to the Information Research Department (IRD) of the British Foreign Office in early 1949. The list included his assessment of whether the person was a potential Stalinist 'fellow traveller'.

This was but one of his contributions to the Cold War in which his authority was exploited by the political Left and Right. In his younger years, Orwell was involved in other conflicts. Together with his first wife Eileen O'Shaughnessy, he participated in the Spanish Civil War where he was badly wounded. As a journalist and writer, he actively supported the withdrawal of the British from the Indian subcontinent where he was born and served in the Indian Imperial Police in Burma.[3] His rejection of colonialism generalized in a critical attitude towards Englishness – a state of culture and mind from which he suffered so much. Of course, he could not accept Scottish nationalism either, but his main concern was totalitarian regimes, whether fascist or communist, socialist or capitalist, and regimes which were on the way to becoming totalitarian and their inclination to 'untruth'. He blamed mass culture for preparing the soil for totalitarianism and moved to the Scottish island of Jura, a rather unpopulated part of the Hebrides. There 'he found that keeping pigs could be a loathsome business' (Hitchens 2002a, p. 133).

Orwell disliked the Scots and the cult of Scotland and is one of the few writers of his period to anticipate the force of Scottish nationalism (see ibid., p. 10). In his novel *Burmese Days*, he lets his British-Indian protagonist

James Flory say to his native friend, Dr Veraswami: 'The British Empire is simply a device for giving trade monopolies to the English – or rather to gangs of Jews and Scotchmen' (Orwell [1934], p. 40). However, one has to be careful with Orwell not to identify his opinion with those of his protagonists. One should not confuse the medium with the message. For instance, it would be a misinterpretation to conclude from this quote that Orwell was an anti-semite. His target was the British and their colonies. In a non-fictional essay of 1940, Orwell observes:

> It is much easier for the aristocrat to be ruthless if he imagines that the serf is different from himself in blood and bone. Hence the tendency to exaggerate race-differences, the current rubbish about shapes of skulls, colour of eyes, blood-counts etc., etc. In Burma I have listened to racial theories which were less brutal than Hitler's theories about the Jews, but certainly not less idiotic. (Quoted in Hitchens 2000a, p. 21)

3 ORWELL'S LIST

With the emergence of the Cold War, the Foreign Office, which had been erring on the side of Stalin for almost a decade, looked for advice on how to determine who was a possible fellow traveller of Stalin and a 'reliable' leftist. Its secret arm, the IRD, contacted Orwell for support. In the Spanish Civil War, Orwell had seen his leftist companions massacred by Stalin's agents.[4] To him, Stalinism was a negation of socialism, and it seems that he was more than willing to be of help to the IRD. He handed over a hand-written list of 35 names. Another story (see Lashmar and Oliver 1998, pp. 95–8) says that Orwell agreed that his notebook containing 130 names, listed and with comments, was sent to the IRD office. At that time, he was terminally ill at a sanatorium in Cranham. The notebook was copied and later returned to his home. According to Ash (1998, p. 12), Peter Davision, editor of a recent edition of *The Complete Works of George Orwell*, 'gives us the true facts, in impeccable detail. In the late 1940s Orwell kept a small, pale blue notebook listing what he called "crypto-communists and fellow-travellers." Davison prints 135 names; another thirty-six have been withheld for fear of libel actions'. According to Hitchens (2002b, p. 28), Davison was 'the only scholar with comprehensive access to the archives', and he points out that Orwell's notebook is not the same as the List. For example, the names of Charlie Chaplin and Stephen Spender are in the notebook, but not on the List as it was received by the IRD.[5] In the List, the names are followed by comments such as 'Political Climber. Zionist (appears sincere about this). Too dishonest to be outright F.T.', where F.T. is the abbreviation for 'fellow traveller'.

Ash (1998, p. 12) concludes from the Davison edition that all Orwell did 'was to pass on thirty-five *names* of people from his notebook. He did this not to get them spied upon by MI5, but so that communists should not inadvertently be used as anticommunist propagandists'. Somehow the puzzle about the number and the process of passing on remains.[6] But does it matter?

Frances Stoner Saunders is very critical about the List, and so were others. Her arguments boil down to the observation 'that by his actions, he demonstrated that he confused the role of the intellectual with that of the policeman' (2000, p. 300). What was the role of an intellectual in the Cold War? Michael Foot, a former leader of the Labour Party and a friend of Orwell, found the 'black-list' amazing. Tony Benn, another prominent Labour Party member, 'was saddened to learn that Orwell "gave in" to the pressure of the intelligence service' (Lashmar and Oliver 1998, p. 98). Although arguments were weak, to see Orwell's List as an act of betrayal enjoyed quite extensive currency. For instance, Lashmar and Oliver (1998, p. 95) remark:

> George Orwell's reputation as a left-wing icon took a body blow from which it may never recover when it was revealed in 1996 that he had cooperated closely with the IRD's Cold Warriors, even offering his own black-list of eighty six Communist 'fellow-travellers.' As the Daily Telegraph noted, 'To some, it was as if Winston Smith had willingly cooperated with the Thought Police in *1984*.'

In a recent comment on the discussion of Orwell's List, Hitchens (2002a,b) observes that Lashmar and Oliver are wholly mistaken, and not just in the number of names. First of all, it seems that Orwell said nothing in private that he did not say in public. The listed names were of public figures, like Congressman Claude Pepper and US Vice President Henry Agard Wallace, and only a few were known to him personally. The information contained in Orwell's List, was public knowledge, only its evaluation was private. To call it a 'black-list' was utterly misleading. Moreover, it seems that this evaluation was given by a person who had enough practical experience and built up sufficient theoretical capacity to be qualified for this job. Peter Smolka, alias Smollett, was the only person on Orwell's List who was accused of being a Soviet agent. He was the very official in the British Ministry of Information who put pressure on the publisher to drop *Animal Farm*. In the sequel it has been 'conclusively established that Smolka was indeed an agent of the Society security' (Hitchens 2002b, p. 26).

Is somebody interested in cutting down the left-wing icon George Orwell and why? George Orwell was a man of the Cold War and he explicitly chose this role. Surprising as Orwell's behaviour may seem, it is clear that, unlike many of his contemporaries, he was cynical towards the Soviet Union and, quite contrary to the belief of many right-wing Cold Warriors, he was never a communist and never went through a phase of Russophilia or Stalin-worship or fellow-travelling. Consequently, he never had to be cured or purged by disillusionment. In 1947, Orwell wrote that in Spain he understood, 'more clearly than ever, the negative influence of the Soviet myth upon the western Socialist movement' (Lashmar and Oliver 1998, p. 98). His concern was that Stalinism corrupted and discredited the socialist movement, and even made use of it to build up its totalitarian regime. However, some influential intellectuals from the Left did not accept this perspective, even before the existence of the List was made public. Hitchens (2002a, pp. 46–53) reports that Raymond Williams, who once defended the Soviet Union's invasion to Finland in the period of the Hitler–Stalin pact in a Cambridge student pamphlet and a leading figure of the New Left of the 1950s, pointed out a paradox which obviously misinterpreted Orwell, but still had a negative impact on the evaluation of Orwell's work and political message. In 'his immensely influential book *Culture and Society*, published in 1958', Williams claimed that the total effect of Orwell's work is paradoxical: 'He was a humane man who committed an extreme of inhuman terror; a man committed to decency who actualized a distinctive squalor' (quoted in ibid., p. 48). Hitchens adds that this comes close to maintaining that Orwell invented the picture of totalitarian collectivism. Again, one has to be careful not to identify Orwell's opinion as that of his protagonists.

One reason why the information about Orwell's List was received with alarm is that in the Cold War period, especially during the reign of Senator Joseph McCarthy, many former Trotskyist or communist intellectuals, for example, James Burnham, excelled in drafting 'one-sided reports for Red-hunting Senate investigation committees' (Tanenhaus 1999, p. 44). It seems that many of these reports were strategic, that is, written to dissuade from the authors' own leftist past. They delivered material for black-lists, banning people from work and public office, even 'casting high officials such as Dean Acheson, George Kennan, and General George Marshall in treasonous roles' (ibid. p. 47). Another possible form of strategic Red-hunting was public declarations, not very different from confessions in Stalin's show trials. The consequences were, however, quite different.

4 ARTHUR KOESTLER AND THE DESTRUCTION OF ANOTHER ICON

The destruction of icons seems a very general experience of the post-Second Word War period. Is this because truth-telling became a major issue in times of secret services and policies which referred to ideologies? Is it because of an even stronger position of the mass media in political life? In old times, heroes lost their reputation when it turned out that they acted cowardly, but not because they lied or were not successful. (The brutal logic of heroism was to inflict harm on your enemies at all costs.)

In March 1983, Arthur Koestler, author of the anti-communist *Darkness at Noon* and listed as a friend of Orwell, killed himself at the age of 77 with an overdose of barbiturates and alcohol in his London flat. Dying with him was his third wife Cynthia Jefferies; she was 20 years younger than her husband. Julian Barnes (2000, p. 24), who calls himself a friend of Koestler, reports that in August 1998, Jill Craigie, filmmaker wife of Michael Foot, told David Cesarani, author of the biography *Arthur Koestler: The Homeless Mind*,

> That in May 1952, after a pub-crawl in Hampstead (during which she drank only ginger beer), Koestler attacked and raped her at her flat. She did not tell anyone, not even her husband, for nearly fifty years; obviously, there were no witnesses, no police report, no corroborating evidence. She died in December 1999. Her account, though it stands by itself, sounds absolutely true.

The result of this disclosure was an outcry of disappointment of Koestler's community of friends and admirers and a redefinition of his reputation in public life. Barnes (ibid.) reports that Edinburgh University, 'which received about a million pounds under the Koestlers' wills for a chair in parapsychology, reacted not by closing the department or returning the money but by removing Koestler's bust from display'. Barnes adds that this was 'an act of statuarial unpersonning worthy of the communism he spent much of his life exposing'. This type of 'unpersonning', one might add, was also the core of Orwell's *Nineteen Eighty-Four*.

In his younger days, Koestler, who was born in Budapest in 1905, was an active communist. After an exciting youth in Vienna and Palestine, he spent the early 1930s as an influential communist journalist at Berlin. Why communism? His explanation was that he was filled with indignation about rich people who did not share the feelings of guilt he suffered from inequality. It was not envy that made him detest the rich, but their indifference to the poor and their spending of large sums of money with a clear conscience (see Scheok 1966, p. 136). Later, perhaps also out of his experience in the Spanish Civil War, Koestler changed his view on inequality and communism: he became rich through his writings and an outspoken anti-communist Cold War protagonist. On the occasion of the first meeting of the Congress of Cultural Freedom on 26 June 1950 in Berlin, Koestler proclaimed 'indifference or neutrality in the face of such a challenge amounts to a betrayal and to the abdication of the free mind' (Lashmar and Oliver 1998, p. 125).

The challenge was Stalin's communism. Perhaps more dramatically, the actor Robert Montgomery cried out that 'there is no neutral corner in the Freedom's room!' at the same meeting (Saunders 2000, p. 79) – a possible reaction to the rather popular suggestion that Germany should be neutralized and then unified. Melvin Lasky declared that 'Neutralism was, as an idea and as a movement, sponsored by the Soviets' (quoted in Saunders 2000, p. 79). As it turned out, the CIA made a large contribution to the financing of the Congress. Nicholas Nabokov, Russian émigré composer and writer, declared:

> Out of this congress we must build an organization for war. We must have a standing committee. We must see to it that it calls on all figures, all fighting organizations and all methods of fighting, with a view to action. If we do not, we will sooner or later all be hanged. The hour has struck 12. (Quoted in Lashmar and Oliver 1998, p. 127)

Lashmar and Oliver (ibid.) report that, at its height, the resulting organization of the Congress of Cultural Freedom would employ 280 members of staff, have representatives in 35 countries organizing conferences and seminars, as well as a network of sponsored journals. 'During the early 1950s . . . the CIA budget for the Congress of Cultural Freedom . . . was about $800–$900,000, which included . . . the subsidy for the Congress's magazine *Encounter*'.[7]

It seems that Orwell shared the younger Koestler's view on inequality, but he was, as already said, never a communist and he did not live long enough to enjoy the financial success from his books and the fame that accompanied them. However, in 1946 he proposed to Mrs Celia Kirwan, a noted beauty and sister-in-law to Arthur Koestler. She rejected his offer. It was the very same Mrs Kirwan who wrote to Orwell on 30 April 1949:

> Dear George, Thanks so much for helpful suggestion. My department were very interested in seeing them . . . they asked me to say they would be grateful if you would let us look at your list of fellow-travelling and crypto-journalists: we would treat it with the utmost discretion. Yours ever, Celia. (Quoted in Lashmar and Oliver 1998, p. 97)

5 TRUTH AND PROPAGANDA

On 6 April 1949, George Orwell wrote to Celia Kirwan:

> I could also, if it is of any value, give you a list of journalists and writers who in my opinion are crypto-Communists, fellow-travellers or inclined that way & should not be trusted as propagandists. But for that I shall have to send

a notebook which I have at home, & if I do give you such a list it is strictly confidential, as I imagine it is libellous to describe somebody as a fellow-traveller. (Quoted in ibid.)

This confirms what has been said about Orwell's motivation and the status of the List: if it were made public it could damage the reputation of persons described as fellow-travellers. To publicly question the integrity of the listed persons, however, was not Orwell's aim, as we see from the quotation.

From his work at the BBC's Indian Service, Orwell was quite experienced in the evaluation of public and secret information and in circumventing censorship. Not everybody shared his view on the liberation of India. To Christopher Hitchens (2002a, p. 25):

[T]here seems no doubt that Orwell made use of his BBC experience in the writing of *Nineteen Eighty-Four*. The room where the editorial meetings of Eastern Services were held was Room 101 in the Portland headquarters, itself one of the likely architectural models for the 'Ministry of Truth' (Minitrue). Moreover, the concept of doublethink and the description of vertiginous changes in political line clearly owe something to Orwell's everyday experience of propaganda.

There was, however, a new style of British propaganda: the ministry's general view was 'that it was more effective to tell the truth, nothing but the truth, and as far as possible, the whole truth. What the propagandists learned was that propaganda was most effective if it was based on accurate factual information' (Lashmar and Oliver 1998, p. 19). This strategy, however, presupposed that accurate factual information was disseminated and that people believed in it. In this, the BBC played a major role: it informed and inspired trust. As George Orwell noted: 'The BBC as far as its news goes has gained enormous prestige since about 1940 . . . "I heard it on the radio" is now almost equivalent to "I know it must be true" ' (ibid.).

Truth is central to *Nineteen Eighty-Four*, although we argued that the story is logically flawed. But the history of its interpretation demonstrates that there is a very fundamental truth in it: the cruelty of totalitarian systems. In *Burmese Days*, Orwell's protagonist James Flory betrayed his native friend Dr Veraswami – and suffered for it. Truth was very important to Orwell in his writing, but also in his life. In his review, Ash (1998, p. 14) observes with respect to Orwell:

In his best articles and letters, he gives us a gritty, personal example of how to engage as a writer in politics. He takes sides, but remains his own man. He will not put himself at the service of political parties exercising or pursuing power, since that means using half-truths, in a democracy, or whole lies in a dictatorship. He gets things wrong, but then corrects them.

This selected portrait concurs with Orwell's view on the relationship between truth and politics. In his 1935 *Politics and the English Language*, he mused that 'Political language – and with variations this is true of all political parties, from Conservatives to Anarchists – is designed to make lies sound truthful and murder respectable, and to give an appearance of solidity to pure wind' (quoted in Hitchens 2002a, p. 71). Of a Russian agent in Barcelona charged with defaming the POUM fighters as Trotskyist Francoist traitors he writes, in *Homage to Calalonia*, 'It was the first time that I had seen a person whose profession was telling lies – unless one counts journalists' (quoted in Ash 1998, p. 11).

The side remark on the truth-telling journalists may express some contempt, but also some irony as Orwell was, for many years, a journalist. This side remark, which to some degree is self-referential, implies a paradox. Perhaps Orwell wanted to demonstrate just how differentiated truth-telling is. In the following section, I shall apply a game-theoretic model to analyse some strategic implications of the truth-telling problem.

6 A FORMAL MODEL OF DOUBTS AND TRUTH-TELLING

Steinbeck ([1941] 1976, p. 147) once commented: 'Even erroneous beliefs are real things, and have to be considered proportional to their spread or intensity. "All-truth" must embrace all extant apropos errors also, and know them as such by relation to the whole, and allow for their effects'. In this section, we shall discuss a simple game-theoretic model in order to illustrate the effect of raising doubts about Orwell's willingness to be sincere about his anti-Stalinist left-wing liberal position and to defend it. John Bayley's (2001) review of a recent book by Jeffrey Mayers entitled *Orwell: Wintry Conscience of a Generation*, was headlined 'The Last Puritan'. To some extent this label summarizes the conclusion that the public draws from the discussion that followed the outcry about the List. Bayley (2001, p. 50) concludes: Orwell's 'death at the age of forty-seven was a sad loss to letters, as it was to writers and public men of conscience and integrity'. Orwell was 'neutral in religious matters' but his friend Anthony Powell could not avoid saying that Orwell 'was in his way a sort of saint' (quoted in Hitchens 2002a, p. 124).

Not everybody saw Orwell as a saint and some have interpreted his cooperation with the IRD, as we have seen, as strategic behaviour – as a submission to the pressure of the intelligence service. Was Orwell of the sincere Cold Warrior type (t_s) or was he a 'weak' strategic opportunist of dubious moral standards (t_w) as it is often said of Koestler?

Now, who is the judge? The press, or, more generally, the public opinion makers including the various reviewers who were quoted above? Of course, to some extent opinion makers reflect the values of their readers and listeners, but sometimes the role and impact of newspaper owners, politicians, and of those who pay for advertisements is essential. However, it is said that in the long run, information can only be successful if it is accurate. Unfortunately, there is no proof for this conjecture, but it seems more or less evident that, *ceteris paribus*, telling the truth could be cheaper. From *Nineteen Eighty-Four* we can see how costly it is to revise history, including the risk that the revision is not completely successful.

For the sake of argument, let us assume that the public opinion makers (POM) draw some benefits from attacking a strategic figure of type t_w (for example, a Koestler) while they run into problems if their attack was directed to a person who turns out to be a sincere figure of type t_s (for example, an Orwell). However, as we have seen, even in Orwell's case, there were doubts about his integrity after the public was informed about his List. Those POMs who argued that Orwell's 'reputation as a left-wing icon took a body blow from which it may never recover' (see above), however, lost face. Obviously, there was a relatively high a priori expectation that Orwell would turn out to be a weak type t_w and thus their attack would be successful.

Let us denote by p^o the probability of t_w that summarizes this expectation. In the case of Orwell, we may assume that each member of the community of POMs had a different value for p^o and those with a high value were more inclined to attack than those with a low value. Let us further suppose that both groups, those who attacked Orwell and those who did not and perhaps even defended his reputation, were informed in a reliable way that he had given the List to the IRD in 1949. The only difference is that each group drew a different conclusion from this action. The latter group interpreted it as a sign (or signal) that he was sincere (of type t_s) about his anti-Stalinism while the other group saw it as sign of opportunistic behaviour (corruption), or that he had to give in to the pressure of the intelligence service (see Tony Benn above), which identified him as weak type t_w.

Mary McCarthy, a former admirer of Orwell, commented 'on what she saw as Orwell's move to the right' that 'it was a blessing he died so early' (see Saunders 2000, p. 301). Obviously, there were people who no longer believed he was sincere. Was it a reasonable strategy of Orwell to give the List, if he was sincere, or was this a signal that he had merely chosen an easy way to please the authorities in times of the Cold War? (The latter has been said of Koestler.) What can POMs conclude from his giving the List? From the exchange of notes with Celia Kirwan we learn that Orwell took an active part in the List project. In his life and writings he gave ample evidence that he can put himself into the shoes of other people and thereby understand their needs and plans. It seems appropriate to assume that he had a similar approach when he developed the idea of passing the List to the IRD. In other words, a game-theoretic approach seems to be adequate for analysing Orwell's behaviour and to evaluate the conclusions which the POMs drew from it.

When I brooded over such an analysis it dawned on me that the strategic situation of the players – Orwell and POMs – is equivalent to the signalling game analysed in Cho and Kreps (1987). Orwell is identical with player A who can be of type t_w, that is, weak, or type t_s, that is, strong. Player A has two possible strategies: 'to give the List' and 'not to give the List'. Player B, a member of the POM, does not know what type player A is. B can attack A by aggressively reporting on A, or abstain from an attack. The common form of attack is 'scandalization', that is, creating a scandal by assuming a more or less hypothetical interest of a third party (for example, the general public or a third-party victim us in the Koestler case).[8] Looking for a sensation is perhaps a less aggressive form of attack.

This model assumes that player A knows his type, that is, Orwell knows whether he is of type t_w and/or t_s, and that this information is 'private'. This implies that B does not know A's type.[9] Consequently, B does not know whether he is playing the game on the left or on the right in the matrices below. B can, however, observe whether A has chosen to give the List or not, before B decides whether to attack.

	Attack	No Attack
List	(−3, 1)	(−1, 0)
No List	(−2, 1)	(0, 0)

Weak A(t_w)

	Attack	No Attack
List	(−2, 0)	(0, 1)
No List	(−3, 0)	(−1, 1)

Strong A(t_s)

Of course, the payoffs given in the matrices for the various outcomes are highly questionable. It is assumed that it is good for B (a POM) to attack, if A (Orwell) is weak, and it is bad for him if A is strong. This is reflected in the two matrices. A positive outcome to B earns a value of 1, a negative a value of 0. The intuition is the following. A journalist (or writer) profits from a scandalous story if it is seen by the readership as adequate (and the attacked person does not respond). It seems that this applies, at least for the time being, to the case of Koestler. However, if the attacked person is strong and the scandalous story is convincingly rejected – either by the person him-/herself or by 'defenders' as in the case of Orwell – the attacking party may lose reputation and regret his choice of strategy.[10]

The payoffs of A (Orwell) are more differentiated. The best he can earn is 0: this is his value if either (i) he is strong and produces the List and there is no attack, or (ii) he is weak, there is no attack and he did not produce the List. Obviously, an attack gives a value of −2 to A, irrespective of whether he is strong or weak. At least for some period of time, the image of Orwell suffered from the press coverage of the List as the reactions of Michael Foot and Tony Benn and the comments of Paul Lashmar and James Oliver and of Frances Stoner Saunders (see above) demonstrate. If the List was inconsistent with his political view, if Orwell was weak, then there would be even more damage as the −3 in the left-hand matrix compared to the −2 in the right-hand matrix indicates. Irrespective of what the reaction of the press will be, a weak A would suffer a loss of −1 by producing the List, while a strong A prefers to give the List if attacked or not attacked. However, even strong A prefers not to give the List and not be attacked, to giving the List and being attacked.

We can only guess that Orwell preferred to remain silent about the fact that he gave the List to the IRD. Had he known that the List would be discussed in the press he might have been more careful in his *wording*, but – as it seems today – hardly about its *content*. It would be highly misguided to assume that Orwell was not concerned about his reputation as a writer and left-wing activist. We noted above that before he died he gave the instruction that *Nineteen Eighty-Four* should *not* be altered in any way – albeit somewhat in vain. He also gave the order that some of his weaker texts should not be reprinted – he did not succeed here either, but for other reasons. Therefore, it is not unfounded to assume Orwell thought about how future generations would evaluate his work and activities. The fact that he was dead for more than 40 years before the media exploited the issue of the List is not of major relevance: the world has not changed so much that the issues of secrecy and truth-telling in politics became irrelevant. The Cold War may be over, but wars themselves are not.

Moreover, the press is even more than ever into the truth issue, if only to increase sales by pointing out or creating a scandal. You need only put yourself into the shoes of a journalist, forget your moral qualms and your good education, and ask yourself whether you would attack the icon Orwell after you heard about the List. Of course, you do not how the 'public' will react, but in the short run it is very likely that news about the List could have a positive effect on the sales of the newspaper you work for. In the medium run, however, it could turn out that the icon is re-established and your reputation as a journalist and the reputation of your newspaper will suffer from the 'scandalization' of the List. Perhaps you will even lose money. Would you attack Orwell after hearing about the List and receiving some names and information from it? What do you conclude from the fact that Orwell has given the List in the first place? Are there any good arguments which support his decision even today, or was it a silly action of a terminally ill man? In other words, can you conclude that he was strong or weak in the way as defined by the above matrices and the underlying story?

In order to give an answer to the latter question we apply a rigorous game-theoretical analysis to the strategic decision situation expressed in the matrices. In what follows we restrict ourselves to the abstract description and leave it to the reader to think of A as Orwell and of B as a journalist or writer who is looking for a sensation or a chance to scandalize. Following Cho and Kreps (1987) we assume that B expects A to be of type t_w or t_s with probabilities $p^o = 0.1$ and $1 - p^o = 0.9$, respectively, but the results remain the same with every probability assumption in which A is more likely to be strong than weak.

Given these priors, B should *not* attack if there is no further information. But there is further information: B can observe whether or not A has given the List. Today it is common knowledge that A did give the List. This raises the question as to whether this is rational within the bounds of our model. If, from a strategic point of view, A wants to evaluate whether or not he should give the List then he has to form expectations about whether B will ultimately attack. The answer to this question is by backward induction. The first step is to find out about the reasoning of B which is at the end of the decision chain. If B has to decide whether or not to attack, then he has to form expectations about whether A is 'strong' or 'weak'. A game-theoretic interpretation of A's giving the List could be helpful in this respect on the grounds that it can be interpreted as a signal in the sense of Spence (1974). However, as we shall see, there are problems with this.

If we consider that the game as depicted in the matrices is played sequentially, A moves first and B can see the choice of B before choosing his strategy, then we can identify two Nash equilibria.[11] Equilibrium I is a pooling equilibrium which is characterized by the fact that A gives the List, irrespective of his type; and B does not attack because the utility[12] to B of 'no attack' is larger than his utility gained from 'attack', that is, u_B(no attack) $= 0.9 \cdot 1 + 0.1 \cdot 0 > u_B$(attack) $= 0.9 \cdot 0 + 0.1 \cdot 1$. To prevent A being identified as weak, if he is weak, we assume that B attacks with a probability $q > 0.5$ or $q = 0.5$ if A does not give the List. Not giving the List is taken as a signal that A is weak. Consequently B updates his priors. If B's posterior beliefs are such that he expects A to be weak with probability $p > 0.5$ then B prefers to attack.[13] Obviously, u_B(no attack) $= (1-p) \cdot 1 + p \cdot 0 < u_B$(attack) $= (1-p) \cdot 0 + p \cdot 1$, if $p > 0.5$. At $p = 0.5$, B is indifferent between attacking and not attacking.

A pooling equilibrium implies that B cannot identify A as being weak or strong. Thus the underlying reasoning is not helpful for B to decide whether to attack or not. It is 'unfortunate' to B that Equilibrium II is also a pooling equilibrium. Here is a situation in which A does not give the List irrespective of his type. In this case B learns nothing: his posterior equals his prior belief. Hence B will not attack. To keep a strong A from preferring the List it suffices that A knows that B will attack with probability 0.5 or more if B learns that A gave the List. But how can we rationalize B's intention to attack in this scenario? We simply assume that B believes A to be weak with probability 0.5 or greater, if A gives the List. This assumption is possible (that is, consistent) because giving the List is out of Equilibrium II.

We assumed a prior belief that A is weak $p^o = 0.1$, however, the above reasoning holds for any $p^o > 0.5$. At $p^o = 0.5$ B is indifferent between attacking and not attacking. If $p^o > 0.5$, then there exists a well-defined separating Equilibrium III: a strong A will always give the List; and B will choose the strategy 'attack if A does not give the List'. If, however, A gives the List, then B will randomize (with probability $q = 0.5$) on attacking or not, such that a weak A will be indifferent between giving and not giving the List. Note that in the case of 'no List' there will be an attack which results in a payoff of -2 for a weak A. Correspondingly, a weak A will randomize (with probability $r = (1 - p^o)/p^o$) on giving or not giving the List such that B is indifferent between attacking and not attacking, if he learns that A gave the List.

The mixed strategies of Equilibrium III contain a serious incentive problem: the equilibrium strategy of a weak A depends exclusively on the payoffs of B and the equilibrium strategy of B depends exclusively on the payoffs of a weak A. Thus the equilibrium behaviour of, for instance, B, will not change if B's payoffs change as long as a mixed strategy equilibrium exists (see Holler 1990). Thus it might be more interesting to focus further analysis on Equilibria I and II which are characterized by pure strategies. Another reason, of course, is that we assumed a prior $p^o = 0.1 < 0.5$.

Equilibrium II (no List, no attack) demonstrates that it could be to the advantage of a weak A not to give the List. But are B's beliefs reasonable for this equilibrium? Cho and Kreps (1987, p. 185) provide an argument that they are not. A weak A will get a payoff of 0 in equilibrium. By giving the List, the best he could get reduces to a payoff of -1. To give the List makes no sense if A is weak, although it will if A is strong: t_s receives a payoff of -1 in the equilibrium by not giving the List but can *conceivably* get 0 from offering the List. If B follows his *intuition* and puts no probability weight on a weak A if B observes the fact that the List was given, then an A who gave the List would be expected to be strong and B would not opt for an attack. More generally, the *intuitive criterion* of Cho and Kreps implies that type t_i would not reasonably be expected by B to send out-of-equilibrium message

m if the best t_i could get from m was less than t_i got at the equilibrium outcome. If a strong A realizes this argument he will always give the List – which 'breaks' Equilibrium II.

The selection of Equilibrium I is also confirmed by the results for very low p^o. In the absence of a weak A, that is, $p^o = 0$, there is no asymmetric information and the strong A will give the List. We would not expect this scenario to significantly differ from the one for very low p^o. This enforces the selection of Equilibrium I.

It is notable that for $p^o < 0.5$ both equilibria suggest that B will not attack. For the given priors, this result coincides with the rational decision of B, if B cannot gain information about A's willingness to give the List. Thus, it seems that, in the given case, giving the List or not does not have any influence on the decision of B. Yet, if we accept Cho and Kreps's intuitive criterion, then Equilibrium I will be selected and we would expect A to give the List, irrespective of his type, and B does not attack. Consequently, B will identify A as weak, if A does not give the List, and thus attack. Hence, Equilibrium I does not provide B with any information as regards A's type, but it forces A to give the List and rationalizes B's renunciation of an attack as a best reply to A giving the List.

The intuitive criterion, which selects Equilibrium I in our game, has been criticized because of the logical difficulties which arise when interpreting disequilibrium messages as signals (see Mailath et al. 1993). However, Equilibrium II can also be excluded by applying the concept of *strategically stable equilibria* by Kohlberg and Mertens (1986) which selects a subset of the equilibria which fulfils the intuitive criterion. Thus, Equilibrium I seems a rather adequate concept to describe the outcome of the game if the two players act rationally. Now what does it say in terms of Orwell and the List? If Orwell was convinced that his giving the List was an appropriate tool in the political battle with Stalinism (and fascism), as we can conclude from his letter to Celia Kirwan, then this was an optimal behaviour. This behaviour, however, could be imitated by a weak type of Orwell who gave the List for strategic reasons hoping that this would not be observed and cause an attack. Of course, even a strong Orwell would not be happy to read the comment on his List in the *Daily Telegraph*: 'To some, it was as if Winston Smith had willingly cooperated with the Thought Police in *1984*.' However, this attack was not supported by the equilibrium analysis if the a priori expectation – the probability p^o – that Orwell is strong (or sincere) was larger than 0.5. Either the *Daily Telegraph* was misled in the a priori value p^o, or was biased in a way such that the payoffs are very different from those shown in the matrices, above, or did not care about its reputation which, by and large, suffered from the discussed attack on Orwell. An alternative interpretation is that those who were responsible for the comment in the *Daily Telegraph* did not understand the game situation.

7 AFTERWORD

Timothy Garton Ash, a British citizen, productive contributor to the *New York Review of Books* and reviewer of George Orwell (see Ash 1998), reproduced an interesting case of truth-telling. *The Times* of 9 July 2002, quoted 'someone told *The Times* journalist that Shirley Williams said that Tony Blair said that President Bush said to him. Blair's spokesman, Alistair Campbell, denied that Bush said anything of the sort' (Ash 2003a, p. 32). The denial was that President George W. Bush said: 'The problem with the French is that they don't have a word for entrepreneur' (Ash ibid., p. 32). It seems too much of an irony that George Orwell was born as Eric Arthur *Blair* in 1903 at Morihari in Bengal.

Orwell made 'the seldom observed distinction between the Cold War and the arms race or . . . between the Stalinization of Eastern Europe and the global ambitions of the United States' (Hitchens 2002a, p. 87). As early as 1947, Orwell wrote: 'In the end, the European peoples may have to accept American domination as a way of avoiding domination by Russia, but they ought to realize, while there is yet time, that there are other possibilities' (quoted in ibid., p. 100). His favoured alternative was obvious: 'a socialist United States of Europe seems to me the only worthwhile political objective today' (quoted in ibid.).

It has been said that Orwell more or less copied his *Nineteen Eighty-Four* from Jewgenij Iwanowitsch Samjatin's utopian fiction *My*.[14] Samjatin wrote this book in 1920, and after its publication in the West he had to leave the Soviet Union; he died in Paris in 1937.

There are strong similarities between *My* and *Nineteen Eighty-Four*. In *My* the secret police are called 'protectors' and the god-like Big Brother is called 'benefactor'. Freedom was bad in both scenarios: in *Nineteen Eighty-Four*, we learn that 'Freedom is Slavery' while in the mathematical world of *My*, freedom is responsible for disorder, crime and destruction. There is also an other-world in which the 'proles' are called 'MEPHIs'; the latter live on the other side of the Green Wall, an area that nobody of the established world has ever seen. In the established world, regular inhabitants are known as numbers and organized accordingly. There is also a love story: Julia and Winston Smith are called I-330 and D-503. However, there also substantial differences. He, D-503, was cured not through love and fear of torture by thought police officer O'Brien but through brain surgery. Unlike Julia, I-330 does not cooperate with the benefactor. She is physically tortured but did resist. Moreover, in *My* there are revolutionary street fights between the MEPHIs and their supporters, on the one hand, and the established world represented by the benefactor, the protectors and the numbers, on the other, and the outcome is not decided before the novel ends. The established world is organized, on the basis of mathematical laws, as the 'Only State', that is, the world is not divided into three great super-states as in *Nineteen Eighty-Four*. However, is this true? In *Nineteen Eighty-Four*, we learn about the division of the world from Goldstein's book. We also learn that this book was possibly produced by the Ministry of Truth. That is where knowledge and information break down. The paradox of information and the impossibility of truth and thus of love are the prominent messages of *Nineteen Eighty-Four*. There seem to be more successful methods to dehumanize people than through brain surgery, which brings us back to the problem of truth. O'Brien would argue that untruth is necessary to avoid world catastrophe.

In the case of Orwell's List 'truth' was, on the one hand, an issue of his opinions about other people – were these opinion justified? – and, on the other, was it appropriate to pass these opinions on 'in secret' for secret usage. Was this infringing the personal rights of the listed public figures, especially if they are not informed about this, and does the public have the moral right to be informed when a public figure like Orwell comments on other public figures to a state agency? Obviously these questions describe a trade-off. Legal rules and political culture provide constraints to possible answers.

NOTES

* Sections 1 and 2 and Section 6 derive from Holler (2002b) and Holler and Lindner (2004), respectively. I would like to thank Waltraud Boxall for her detailed material on British culture and politics and her critical remarks on the logic of the chapter. I would also like to thank Alain Marciano for his help in refocusing the chapter.
1. For recent references on British policy in India, see Darnton (2001).
2. The logical structure of the book can be illustrated by the famous statement by Epimenides: 'All Cretians are liars'. Since Epimenides was a Cretian, the logical structure of this statement is self-referential and its truth value concurs with the sentence 'I am lying' if we assume that Cretians lie all the time. Douglas Hofstadter (1990) used the term 'strange loop' for a self-referential system of statements.
3. George Orwell (1903–50), a pseudonym for Eric Arthur Blair, was born in 1903 at Morihari in Bengal, India, the son of a minor customs official who was probably involved in the opium trade between British India and China (see Hitchens 2002a, p. 6). The family moved to England in 1907 and in 1917 he entered Eton. In 1921, he joined the Indian Imperial Police in Burma, from which he retired in 1927 (or 1928) determined to make his living by writing. His novel *Burmese Days*, first published in 1934, reflects his experience.
4. Phillip Deery, an Australian historian, wrote: 'Orwell's opposition to Soviet totalitarianism predated the Cold War. Its genesis lay in the Spanish Civil War. It was there that he witnessed at first hand how Stalinists and NKVD agents brutally trampled the tender

shoots of libertarian socialism and how they deliberately falsified history', quoted in Lashmar and Oliver (1998, p. 98). Orwell and his wife Eileen O'Shaughnessy were both enlisted in the militia of the heterodox Marxist POUM, the Workers' Party of Marxist Unification, which took an anti-Stalin position – rather than the communist-run International Brigade. Hitchens (2002a, p. 67) conjectures that 'Orwell never knew it, but had he and his wife not managed to escape from Spain with the police at their heels they might well have been placed in the dock as exhibits for that very show trial. A memorandum from the archives of the KGB (then known as NKVD), dated 13 July 1937, describes him and Eileen O'Shaughnessy as "pronounced Trotskyites" operating with clandestine credentials. It also asserts, with the usual tinge of surreal fantasy, that the couple maintained contact with opposition circles in Moscow'. None of this was true.

5. However, only recently Ash (2003b) had a chance to see a copy of Orwell's List in the files of the IRD; he reports that it includes Charlie Chaplin's name.
6. Ash (2003b) reports that the copy of the List contains 38 names, however, since 'someone typed up this official copy of the original list that Orwell dispatched from his sickbed on May 2, 1949, to a close friend' (p. 6) the identity of the List can still be questioned.
7. Information given by Tom Bradon in an interview in 1994 (quoted in Lashmar and Oliver 1998, p. 132). Tom Bradon was an OSS (Office of Strategic Services) officer in his youth and former head of the IOD58, the greatest single concentration of covert political and propaganda activities of the CIA; he confirmed the CIA financing of the Berlin meeting (see Saunders 2000, p. 82).
8. See Holler (1999, 2002a) for the analysis of the scandal phenomenon.
9. By the introduction of alternative types for a player we apply Harsanyi's (1967/68) approach to the modelling of incomplete information.
10. In his comments to an earlier version of this chapter, Alain Marciano pointed out that the attitude of the other journalists should be important to the payoffs of B: 'One journalist may find an interest in revealing the existence of the list but his attitude will provide him with great benefits if his or her colleagues follow him and use the disclosed information. On the contrary, if he is not followed, he may suffer from professional sanctions (for instance, for having tried to destroy an icon)'. This supports, by and large, the structure of the payoffs assumed for player B.
11. These are sequential equilibria because the game is sequential and one player has incomplete information so that the equilibria are subject to beliefs. (See Kreps and Wilson, 1982, for the pioneer paper.)
12. In game-theoretical terms, payoffs are (von Neumann–Morgenstern) utilities which satisfy the expected utility hypothesis. As a consequence, we do not have to distinguish between expected utilities, utilities and payoffs.
13. Cho and Kreps (1987, p. 185) point out that we cannot update B's beliefs (that is, calculate his posterior beliefs) by using Bayes's rule, since there is a probability of zero that B will experience that A will give the List, the event 'that is meant to condition upon'. However, as we have seen, there exist consistent beliefs that rationalize B's claim for damages outside equilibrium, that is, the equilibrium satisfies the definition in Kreps and Wilson (1982) of a sequential equilibrium.
14. 'My' is Russian for 'We'. A German version of this book has been published as *Wir*, Heyne-Buch No. 3118, by Wilhelm Heyne Verlag, Munich. The copyright of the German version is with Kiepenheuer & Witsch (Cologne and Berlin), dated 1970.

REFERENCES

Ash, T.G. (1998), 'Orwell in 1998', *New York Review of Books*, 45 (October 22), 10–14.

Ash, T.G. (2003a), 'Anti-Europeanism in America', *New York Review of Books*, 50 (February 13), 32–4.

Ash, T.G. (2003b), 'Orwell's List', *New York Review of Books*, 50 (September 25), 6–12.
Barnes, J. (2000), 'The Afterlife of Arthur Koestler', *New York Review of Books*, 47 (February 10), 23–5.
Bayley, J. (2001), 'The Last Puritan', *New York Review of Books*, 48 (March 29), 47–50.
Cho, I.K. and D. Kreps (1987), 'Signalling games and stable equilibria', *Quarterly Journal of Economics*, **102**, 179–221.
Darnton, R. (2001), 'Un-British activities', *New York Review of Books*, 48 (April 12), 84–8.
Harsanyi, J.C. (1967/68), 'Games with incomplete information played by "Bayesian" players', *Management Science*, **14**, 159–82, 320–34, 486–502.
Hitchens, C. (2002a), *Why Orwell Matters*, New York: Basic Books.
Hitchens, C. (2002b), 'Orwell's List', *New York Review of Books*, 49 (September 26), 26–8.
Hofstadter, D.R. (1990), *Gödel, Escher, Bach: An Eternal Golden Braid*, New York: Vintage Books.
Holler, M.J. (1990), 'Unprofitability of mixed strategy equilibria in two-person games: a second folk-theorem', *Economics Letters*, **32**, 319–32.
Holler, M.J. (ed.) (1999), *Scandal and Its Theory I* (Homo Oeconomicus, 16), Munich: Accedo Verlag.
Holler, M.J. (ed.) (2002a), *Scandal and Its Theory II* (Homo Oeconomicus, 19), Munich: Accedo Verlag.
Holler, M.J. (2002b), 'Artists, secrets, and CIA's cultural policy', in B. Priddat and H. Hegmann (eds), *Finanzpolitik in der Informationsgesellschaft. Festschrift für Gunther Engelhardt*, Marburg: Metropolis-Verlag, pp. 13–33.
Holler, M.J. and I. Lindner (2004), 'Mediation as signal', *European Journal of Law and Economics*, **17**, 165–73.
Kohlberg, E. and J.-F. Mertens (1986), 'On the strategic stability of equilibria', *Econometrica*, **54**, 1003–37.
Kreps, D.M. and R. Wilson (1982), 'Sequential equilibrium', *Econometrica*, **50**, 863–94.
Lashmar, P. and J. Oliver (1998), *Britain's Secret Propaganda War*, Stroud: Sutton.
Mailath, G.J., M. Okuno-Fujiwara and A. Postlewaite (1993), 'Belief-based refinements in signalling games', *Journal of Economic Theory*, **60**, 241–76.
Orwell, G. ([1934] no date given), *Burmese Days*, San Diego, New York, and London: Harvest.
Orwell, G. ([1938] 2003), *Homage to Catalonia*, Harmondsworth: Penguin Books.
Orwell, G. ([1945] 1980), *Animal Farm*, Harmondsworth: Penguin Books.
Orwell, G. ([1949] 1981), *Nineteen Eighty-Four*, Harmondsworth: Penguin Books.
Saunders, F.S. (2000), *The Cultural Cold War: The CIA and the World of Arts and Letters*, New York: Free Press. (Revised version of *Who Paid the Piper: The CIA and the Cultural Cold War*, London: Granta Publications, 1999, by the same author.)
Schoeck, H. (1966), *Der Neid und die Gesellschaft [Envy and Society]*, Freiburg i. Br.: Herder.
Spence, A.M. (1974), *Market Signaling*, Cambridge, MA: Harvard University Press.
Steinbeck, J. ([1941] 1976), *The Log from the Sea of Cortez*, Harmondsworth: Penguin Books.
Tanenhaus, S. (1999), 'The red scare', *New York Review of Books*, 48 (January 14), 44–8.

6. Measuring terrorism
Bruno S. Frey and Simon Luechinger*

1 INTRODUCTION

Terrorism may well be the curse of our times. Recent events suggest that the topic will be high on the political agenda for many years to come. Terrorism is nothing new, however. In many countries in the world, the phenomenon has been prevalent for many decades. Pertinent examples are the acts of terrorism taking place in the Basque Country, Northern Ireland and Palestine. France exemplifies the situation faced by many countries: besides domestic separatist groups, like the Front de Libération Nationale de la Corse and the Armée de Libération de la Bretagne and domestic (left-wing) terrorist organizations like *Action Directe*, to name just a few, various foreign terrorist organizations committed acts of terrorism (see also Figure 6.2, below). But, since September 11, issues of terrorism have become even more prominent.[1]

There are virtually hundreds of definitions of terrorism, and there is no consensus of opinion as to which is the most relevant one (see, for example, Schmid and Jongman 1988; Badey 1998; and Hoffman 1998). We follow a pragmatic approach to determine what terrorism is. This allows us to interpret and integrate new phenomena, and provoke further thought on the matter. Moreover, any definition should depend on the issue to be analysed and therefore cannot be generalized.

For the purpose of measuring terrorism, the following elements are crucial: the perpetrators

1. use force on civilians;
2. act in an unofficial capacity. They are, in particular, not part of the national army and do not wear any national uniform;
3. want to achieve political goals; and
4. aim to have far-reaching effects beyond the immediate victims, particularly through the media.

Why is it important to measure terrorism? The fundamental reason for the existence of the state is to overcome the brutish fight of everyone against everyone, because this represents a negative sum game strongly reducing the welfare of everyone. One of the basic elements of any constitutional consensus is therefore to give government the unique right to use force. All other actors in society must seek to achieve their goals by using peaceful means. Terrorists deliberately undermine this consensus by using force on other people. The government therefore has the task given by the constitution to deal with terrorism. In many cases, governments try to reduce the incidence of terrorism by using counter-force, in particular deterrence policy, imposing negative sanctions on actual and presumptive terrorists. However, deterrence policy has proved to be rather ineffective, and sometimes even counterproductive. But there are alternative means of dealing with terrorism by using a more positive approach (see more fully Frey and Luechinger 2003, 2004; Frey 2004). In any case, government policy against terrorism involves costs. It is therefore necessary to know the costs imposed on the people by terrorist activities.[2] Only then can the government decide what resources should be mustered to deal with terrorism. If the utility loss is underestimated, the government tends to undertake too little, and if it is overestimated, the government tends to overreact and activate too many resources against terrorism. This holds even if the government is not viewed as a social welfare-maximizing agent, but is rather seen to act in a setting characterized by political competition, most importantly the need to stay in power (in a democracy to be re-elected).

The appropriate sample of individuals depends on the goal of the analysis. It should be noted that some persons derive benefits from a decrease of terrorism while others – the terrorists and their supporters, but probably also the police and the armed forces expecting higher allocation of public means – benefit from an increase in terrorism. A classical benefit–cost analysis would take an overall view for a specific territory (country, region or town). In that case, a representative sample of inhabitants (which may include some supporters of terrorism) should be considered. But, in other cases, the government supposed to pursue an anti-terrorist policy is only interested in knowing the benefits from a reduction in terrorism.

The preceding discussion makes it clear that measurement of terrorism does not only include the *number of terrorist acts*. More important are the *consequences for people* reflected in economic losses and, above all, utility losses incurred by the individuals as a result of terrorist activity. This chapter discusses seven different methods of evaluating the intensity and subjective evaluation of terrorism. However, most of the approaches presented below rely on the evolution of terrorism over time or differences in the intensity of terrorist campaigns between various countries or regions to identify the consequences of terrorism. Both can be captured by the number of terrorist acts or casualties at different locations and/or periods of time. We shall, therefore, first address some issues regarding series that contain the number of terrorist acts and number of victims (Section 2). Section 3 briefly discusses impact studies. Section 4 considers the hedonic market approach and two variants of the averting behaviour approach, which all rely on revealed behaviour. The contingent valuation method, the most prominent stated preference method, is discussed in the following Section 5. Section 6 discusses the possibility of resorting to aggregate evaluation functions based on popularity and election data and on reported subjective well-being measures. A substantially different approach, combining measurement and decision making, is used in popular referenda (Section 7). Conclusions are offered in Section 8.

2 TRADITIONAL MEASUREMENT

Given a definition of terrorism, the *number of terrorist events* can easily be measured. But this means that terrorist activities of quite different size are indiscriminately lumped together. The attacks against the World Trade Center would be counted as one (or perhaps two) event(s), the same as taking one person as a hostage. It can be asked whether it makes sense to place such widely differing incidents on a common scale. Such measurement can at best capture general developments. But even then, they are useful only if the structure of terrorist events remains more or less unchanged. Thus, measuring the number of incidents makes sense if the share of terrorist hostage-takings and major attacks remains approximately constant.[3] In contrast, if in one year (such as in 2001) a major attack occurred, although there have been none of that magnitude in preceding or later years, a time series based on the number of incidents is of little value. Therefore, in order to capture the unequal importance of different terrorist events, most series additionally measure the *number of casualties*. Some data take the number of persons killed, while others consider the number of people injured. In the latter case, the problem arises that being seriously injured, with permanent disabilities persisting for the rest of one's life (for example, if victims lose their eyesight) differs markedly from being only lightly injured. There can be no strict rule as to what to count and what to disregard.

The US Department of State (various years) issues a series covering the number of terrorist events, persons killed and injured. Figure 6.1 shows the annual time series for the number of incidents and the number of persons killed in the 1977–2000 period (see also Table 6A.1 in the appendix).[4] The number of events recorded in this statistic exhibits strong fluctuations. It varies between 274 and 665. A high was reached in 1987 and a somewhat lower level again in 1991 and since then it has been declining quite markedly. This finding certainly contradicts the general notion that terrorism has

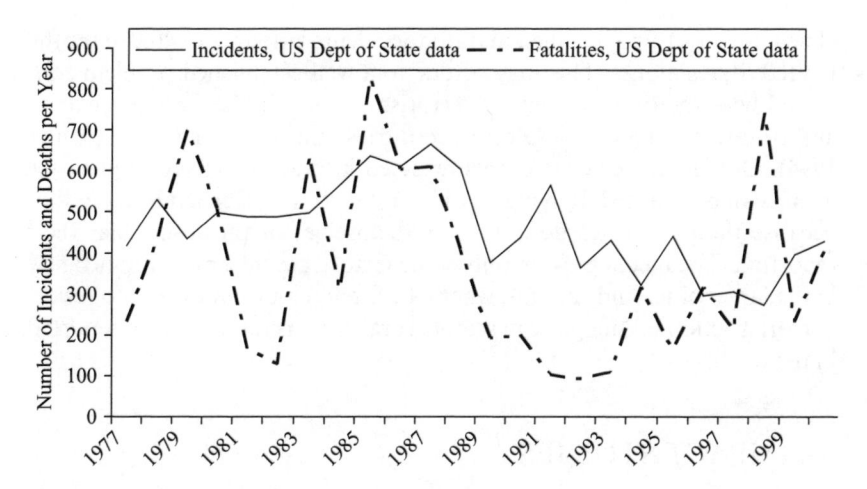

Sources: US Department of State, *Patterns of Global Terrorism* (various years) and Sandler and Enders (2004), Table 1.

Figure 6.1 Transnational terrorism, 1977–2000: number of events and persons killed

become an increasing threat. As is the case with the number of events, the number of persons killed shows considerable fluctuations. It ranges from 93 in 1992 to 825 in 1985. There are peaks around 1979 and the mid-1990s, but no trend is visible. The same applies to the number of persons injured (see Table 6A.1), which varies between 233 in 1979 and 6,291 in 1995. As these series exhibit, the level of transnational terrorist acts has been declining since the early or mid-1990s, while the number of persons killed and injured has not been reduced as much. This implies that terrorism has become increasingly lethal – a common observation made by scholars studying terrorism. According to Enders and Sandler (2002), in recent years an act of terrorism is about 17 percentage points more likely to result in casualties than in the 1970s. This increased lethality has been attributed to the increasing proportion of fundamentalist religion-based terrorist groups seeking mass casualties of innocent people to make their cause widely known. In contrast, the leftist-based and nationalist terrorists want to instigate a revolution and aim at winning the hearts of the people. They therefore avoid killing or maiming innocent people not directly connected with the existing political and economic regime (Hoffman 1997 and 1998; Juergensmeyer 1997).

Overall, the series on transnational terrorism compiled by the US Department of State seems to cover only a rather restricted part of overall terrorist activities throughout the world. The number of persons killed is rather small compared with, for example, those killed in traffic accidents.

(The number of people killed in traffic accidents amounts to 40,000 for the United States alone.) This may be due to a well-established problem connected with the measurement of terrorism, which applies in particular to authoritarian and less-developed countries, the reporting bias (Miller 1994). Only those terrorist events reflected in official statistics and in the media can be counted. Relying on official statistics is often a mistake, either because the authorities do not know themselves or purposely bias their reporting. The media pick up only some terrorist events, most importantly in the larger cities and capitals, where the foreign journalists tend to reside. Terrorist action taking place in remote rural areas is rarely, if ever, reported in the media.

3 IMPACT STUDIES

One of the consequences of terrorism is the losses incurred by individuals in terms of monetary revenues, for instance because the number of tourists declines or investors are less prepared to build up or buy firms in countries affected by terrorism. Over the last few years, economics scholars have analysed the effects terrorist acts have on various aspects of the economy.[5]

Terrorists have often used *tourists* as targets because they are easy to attack. The effect on the choice of tourist location is extensive. The expected cost of a holiday in a country under threat of terrorist attacks is higher than for vacations in an alternative location without the threat of terrorism. The host country is therefore substantially negatively affected by terrorist attacks. At the same time, the resonance in the media is huge. Bombing, shooting and kidnapping tourists often has a highly positive expected net benefit to terrorists and is therefore often undertaken. An example is the Luxor massacre, in which terrorists of the Al-Gama'a al-Islamiyya shot dead 58 foreign tourists visiting the temple of Queen Hatshepsut in the Valley of the Queens in 1997. Another example is the bombing of a disco in Bali in 2002, which cost the lives of almost 200 tourists. Careful econometric analyses using advanced time-series methods (vector auto-regression: VAR) have been used to study the relationship between terrorism and tourism (Enders and Sandler 1991). The causal direction was found to run from terrorism to tourism and not the reverse.[6] For Spain, in which not only the Basque ETA movement but also other (mostly left-wing) groups have committed terrorist acts, it has been estimated that a typical terrorist act scares away over 140,000 tourists when all the monthly impacts are combined. Similar results have been found for other tourist destinations such as Greece, Austria, Turkey and Israel

(Enders et al. 1992; Pizam and Smith 2000; Drakos and Kutan 2003). Terrorism thus has a substantial effect on tourism. It is transitory but, compared to a situation in which no, or fewer, terrorist acts are committed, the income loss for the host country is large. The relevant comparison is not the number of tourists before the event, because without the event the number of tourists would most likely have risen.

The effect of terrorism on *foreign firms investing money into real foreign assets* must also be expected to be considerable. Terrorists can quite easily attack and damage foreign-owned firms, seriously disrupting their activities. As foreigners have a large choice of countries to invest in, even quite mild terrorist activities in a particular country may strongly affect the inflow of capital to that country. This has indeed been found to be the case for Spain and Greece, again using the VAR methodology (Enders and Sandler 1996). In Spain, terrorism is estimated to have reduced annual direct foreign investment inflow by 13.5 per cent on average over the 1968–91 period. This translates into a decline in real direct foreign investment of almost $500 million. In the same period, Greece was plagued by two major terrorist organizations, 17 November and the Revolutionary Popular Struggle. Both are extreme left-wing movements. The reduction of direct foreign investment was estimated to be on average 11.9 per cent annually. This translates into a loss amounting to almost $400 million. These economic costs are substantial. As foreign direct investment is an important source of saving, investment and economic growth are negatively affected. Moreover, the transfer of technological know-how into these countries was reduced, again dampening growth.

In the light of these substantial impacts, one expects terrorism to have strong adverse effects on economic prosperity. Abadie and Gardeazabal (2003) estimate the overall economic effects of conflict in the Basque Country. The authors construct a 'synthetic' control region – using a combination of other Spanish regions – which resembles the Basque Country before the onset of the terrorism campaign. The economic evolution of the 'counterfactual' Basque Country is compared to the economic evolution of the actual Basque Country. After the outbreak of the ETA campaign in 1975, GDP per capita in the Basque Country declined about 12 percentage points relative to the synthetic control region in the late 1970s and about 10 percentage points during the 1980s and 1990s. Moreover, this gap correlates highly with the fluctuating intensity of terrorism.

Impact studies are confronted with a major problem: non-market values are, by definition, excluded from this measure. It follows that the damage done by terrorism may be considerably underestimated. If policy makers take the estimates seriously, they would allocate too little money to dealing with terrorism but rather use the funds and their energy for pursuing other goals.

This problem suggests that impact studies do not measure the overall consequences of terrorism adequately. In the following sections, therefore, different methods are presented to capture total utility losses suffered by the people due to terrorist activities.

4 HEDONIC MARKETS AND AVERTING BEHAVIOUR

The two approaches discussed in this section are based on actual behaviour, or revealed preferences, in contrast to stated preferences, as is the case with contingent valuation. When choosing between different (public and private) goods, individuals make a trade-off that reveals something about the value they place on these goods. In the case of either a complementary or substitutive relationship between the public good and a private good, individuals' willingness to pay (WTP) for the public good (or the marginal willingness to accept (WTA) in the case of a public bad) can be inferred from market transactions in the private good. There are two prominent approaches based on these relationships that seem promising for evaluating the WTP for security from terrorism: the hedonic market approach (based on complementarity) and the averting behaviour method (based on perfect substitutability).[7]

4.1 The Hedonic Market Approach

Private markets to some extent reflect the indirect utility losses imposed on individuals by terrorist activity. A pertinent market value is the higher wages to be paid to compensate employees for the disamenities incurred by working in an environment affected by terrorism. Another is the rent for housing and land to be paid, which is negatively affected by terrorism. The wage and rent differentials due to terrorist activities reflect the implicit compensations for the disamenities. In equilibrium, the marginal implicit compensations associated with working or housing in a region plagued by terrorism must be equal to the corresponding marginal WTA. In both cases, the effect of the extent and intensity of terrorism must be isolated from other influences on wages and rents. With sufficient data available, this is possible by running carefully designed multiple regressions. To our knowledge, no study directly examines the influence of terrorism on wages and rents. But results regarding the effects of violent crime suggest that wage and rent differences across regions could be considerably affected by terrorism.

Investigating marginal implicit prices for various local amenities in the housing and labour market[8] across different counties of the United States, Blomquist et al. (1988) find that individuals living in the county with the most crime are compensated by $2,267 in the labour and housing markets compared to those living in the county with least crime, and $1,600 compared to those living in the county with the average rate of violent crime.

The hedonic market approach is faced with four major problems:

1. The hedonic market approach is based on the assumption that the market is in equilibrium. This would require individuals to be informed regarding all housing prices and wages, as well as attributes of the jobs and houses and require that transactions and moving costs are low. Price distortions due to market imperfections and illiquid markets may seriously bias the estimates (Pommerehne 1987, pp. 73–4; Freeman 2003, p. 393). But in many countries affected by terrorism, markets do not work well, partly due to government regulations. In that case, the hedonic market approach may at best provide some general idea on the gravity of terrorism. But already this may be useful.
2. The adjustment that people are likely to make in response to changes in intensity of a terrorist campaign, as well as changes in the supply side of the hedonic property market, needs to be accounted for (Freeman 2003, pp. 373 and 381).
3. Similarly, it might be difficult to isolate the effects of terrorism from those caused by government reactions. Government-imposed curfews and curtailing of civil liberties entail utility losses that, if not accounted for, bias the estimated utility losses due to terrorism upwards.
4. Only reductions in terrorism in one region compared to another, but not an overall reduction in terrorism, can be measured. The two last mentioned problems, however, also apply to other methods of valuing utility losses.

4.2 The Averting Behaviour Method

This method measures the expenditures incurred to avoid, or mitigate, the effects of terrorism and hence are a substitute for government policies. An increase in security leads to a reduction of these expenditures; the marginal change in spending due to improved security reflects the marginal WTP for the change in security. Two costs may be identified.

Cost of exit
Individuals are prepared to undertake expenditures in order to leave a region or country where terrorist acts make life unattractive. These exit

costs may be substantial. They involve monetary costs, such as losing one's job and having to sell one's property at a low price and may, moreover, include bribes to secure an exit permit. These costs indicate a minimum only. It may well be that the monetary cost of exit may be low, but that the utility loss suffered by terrorism may nevertheless be high.

This measure relies on two assumptions:

1. The cost figures only reflect the (minimum) utility loss if the exit is caused solely by terrorist activity. In case other factors are relevant also (for example, that the employment prospects elsewhere are much better) their size must be evaluated and deducted which is difficult to do.
2. All barriers to mobility must be reflected in market prices, that is, in monetary costs. But emigration also imposes psychic costs, most importantly the loss of one's social environment of family and friends, but also the great uncertainty accompanying the act of leaving one's country.

Security expenditures

In environments characterized by terrorism, individuals spend money in order to reduce the impact of terrorist acts on themselves. They invest in tightening the security of their homes, employing private bodyguards, using fortified cars, and sending their children to specially protected schools. Private enterprises spend considerable amounts of money on protecting themselves against terrorist attacks, particularly by establishing their own police forces and safeguarding their buildings by electronic means (Hobijn 2002). The premiums paid for insurance (if they exist at all) against terrorist attacks provides another indicator of the perceived probability of a terrorist attack occurring, and of the monetary evaluation of the insured objects, including persons.

Three requirements must be satisfied for the averting behaviour method to provide reliable estimates:

1. Decisions regarding the optimal amount of a particular averting behaviour are governed by the risk-reduction capability of a particular averting behaviour, as perceived by the individuals and firms. This implies that either the risk-reduction capability is generally known or the researcher knows individuals' and firms' perceptions (Freeman 2003, p. 337). Both premises are highly questionable in the case of defence expenditures against terrorism.
2. The averting behaviour method relies on the assumption of perfect substitutability between a public good (or a government programme that provides that good) and the private good. According to Pommerehne (1987, p. 25), privately provided security services are substitutes for the

police in the case of property crimes, but by no means perfect substitutes; this is likely to be even more true in the case of terrorism.
3. Averting behaviour should not affect utility directly, either positively or negatively.

The government undertakes similar expenditures. Public money is spent on the police, the army and the secret service in order to fight terrorism and to protect public buildings, politicians and public officials. If terrorism is dealt with by a positive approach (see Frey and Luechinger 2003; Frey 2003), in particular when offering incentives to leave terrorist groups, the respective outlays also reflect the utility loss due to terrorism. In the case of public expenditures, the deadweight loss incurred due to additional distortions in the allocation of resources must also be counted. But care should be taken when these expenditures are used as reflections of the (minimum) WTP of the population. This implicitly assumes a perfect political market in which the government adjusts to citizens' preferences. This is, of course, not generally so, in particular in countries torn by terrorism. Normatively, measuring the government expenditures to fight terrorism should not be taken as an indicator of the WTP, because the aim of a benefit–cost analysis is to establish what these expenditures should be.

In addition to the problems connected with the approaches put forward, there are two further obstacles that hamper an evaluation of terrorism based on revealed preferences:

1. Indirect estimations of utility losses can only be applied if the individuals are aware of changes in the terrorism risk over time and/or differences across regions (Pommerehne 1987, p. 74; Freeman 2003, p. 100). Several studies show, however, that people have difficulty in assessing the terrorism risk. According to Viscusi and Zeckhauser (2003), people are subject to a propensity to predict worst-case scenarios and anomalies known from other risk perception contexts. Hindsight bias and embeddedness effects are particularly evident for terrorism-risk perception. Much higher probabilities are accorded to terrorism than to other life-threatening acts (Hoffman 1998, p. 149). This also implies that unanticipated and cataclysmic terrorist acts cannot be evaluated. Further, revealed behaviour may reflect anticipated future risk rather than current risk. Some of these qualifications also apply to the aggregate evaluation function presented below.
2. Only the use values of reduced terrorism are captured, but not negative external effects of various sorts. Following the literature on estimating individual utility gains and losses, one may distinguish between existence value (individuals value peace even if they are not affected by a

conflict), option value (individuals wish to have the option of living and working in areas free of, or with a lower level of terrorism), educational value (it is important that everyone learns that not only is a peaceful resolution of conflicts possible, but it also raises welfare, while terrorism is a destructive force for all involved), and prestige value (a region or country is proud of being peaceful and secure). These values are public goods and therefore subject to a tendency to free ride in a market setting. Non-use values can be captured by the contingent valuation method and, to some extent, by aggregate evaluation functions.

5 CONTINGENT VALUATION SURVEYS

The contingent valuation method enables researchers to assess total value that includes non-use value of a reduction in terrorism.[9] The credibility and validity of results based on this method are the subject of heated controversy in the economic literature. This debate, which became accentuated in the aftermath of the *Exxon Valdez* oil spill in March 1989 and related attempts of damage evaluation, has stimulated a substantial body of research on practical issues and credibility and validity of estimated values.

In a contingent valuation survey, respondents are asked to value a specific public good. This is an unfamiliar situation and entails problems of strategic responses. Two key design issues, therefore, have been found to be the presentation of adequate information and the choice of a credible (hypothetical) payment mechanism, in order to confront subjects with a specific and realistic situation and make them believe that they actually could have to pay for the good. Another important design issue is the choice of an adequate elicitation method. In environmental economics, respondents are usually asked to value a policy programme that provides a public good rather than to value the public good itself, in order to avoid treating the valuation as symbolic. A survey must, therefore, contain a detailed description of a hypothetical policy programme, which the respondent believes to be capable of providing the public good in question. In light of the failure of most traditional anti-terrorism policies, this is likely to be a difficult task in designing a reliable survey to value utility losses due to terrorism. Furthermore, respondents must be reminded of the availability of substitutes and their budget constraint. In the literature the referendum format is usually recommended as the appropriate elicitation method, that is, subjects should be asked whether they are willing to pay a specific amount for a specific government programme. Only this format is – under certain circumstances – incentive compatible. Furthermore, the dichotomous decision is relatively simple and similar to many real-life decisions (see

Pommerehne 1987; Arrow et al. 1993; Hanemann 1994; Portney 1994; Carson et al. 2001, 2003; Freeman 2003).[10]

Much of the discussion in the literature focuses on whether the hypothetical nature of the question inevitably leads to biased and unreliable answers. Critics as well as proponents of the contingent valuation method rely on various approaches to assess the validity and credibility of WTP estimates of a particular study or contingent valuation studies in general. A first validity assessment approach is the comparison between the answers to the hypothetical survey question and real-life market transactions (criterion validity), where this is possible (see List and Gallet 2001 for a meta-analysis). A second validity assessment approach is the comparison with results from revealed preference methods (convergent validity); this approach was already used in one of the first contingent valuation studies (Davis 1963). The differences can be huge, as exemplified by the evaluation of the utility losses due to the *Exxon Valdez* oil spill. Using the travel cost method, Hausman et al. (1995) estimate the utility losses to be less than $5 million compared to $2.8 billion, the estimate of Carson et al. (2003) using the contingent valuation method. In their literature review, however, Carson et al. (1996) find rather small discrepancies. Furthermore, discrepancies may be due to a lack of validity of the revealed preference method, the contingent valuation study or both (Freeman 2003). A third possibility is to control whether estimates of WTP react to different factors, as predicted by economic theory (construct validity).[11] This includes a test as to whether the income elasticity of the WTP is reasonable (Pommerehne 1987; Carson et al. 2001). The 'embedding effect', which traces back to Kahneman and Knetsch (1992), is seen as the 'major contingent valuation anomaly' (Diamond and Hausman 1994, p. 46) in the literature. The 'embedding effect' refers to an insensitivity of expressed values to changes in the quantity of the good being valued. Literature reviews and meta-analysis, however, reject the hypothesis of inadequate responsiveness to changes in scope and scale (see, for example, Smith and Osborne 1996; Carson 1997). Overall, there is substantial evidence for the validity of contingent valuation survey responses. In light of the serious difficulties connected with the evaluation of terrorism based on revealed preference methods, contingent valuation seems to be a promising approach.

Viscusi and Zeckhauser (2003) survey students to examine the trade-off between money and terrorism risk. Their main research interest, however, is whether the answers reflect a rational response to terrorism risks. They asked their subjects what increase in the price of a plane ticket they would be willing to pay if the risk of a terrorist attack on an aeroplane were to be reduced (a) by 50 per cent, (b) to one in a million per flight, (c) to one in 10 million per flight or finally (d) to zero. The average increase subjects are willing to pay for plane tickets is (a) ca. 25 per cent, (b) ca. 38 per cent, (c) ca. 53 per cent and (d) ca. 70 per cent, respectively. These estimates reflect a well-known premium for reaching a zero risk level (see Kahneman and Tversky 1979 for the 'certainty effect'). Ludwig and Cook (2001) investigate the WTP, not for a reduction in terrorism risk, but for a reduction in crime. They estimate that the Americans' WTP to reduce gun assaults by 30 per cent equals $24.5 billion, or around $1.2 million per injury. Both these studies suggest that the contingent valuation method can be applied to evaluate utility losses due to terrorism. Nevertheless, beside design and implementation issues, two further problems have to be kept in mind.

5.1 What Value for Whom?

It is not obvious *what* preferences should enter contingent valuation studies of terrorism. Three aspects are of particular importance.

First, *psychological anomalies* play a major role. Most importantly, the disparity between gains and losses matters. This 'endowment effect' leads to a major difference between WTP and WTA.[12] It is therefore important whether one asks what people are prepared to pay to reduce terrorism, or what they would be prepared to accept in order to tolerate some extent of terrorism. A review of more than 200 studies indicates that WTA is about seven times higher than WTP. This ratio is even higher in the case of publicly provided goods and the highest for safety and health (Horowitz and McConnell 2002). The question is what evaluation is to count, or equivalently, what initial state is envisaged. Much speaks for taking the status quo and inquiring how high a loss would be evaluated.

Second, terrorism is an *international* phenomenon and terrorists often have no difficulty in moving from one country to another. For this reason, anti-terrorism policies by a particular country produce international or even global externalities. On the one hand, an anti-terrorism policy that successfully deters terrorists from attacking a particular country increases the probability of attacks in other countries, because of a substitution of targets on the part of the terrorists (Sandler and Lapan 1988). The same applies when a government chooses the 'paid-rider' option (Lee 1988; Lee and Sandler 1989), that is, offers terrorists a safe haven in return for the promise not to attack the country. On the other hand, anti-terrorism policies based on positive incentives (Frey and Luechinger 2003, 2004) entail positive externalities for other countries. The dimension of the relevant population, whose values for security from a specific terrorist campaign should be sought, is ultimately an empirical question. Politico-economic and legal considerations suggest, however, that for politicians, only the opinion of the domestic population will be relevant.

Third, a similar problem arises with *future generations* who cannot be surveyed at all. Part of the value is taken into account by the bequest motive of the respondents, but the questionnaire has to be very carefully designed.

5.2 Specific versus Statistical Values

Individuals evaluate specific objects quite differently from a non-specified, or statistical, object. This disparity has first been found for human lives (Schelling 1984), which play a major role when evaluating the utility loss due to terrorism. People are prepared to spend enormous sums of money to save the life of an identified person, such as of a child who has fallen into a well (see also Small and Loewenstein 2003). They are prepared to spend much less on efforts to save as yet unidentified lives by terrorist attacks.

Despite these difficulties, contingent valuation surveys are useful. They provide major insights into the utility losses imposed by terrorism. Compared to the approaches discussed so far, the contingent valuation studies have the major advantage of being able to capture existence, option and bequest values: 'the contingent valuation method would appear to be the only method capable of shedding light on [such] potentially important values' (Portney 1994, p. 14). These non-use values are of great importance in evaluating the utility losses imposed by terrorism.

6. AGGREGATE EVALUATION FUNCTIONS

Individuals' evaluations of terrorism may be captured at the *aggregate level* by focusing on the political reactions of the voters or on the induced changes in reported subjective well-being (or happiness).

6.1 Vote and Popularity Functions

In many democracies, the vote a citizen casts for a certain party is the strongest instrument he or she can use to show approval or disapproval of past policy or proposed political programmes. This also applies to anti-terrorist policy. Voting reflects the citizens' evaluation of the outcome of the anti-terrorist policy. Thus, a government's or party's popularity, as measured by regular surveys or by its re-election, also signals the satisfaction of the people with the government's policy towards terrorism.

This idea lies behind the empirical analysis of so-called vote and popularity functions. The evaluation of economic conditions by the voters, or in regular political surveys, is the subject of an immense literature (it is surveyed, for example, by Paldam 1981; Schneider and Frey 1988; and

Nannestad and Paldam 1994). While these reactions can be attributed to various models of individual behaviour, the 'responsibility hypothesis' has fared best in empirical analyses. Voters are taken to express a general dissatisfaction when the economy is in a bad state, and hold the government responsible. Citizens thus tend to vote in a socio-tropic way, that is based on their perception of the state of the macro economy rather than on their own economic experience. They also tend to vote retrospectively. Vote and popularity functions have been estimated for a large number of countries and periods primarily to analyse the effect of economic conditions on voters. The estimated coefficients differ greatly in magnitude both over time and across countries, but it is nevertheless possible to indicate broad magnitudes: a one-percentage point increase in the unemployment or inflation rate lowers the voting or popularity percentage of the government by between 0.4 and 0.8 percentage points (Nannestad and Paldam 1994).

It is to be expected that voters systematically reveal their reaction to how the government deals with terrorism by increasing or decreasing the support of the party in power. Such an approach only makes sense for non-authoritarian countries, in which the citizens may freely vote and where they are not afraid to answer survey questions truthfully. The citizens may consider two different aspects: (i) they may evaluate the effort the government makes to deal with terrorism; (ii) they may consider the result of these policies. The procedural and the outcome aspects need not be the same. It may well be that the government makes a determined effort to come to grips with terrorism, but is not successful; or the government undertakes nothing but, due to some other beneficial factors, terrorism declines. Rational choice theory suggests that the voters should make the government responsible only for the policies undertaken. If voters solely evaluate outcomes, a government may benefit by pure luck, and not necessarily because it acted well. But the research on vote and popularity functions clearly shows that the voters also tend to react to outcomes. In particular, a government lucky enough to be in power during good economic conditions gets a higher level of support, even if the government has done nothing to bring about these favourable conditions (Wolfers 2002). It will be interesting to see to what extent the citizens follow a responsibility hypothesis when evaluating terrorism, and to what extent they also consider government's effort.

Another finding of vote and popularity functions is that voters prefer different parties, depending on the predominant economic problem. Voters assess left-wing parties to be more competent in dealing with unemployment and right-wing parties to be more competent in dealing with inflation (Rattinger 1980). Similarly, it might be possible to ascertain which party and, consequently, which anti-terrorism policy voters assess to be the most promising.[13]

In one of the first popularity functions, Mueller (1970) investigates the effect of international conflicts on the popularity of American presidents. He finds evidence for a rally-round-the-flag effect, that is, a surge in popularity in times of international crises, which is largely independent of government reaction to the crises. Similar observations have been made in the case of international terrorist attacks in studies using less sophisticated techniques (see, for example, Nacos 1994). The rally-round-the-flag effect could hamper the evaluation of terrorism or anti-terrorism policies. No inferences can be drawn concerning the importance of terrorism relative to other problems, if terrorist attacks have a positive effect on popularity. Furthermore, if this positive effect is independent of the government reaction to a terrorist attack, different anti-terrorism policies cannot be evaluated using vote and popularity functions.

6.2 Happiness Functions

People's assessment of their overall well-being is directly captured in the subjective well-being approach (for surveys of this approach in economics, see Frey and Stutzer 2002a,b and 2003). In large representative questionnaire studies, individuals are asked about their level of life satisfaction, happiness or positive and negative affects. In happiness functions, reported subjective well-being is related to individual factors, as well as to economic and political characteristics of the environment. Citizens' well-being is systematically influenced by the political process. This includes terrorism. It stands to reason that people living in a country rife with terrorism are less happy than those living under more orderly political conditions.

The general level of happiness is affected by many different events, among them political ones. Typically, such an event could be the assassination of a dictator, the overthrow of a constitutional government, or also the deep uncertainty created by terrorism, or by not having any firmly established government. A good example is the Dominican Republic in 1962 where, after President Rafael Trujillo's murder, the political situation was very unsettled and political chaos was a real threat. The level of life satisfaction recorded in that country was the lowest ever recorded, namely 1.6 on the normal 0 to 10 scale. By way of contrast, in politically stable democracies, such as Switzerland, Norway or Denmark, the population expresses high life satisfaction. The corresponding values in the 1990s, for example, were 8.16 for Denmark, 8.02 for Switzerland and 7.66 for Norway. Thus, happiness and political stability seem to be closely related.

The causation may, however, run in both directions: while it seems obvious that political unrest is dissatisfying to people, it also stands to reason that dissatisfied people resort to demonstrations, strikes and terrorist actions, therewith creating political instability. But it would be a romantic view (see Tullock 1971) to assume that revolutions are normally caused by people's unhappiness with existing political conditions. Most *coups d'état*, and even revolutions, are undertaken by competing political clans, parties or the military. There is an exchange of rulers *within* the '*classe politique*' itself, only partially fuelled by the people's unhappiness with their rulers. The people's dissatisfaction is often taken merely as an excuse to seize power (see Weede and Muller 1998; Wintrobe 1998; Galetovic and Sanhueza 2000).

The people may also experience unhappiness during periods of national stress caused by unfavourable foreign policy developments and terrorism. In Israel, for example, in the period between June 1967 and August 1979, lower levels of well-being were reported by large segments of the population, in particular women, the less well-educated, the elderly and those not of European or American origin (Landau et al. 1998).

Using happiness data to assess the utility losses of the people due to terrorist activity has several important advantages over the approaches discussed so far.[14] Contrary to contingent valuation surveys, this approach does not rely on asking people how they value a public good. The hypothetical nature of these questions is the principal reason for most of the scepticism about, and problems concerning, the contingent valuation method. The evaluation of a public good or a policy programme is likely to be an unfamiliar situation for most of the subjects. It is a demanding cognitive task, and superficial or socially desirable responses, without adequate consideration of the budget constraint or substitutes, can result. To correctly state one's own current level of life satisfaction, in contrast, considerably reduces the 'informational and computational burden' on the respondents (Di Tella et al. 2002, p. 9). The possibility of strategic response biases is another problem of contingent valuation. There is no reason to expect a strategic response bias when using life satisfaction data.

While approaches based on revealed preferences rely on a number of strict assumptions, like housing or labour market equilibrium in the case of the hedonic market approach, or perfect substitutability in the case of the averting behaviour approach, these stringent conditions do not have to be met in order to evaluate welfare effects through the use of happiness data.[15] This last approach also captures non-use values. However, it shares, with revealed preference methods, the problem that utility losses may partly reflect the effects of government reactions rather than solely the effects of terrorism.

Several avenues of valuing the utility losses caused by terrorist activity using life satisfaction data can be pursued. One possibility is to follow the lead taken by macro-happiness functions based on international cross-section and time-series analyses, for instance trying to identify the effect of environmental conditions (see, for example, Welsch 2002). Alternatively, the subjective well-being of the population in particular regions and cities affected by terrorism may be compared to the rest of a country. Frey et al. (2004b) pursue this latter approach. In the following, the approach is applied to the case of France.

Life satisfaction data are taken from the Euro-Barometer Survey Series (1970–99); the variable is the categorical response to the following question: 'On the whole, are you very satisfied [4], fairly satisfied [3], not very satisfied [2], or not at all satisfied [1] with the life you lead?'. Moreover, the Euro-Barometer Survey Series contains information about the household income and various other socio-demographic and socio-economic characteristics of the respondents. Three indicators of the level and intensity of terrorist activity are constructed on the basis of the 'RAND–St. Andrews Chronology of International Terrorism' and the 'Terror Attack Database' of the International Institute for Counter-Terrorism (see note 4): the number of attacks, the number of persons killed and the number of persons injured. The regions to be compared with each other are Île-de-France (including Paris), Provence-Alpes-Côte-d'Azur (which includes Corsica in the Euro-Barometer Surveys Series) and the rest of France; the data are available for the years 1973 to 1998. Figure 6.2 depicts average satisfaction with life and the three terrorism indicators.

Based on these data sets, a microeconometric happiness function is specified. Individual life satisfaction y_{itr}, that is, the life satisfaction y of individual i living in region r at time t, is explained by differences in the level of terrorism q_{tr} across regions and over time, the individual's household income m_{itr} other personal and socio-demographic characteristics $\bar{Z}_{itr}$, as well as region and time fixed effects. The specification is summarized in the following equation:[16]

$$y_{itr} = \beta_0 + \beta_1 q_{tr} + \beta_2 \ln(m_{itr}) + \beta_3 \bar{Z}_{itr} + \beta_4 D_t + \beta_5 D_r + \varepsilon_{itr} \qquad (6.1)$$

Table 6.1 shows the estimation results. The number of terrorist attacks and the number of people killed both have a statistically significant negative effect on reported life satisfaction. For 25 terrorist attacks (that is, approximately the average number of attacks in France during the period studied), an average reduction in satisfaction with life by 0.07 units on the four-point scale is estimated. This effect is of similar size to the difference in life satisfaction between singletons and married people (see Table 6A.2 in the appendix). For a change in the number of fatalities by one standard deviation (that is, 16 fatalities), satisfaction with life is reduced by 0.06 points. Thus, two frequently used indicators for terrorism are correlated with people's subjective well-being in a sizeable way. However, life satisfaction seems not to be

160   How to shape a democratic state

(a) *Mean level of life satisfaction in France, 1975–1998*

(b) *Number of incidents in France, 1975–1998*

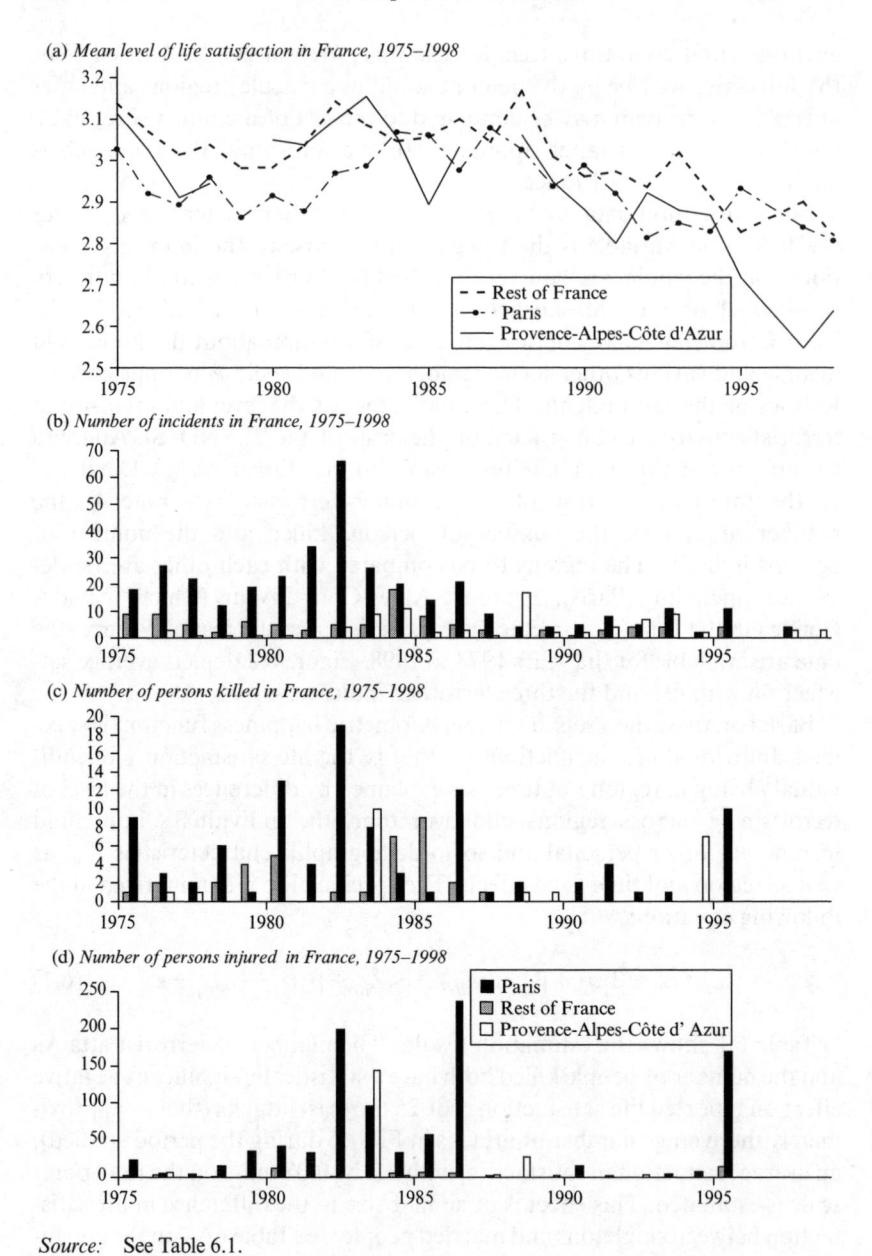

(c) *Number of persons killed in France, 1975–1998*

(d) *Number of persons injured in France, 1975–1998*

Source: See Table 6.1.

Figure 6.2 Average satisfaction with life, and the three terrorism indicators

Table 6.1 Terrorism and life satisfaction in France, 1973–1998: summary

Dependent variable	(1)		(2)		(3)	
Life satisfaction	Coefficient	t-value	Coefficient	t-value	Coefficient	t-value
Terrorism indicators						
Number of incidents	−0.003**	−4.49				
Number of persons killed			−0.004(*)	−1.97		
Number of persons injured					0.000	0.02
Income						
ln(income)	0.234**	20.00	0.234**	19.93	0.234**	19.97
Individual characteristics	Yes		Yes		Yes	
Year dummies	Yes		Yes		Yes	
Region dummies	Yes		Yes		Yes	
Constant	Yes		Yes		Yes	
Number of observations	46,763		46,763		46,763	
Number of clusters	70		70		70	
Prob > F	0.000		0.000		0.000	
R^2 adj.	0.08		0.08		0.08	

Notes:
1. Least squares estimations;
2. Standard errors are adjusted for clustering within regions per year;
3. ** is significant at the 99 per cent level, and (*) at the 90 per cent level.

Sources: Euro-Barometer Survey Series, 1970–1999; 'RAND–St. Andrews Chronology of International Terrorism, 1968–2000', provided by the Oklahoma City National Memorial Institute for the Prevention of Terrorism (www.mipt.org); 'Terror Attack Database' of the International Institute for Counter-Terrorism (www.ict.org.il).

affected by variation in the number of persons injured across regions (column 3). A possible explanation for the inability to find an effect of the number of injured persons on well-being is that the severity of injuries differs considerably. However, this problem also applies to the number of terrorist attacks. But, in contrast to the number of attacks (and the number of persons killed), the number of injuries is a much more random event. Therefore, the number of injured persons is likely to be an inaccurate indicator for the intensity of the terrorist campaigns in general.

The estimated coefficients (β_1 and β_2) in equation (6.1) can be used to calculate the WTP for a discrete change in the level of terrorism. The decrease in annual household income necessary to offset a hypothetical reduction in terrorism is calculated. Estimates are presented for an individual living in the region Île-de-France (Paris) with an average of 12.2 attacks or 3.6 persons killed (a) vis-à-vis an individual living in the rest of France (except Provence-Alpes-Côte d'Azur), with an average of 3.3 attacks or 1.1 persons killed and (b) vis-à-vis an individual living in a hypothetical region without any terrorism. The respective WTPs are calculated for an individual with the average household income, that is, €20,573 per year (1998 euros).[17]

An individual would be willing to pay €3,090 per year (approx. 15 per cent) for a decrease of 12.2 attacks per year or €1,192 per year (approx. 6 per cent) for a decrease of 8.9 attacks per year, respectively. An offsetting decrease in annual household income of €2,263 (approx. 11 per cent) would be required if the number of persons killed is reduced by 3.6 per year and a decrease of €828 (approx. 4 per cent) if it is reduced by 2.5 per year. These WTPs seem to be high. However, they are comparable to the compensations which Blomquist et al. (1988) identified on the labour and housing markets for individuals living in the US county with the highest rate of violent crime.[18] This exploratory application demonstrates that life satisfaction or happiness data are well suited to assess the utility loss of the population due to terrorism.

7 POPULAR REFERENDA

Public decisions on dealing with terrorism are taken in the politico-economic process in which politicians, public officials, interest groups and citizens/taxpayers interact within a given constitutional framework. These decisions are normally highly complex due to the many interactions. But the budgetary situation and the administrative constraints are always highly important and determine to a large extent how much money is spent in what ways for dealing with terrorism. In contrast, studies relating to social welfare, and not to political exigencies, are of little importance in the current political process. *Some* actors may under *some* circumstances use the results of such studies to bolster their arguments, provided it suits them. The major problem with the social welfare-based studies is that they are *divorced from political decisions*. It is therefore proposed here that the WTP is revealed, and at the same time the decision taken, by *popular referenda*. As a decision mechanism, referenda have many advantages over democratic decisions via representation. In particular, it avoids the principal–agent problem and constitutes an effective barrier against the *classe politique* (see, for example, Bohnet and Frey 1994; Frey 1994). Both aspects are of particular importance with respect to domestic security decisions, because the politicians and bureaucrats tend to have a larger discretionary room in this area than elsewhere.

In countries torn by terrorism, the government may ask the citizens whether they support particular measures against terrorism. They may refer to specific security measures (such as the establishment of a special anti-terrorism police force) and, even more importantly, to a reduction of civil liberties (such as the implementation of a systematic and computerized search for wanted persons by means of descriptive profiles – for example, the *Rasterfahndung* of the German police against members of the Rote Armee Fraktion (RAF), the revocation of *habeas corpus*, or the imposition of a curfew).

Italy is the only country where anti-terrorism legislation was subject to referenda (Bogdanor 1994; Butler and Ranney 1994; Uleri 1996). In 1969, the Brigate Rosse was formed out of the student protest movement. It advocated violence in the service of class warfare and attacked symbols of 'the establishment' such as businessmen, politicians and unionists. In 1979, in what became a hallmark of Italian terrorism, the Brigate Rosse kidnapped the former prime minister, Aldo Moro. He was killed after being held captive for nearly two months. As a response to the group's terrorist campaign, repressive anti-terrorism laws have been enacted, such as the *'legge Reale sull'ordine pubblico'* of 1975 and the *'legge Cossiga'* or *'legge antiterrorismo'* of 1979. The *legge antiterrorismo* justified nearly any kind of violation of individual rights; besides the use of the stick, a carrot in the form of a principal witness programme was offered. Both acts were subject to a referendum, because of initiatives to repeal them. The referendum on the *legge Reale* was held in June 1978, shortly after the murder of Aldo Moro; 76.5 per cent of the electorate were in favour of the act (with a turnout of 81.4 per cent). The referendum on the *legge Cossiga* was held in May 1981, with 85.1 per cent of the electorate in favour of the act (with a turnout of 79.4 per cent).

The following counter-arguments are often raised against the use of popular referenda.

7.1 Incapable Citizens

Voters are charged with being both uninformed and unintelligent and therefore cannot be trusted to make 'good' decisions. The criticism concerning the lack of information is doubtful, because when citizens are given the power to decide, they will inform themselves; they do not acquire much information today as they cannot decide anything. The state of information is not given, but endogenous (see the empirical evidence in Benz and Stutzer 2004). The discussion process *induced* by the referendum produces the necessary information to decide, a service which the researcher has to artificially perform when undertaking a contingent valuation survey. With respect to the lack of intelligence, referenda are, of course, in exactly the same position as all WTP methods: in each case, individual preferences – and not the (supposedly) superior insights of a cultural/political elite – count. As one of the major goals of terrorist attacks is to attract media attention, the citizens can be assumed to be quite well informed about terrorist attacks occurring in their location. They are likely to have a good sense for evaluating the usefulness of various measures to deal with terrorism.

7.2 Superficial Citizens

Voters are charged with not taking referendum decisions seriously. It is quite true that they are 'low cost' (see Kliemt 1986; Kirchgässner and Pommerehne 1993), but this equally applies to contingent valuation procedures (but not to revealed preference methods). One may even argue that individuals respond to a survey even more lightly because the situation is purely hypothetical. Referendum voting is, moreover, connected with significant personal cost when the pre-referendum discussion is intense. In that case, not to have, and not to be able to defend, a particular position is negatively sanctioned by the citizen's social environment (see Frey 1994). To the extent that terrorism is a serious issue, the citizens are certainly concerned about it and will have an incentive to take a well-reasoned decision at the polls. The fact that one's revelation of preference is connected with a binding democratic decision tends to raise the seriousness with which the decision is taken.

7.3 Propaganda Influence

In referenda, the interest groups and parties seek to affect the vote via newspaper, radio and television campaigns. A precondition is an open society, which is defined by admitting propaganda from *all* sides, and it is therefore not a priori clear what the effect is. Normally, the police and the military interests are well organized and motivated and are therefore likely to significantly influence the discussion process. But there are also opposing groups, such as peace movements, which make their views known and which may support alternative measures, such as trying to reintegrate terrorists and their supporters back into the legitimate political process.

7.4 Restricted Participation

Referendum participation is constrained in two ways:

1. Citizens decide not to vote. The major reason for non-participation is the lack of interest, and it may therefore be argued that it is not so bad if such people do not vote.
2. Some people, especially foreigners and future generations, are formally excluded from voting. But this restriction also applies to many approaches to assess the WTP for security from terrorism.

These arguments suggest that there are circumstances in which referenda are a suitable means to identify the citizens' evaluation of terrorism and to implement the consequent policies. An important precondition is that the terrorists may not disrupt the vote by using force. The voters must be able to cast their vote freely according to their preferences. Even in a country torn by terrorism, this condition may be met if foreign observers are able to guarantee a fair voting procedure.

8 CONCLUSIONS

The major result of our discussion has been that the hedonic market approach, the averting behaviour method, the contingent valuation method as well as vote and popularity functions and, in particular, happiness functions may be useful approaches to evaluate the utility loss caused by terrorism. Each of the approaches has particular advantages and disadvantages and should be used depending on the goal of the analysis. The methods based on revealed preferences rely on stringent assumption and requirements, the unfamiliar and hypothetical situation in contingent valuation surveys may entail unreliable results and strategic behaviour, and the evaluation of terrorism using vote and popularity functions may be hampered because of the rally-round-the-flag effect. The calculation of the utility loss due to terrorism based on happiness and life satisfaction data shares with revealed behaviour methods the problem that people's perception, rather than some objective measure of the intensity of terrorism, affects their utility. Further, government reactions, which cannot be accounted for, may bias the results. In many cases, it may be useful to apply various methods in order to capture the different dimensions.

When the evaluation of the utility losses induced by terrorism are used in the context of a benefit–cost analysis, it is useful to compare the benefit–cost ratio to government activities in other cases. The decrease in casualties due to particular anti-terrorist expenditures can be compared to the decrease in casualties, for instance, with traffic control. It is important how much money is spent on reducing the number of deaths due to terrorism, compared to those due to traffic accidents and other reasons (see Viscusi and Aldy 2003 for a critical review of studies that provide estimates of the value of a statistical life using revealed preference methods). But it remains open whether the individuals place the same value on a death due to terrorism as on a death due to a traffic accident. It may well be that the deaths caused by mobility are taken to be (more or less) immutable, while those caused by terrorism are judged to be subject to government measures.

But these approaches have a decisive disadvantage: they are not connected to political decisions. Popular referenda combine the evaluation of competing alternatives with democratic decisions. It has been argued that this combination is relevant for decisions on how to deal with terrorism. Economists wanting to contribute to dealing with terrorism should suggest constitutional changes allowing and prescribing the use of popular referenda for the respective political decisions.

APPENDIX 6A

Table 6A.1 Transnational Terrorism, 1977–2000: number of incidents, persons killed and injured

Year	US Dept of State data			RAND data		
	Incidents	Fatalities	Wounded	Incidents	Fatalities	Wounded
1968	–	–	–	132	32	191
1969	–	–	–	155	12	110
1970	–	–	–	215	105	161
1971	–	–	–	150	66	91

Table 6A.1 (continued)

Year	US Dept of State data			RAND data		
	Incidents	Fatalities	Wounded	Incidents	Fatalities	Wounded
1972	–	–	–	171	191	166
1973	–	–	–	193	72	504
1974	–	–	–	237	229	690
1975	–	–	–	221	102	556
1976	–	–	–	325	346	805
1977	419	230	404	242	80	299
1978	530	435	629	242	263	405
1979	434	697	542	271	290	1,060
1980	499	507	1,062	268	156	332
1981	489	168	804	318	329	1,187
1982	487	128	755	384	188	637
1983	497	637	1,267	317	589	1,045
1984	565	312	967	326	182	502
1985	635	825+	1,217	438+	688+	1,255
1986	612	604	1,717	379	346	1,221
1987	665+	612	2,272	355	358	1,219
1988	605	407	1,131	377	593	1,869
1989	375	193	397	367	170	507
1990	437	200	675	302	121	366
1991	565	102	233−	436	175	284
1992	363	93−	636	310	154	751
1993	431	109	1,393	320	464	2,806
1994	322	314	663	58−	5−	53−
1995	440	163	6,291+	258	245	6,007+
1996	296	314	2,652	267	516	3,192
1997	304	211	693	200	230	887
1998	274−	741	5,952	–	–	–
1999	395	233	706	–	–	–
2000	426	405	791	–	–	–

Note: + denotes the highest value in a row, − the lowest value.

Sources: US Department of State, *Patterns of Global Terrorism* (various years); Sandler and Enders (2004), Table 1; and 'RAND–St. Andrews Chronology of International Terrorism, 1968–2000', provided by the Oklahoma City National Memorial Institute for the Prevention of Terrorism (www.mipt.org).

Table 6A.2 Terrorism and life satisfaction in France, 1973–1998; including control variables

Dependent variable	(1) Coefficient	(1) t-value	(2) Coefficient	(2) t-value	(3) Coefficient	(3) t-value
Life satisfaction						
Terrorism indicators						
Number of incidents	−0.003**	−4.49				
Number of persons killed			−0.004(*)	−1.97		
Number of persons injured					0.000	0.02
Income (household)						
ln(income)	0.234**	20.00	0.234**	19.93	0.234**	19.97
Income not available	2.289**	19.98	2.286**	19.92	2.286**	19.96
Size of household$^{1/2}$	−0.096**	−8.59	−0.095**	−8.51	−0.095**	−8.49
Size of household not available	−0.137	−1.38	−0.136	−1.38	−0.135	−1.36
Individual characteristics						
Male	Reference group					
Female	0.034**	4.02	0.034**	4.04	0.034**	4.03
Age	−0.020**	−11.19	−0.020**	−11.20	−0.020**	−11.21
Age^2	0.000**	12.60	0.000**	12.62	0.000**	12.64
Education, 15 years and less	Reference group					
Education, 16–19 years	0.078**	7.42	0.078**	7.42	0.078**	7.43
Education, 20 years and more	0.204**	14.60	0.205**	14.59	0.205**	14.57
In education	0.185**	9.44	0.185**	9.46	0.185**	9.47
Education not available	0.065	0.77	0.066	0.78	0.066	0.79
No children	Reference group					
One child	0.001	0.07	0.000	0.00	−0.000	−0.03
Two children	0.022	1.29	0.021	1.21	0.020	1.18

Three children	0.023	0.86	0.022	0.79	0.021	0.77
Four children and more	−0.071	−1.51	−0.073	−1.56	−0.073	−1.57
Number of children not available	−0.146	−1.63	−0.144	−1.60	−0.143	−1.60
Single	Reference group					
Married	0.071**	5.60	0.071**	5.59	0.071**	5.57
Living together	0.002	0.11	0.001	0.09	0.001	0.08
Divorced	−0.147**	−6.72	−0.148**	−6.78	−0.148**	−6.77
Separated	−0.182**	−5.43	−0.183**	−5.46	−0.183**	−5.45
Widowed	−0.079**	−4.24	−0.079**	−4.26	−0.079**	−4.25
Marital status not available	−0.119	−1.48	−0.117	−1.45	−0.116	−1.44
Employed	Reference group					
Unemployed	−0.197**	−8.57	−0.198**	−8.57	−0.198**	−8.57
Retired	0.165**	10.26	0.165**	10.26	0.165**	10.28
Housewife	0.068**	5.56	0.068**	5.54	0.068**	5.55
Other occupation	0.166**	6.08	0.166**	6.08	0.165**	6.09
Occupational status not available	0.043	1.18	0.043	1.19	0.043	1.19
Living in a rural area	Reference group					
Living in a small town	−0.066**	−5.78	−0.066**	−5.80	−0.066**	−5.80
Living in a big town	−0.084**	−7.33	−0.085**	−7.42	−0.085**	−7.38
Size of community not available	0.012	0.81	0.012	0.81	0.012	0.83
Year dummies	Yes		Yes		Yes	
Region dummies	Yes		Yes		Yes	
Constant	1.095**	5.45	1.096**	5.48	1.090**	5.45

Table 6A.2 (continued)

Dependent variable	(1)		(2)		(3)	
Life satisfaction	Coefficient	t-value	Coefficient	t-value	Coefficient	t-value
Number of observations	46,763		46,763		46,763	
Number of clusters	70		70		70	
Prob > F	0.000		0.000		0.000	
R^2 adj.	0.08		0.08		0.08	

Notes: 1. Least squares estimations; 2. Standard errors are adjusted for clustering within regions per year; 3. ** is significant at the 99 per cent level, and (*) at the 90 per cent level.

Sources: Euro-Barometer Survey Series, 1970–1999; 'RAND–St. Andrews Chronology of International Terrorism, 1968–2000', provided by the Oklahoma City National Memorial Institute for the Prevention of Terrorism (www.mipt.org); 'Terror Attack Database' of the International Institute for Counter-Terrorism (www.ict.org.il).

Measuring terrorism 171

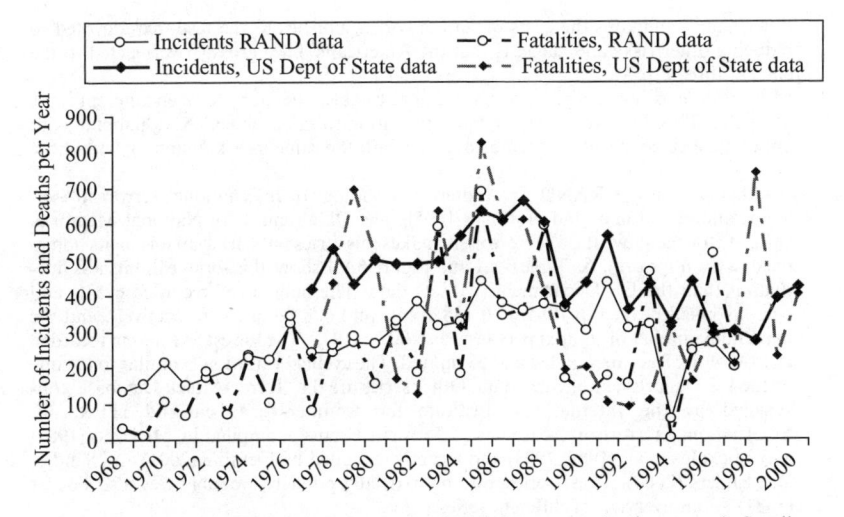

Sources: US Department of State, *Patterns of Global Terrorism* (various years); Sandler and Enders (2004), Table 1; and 'RAND–St. Andrews Chronology of International Terrorism, 1968–2000', provided by the Oklahoma City National Memorial Institute for the Prevention of Terrorism (www.mipt.org).

Figure 6A.1 Transnational terrorism, 1968–2000: comparison of US Department of State vs. RAND data

NOTES

*   We are grateful for helpful comments from Matthias Benz, Reto Jegen, Stephan Meier, Alois Stutzer and the participants of the 4th Corsica Workshop on Law and Economics in Reims, in particular Léonard Dudley, Manfred Holler and Alain Marciano.
1. See, for example, Kushner (2002); Wilkinson (2002); and Wilkinson and Jenkins (2003). These books provide extensive references to the literature on terrorism in political science, psychology, sociology, law and history. There are fewer contributions to the study of terrorism by economists. Forerunners are Schelling (1960, 1966); Boulding (1962); Selten (1977); and Landes (1978). Important more recent contributions are Kirk (1983); Atkinson et al. (1987); Im et al. (1987); Cauley and Im (1988); Lapan and Sandler (1988, 1993); Lee (1988); Sandler and Lapan (1988); Islam and Shahin (1989); Shahin and Islam (1992); Enders and Sandler (1993, 1995 and 2000); Rathbone and Rowley (2002); Sandler and Enders (2004); Arce M. and Sandler (2003); and Schneider (2004). See also Frey (1988, 2004) and Frey and Luechinger (2003 and 2004).
2. According to economic methodology, the preferences of the individuals are the normative basis to evaluate different policies (Brennan and Buchanan 1985). This holds in the case of expenditures in the fight against terrorism as well. Congleton (2002) and Hobijn (2002) both assess the adequacy of resources devoted to anti-terrorism in the aftermath of September 11, without reference to individuals' preferences. Their different assessments reflect the – to some extent – arbitrariness of their reference points. Hobijn takes as a reference point the military expenditures during the Cold War era and concludes on this basis 'that the economic costs of homeland security will be small' (p. 31) and will not evaporate the peace dividend of the 1990s. Congleton, on the

other hand, compares the costs of anti-terrorism policies to the resources devoted to reducing other risks and suggests that the Americans 'have grossly overreacted to the current threat' (p. 48).
3. Most of the existing data series on terrorism distinguish therefore between different types of attack. This, however, is only a partial solution to the problem. A kidnapping with only one hostage is still counted as one incident, the same as a kidnapping with more hostages.
4. Another series is the 'RAND–St. Andrews Chronology of International Terrorism' (see, for example, Hoffman and Hoffman 1995). The Oklahoma City National Memorial Institute for the Prevention of Terrorism makes this series publicly available on its homepage (www.mipt.org). As Table 6A.1 and Figure 6A.1 show, this series exhibits less fluctuation than the US Department of State data. The number of recorded events and persons killed peaked in 1985 with 438 events and 688 fatalities, respectively, and the maximum number of injured persons was 6,007 in 1995. The lowest levels were recorded in 1994 with 58 events, 5 killed and 53 injured. The cyclical variation is similar to the one of the US Department of State data. Other series are the 'Terror Attack Database' constructed by the International Institute for Counter-Terrorism and ITERATE, 'International Terrorism: Attributes of Terrorist Events', compiled by Mickolus (1982) and Mickolus et al. (1989, 1993) and recently extended by Fleming (2001) and Sandler and Enders (2004). These series are only partially publicly available. See also Fowler (1981) for an overview of different series.
5. Other impact studies than the ones presented below are Abadie and Gardeazabal (2003), Chen and Siems (2004) and Drakos (2004), which investigate the effects of terrorism on stock markets, Nitsch and Schumacher (2004), which analyses the repercussions on international trade, and Glaeser and Shapiro (2002), which examines the impact on urbanization. Navarro and Spencer (2001) estimate the consequences of the attacks of September 11 on the United States to be in excess of $100 billion in direct cost, and as much as $2 trillion in total costs (see also Becker and Murphy 2001, IMF 2001 and Saxton 2002). For a review see Frey et al. (2004a).
6. Pizam (1978) and Aziz (1995) – among others – hypothesize that tourism causes criminality and particularly terrorism in the host countries.
7. The averting behaviour method has been used to estimate the benefits of a reduction in pollution (Courant and Porter 1981), of ozone control policies (Dickie and Gerking 1991), of reduced soiling (Harford 1984) and of a reduction in the rates of non-melanoma skin cancers (Murdoch and Thayer 1990). The hedonic market approach has been applied to estimate the WTP for a reduction in air pollution (for example, Harrison and Rubinfeld 1978 and Chay and Greenstone 2000; see also Smith and Huang 1995 for a meta-analysis), distance from toxic waste sites (Kohlhase 1991), visibility of surrounding land (Paterson and Boyle 2002), improvements in cultural amenities (Clark and Kahn 1988) and safety at work (Gegax et al. 1991).
8. The marginal implicit price for a local amenity reflected in either the housing or the labour market is an underestimate of the individuals' valuation of this amenity if purchased simultaneously through both these hedonic markets.
9. See Carson et al. (2003) for an application of contingent valuation in environmental economics. Meta-analyses, debates and controversies concerning the contingent valuation are the subject of Arrow et al. (1993), Diamond and Hausman (1994), Hanemann (1994), Portney (1994), Carson et al. (1995), Smith and Osborne (1996), Carson (1997) and Carson et al. (2001). The contingent valuation method in cultural economics is the subject of Frey (1997), Frey and Oberholzer-Gee (1998), Santagata and Signorello (2000), Thompson et al. (2002), Willis (2002) and Cuccia (2003).
10. To increase validity, one may also consider statistically based probability sampling instead of convenience sampling, in-person interviews instead of interviews conducted by mail or over the telephone and follow-up questions or a 'debriefing' section. This ensures that respondents understood the choice and helps to discover the reasons for their answer; information that can be usefully exploited in the data analysis.

11. Several critics of contingent valuation reject the method because they think it to be incompatible with economic theory; they make a number of statements about what, according to their view, are permissible arguments in the utility function (see, for example, Diamond and Hausman 1994). As Hanemann observes, '[critics] argue that people should care about outcomes, not about the process whereby these are generated . . . [and] should value things for purely selfish motives' (1994, pp. 32–3). According to this reasoning, it should make no difference whether a certain number of persons are killed by terrorist attacks or inevitable accidents.
12. Various authors try to explain differences between WTP and WTA in a neoclassical framework. Hanemann (1991), for example, shows that the difference may be governed by a substitution effect and not only a minor income effect. In the case of imposed quantity changes, where the individual is not free to trade to the desired quantity level, 'there is no reason why WTP and WTA could not differ vastly: in the limit, WTP could equal the individual's entire (finite) income, while WTA could be infinite' (pp. 635–6). However, even in the case of inexpensive and ordinary market goods, persistent, albeit smaller, differences between the two measures can be found (Horowitz and McConnell 2002). From a meta-analysis of more than 200 WTA/WTP ratios, Horowitz and McConnell (2003) infer that the available data are not consistent with neoclassical preferences. Thaler (1980) ascribes this finding to the 'endowment effect', which he sees as an extension of the prospect theory from Kahneman and Tversky (1979). See also Gordon and Knetsch (1979), Knetsch (1989, 1995a, 1995b) and Knetsch and Sinden (1984). For psychological anomalies in general, see, for example, Kahneman et al. (1982); Arkes and Hammond (1986); Bell et al. (1988); Dawes (1988); Frey and Eichenberger (1989); and Thaler (1992)
13. See, for example, Berrebi and Klor (2004). Studying the relationship between terrorist attacks in Israel and the occupied territories from 1990 and 2003 and electoral outcomes in Israel, they find that relative support for the rightist party increases after periods with high levels of terrorism and decreases after relatively calm periods.
14. So far, happiness or reported subjective well-being data are rarely used to determine the WTP or WTA for public goods and bads. Van Praag and Baarsma (2001) assess the WTA for noise nuisance effects around the airport of Amsterdam, Welsch (2002) estimates the WTA for urban air pollution in a cross-country analysis and Di Tella et al. (2002) investigate the relationship between various macro variables such as environmental indicators, crime rate, divorce rate and macroeconomic variables, and life satisfaction.
15. However, there are the conditions of cardinality and interpersonal comparability of the individual statements of well-being. Although economists are likely to be sceptical about both claims, there is a lot of evidence that both of them may be less of a problem on a practical level than on a theoretical level (see, for example, Kahneman 1999; Frey and Stutzer 2002b).
16. In order to control for potential correlation of the error terms across observations that are contained within a cross-sectional unit at any given point in time, robust standard errors are estimated.
17. The WTP for a decrease in the level of terrorist activity from q_0 to q_1 is measured by the compensating surplus (CS). The CS is the decrease in income necessary to hold utility constant. In other words, the CS is the solution to the following expression: $v(m_0; q_0) = v(m_0 - CS; q_1)$, where $v(\cdot)$ is the utility function. In a first step, using the coefficient β_1 of table 6.1, utility gains Δv for a discrete change in terrorism from q_0 to q_1 are estimated. The utility gain amounts to $\beta_1 \cdot (q_0 - q_1)$, that is, to $-0.0029 \cdot (q_1 - q_0)$ in the case terrorism is measured by the number of incidents (panel 1 in Table 6.1) and to $-0.0038 \cdot (q_0 - q_1)$ in the case terrorism is measured by the number of persons killed (panel 2 in Table 6.1). In a second step, the marginal utility of income $\partial v/\partial m_0$ at mean household income is calculated. The marginal utility of income is $\beta_2 \cdot (1/m_0)$, that is 0.2345·(1/20573.4) and 0.2342·(1/20573.4), respectively. Finally, the estimated utility gain Δv and marginal utility of income $\partial v/\partial m_0$ are used to compute the WTP, or CS: $CS = \Delta v / \partial v / \partial m_0$.

18. According to Blomquist et al. (1988), the compensation amounts to $2,267 for those living in the county with the highest crime compared to those individuals living in the county with the least crime, and then to $1,600 compared to those living in the county having the average rate of violent crime. This corresponds to 11 and 8 per cent, respectively, of annual household income. Compensation relative to a hypothetical county with no violent crime is not estimated.

REFERENCES

Abadie, Alberto and Javier Gardeazabal (2003), 'The economic costs of conflict: a case study for the Basque Country', *American Economic Review* **93** (1): 113–32.

Arce M., Daniel G. and Todd Sandler (2003), 'An evolutionary game approach to fundamentalism and conflict', *Journal of Institutional and Theoretical Economics* **159** (1), 132–54.

Arkes, Hal R. and Kenneth R. Hammond (eds) (1986), *Judgement and Decision Making: An Interdisciplinary Reader*, Cambridge: Cambridge University Press.

Arrow, Kenneth J., Robert S. Solow, Edward Leamer, Paul Portney, Ray Radner and Howard Schuman (1993), 'Report of the NOAA-Panel on contingent valuation', *Federal Register* **58** (10): 4601–14.

Atkinson, Scott E., Todd Sandler and John Tschirhart (1987), 'Terrorism in a bargaining framework', *Journal of Law and Economics* **30** (1): 1–21.

Aziz, Heba (1995), 'Understanding attacks on tourists in Egypt', *Tourism Management* **16** (2): 91–5.

Badey, Thomas J. (1998), 'Defining international terrorism: a pragmatic approach', *Terrorism and Political Violence* **10** (1): 90–107.

Becker, Gary S. and Kevin Murphy (2001), 'Prosperity will rise out of the ashes', *Wall Street Journal*, 29 October p. A22.

Bell, David E., Howard Raiffa and Amos Tversky (eds) (1988), *Decision Making: Descriptive, Normative and Perspective Interactions*, Cambridge: Cambridge University Press.

Benz, Matthias and Alois Stutzer (2004), 'Are voters better informed when they have a larger say in politics? Evidence for the European Union and Switzerland', *Public Choice* **119** (1–2), 31–59.

Berrebi, Claude and Esteban F. Klor (2004), 'On terrorism and electoral outcomes: theory and evidence from the Israeli-Palestinian Conflict', working paper series of the Princeton University Industrial Relations Section no. 480, New Jersey.

Blomquist, Glenn C., Mark C. Berger and John P. Hoehn (1988), 'New estimates of quality of life in urban areas', *American Economic Review* **78** (1): 89–107.

Bogdanor, Vernon (1994), 'Western Europe', in Butler and Ranney (eds), p. 24–97.

Bohnet, Iris and Bruno S. Frey (1994), 'Direct-democratic rules: the role of discussion', *Kyklos* **47** (3): 341–54.

Boulding, Kenneth E. (1962), *Conflict and Defense*, New York: Harper & Row.

Brennan, Geoffrey and James M. Buchanan (1985), *The Reason of Rules: Constitutional Political Economy*, Cambridge: Cambridge University Press.

Butler, David and Austin Ranney (eds) (1994), *Referendums around the World. The Growing Use of Direct Democracy*, Washington, DC: AEI Press.

Carson, Richard T. (1997), 'Contingent valuation surveys and tests of insensitivity to scope', in Raymond J. Kopp, Werner W. Pommerehne and Norbert Schwarz (eds), *Determining the Value of Non-Marketed Goods: Economic, Psychological, and Policy Relevant Aspects of Contingent Valuation Methods*, Boston, MA: Kluwer Academic: 127–63.

Carson, Richard T., Nicholas E. Flores, Kerry M. Martin and Jennifer L. Wright (1996), 'Contingent valuation and revealed preference methodologies: comparing the estimates for quasi-public goods', *Land Economics* **72** (1): 80–99.

Carson, Richard T., Nicholas E. Flores and Norman F. Meade (2001), 'Contingent valuation: controversies and evidence', *Environmental and Resource Economics* **19**: 173–210.

Carson, Richard T., Robert C. Mitchell, W. Michael Hanemann, Raymond J. Kopp, Stanley Presser and Paul A. Ruud (2003), 'Contingent valuation and lost passive use: damages from the *Exxon Valdez* oil spill', *Environmental and Resource Economics* **25** (3): 257–86.

Carson, Richard T., Jennifer L. Wright, Nancy C. Carson, Nicholas E. Flores and Anna Alberini (1995), *A Bibliography of Contingent Valuation Studies and Papers*, San Diego: Natural Resources Damage Assessment, Inc.

Cauley, Jon and Eric-Iksoon Im (1988), 'Intervention policy analysis of skyjackings and other terrorist incidents', *American Economic Review* **78** (2): 27–31.

Chay, Kenneth Y. and Michael Greenstone (2000), 'Does air quality matter? Evidence from the housing market', mimeo (revised version of NBER 6826), University of California at Berkeley.

Chen, Andrew H. and Thomas F. Siems (2004), 'The effects of terrorism on global capital markets', *European Journal of Political Economy*, **20** (2), 349–66.

Clark, David E. and James R. Kahn (1988), 'The social benefits of urban cultural amenities', *Journal of Regional Science* **28** (3): 363–7.

Congleton, Roger D. (2002), 'Terrorism, interest-group politics, and public policy: curtailing criminal modes of political speech', *The Independent Review* **7** (1): 47–67.

Courant, Paul N. and Richard C. Porter (1981), 'Averting expenditure and the cost of pollution', *Journal of Environmental Economics and Management* **8** (4): 321–9.

Cuccia, Tiziana (2003), 'Contingent valuation', in Ruth Towse (ed.), *A Handbook of Cultural Economics*, Cheltenham, UK, Northampton, MA, USA: Edward Elgar: 119–31.

Davis, Robert (1963), 'The value of outdoor recreation: an economic study of the Maine Woods', PhD Dissertation, Harvard University.

Dawes, Robyn M. (1988), *Rational Choice in an Uncertain World*, San Diego and New York: Harcourt, Brace, Jovanovich.

Di Tella, Rafael, Robert MacCulloch and Richard Layard (2002), 'Income, happiness and inequality as measures of welfare', mimeo, Harvard Business School.

Diamond, Peter A. and Jerry A. Hausman (1994), 'Contingent valuation: is some number better than no number?', *Journal of Economic Perspectives* **8** (4): 45–64.

Dickie, Mark and Shelby Gerking (1991), 'Willingness to pay for ozone control: inferences from the demand for medical care', *Journal of Environmental Economics and Management* **21** (1): 1–16.

Drakos, Konstantinos (2004), 'Terrorism-induced structural shifts in financial risk: airline stocks in the aftermath of the September 11th terror attacks', *European Journal of Political Economy* **20** (2): 435–46.

Drakos, Konstantinos and Ali M. Kutan (2003), 'Regional effects of terrorism on tourism: three Mediterranean countries', *Journal of Conflict Resolution* **47** (5): 621–41.

Enders, Walter and Todd Sandler (1991), 'Causality between transnational terrorism and tourism: the case of Spain', *Terrorism* **14**: 49–58.
Enders, Walter and Todd Sandler (1993), 'The effectiveness of antiterrorism policies: a vector-autoregression-intervention analysis', *American Political Science Review* **87** (4): 829–44.
Enders, Walter and Todd Sandler (1995), 'Terrorism: theory and applications', in Keith Hartley and Todd Sandler (eds), *Handbook of Defense Economics. Volume 1. Handbooks in Economics. Volume 12*, Amsterdam, New York and Oxford: Elsevier: 213–49.
Enders, Walter and Todd Sandler (1996), 'Terrorism and foreign direct investment in Spain and Greece', *Kyklos* **49** (3): 331–52.
Enders, Walter and Todd Sandler (2000), 'Is transnational terrorism becoming more threatening? A time-series investigation', *Journal of Conflict Resolution* **44** (3): 307–32.
Enders, Walter and Todd Sandler (2002), 'Patterns of transnational terrorism, 1970–99: alternative time series estimates', *International Studies Quarterly* **46**: 145–65.
Enders, Walter, Todd Sandler and Gerald F. Parise (1992), 'An econometric analysis of the impact of terrorism on tourism', *Kyklos* **45** (4): 531–54.
Fleming, Peter (2001), 'International terrorism: attributes of terrorist events 1992–1998' (ITERATE 5 update), mimeo.
Fowler, William Warner (1981), 'Terrorism data bases: a comparison of missions, methods, and systems', A RAND Note N-1503-RC, RAND–St. Andrews.
Freeman, A. Myrick (2003), *The Measurement of Environment and Resource Values: Theory and Method*, 2nd edn, Washington, DC: Resources for the Future.
Frey, Bruno S. (1988), 'Fighting political terrorism by refusing recognition', *Journal of Public Policy* **7**: 179–88.
Frey, Bruno S. (1994), 'Direct democracy: politico-economic lessons from Swiss experience', *American Economic Review* **84** (2): 338–48.
Frey, Bruno S. (1997), 'Evaluating cultural property: the economic approach', *International Journal of Cultural Property* **6** (2): 231–46.
Frey, Bruno S. (2004), *Dealing With Terrorism: Stick or Carrot?*, Cheltenham, UK, and Northampton, MA, USA: Edward Elgar.
Frey, Bruno S., Matthias Benz and Alois Stutzer (2004), 'Introducing procedural utility: not only what, but also how matters', *Journal of Institutional and Theoretical Economics*, **160** (3): 377–401.
Frey, Bruno S. and Reiner Eichenberger (1989), 'Should social scientists care about choice anomalies?', *Rationality and Society* **1**: 101–22.
Frey, Bruno S. and Simon Luechinger (2003), 'How to fight terrorism: alternatives to deterrence', *Defence and Peace Economics* **14** (4): 237–49.
Frey, Bruno S. and Simon Luechinger (2004), 'Decentralization as a disincentive for terror', *European Journal of Political Economy* **20** (2): 509–15.
Frey, Bruno S., Simon Luechinger and Alois Stutzer (2004a), 'Calculating tragedy: assessing the costs of terrorism', CESifo working paper series no. 1341, Munich: CESifo.
Frey, Bruno S., Simon Luechinger and Alois Stutzer (2004b), 'Valuing public goods: the life satisfaction approach' CESifo working paper series no. 1158, Munich: CESifo.
Frey, Bruno S. and Felix Oberholzer-Gee (1998), 'Public choice, cost–benefit analysis, and the evaluation of cultural heritage', in Alan Peacock (ed.), *Does the Past*

have a Future? The Political Economy of Cultural Heritage, London: Institute of Economic Affairs: 27–53.
Frey, Bruno S. and Alois Stutzer (2002a), *Happiness and Economics: How the Economy and Institutions Affect Human Well-Being*, Princeton, NJ: Princeton University Press.
Frey, Bruno S. and Alois Stutzer (2002b), 'What can economists learn from happiness research?', *Journal of Economic Literature* **40** (2): 402–35.
Frey, Bruno S. and Alois Stutzer (2003), 'Testing theories of happiness', working paper no. 147, Institute for Empirical Research in Economics, University of Zurich.
Galetovic, Alexander and Ricardo Sanhueza (2000), 'Citizens, autocrats, and plotters: a model and new evidence on coups d'état', *Economics and Politics* **12** (2): 183–204.
Gegax, Douglas, Shelby Gerking and William Schulze (1991), 'Perceived risk and the marginal value of safety', *Review of Economics and Statistics* **73** (4): 589–96.
Glaeser, Edward L. and Jesse M. Shapiro (2002), 'Cities and warfare: the impact of terrorism on urban form', *Journal of Urban Economics* **51** (2): 205–24.
Gordon, Irene M. and Jack L. Knetsch (1979), 'Consumers' surplus measures and the evaluation of resources', *Land and Economics* **55** (1): 1–10.
Hanemann, W. Michael (1991), 'Willingness to pay and willingness to accept: how much can they differ?', *American Economic Review* **81** (3): 635–47.
Hanemann, W. Michael (1994), 'Valuing the environment through contingent valuation', *Journal of Economic Perspectives* **8** (4): 19–43.
Harford, Jon D. (1984), 'Averting behavior and the benefits of reduced soiling', *Journal of Environmental Economics and Management* **11** (3): 296–302.
Harrison, David and Daniel L. Rubinfeld (1978), 'The distribution of benefits from improvements in urban air quality', *Journal of Environmental Economics and Management* **5** (4): 313–32.
Hausman, Jerry A., Gregory K. Leonard and Daniel McFadden (1995), 'A utility-consistent, combined discrete choice and count data model: assessing recreational use losses due to natural resource damage', *Journal of Public Economics* **56** (1): 1–30.
Hobijn, Bart (2002), 'What will homeland security cost?', *Federal Reserve Bank of New York Economic Policy Review* **8** (2): 21–33.
Hoffman, Bruce (1997), 'The confluence of international and domestic trends in terrorism', *Terrorism and Political Violence* **9** (2): 1–15.
Hoffman, Bruce (1998), *Inside Terrorism*, New York: Columbia University Press.
Hoffman, Bruce and Donna K. Hoffman (1995), 'The RAND–St. Andrews Chronology of International Terrorism, 1994', *Terrorism and Political Violence* **7** (4): 178–229.
Horowitz, John K. and Kenneth E. McConnell (2002), 'A review of WTA/WTP studies', *Journal of Environmental Economics and Management* **44** (3): 426–47.
Horowitz, John K. and Kenneth E. McConnell (2003), 'Willingness to accept, willingness to pay and the income effect', *Journal of Economic Behavior and Organization* **51** (4): 537–45.
Im, Iksoon Eric, John Cauley and Todd Sandler (1987), 'Cycles and substitutions in terrorist activities: a spectral approach', *Kyklos* **40** (2): 238–55.
International Monetary Fund (IMF) (2001), 'How has September 11 influenced the global economy?', *World Economic Outlook*, Washington, DC: IMF: Chapter 11.

Islam, Muhammad Q. and Wassim N. Shahin (1989), 'Economic methodology applied to political hostage-taking in light of the Iran–Contra affair', *Southern Economic Journal* **55** (4): 1019–24.
Juergensmeyer, Mark (1997), 'Terror mandated by God', *Terrorism and Political Violence* **9** (2): 16–23.
Kahneman, Daniel (1999), 'Objective happiness', in Daniel Kahneman, Ed Diener and Norbert Schwarz (eds), *Well-Being: The Foundations of Hedonic Psychology*, New York: Russell Sage Foundation: 3–25.
Kahneman, Daniel and Jack L. Knetsch (1992), 'Valuing public goods: the purchase of moral satisfaction', *Journal of Environmental Economics and Management* **22** (1): 57–70.
Kahneman, Daniel, Paul Slovic and Amos Tversky (eds) (1982), *Judgement under Uncertainty: Heuristics and Biases*, Cambridge: Cambridge University Press.
Kahneman, Daniel and Amos Tversky (1979), 'Prospect theory: an analysis of decision under risk', *Econometrica* **47** (2): 263–91.
Kirchgässner, Gebhard and Werner W. Pommerehne (1993), 'Low-cost decisions as a challenge to public choice', *Public Choice* **77** (1): 107–15.
Kirk, Richard M. (1983), 'Political terrorism and the size of government: a positive institutional analysis of violent political activity', *Public Choice* **4** (1): 41–52.
Kliemt, Hartmut (1986), 'The veil of insignificance', *European Journal of Political Economy* **2/3**: 333–44.
Knetsch, Jack L. (1989), 'The endowment effect and evidence of nonreversible indifference curves', *American Economic Review* **79** (5): 263–91.
Knetsch, Jack L. (1995a), 'Assumptions, behavioral findings, and policy analysis', *Journal of Policy Analysis and Management* **14** (1): 68–78.
Knetsch, Jack L. (1995b), 'Asymmetric valuation of gains and losses and preferences order assumptions', *Economic Inquiry* **33** (1): 134–41.
Knetsch, Jack L. and Paul Sinden (1984), 'Willingness to pay and compensation demanded: experimental evidence of an unexpected disparity in measures of value', *Quarterly Journal of Economics* **99** (3): 507–21.
Kohlhase, Janet E. (1991), 'The impact of toxic waste sites on housing values', *Journal of Urban Economics* **30** (1): 1–26.
Kushner, Harvey W. (2002), *Encyclopedia of Terrorism*, New York: Sage Publications.
Landau, Simha F., Benjamin Beit-Hallahmi and Shilomit Levy (1998), 'The personal and the political: Israelis' perception of well-being in times of war and peace', *Social Indicators Research* **44** (3): 329–65.
Landes, William A. (1978), 'An economic study of US aircraft hijackings, 1961–1976', *Journal of Law and Economics* **21** (1): 1–31.
Lapan, Harvey E. and Todd Sandler (1988), 'To bargain or not to bargain: that is the question', *American Economic Review* **78** (2): 16–21.
Lapan, Harvey E. and Todd Sandler (1993), 'Terrorism and signalling', *European Journal of Political Economy* **9** (3): 383–97.
Lee, Dwight R. (1988), 'Free riding and paid riding in the fight against terrorism', *American Economic Review* **78** (2): 22–6.
Lee, Dwight R. and Todd Sandler (1989), 'On the optimal retaliation against terrorists: the paid-rider option', *Public Choice* **61** (2): 141–52.
List, John A. and Craig A. Gallet (2001), 'What experimental protocol influence disparities between actual and hypothetical stated values?', *Environmental and Resource Economics* **20** (3): 241–54.

Ludwig, Jens and Philip J. Cook (2001), 'The benefits of reducing gun violence: evidence from contingent-valuation survey data', *Journal of Risk and Uncertainty* **22** (3): 207–26.
Mickolus, Edward F. (1982), 'International Terrorism: Attributes of Terrorist Events 1968–1977' (ITERATE 2), Ann Arbor, MI: Inter-University Consortium for Political and Social Research.
Mickolus, Edward F., Todd Sandler, Jean M. Murdock and Peter Fleming (1989), 'International Terrorism: Attributes of Terrorist Events, 1978–1987' (ITERATE 3), Dunn Loring, VA: Vinyard Software.
Mickolus, Edward F., Todd Sandler, Jean M. Murdock and Peter Fleming (1993), 'International Terrorism: Attributes of Terrorist Events, 1988–1991' (ITERATE 4), Dunn Loring, VA: Vinyard Software.
Miller, Abraham H. (1994), 'Comment on terrorism and democracy', *Terrorism and Political Violence* **6** (4): 435–9.
Mueller, John E. (1970), 'Presidential popularity from Truman to Johnson', *American Political Science Review* **64** (1): 18–34.
Murdoch, James C. and Mark A. Thayer (1990), 'The benefits of reducing the incidence of nonmelanoma skin cancers: a defensive expenditures approach', *Journal of Environmental Economics and Management* **18** (2): 107–9.
Nacos, Brigitte L. (1994), *Terrorism and the Media*, New York: Columbia University Press.
Nannestad, Peter and Martin Paldam (1994), 'The VP-function: a survey of the literature on vote and popularity functions after 25 years', *Public Choice* **79** (3–4): 213–45.
Navarro, Peter and Aron Spencer (2001), 'September 2001: assessing the costs of terrorism', *Milken Institute Review* **2,** 16–31.
Nitsch, Volker and Dieter Schumacher (2004), 'Terrorism and international trade: an empirical investigation', *European Journal of Political Economy* **20** (2): 301–16.
Paldam, Martin (1981), 'A preliminary survey of the theories and findings on vote and popularity functions', *European Journal of Political Research* **9** (2): 181–99.
Paterson, Robert W. and Kevin J. Boyle (2002), 'Out of sight, out of mind? Using GIS to incorporate visibility in hedonic property value models', *Land Economics* **78** (3): 417–25.
Pizam, Abraham (1978), 'Tourism impacts: the social costs to the destination community as perceived by its residents', *Journal of Travel Research* **16** (4): 8–12.
Pizam, Abraham and Ginger Smith (2000), 'Tourism and terrorism: a quantitative analysis of major terrorist acts and their impact on tourism destinations', *Tourism Economics* **6** (2): 123–38.
Pommerehne, Werner W. (1987), *Präferenzen für öffentliche Güter. Ansätze zu ihrer Erfassung [Preferences for Public Goods: Elicitation Approaches]*, Tübingen: Mohr (Siebeck).
Portney, Paul R. (1994), 'The contingent valuation debate: why economists should care', *Journal of Economic Perspectives* **8** (4): 3–17.
Rathbone, Anne and Charles K. Rowley (2002), 'Terrorism', *Public Choice* **111** (1–2): 9–18.
Rattinger, Hans (1980), *Wirtschaftliche Konjunktur und politische Wahlen in der Bundesrepublik [Economic Cycles and Political Elections in the Federal Republic of Germany]*, Berlin: Duncker & Humblot.
Sandler, Todd and Walter Enders (2004), 'An economic perspective on transnational terrorism', *European Journal of Political Economy* **20** (2), 301–16.

Sandler, Todd and Harvey E. Lapan (1988), 'The calculus of dissent: an analysis of terrorists' choice of targets', *Synthese* **76** (2): 245–61.
Santagata, Walter and Giovanni Signorello (2000), 'Contingent valuation of a cultural public good and policy design: the case of "Napoli Musei Aperti"', *Journal of Cultural Economics* **24** (3): 181–200.
Saxton, Jim (2002), 'The economic costs of terrorism', Joint Economic Committee Working Paper, United States Congress.
Schelling, Thomas C. (1960), *The Strategy of Conflict*, Oxford: Oxford University Press.
Schelling, Thomas C. (1966), *Arms and Influence*, New Haven, CT: Yale University Press.
Schelling, Thomas C. (1984), 'The life you save may be your own', in *Choice and Consequence: Perspectives of an Errant Economist*, Cambridge, MA and London: Harvard University Press: 113–46.
Schmid, Alex P. and Albert J. Jongman (1988), *Political Terrorism: A New Guide to Actors, Authors, Concepts, Data Bases, Theories, and Literature*, New Brunswick, NJ: Transaction Books.
Schneider, Friedrich (2004), 'The financial flows of Islamic terrorism', in Donato Masciandaro (ed.) *Global Financial Crime? Terrorism, Money Laundering and Offshore Centres*, Aldershot: Ashgate, pp. 97–124.
Schneider, Friedrich and Bruno S. Frey (1988), 'Politico-economic models of macroeconomic policy: a review of the empirical evidence', in Thomas D. Willett (ed.), *The Political Economy of Money, Inflation and Unemployment*, Durham, NC and London: Duke University Press: 240–75.
Selten, Reinhard (1977), 'A simple game model of kidnapping', in Rudolf Henn and Otto Moeschlin (eds), *Mathematical Economics and Game Theory: Lecture Notes in Economics and Mathematical Systems*, Vol. 141, Berlin: Springer: 139–56.
Shahin, Wassim N. and Muhammad Q. Islam (1992), 'Combating political hostage-taking: an alternative approach', *Defence Economics* **3** (4): 321–7.
Small, Deborah A. and George Loewenstein (2003), 'Helping *a* victim or helping *the* victim', *Journal of Risk and Uncertainty* **26** (1): 5–16.
Smith, V. Kerry and Ju Chin Huang (1995), 'Can markets value air quality? A meta-analysis of hedonic property value models', *Journal of Political Economy* **103** (1): 209–27.
Smith, V. Kerry and Laura Osborne (1996), 'Do contingent valuation estimates pass a "scope", test? A meta analysis', *Journal of Environmental Economics and Management* **31** (3): 287–301.
Thaler, Richard H. (1980), 'Toward a positive theory of consumer choice', *Journal of Economic Behavior and Organization* **1** (1): 39–60.
Thaler, Richard H. (1992), *The Winner's Curse: Paradoxes and Anomalies of Economic Life*, New York: Free Press.
Thompson, Eric, Mark Berger, Glenn Blomquist and Steven Allen (2002), 'Valuing the arts: a contingent valuation approach', *Journal of Cultural Economics* **26** (2): 87–113.
Tullock, Gordon (1971), 'The paradox of revolution', *Public Choice* **11** (Fall): 88–99.
Uleri, Pier Vincenzo (1996), 'Italy: referendums and initiatives from the origins to the crisis of a democratic regime', in Michael Gallagher and Pier Vincenzo Uleri (eds), *The Referendum Experience in Europe*, Basingstoke: Macmillan pp. 106–25.
US Department of State (various years), *Patterns of Global Terrorism*, Washington, DC: US Department of State.

Van Praag, Bernard M.S. and Barbara E. Baarsma (2001), 'The shadow price of aircraft noise nuisance: a new approach to the internalization of externalities', Tinbergen Institute discussion paper TI 2001–010/3.

Viscusi, W. Kip and Joseph E. Aldy (2003), 'The value of a statistical life: a critical review of market estimates throughout the world', *Journal of Risk and Uncertainty* **27** (1): 5–76.

Viscusi, W. Kip and Richard J. Zeckhauser (2003), 'Sacrificing civil liberties to reduce terrorism risks', *Journal of Risk and Uncertainty* **26** (2–3): 99–120.

Weede, Erich and Edward N. Muller (1998), 'Rebellion, violence and revolution: a rational choice perspective', *Journal of Peace Research* **35** (1): 43–59.

Welsch, Heinz (2002), 'Preferences over prosperity and pollution: environmental valuation based on happiness surveys', *Kyklos* **55** (2): 473–94.

Wilkinson, Paul (2002), *Terrorism Versus Democracy: The Liberal State Response*, London: Frank Cass.

Wilkinson, Paul and Brian M. Jenkins (2003), *Aviation Terrorism and Security*, London: Frank Cass.

Willis, K.G. (2002), 'Iterative bid design in contingent valuation and the estimation of the revenue maximising price for a cultural good', *Journal of Cultural Economics* **26** (4): 307–24.

Wintrobe, Ronald (1998), *The Political Economy of Dictatorship*, Cambridge: Cambridge University Press.

Wolfers, Justin (2002), 'Are voters rational? Evidence from gubernatorial elections', Stanford Graduate School of Business working paper no. 1730, Stanford University.

PART II

How to control a democratic state: the legal constraint

7. Rule of law, finance and economic development: cross-country evidence*

Stefan van Hemmen and Frank H. Stephen

1 INTRODUCTION

Starting with the contributions of La Porta, Lopez-de-Silanes, Shleifer and Vishny (1997a, 1998), and concerned with the production of economically efficient laws, law and economics scholars have increasingly focused their attention on the chain which connects legal rules (that is, formal institutions) and their enforcement to financial and economic growth. This approach has potential interest for policy makers and responds to the needs of governments involved in large-scale economic reform programmes. The focus on institutions and their importance for economic development (Davis and North 1971; North 1981, 1990) connects with the so-called 'structural reforms' that have been actively encouraged by the World Bank and the International Monetary Fund (IMF) in the last ten years or so. In terms of Williamson's (2000) conceptual framework, reforms have effects on both the *institutional environment* and on *governance*. Changes in the former may take 10 to 100 years to evolve (or are socially and economically too costly to be achieved in the short term), setting the context within which governance structures are designed. Policy makers are conditioned by institutions that can be taken as exogenous in the short term. Rodrik et al. (2004) find it helpful to think of policy as a *flow* variable, in contrast to institutions, which is a *stock* variable. They view institutions as the cumulative outcome of past policy actions:

> Policies pursued over a short time span, say 30–40 years, are like a flow variable, whereas development, the result of a much longer cumulative historical process, is more akin to a stock variable. (p. 136, note 3)

In this context, can governance reforms contribute to effectively promoting economic performance? Which aspects of the economic system should be given priority?

Finance literature suggests that efficient resource allocation relies heavily on governance aspects such as firms rewarding and returning funds to investors, banks having access to information that facilitates selection of projects, and tribunals enforcing laws when there is a conflict between debtor and creditors (Harris and Raviv 1991; Shleifer and Vishny 1997). Microeconomic studies show that external financing causes faster growth of industries and firms (Rajan and Zingales 1998; Demirgüç-Kunt and Maksimovic 1998). La Porta et al. (1997a, p. 1131) start their seminal work with questions like: 'Why do some countries have so much bigger capital markets than others? . . . why in fact do we see huge differences in the size, breadth and valuation of capital markets?'. In their empirical analysis, they show that the differences are largely explained by the degree with which the legal and enforcement institutions protect investors, which differ greatly and systematically across countries. Then, if external finance promotes economic growth, it is crucial for policy makers and researchers to understand which legal and enforcement institutions facilitate the access to external finance (Levine 1998, 1999, 2002, 2003a).

Following the empirical methodology used in the country growth literature (Barro and Sala-i-Martin 1995) and La Porta et al.'s (1997a, 1998) legal binary and aggregate variable approach, some authors have concentrated on the link between financial and economic growth (Azfar and Matheson (2003); Levine, 1998, 1999, 2002, 2003a; Stephen and van Hemmen 2003). Their studies find evidence that the link can be found through the institutions that contribute to financial market development. Previous analysis used financial development as a predictor of future growth (King and Levine 1993b; Levine and Zervos 1998). A problem is that they do not tackle the issue of causality, as pointed out by Rajan and Zingales (1998), who suggest that financial development may simply be a leading indicator of growth. It is agreed that causality, plausibly, runs in both directions (access to finance promotes growth, and economic growth produces higher demand for external funds). As a way of circumventing this problem, Levine and other authors use La Porta et al. institutional investor protection variables, which can be taken as instruments for the exogenous component of financial development. To the extent that laws that protect banks and investors and the quality of their enforcement are historically inherited, it seems reasonable to characterize them as exogenous (that is, shaping the *institutional environment*).

Some growth scholars, however, have taken a much wider approach in which institutions are considered a part of economic development. Among them, Rodrik et al. (2004, p. 134) have warned of the difficulty of showing that 'improvements in property rights, the rule of law and other aspects of the institutional environment are an independent determinant of incomes and are not simply a consequence of higher incomes or of greater [trade] integration'. In particular, their paper uses mortality rates of colonial settlers as the valid instrument for institutions.

Concerned with testing competing theories of development, some economic growth scholars (Rodrik et al. 2004; Acemoglu et al. 2003; Easterly and Levine 2003) have focused on looking for instruments that capture the exogenous source of variation in institutions. Once the importance of institutions is highlighted, however, little is said about the way institutions can be improved. On the other hand, La Porta et al. (1998) and, more recently, Beck et al. (2001a) show that legal rules and the quality of enforcement are strongly correlated with legal origin.

It has been argued that legal traditions developed in the eighteenth and nineteenth centuries in Europe as a result of differences in the relative power of the crown and property holders. Countries with weaker state power and independent courts produced positive institutional environments for economic transactions and for financial development (North and Weingast 1989). Borrowing from Reynolds and Flores (1996), La Porta et al.'s division of countries into legal families (English, French, German and Scandinavian), which mainly originated from adoption, occupation or colonization, is widely used as an instrument for the characteristics of the financial system. Legal origin is viewed by Levine (1998) and Levine et al. (2000) as an exogenous *endowment* which has influenced banking development. The validity of the instrument is justified in La Porta et al. (1998), who trace the connection between legal origin and financial laws. As Beck et al. (2004) put it, law and finance theory predicts that historically determined differences in legal origin can explain cross-country differences in financial development today. In their analysis, legal origin and other endowments (which are related to the initial disease and geographical conditions encountered by colonizers) are shown to be jointly significant in explaining the size of external financial markets. La Porta et al., Levine and other authors tend to suggest that financial development and economic growth are not a dominant influence in the production of laws: it is legal origin that better explains the differences in legal codes and enforcement efficiency. Anywhere legal origin is substituted for legal rules and enforcement, similar results are found. Nevertheless, it must be pointed out that stress on the rights of individual investors (that is, law and finance approach) is only one of the competing historical determinants of financial development. Beck et al. (2001a) also consider a *dynamic law and finance* explanation. While accepting the law and finance (legal origin) approach, the dynamic law and finance view puts its emphasis on the ability of the legal and court system to adapt to changing conditions. Common law (case-by-case approach) and German law (based on dynamic law production), it is suggested, outperform French legal tradition (at least in its static version, which consists of rigidly sticking to codes and laws) in adapting quickly to the needs of the economic agents. Two other determinants are also studied by Beck et al. (2001a): the 'politics and finance' and the 'endowment' views. The first hypothesizes that where a state has responded to pressures by a particular dominant elite, more control will be exerted on financial markets, reducing development opportunities. The endowment view is concerned with the role played by initial conditions (land, climate, diseases and so on) found by Europeans in the lands they colonized: when they settled successfully, institutions that promoted long-run development took root.

The evidence presented on particular measures of rule of law and legislation on investors' protection against expropriation by insiders introduces new possibilities for testing financial theories and analysing the impact of financial markets on economic growth. It is not clear whether the econometric cross-country models are able to show the macro-level effect of changing a particular law or improving the mechanisms by which laws are enforced; however, it helps to identify contexts where wide programmes of reforms may produce major economic improvements and promises to help orientate successful policy strategies. Alternatively, as Levine (1998) suggests, if the exogenous component of financial development were to be unrelated to economic growth, it lowers the priority given to these legal factors.[1]

While the improvement of *formal* institutions is policy makers' major concern, it is worth noting that *informal* institutions should also be taken into account. La Porta et al. (1997b) suggest that low levels of trust may condition the effectiveness of institutions. Actually, even if enforcement is generally considered as being closer to formal rather than to informal institutions, it is evident that the latter dimension is present in variables such as the rule of law, legality, judicial efficiency and so on, not to mention corruption. That is, enforcement depends on both how the formal mechanisms (the judicial system, existence of the so-called 'checks and balances' and control on government action) are designed and societal elements such as the level of trust or individualism (that is, how economic agents behave within the system). These elements have been used by Guiso et al. (2001), Calderón et al. (2002) and Garretsen et al. (2003) to produce interesting results in the explanation of financial and economic performance. Nevertheless, their analysis is relevent to us because it provides additional evidence on the role played by formal institutions after controlling for the quality of informal institutions.

In contrast to cross-country methodology, micro-level approaches do not offer a direct connection between a specific institution or law and its impact on financial and economic development. After a law has been changed or replaced by a new one, policy makers may observe how economic agents (firms or individuals) react to the reform, but they seldom have a clear indication of its final, net, impact at the macro level. Furthermore, an analysis at the micro level is always constrained to one particular institutional environment, which is country specific. Comparative law has traditionally orientated legislators to the different possibilities at hand, but no connection to economic growth is found either. While Azfar and Matheson (2003) suggest that a combination of impact analysis of commercial law reform in individual countries and rich historical investigation may produce interesting hints, we cannot reject the possibility that further improvements are to come from cross-country studies.

Our survey focuses on financial laws and enforcement mechanisms ('market augmenting government', in Azfar and Matheson's (2003) terminology) that influence: (a) the development of financial markets, and (b) economic growth.[2] As to the development of financial markets, our aim is to go beyond the traditional bank- versus market-based debate, finding it useful to provide an extensive view on how legal institutions affect more specific measures such as the number of initial public offerings (IPOs), firms' ownership concentration, the number of bankruptcies resolved judicially and so on. With regard to economic growth, the studies reviewed belong to the law and finance view, where the role of the legal system in promoting growth is highlighted. These authors tend to support the view that it is more useful to focus on the elements that define financial contracts (laws and enforcement mechanisms) rather than distinguishing countries as bank or market based.[3]

The studies surveyed here use the cross-country analysis method and are concerned with the role that institutions play in the development of financial markets and the economy. An increasing number of relevant papers also contrast the influence of legal institutional variables at the microeconomic level (La Porta et al. 2000b, 2002; Dyck and Zingales 2004; Himmelberg et al. 2002; Utrero 2002; Esty and Megginson 2003, among others); however, even if many of these studies provide international data, for comparison purposes and space, they have not been included in this survey: our focus is on results obtained with countries as units of analysis.

At this point, our aim is to answer questions such as: where in the finance literature have La Porta et al.'s variables (and other derived measures) been used? Under what theoretical backgrounds have they been introduced in the models? Do the different studies generally present consistent results (signs, significance and so on)? Are the results sensitive to model specification?

Section 2 is methodological. We present the variables which have been used in the models, and show that some definition and interpretation problems have motivated further refinements. In Section 3, we discuss the hypotheses behind the models and analyse the coherence of the empirical results. Section 4 concludes.

2 DEFINITION AND BACKGROUND TO THE VARIABLES USED IN THE MODELS

In this section, three types of variables will be considered: measures of economic development; financial markets indices; and legal rules and enforcement institutions that protect investors. This classification is behind the tables included in the appendix, through which we can appreciate the studies in which they appear, whether as dependent or explanatory variables. As we shall see in Section 3, type 3 variables are used as instruments for type 2 in explaining the variance of economic growth (type 1). Studies concerned only with financial markets regress type 2 on type 3 variables.

2.1 Economic Development

Type 1 variables are used to capture the 'real' consequences of financial markets and institutions. Per capita GDP growth is generally used to measure economic development. Researchers are interested in measuring how fast countries have grown in the last one or two decades, so series of data of these periods are averaged producing one observation per country, which is easily calculated and used for comparisons.

Additionally, it is worth noting that other measures can be used to contrast the robustness of the results obtained with per capita GDP growth. To this end, Levine's (1998) paper includes per capita capital stock growth (that is, capital accumulation) and productivity growth, which act as channels of influence on economic development.

2.2 Financial Markets Indices

Type 2 variables characterize financial markets, their size, level of activity, complexity and so on. The size of equity and debt markets are the most used among them. Aggregate data are used due to the difficulty of having access to direct measures of external financing for smaller companies.

Other variables, such as IPOs and venture capital, indicate the availability and degree of sophistication that firms face in looking for sources of finance. Some measures respond to specific research interests (for instance, the use of courts for resolving financial distress).

Credit

A credit market should be evaluated for its ability to identify and fund profitable investment projects, to efficiently supervise resource management, to minimize transaction costs and so on. However, as pointed out by Levine (1999, p. 11), if finding evidence on these aspects for one country is difficult, doing it for a broad cross-section of countries is virtually impossible. La Porta et al. (1997a, pp. 1135–6) use data on the total bank debt of the private sector and on the total face value of corporate bonds. Data on debt used by small companies are not available, which eliminates the possibility of identifying where financial resources are allocated. However the authors believe that looking at the whole private sector rather than firms may be an advantage, since frequently in many countries entrepreneurial projects are financed on personal accounts.

Borrowing from King and Levine (1993b), methodological improvement is observed in Levine (1998, 1999). Levine uses several measures of banking development: (i) the value of loans made by commercial banks and other deposit-taking banks to the private sector divided by GDP; this variable allows the isolation of credit issued by banks to the private sector, as opposed to credit issued to governments or public enterprises; it captures the level of financial intermediary development (Levine 1998); (ii) credit allocated to the private sector divided by GDP, now including credit initiatives and government subsidy programmes; (iii) ratio of credit allocated to the private sector to total domestic credit (excluding credit to banks); (iv) liquid liabilities of the financial system (currency demand and interest-bearing liabilities of banks and nonbank financial intermediaries);[4] (v) ratio of bank credit divided by bank credit plus central bank domestic assets, which captures the ability of banks to provide finance.[5] Variables (ii) to (iv) are used in Levine (1999). On the other hand, the paper by Levine et al. (2000) uses similar variables, and provides a measurement improvement in that nominal financial intermediary assets and liabilities are accurately deflated, to deal with possible distortion caused by high inflationary environments. See Table 7A.1 for a detailed description and sources of the specific measures used in the reviewed studies.

Equity

A common measure for the size of secondary markets and for equity finance (see Table 7A.2) is the ratio of stock-market capitalization to GNP: that is, the value of listed domestic shares on domestic exchanges divided by GNP. Levine (2003a) points out that 'although large markets do not necessarily function well, and taxes may distort incentives to list on the exchange, many observers use Capitalisation as an indicator of market development' (p. 56).

La Porta et al. (1997a) scale this variable by a measure of the fraction of the stock market held by outside investors. They estimated the average equity held by insiders (three largest shareholders) in each country's ten largest publicly traded non-state firms. The authors acknowledge that it is an imperfect measure, since only the ten largest firms are considered, and since they do not take account of cross-holdings, which result in overestimating the share of equity held by true outsiders. Nevertheless, in spite of all the roughness, La Porta et al. conceptually prefer this procedure to looking at the uncorrected ratio of market capitalization to GNP. Other authors (see Beck et al. 2003b, footnote 10) point out that making this adjustment reduces substantially their data set, which is why they report results using the standard unadjusted indicator. In Table 7A.2, a detailed description of the specific measures used by several authors is included.

Market-mobilized capital

Consistent with Modigliani and Miller's (1958) financial structure irrelevance theorem, Azfar and Matheson (2003) introduce the concept of *market-mobilized capital* (that is, the level of capital mobilized by market mechanisms) which is calculated by adding the levels of debt (stock of credit by commercial and deposit-taking banks to the private sector divided by GDP) to equity (average value of listed domestic shares on domestic exchanges in a year divided by GDP that year).[6] The reason for aggregating debt and equity is that they feel that the distinction between capital that is allocated via the market and capital that is allocated by non-market means is more important for economic growth than the distinction between debt and equity: debt and equity both perform essentially similar functions by channelling finance to projects.

Other financial system measures

Table 7A.4 presents other variables that complement the size of equity and debt in shaping the characteristics of the financial system. Variables that reflect credit system characteristics are: financial system and intermediaries' liquid liabilities and assets (Levine 1999; Levine et al. 2000; Calderón et al. 2002), government ownership of banks (La Porta, Lopez-de-Silanes and Shleifer 2002), the number of bankruptcies to total number of firms (Claessens et al. 2003; Claessens and Klapper 2002: economic agents rely on judicial institutions when the judiciary is trusted); venture capital to GDP (Allen and Song 2002: it is a major source of external capital for high-technology firms); and the existence of public credit register (Jappelli and Pagano 2002: governments promote information sharing to reduce adverse selection and moral hazard problems).

As to the equity market, La Porta et al. (1997a) introduce the number of IPOs relative to the population (between mid-1995 and mid-1996). This variable, together with the number of listed domestic firms in each country relative to its population, reflect both the flow and stock of companies obtaining equity finance externally. La Porta et al. (1997a, pp. 1132–4) justify their interest on the recent accelerated development of financial markets and on the excessive dominance that large firms have in the values of equity and debt markets.

On the other hand, Levine (2003a) uses two measures of stock market liquidity: (i) *value traded* (total value of the trades of domestic stock on domestic stock exchanges divided by GDP) and (ii) *turnover* (value of domestic shares traded on domestic exchanges divided by the value of listed shares). While value traded captures trading relative to the size of the economy, turnover measures trading relative to the size of the market (Levine 2003a, p. 56). The easier it is to trade, it is argued, the larger are the values of both market liquidity measures. Change in stock market value during the Asian crisis is also analysed (Johnson et al. 2000; investors adjust their decisions to the quality of the institutions).

In another paper, La Porta et al. (1998) explore the reasons behind the differences in ownership concentration in the largest firms across different countries. *Ceteris paribus*, the higher the concentration, the easier it will be for owners to control and supervise management. Then, strong antidirector protection guarantees that dispersed ownership will not suffer from high agency costs. Closely related to that variable is ownership separation, which is an index produced by La Porta et al. (1999) which calculates how many of the twenty firms with just above $500 million in rich countries do not have a stockholder owning 20 per cent or more of the firm's stock.

Also related to ownership, Nenova (2003) measures the lower bound of private benefits of control through the value of control-block votes, that is, the value of all votes comprising 50 per cent of corporate voting power. This value is expected to increase with the possibility of expropriation by insiders so that the private benefits of control become a substantial share of the firm's value (also see La Porta et al. 2000a, p. 27).

Finally, Leuz et al. (2003) consider earnings management as a key variable in characterizing a country's financial system. In particular, they analyse the use of earnings management by insiders as a tool to protect their private control benefits: insiders may conceal their private control benefits by managing the level and variability of reported earnings, reducing the likelihood of outside intervention. Variability management, commonly known as income smoothing, is measured by relating the behaviour (that is, changes and standard deviation) of earnings to that of cash flows from operations. The magnitude of accruals (the accounting component of earnings) and the avoidance of small losses, constitute additional indices of earnings management. After computing country medians, all these measures are merged into an aggregate earnings management variable.

2.3 Legal Rules and Enforcement Mechanisms

Type 3 variables cover the differences across legal regimes and enforcement mechanisms. La Porta et al. (1997a) were the first to construct variables that capture 'the legal rights that shareholders and creditors have that enable them to extract a return on their investment from insiders' (p. 1136). Interestingly, Levine (2003a, p. 72) points out that shareholder rights are not highly correlated with banking sector development nor are the legal rights of creditors highly correlated with stock market development. The evidence suggests that they are not proxying for overall legal efficiency; rather, each group of rights capture particular aspects of the legal environment.

Creditor protection
La Porta et al. cover creditors' rights (basically, secured creditors rights) in liquidation and reorganization procedures. Four binary variables are aggregated and contribute to an index which ranges from 0 to 4: restrictions on the managers' ability to file for reorganization (such as creditors' consent or minimum dividends requirement); whether management stays or not in reorganization (which affects who keeps control on firms' assets); lack of automatic stay on assets (secured creditors' ability to gain possession of their security); and absolute priority for secured creditors (secured creditors are ranked first in the distribution of the proceeds).

In order to adapt the La Porta et al. approach to transition economies, Pistor et al. (2000, p. 10) reformulate creditor protection variables by creating alternative aggregate measures which are concerned with the functioning of the credit market. First, in transition economies bankruptcy procedures lack clear separation of liquidation and reorganization procedures similar to the US model; consequently, creditor consent for going into reorganization as opposed to liquidation cannot be considered for this type of country. Second, in transition economies it is pertinent to know whether there is the possibility of: using land as collateral; creating securities on movable assets without transference of the asset; and having access to registered information about the existence of security interests in an asset possessed by the debtor. Third, the fact that creditors may hold management liable for violating bankruptcy rules, or that they may challenge the validity of pre-bankruptcy transactions between the debtor and other parties is also considered.

Shareholder protection
In La Porta et al.'s work, shareholder protection generally refers to minority owners putting representatives on boards of directors and the possibility of making claims against the corporation. They construct binary variables for each specific aspect of minority shareholder protection, so that they can be aggregated as a more general index. This ranges from 0 to 5 and includes: the ability to vote by proxy; whether control of shares is retained during the shareholders' meeting (if shareholders are required to deposit their shares practices such as selling shares for a number of days are then prevented, and costs of voting increase); the possibility of cumulative voting for directors (which makes it easier for minority shareholders to be represented); whether the minimum percentage of share capital required allows minority shareholders to call an extraordinary shareholder meeting; and allowing oppressed minority shareholders to make legal claims against the directors.

La Porta et al. also use another shareholder rights variable: the requirement that each ordinary share carry only one vote; in fact, minority rights are reduced with multiple voting and when some groups of ordinary shares owners are not entitled to vote.

Interestingly, Pistor (2000) and Pistor et al. (2000, p. 7) warn that corporate law not only aims at protecting minority shareholders; other groups may also be given preference, and the differences observed in shareholder protection in different systems may be functional substitutes (Coffee 1999; La Porta et al. 1999). Indeed, Pistor et al. reformulate shareholders' rights by also including the more general manager and shareholders' agency problem, in spite of focusing only on the shareholders' coordination problem (conflict between large and small investors). Aspects such as voting or internal information can be used to control management decisions (voice mechanisms), and how easy it is for shareholders to leave the corporation (exit mechanisms) are considered in the agency context. These authors agree, however, that in countries with highly concentrated ownership the real conflict is between minority shareholders and block holders.[7] In addition, a stock market integrity index is also created.[8] Unfortunately, since Pistor et al.'s efforts focus on one type of economy, it is not possible to use their variables in a wider context.

As a complement to La Porta et al. investor protection variables, Nenova (2003) constructs two variables which capture take-over law characteristics and corporate charter provisions respectively. Take-over regulation results from considering whether a control contestant is required to offer all classes the same tender price or not, if the law requires the buyer of a large or majority block to pay minority shareholders the same price as for the block shares by share class; and the level at which a dominant vote-owner is legally required to make an open market bid for all shares. Charter provisions include all those aspects that concentrate power in the hands of dominant shareholders: among them, special decision making in the hands of dominant shareholders (golden shares) and provisions that make it costly for outsiders to purchase large stakes (poison pills).

Accounting regulation
As an additional legal measure of investor and creditor protection, La Porta et al. (1998) use an index of the quality of accounting information constructed by the Center for International Financial Analysis and Research, which is based on the inclusion or omission of 90 items in companies' reports. The availability of useful information allows better investment analysis (facilitating better comparisons) and better control by creditors and investors of insiders, thus reducing agency costs. When financial reports are reliable, creditors include covenants based on accounting measures, acting as an additional guarantee that financing contracts will be fulfilled. In contrast, Leuz et al. (2003) suggest that this variable cannot be treated as exogenous, since the quality of disclosure might be a consequence of investor protection laws: strong protection laws discourage insiders from concealing firm performance from outside investors. In fact, as has been discussed in Section 2.2, accounting quality (earnings management) is an endogenous variable reflecting a characteristic of the financial system. Analysing accounting regulation on accruals might be a better approach: actually, Leuz et al. include an index constructed by Hung (2001) as a control variable which proxies for the extent to which accounting rules limit accrual accounting and is orientated towards producing informative reports.

Legal origin
Methodologically, the fact that many laws and codes result from historical external influence is interesting because it allows them to be treated as exogenous, and to be used as instruments for financial markets in the equations in which economic development is explained. Based on Reynolds and Flores (1996), La Porta et al. (1998) find that legal rules protecting investors and its enforcement by the judiciary vary systematically by legal origin (English, French, German or Scandinavian). As the authors point out, 'English law is common law, made by judges and subsequently incorporated into legislation. French, German, and Scandinavian laws, in contrast, are part of the scholar and legislator-made civil law tradition, which dates back

to Roman law' (La Porta et al. 1997; p. 1131). With regard to protection against expropriation by insiders,

> [C]ommon law countries protect both shareholders and creditors the most, French civil law countries the least, the German civil law and Scandinavian civil law countries somewhere in the middle . . . richer countries enforce laws better than poorer countries, but, controlling for per capita income, French civil law countries have the lowest quality of law enforcement as well. (La Porta et al. 1997a, p. 1132)

On the other hand, Beck et al. (2001a), after controlling for several variables (GDP per capita, endowment indicators such as climate and latitude), confirm that British legal origin countries have better outsider rights (where 'outsider' refers to both minority shareholder and creditor rights), and better accounting standards, and French the worst. German origin, however, tends to have stronger contract enforcement than British or French legal origin countries.

Other regulations
Another legal-based variable is used by Roe (2003), who turns to labour market characteristics and looks for a variable that measures employee protection. It is an OECD index which measures how easy it is to fire an employee in OECD countries, showing that the least protected employees are those in the United States, while continental European countries' legislation tends to provide the strongest protection. Roe argues that this variable parallels the common law/civil law divide yet provides a more valid historical explanation. On the other hand, based on Holmes et al. (1997), regulation on opening and keeping open a business and banking regulation can also be found in La Porta, Lopez-de-Silanes and Shleifer (2002).

Enforcement and the judicial system
La Porta et al. use several survey-based indices scaled from 0 to 10 as measures of the quality with which laws are enforced: rule of law, corruption, risk of expropriation and repudiation of contracts by government. They are obtained from the *International Country Risk Guide*.[9] The most widely used estimate in the literature is 'rule of law', which captures investors' assessment of law and order. La Porta et al. also consider an efficiency of the judiciary index, which is taken from the Business International Corporation. La Porta et al. (1999) and La Porta, Lopez-de-Silanes and Shleifer (2002) add another variable to the list: a property rights index of the degree to which a government protects and enforces laws that protect private property, as assessed by Freedom in the World (1996).[10] Table 7A.5 shows that alternative measures are used by other authors. Levine (1998) averages La Porta et

al.'s rule of law and a measure of the risk that a government modifies a contract after it has been signed. As Pistor et al. (2000) point out, the credibility of the commitment by the state that private rights will be enforced ('Legality') is crucial in transition economies. Among other indices, they use the Central European Economic Review index for the risk of government expropriation, which is higher in the absence of effective legal institutions. In the context of international portfolio investments, enforcement of insider trading laws (as reported by Bhattacharya and Daouk 2002) is considered as an explanatory variable by Dahlquist et al. (2003).

Closely connected with enforcement is the independence of the judiciary relative to the state, which has been measured by La Porta, Lopez-de-Silanes, Pop-Eleches, and Shleifer (2002) through: (i) *tenure of Supreme Court judges*, which takes the value of one if tenure is between six years and lifelong and zero otherwise; (ii) *Supreme Court power*, which equals one if Supreme Court judges have lifelong tenure *and* have power over administrative cases (taking the value of zero otherwise). According to the political channel theory (see Beck et al. 2003a), the independence of judges is one of the paths through which legal origin contributes to financial development. Judicial system independence guarantees that higher priority will be attached to protecting the rights of private investors *vis-à-vis* the state, which in turn should contribute to financial development.

As to the reasons why legal origin may have an effect on laws and contract enforcement, one that is frequently mentioned is that in common law countries judicial decisions are a source of law: this circumstance is captured in *case law*, a variable created by La Porta, Lopez-de-Silanes, Pop-Eleches, and Shleifer (2002). Since it may affect the ability to adapt laws to the changing financial and economic conditions, Beck et al. (2003a) analyse its effect on financial development. Similarly, they also profit from a variable which appears in Djankov et al. (2003): *legal justification*, which (based on a survey distributed to law firms in 109 countries) indicates whether judgments have been based on statutory law rather than on principles of equity. Attaching to statutory law is hypothesized to constrain judges' ability to efficiently adapt incomplete contracts to the economic environment.

2.4 Discussion: Methodological Issues

We have seen that, after the first La Porta et al. papers appeared, their variables have been the subject of refinements by other authors. Further discussion includes the meaning of some measures, the loss of information caused by simple aggregation of binary variables to construct general indices, and some improvements that may come from interacting commercial laws and enforcement variables.

Legal origin, laws and endogeneity

Investors and creditor protection are presumably influenced by the rate and degree of development of the financial system: the larger the size and complexity of banking and equity markets, the higher the pressure to reform and change laws. A similar argument holds for enforcement mechanisms. Furthermore, the quality of laws and enforcement may be a consequence of economic development. Consequently, as a way of controlling for the simultaneity bias, legal origin variables have been treated as exogenous and used as instruments in models that explain financial development (Levine 1998, 1999; Levine et al. 2000) and economic growth (Levine 1999; Levine et al. 2000).[11] In Levine's studies, the validity of instrumental variables is tested through the overidentifying restrictions test (Hansen 1982). To be valid, it is necessary that instruments are uncorrelated with the error term: that is, legal origin dummy variables may affect growth only through the financial development indicators and the variables in the conditioning information set (see Levine et al. 2000; Levine, 2003b). Levine (2002) devotes less attention to causality, convinced that it is more likely that the way laws are produced depends upon legal origin and not on development. Beck et al. (2003a) find that the legal origin influences financial development through the ability to adapt to the needs that arise with changing commercial circumstances and minimize the gap between the contracting needs of the economy and the legal system's capabilities. In other words, laws and enforcement are a consequence of the legal system adaptability which, in turn, is determined by legal origin (more static in the French tradition, compared with the British and German legal origins). If this adaptability hypothesis is right, then large gaps will appear between financial needs and the legal system's ability to support those needs. Roe (2003), however, has argued that the greater creditor and investor protection laws seen in common law jurisdictions have been the result of legislation rather than the adaptability of the common law.

Although La Porta et al. (1998) report the strong relation between legal origin and laws, legal origin has been found, however, to be an imperfect predictor of enforcement. Berkowitz et al. (2003) show that the 'transplant effect' (which captures the degree to which countries that received their legal order externally adapted successfully to it) is a better predictor of different measures of enforcement (efficiency of the judiciary, rule of law, corruption, risk of expropriation and risk of contract repudiation) than legal origin: countries that did not adapt to the external influence (that is, the legal order supplied did not match the demand by domestic users of the legal system) show worse contract enforcement. As far as we know, the transplant effect has not been used in models of financial development. Instead, and concerned with the endogeneity problems that the presence of 'origin' countries (that is, those where legal traditions originated) may cause, Beck et al. (2003a) test the validity of the results by reducing the sample through eliminating origin countries.

Background to legal protection
Some authors warn that we must be cautious about the meaning of the protection that commercial laws afford. For instance, Azfar et al. (1999, p. 15) take the variable 'one share–one vote' as an example:

> This variable takes the value 1 if the law requires (rather than allows) that the votes of all shareholders carry an equal weight per share. Almost all countries *allow* that shareholders have equal rights. Why would *requiring* such a law have significant effect on shareholder values? After all if firms found it easier to raise capital by reassuring shareholders that each share would carry an equal weight they could write it into their corporate charter.

Creditor variables may also be subject to criticism, as only *secured* creditors are considered. In countries where a judicial reorganization procedure exists (for example, in the US), it is true that secured creditors may receive less than their face value if managers retain control (see Warner 1977 and Eberhart et al. 1990). However, ordinary creditors may also expect to receive more if the firm survives compared to liquidation.

On the other hand, using aggregate indices means imposing the equality of their coefficients in regressions, a hypothesis which is seldom tested (Stephen and van Hemmen 2003). Conceptually, hidden aspects may result from composite indices and, although using too many binary variables would cause multicollinearity, clearer results may emerge.

Interaction of commercial laws and enforcement
A number of recent papers pay more specific attention to the relationship between legal rules and their enforcement, which results in using interaction variables in econometric tests. One reason for doing so is to check whether there might be a distinctive impact of laws depending on the degree with which they are enforced (Stephen and van Hemmen 2003). If certain laws are found to be important for financial and economic development, policy makers should make sure that these rules will be enforced. If laws are only effective in countries with very high levels of enforcement, then it would be worthless to introduce them in low-enforcement countries. The evidence suggests that such low-enforcement countries are developing countries. Claessens et al. (2003) interact the efficiency of the judiciary system and an index of creditor rights. They suggest that effective contractability strengthened with credible threat of bankruptcy enforcement increases the likelihood of bankruptcy. On the other hand, Rossi and Volpin (2001, p. 9)

follow Johnson et al. (2000) and define Shareholder Protection as the product of Antidirector Rights and Rule of Law [both of them constructed following La Porta et al. 1998], normalised to ten. Shareholder Protection measures the rights that minority shareholders effectively hold after controlling for their enforcement by the legal system. In countries with lower shareholder protection, minority shareholders are expropriated more. Hence Shareholder Protection is a proxy for the quality of the corporate governance.

With regard to creditors,

> Similarly, we define as Creditor Protection the product between Creditor Rights and Rule of Law [again, taken from La Porta et al. 1998], divided by 10. Creditor Protection measures the rights that creditors effectively hold in a bankruptcy procedure. We interpret this variable as a proxy for the ease of access to credit markets.

In their study of the impact of the 1990s' Asian financial crisis on 25 emerging markets, Johnson et al. (2000, 172–77) argue:

> We look at each measure [that is, La Porta et al.'s 'anti-director' and 'creditor' rights] in turn and also evaluate the product of these rights and three measures of contract enforceability. Rights on paper are good, but we are particularly interested in evaluating the implications of how these rights are enforced. We use a very simple measure, the product of legal *de jure* rights and the enforceability of these rights. Because it is hard to know exactly how rights are enforced we use the three indices of general legal environment used in the previous section: judicial efficiency, corruption, and the rule of law [taken from La Porta et al. 1998]. This enables us to check for a robust pattern in the data.

Finally, Stephen and van Hemmen (2003) separate countries into those where enforcement is high (with the measure constructed by Levine 1998, higher than 8.00), those where it is moderate (between 6.00 and 8.00) and those where it is low (below 6.00). Thus three dummy variables are created for these levels of enforcement, which are then interacted with each legal rule variable.

3 HYPOTHESIS, ECONOMETRIC TESTS AND GENERALITY OF THE RESULTS

This section is organized following the general framework that is behind legal–financial theories of growth: legal and enforcement institutions determine the differences in financial markets across countries (3.1) and financial markets influence economic development (3.2).

3.1 Legal and Enforcement Institutions and Financial Markets

The legal institutions that regulate debt markets have been described as being different from those that protect small investors (La Porta et al. 1998). In turn, laws that regulate debt markets differ across countries: for example, there are markets where creditors take over insolvent firms' management once a bankruptcy procedure is filed for (UK), and markets where management stays and controls the procedure. Similar variance is found in external equity institutions. Furthermore, the size and quality of these two components of external finance, it is argued, is determined by the characteristics of these distinctive legal institutions.

Size of credit market and legal rules

Do legal rules have any effect on the banking sector development? If banks act in a legal environment that protects their funding to investment projects, a lower financial cost will be offered to entrepreneurs, who in turn will tend to assume more debt. The literature has tested empirically whether giving the highest priority to credit recovery helps develop credit markets. Table 7A.1 shows that the evidence on the impact of legal rules as determinants of the size of credit markets is somewhat mixed: when the La Porta et al. aggregated index is used, only Jappelli and Pagano (2002) find a positive coefficient at below 5 per cent significance, while in La Porta et al. (1997a), and Garretsen et al. (2003) apparently the size of external debt is not influenced by creditor protection. A slightly different definition of the creditors' protection variable in Azfar and Matheson (2003) and Levine (1998) produces a positive and significant relationship at the 5 per cent level.[12] In another paper, Levine (1999) finds that the exogenous component of creditor rights, enforcement and accounting standards are also significant (and with the predicted signs), which suggests that the relationship with financial development is not dominated by any endogeneity bias. On the other hand, the above described, Pistor et al. (2000) creditor variables do not show any significance for transition economies. Finally, Azfar and Matheson (2003) decompose the La Porta et al. index but no component seems to have any individual effect. Stephen and van Hemmen (2003) decompose the creditor index but find that only secured lender protection has any effect and then only in a limited context (see further below).

Ergungor (2004) also finds that creditor rights affect positively the size of credit markets. However, he additionally separates the countries into two subsamples by legal tradition, allowing for the possibility that each tradition corresponds to a separate economic environment where laws play different roles. Laws that protect creditors are found to have a greater impact on the size of credit markets in common law countries than in civil law countries, where no effect is observed. Presumably, common law countries benefit more from detailed creditor protection in comparison to civil law countries because courts in the former will be able to use that regulation to deal with debtors' moral hazard behaviour once they are produced. This connects with the question of whether differences in banking development can be traced back to the legal origin of the country. La Porta et al.'s (1997a) descriptive analysis shows that French legal origin countries have lower ratio of debt to GDP (that is, 0.45) in comparison to common law countries (0.68), whereas German origin show the highest figure (0.97).[13] Thus the authors hypothesize that legal origin accounts for some of the variance observed in credit markets: when other variables are controlled for, French and Scandinavian legal origin affects levels of credit negatively. Jappelli and Pagano (2002) show similar results. Levine (1998) finds that countries with the German legal system have better developed banks, even after controlling for the level of economic development. French tradition is also found to be negatively related with credit market size in an extensive econometric exercise performed by Beck et al. (2003a,b), where political structure and other endowments (settler mortality by colonizers, latitude) are controlled for.

The legal system is important for banking development, although Ergungor's (2004) suggestion that what matters is not how these traditions produce laws but how laws are applied by courts connects with the law and finance 'adaptability' hypothesis. We return to this issue below.

Although many studies show that laws protecting secured creditors' contribute to explaining cross-country variance in the credit market size: (a) this evidence depends on how the model is specified; (b) the fact that mainly aggregate measures have explanatory power, does not help in understanding which particular aspects are important for fostering credit; and (c) the impact of creditor protection laws may depend on legal tradition, when connected to interpretative powers of the judges.

Size of equity market and legal rules

A major motivation in La Porta et al. (1997a) is finding why countries like France and Germany have much smaller equity markets than the United States and the United Kingdom. They suggest that one of the causes can be found in the differences in shareholders' legal protection: the willingness of an entrepreneur to sell his/her equity depends on the terms at which he/she can find a good valuation relative to the underlying cash flows. This valuation increases if small investors are well protected.

This concern especially affects countries like the Latin American ones, where weaker legal codes (in terms of the protection of minority shareholders) are observed (Levine 2003a). Therefore, as shown in Table 7A.2, small investors' protection is included in models where the size of equity markets in different developed and developing countries is explained. The results obtained by La Porta et al. (1997a), Azfar and Matheson (2003), Garretsen et al. (2003), Levine (2003a) and Ergungor (2004) and support the idea that overall market size (whether it is scaled by the fraction of shares held by outside investors or not) is strongly and positively connected to shareholder rights when they are aggregated in a synthetic index.[14] Furthermore, some individual binary variables which capture specific aspects such as 'one share – one vote' (La Porta et al. 1997a; Azfar and Matheson 2003) and 'oppressed minority' show a positive and significant effect. However, when the variables are defined differently (see Subsection 2.3, above) and the analysis is focused on transition economies, no effect is found (Pistor et al. 2000). Stephen and van Hemmen (2003) show that while it is valid to aggregate La Porta et al.'s investor protection variables, it is only so where legal rules are at least moderately enforced.

On the other hand, Levine (2003a) includes a variable that is not strictly legal:[15] the quality of accounting. Countries where companies tend to publish higher-quality and more comprehensive financial statements have larger capital markets.

With regard to legal origin, it is shown that belonging to the French legal family has a negative impact on the size of stock markets (La Porta et al. 1997a; Beck et al. 2003a,b).

Market mobilized capital and legal rules

As a prior step to a more general model, we have seen (Tables 7A.1 and 7A.2) that Azfar and Matheson (2003) replicate La Porta et al. (1997a) by separating equity and debt equations. However, if the structure of corporate finance is irrelevant and the role that both sources of finance play in an economy is similar (that is, they act as substitute sources of finance), it might make sense to analyse how legal rules affect *market-mobilized capital* (MMC). When MMC is used as a dependent variable (see Table 7A.3), the model includes both types of laws. Both aggregate corporate and collateral law variables show significant and positive coefficients in explaining MMC. When decomposed, no specific creditor protection laws shows any effect. However, one share–one vote has a positive impact on MMC.

The implication of Stephen and van Hemmen (2003) is that this result arises from a mis-specification. However, these authors do find that it is MMC that influences growth not its individual components.

Other financial system variables and legal variables

As a consequence of the methodological innovation of the introduction of legal environment variables by La Porta et al. in cross-country analysis, other authors have included them in explaining specific dependent variables which capture different dimensions of the financial system (Table 7A.4). Among these variables, there is a group that belongs or presents closer connection to the credit market than to the equity market (Panel A), and vice versa (Panel B). Within these two groups, some variables have been interpreted as alternative measures of the size of the market (such as the number of listed firms to total population, in the case of equity market). Again, the effect of belonging to a particular legal tradition is also tested in many of these studies (Panel C).

Characteristics of the credit market and legal rules As an additional measure of the financial system size, we find liquid liabilities of the financial system. In Levine (1999) we find that only 'management stays in reorganisation' is negatively and strongly related to liquid liabilities; later, Levine et al. (2000) show that the aggregated creditors protection index (where 'management stays' enters negatively) has a positive effect on liquid liabilities. Government ownership of banks is also an important characteristic of the financial system. La Porta, Lopez-de-Silanes and Shleifer (2002a) show that government ownership of banks may cause both financial market and economic underdevelopment, which is consistent with the view that such ownership politicizes the resource allocation process and reduces efficiency. Among other factors, investor protection laws (minority shareholders and creditors protection index separately) are regressed on government ownership of banks: no effect is found, however. It is more business regulation (on opening and maintaining a business) and specific banking regulation which are significantly related to banks ownership. On the other hand, it is worth remarking that La Porta et al.'s creditor protection variables are concerned with how laws protect creditors when a bankruptcy procedure is initiated. This protection mainly addresses the problem of how creditors deal with *ex post* moral hazard in financial contracts.

Furthermore, La Porta et al. are especially sensitive to secured creditors' debt recovery through asset control and repossession. Claessens and Klapper (2002) suggest that these laws may contribute to explaining the rate of bankruptcies in an economy: if creditors feel protected by insolvency laws, their willingness to file for a bankruptcy procedure (in contrast to private renegotiation of contracts) increases. The authors, however, do not find any effect of the La Porta et al. aggregated protection index on the number of judicial bankruptcies.

On the other hand, Jappelli and Pagano (2002) analyse another dimension of the financial system: the amount of information that is available to creditors, which is of importance when dealing with *ex ante* adverse selection problems (that is, discriminating good and bad entrepreneurs). Some countries may need the government impulse to create a public credit register to foster information sharing and compensate for weak creditors' laws: reliable information may contribute to reducing the overall costs of insolvency if banks correctly discriminate potential debtors *ex ante*. Actually, as is shown by their empirical analysis, this is what happens: La Porta et al. creditors protection aggregated index is strongly and negatively related to the existence of a public information sharing mechanism. Public credit registers 'have been introduced to compensate, at least partly, for the weak protection that the state offered to creditors' interests, and thus to remedy heightened moral hazard in lending' (p. 2039).

Finally, Levine (1999) and Levine et al. (2000) complement the abovementioned financial development variables with liquid liabilities of the financial system, which is shown to be negatively related to the fact that management stays: financial intermediaries develop less if they cannot control the firm during the bankruptcy procedure.

Characteristics of the equity market and legal rules La Porta et al. (1997a) complement their study of the equity market with the analysis of two additional variables: number of IPOs to total population and number of domestic listed companies to total population. These variables complement market capitalization (value of equity) as additional measures for the degree with which firms have access to capital markets. The hypothesis is the following: the better the protection of investors, the easier it will be for firms to offer equity, and the broader the equity market. Regressions show a strong and positive relation between the aggregate creditor protection variable and primary market issues, a result that is also found in Levine (2003a). Again, one share–one vote is positive and significant in La Porta et al. (1997a) and the quality of accounting information is shown to positively influence the number of IPOs. As to the relative number of domestic listed companies in the economy, La Porta et al.'s aggregate index is found to be positive and statistically significant.

Another measure of size and breadth of the stock market is analysed by Levine (2003a): market liquidity. He raises the question of whether investor protection helps to increase activity and trade in stock markets, a question that is of particular interest for policy makers in developing countries. Multivariate analysis shows, however, that shareholder rights do not have a robust link with stock market liquidity as measured by a *turnover* index and the *value traded*. Only accounting transparency seems to positively influence these measures.

With regard to ownership concentration in the largest publicly traded non-financial domestic non-government firms, on the other hand, La Porta et al. (1998) expect a lower ownership concentration in countries with higher investor protection, where the risk of expropriation by insiders is reduced.

The authors suggest that heavily concentrated ownership may result from, and perhaps substitutes for, weak protection of investors in a corporate governance system; that is: (i) shareholders who monitor the managers might need to own more capital to exercise their control rights; and (ii) small investors might be willing to buy corporate shares only at such low prices that make it unattractive for corporations to issue new shares to the public, which would indirectly cause ownership concentration (La Porta et al. 1998, p. 1145). The evidence supports that view: the anti-director rights aggregate index shows a negative and strong relation with ownership concentration. However, different decomposed measures and, specifically, one share–one vote, do not seem to have any individual impact. Nor does the creditor protection index have any influence on ownership concentration. The regression shows, however, 'a large negative effect of the legal reserve requirement on ownership concentration' (ibid. p. 1150). Additionally, (ibid., p. 1150) test the possible impact of accounting quality, although no statistical effect is found. The authors warn that accounting standards might be endogenous:

> Countries that for some reason have heavily concentrated ownership and small stock markets might have little use for good accounting standards, and so fail to develop them. The causality in this case would go from ownership concentration to accounting standards rather than the other way around. Since we have no instruments that we believe determine accounting but not ownership concentration, we cannot reject this hypothesis.

Another dimension where ownership matters is the so-called private benefits of control: as Nenova (2003) suggests, the opportunity of expropriation by investors who own control-block votes decreases substantially in strong minority shareholder legal protection environments. Accordingly, control-block votes should be significantly less valuable given stricter legal environments. At the firm level (not reported in Table 7A.4) she finds that investor protection is negative and significantly related to control-block value. However, no significance is found at the cross-country level, when both takeover and charter provisions are controlled for. Particularly in cross-country regressions, charter provisions that concentrate less power in the hands of dominant shareholders show a strong negative relation with the lower bound of private benefits.

A consequence of limiting private benefits of control is that the incentives to manage earnings decrease. That is, insiders will not be interested in concealing the firm's performance from outsiders because there is little to conceal. Accordingly, Leuz et al. (2003) find a lower measure of earnings management in countries with stronger minority shareholder protection: insiders' incentives to manage earnings decrease with low private benefits. On the contrary, when there are large private benefits of control, accounting practices such as income smoothing, the use of discretionary accruals and small loss avoidance will be in place.

Private benefits of control produce another effect: as Dahlquist et al. (2003) point out, shares held by controlling investors cannot generally be bought by portfolio investors; since they are not interested in control, they are not willing to pay the premium that is associated with it. The authors examine the determinants of a country's portfolio share in the portfolio of stocks of US investors. They find that US investors do not invest less in a country with poor investor protection regulation. This result is perhaps explained by the fact that stock prices already take the risk of expropriation into account.

Roe (2003) shows that labour legislation might also contribute to explaining ownership characteristics. Focusing only on OECD countries, he finds that the degree of employee protection is a stronger predictor of La Porta et al. (1999) ownership separation index than the anti-director protection index: in countries where it is costly to fire employees (which proxies for the difficulties owners and managers will have in aligning their interests), owners prefer to hold larger stakes of the firm's stock.

On the other hand, different measures of shareholder protection are used in the analysis by Johnson et al. (2000) of the changes in stock market value in emerging markets during the Asian crisis: countries where investors are better protected should suffer relatively less from the loss of confidence which affected those markets and resulted in a fall of asset prices during and after the crisis. This fall is a consequence of the reassessment by outside investors of the probability of expropriation by managers. Their results partially confirm this hypothesis: La Porta et al.'s shareholder protection index shows no effect on the maintenance of stock market; however, an alternative measure of shareholder protection is found to positively affect this value.

Finally, Allen and Song (2002) provide evidence regarding the factors that have helped venture capital markets develop in different countries. Several reasons are argued to predict that corporate governance (that is, investor protection) is important in explaining venture capital development. Among them, it is argued that: (a) there is much more involvement of the providers of funds; (b) contractual complexity is higher in this type of financing; and (c) since IPOs are an important mechanism by which investors obtain their return, an active IPO market is needed to develop venture capital. All this suggests that strong investor protection should be positively related to the amount of venture capital. The results, however, contradict this hypothesis: the aggregated index of shareholder rights does not show any effect on this sophisticated form of finance. In contrast, the aggregated measure for creditor rights actually has a positive effect: the authors suggest that 'venture capital claims often more closely resemble creditor claims than equity claims. Therefore, creditor protection is more important for venture capital activities' (ibid., p. 15). However, no further explanation is given.

Characteristics of the financial markets and legal origin Panel C in Table 7A.4 shows the result of testing how legal tradition influences the characteristics of the financial system. The general picture seems to confirm that legal origin matters, and that civil law tradition (particularly French and German origin) accounts for the reduced complexity and sophistication in many countries' financial systems.

Calderón et al. (2002) observe that British legal origin results in smaller deposit money bank assets. Claessens and Klapper (2002) find that firms in French and German legal origin countries tend to avoid judicial procedures to renegotiate contracts in insolvency. Contrarily, Scandinavian countries rely more on the judiciary. French origin reduces banking activities efficiency, as measured in terms of net interest margin (Calderón et al. 2002). There is also a higher probability that governments in French and German tradition countries introduce a public credit register (Jappelli and Pagano 2002). La Porta et al. (1997a) confirm that French and German tradition is associated with narrower equity markets, as measured in terms of relative number of IPOs and listed companies. They also find that Scandinavian origin impacts negatively on the number of listed firms. French origin has a positive effect on firm ownership concentration (La Porta et al. 1998). German origin countries are found to have narrower venture capital markets (Allen and Song 2002). Finally, Beck et al. (2003a) show the effect of legal origin on other financial market indicators, such as liquid liabilities (larger in German origin countries, consistent with the presence of well-developed banks) and turnover (higher in common law countries).

Financial dependent variables, enforcement and the judicial system
Enforcement variables capture the degree with which contracts are respected, which increases external investors' and creditors' willingness to provide funds to entrepreneurs. To be effective, legal protection of creditor and investor rights must be accompanied by a system that guarantees enforcement. In many countries, improving enforcement involves reforming government, courts and financial regulating institutions. As Pistor et al. (2000) point out, the absence of developed financial markets in transition economies cannot be solved only with radical changes in the legal framework: a credible commitment by the state that private rights will be honoured and enforced is also needed. While La Porta et al. (1998) show that

effective law enforcement is not a substitute for poor laws on the books, Pistor et al. (2000) suggest that the reverse is also true: good laws cannot substitute for poor enforcement.

Table 7A.5 presents evidence on the role that different measures of enforcement and the judicial system play in developing financial markets. Almost all the studies show that enforcement significantly affects the characteristics of the financial system. Azfar and Matheson (2003) show that the capital which is mobilized by the market increases with enforcement. Other studies find that credit markets are larger in high enforcement environments. However, when common and civil law countries are separated, a different picture emerges: as shown by Ergungor (2004), enforcement appears to be important only in the latter; that is, only in bank-orientated financial systems does better enforcement produce higher incentives for banks to lend. When the sample is restricted to common law countries, the result might also be a consequence of less variance of enforcement levels within the countries belonging to that legal tradition. With regard to judicial system variables, Beck et al. (2003a) find that the exogenous component of case law and legal justification (defined in Subsection 2.3) are significantly correlated with the size of the credit market (with positive and negative signs, respectively). This evidence (which is obtained after controlling for the level of independence of the judicial system) supports the hypothesis that adaptability of the judicial system contributes to financial development, and confirms the indirect evidence found in an earlier work (see Beck et al. 2001a) supporting the 'dynamic' law and finance view.

When government ownership of banks is considered (which, in turn, is shown to negatively affect financial development and economic efficiency), property rights index and government repudiation of contracts index are found to be negatively associated with government participation (La Porta, Lopez-de-Silanes and Shleifer 2002): it is a consequence of poorly protected property rights and heavy government economic intervention that banks are also owned by the government. On the other hand, when contracts are better enforced, bank liquid liabilities tend to be larger, economic agents make relatively more use of courts in insolvency, the banking system is more efficient (measured in terms of net interest margin charged), and there is less perceived credit risk.

With regard to equity finance, when enforcement is high, capital markets tend to be larger (a result that also holds when the focus is put on transition economies). Again, Ergungor (2004) suggests that this is a differential characteristic of civil law countries, which probably shows that only in this group of countries is there enough variance to explain different levels of equity market development. In any case, higher enforcement is a characteristic of common law countries, where capital markets are more developed. It is precisely in common law countries where the judicial system shows more ability to adapt to changing financial and economic environment: adaptability is shown by Beck et al. (2003a) to increase the size of external equity. This result is obtained after the independence of the judicial system is controlled for.

On the other hand, high enforcement leads to more domestic firms listing on stock markets and offering their equity publicly, there are less incentives to manage earnings, merger and acquisition activity increases, and investors stay more confident that their funds will be returned (that is, there is less risk of insiders' expropriation) under macroeconomic financial shocks. Less expropriation risk, less corruption and effective enforcement of the insider trading laws is shown to increase the share of a foreign country portfolio in US investors' portfolio.

In contrast to these results, Allen and Song (2002) observe that venture capital financing develops more in low-enforcement countries. They suggest that venture capital differs from standard forms of financing in that there is much more involvement of providers of funds, implying that implicit relationships provide a good substitute for weak enforcement.

Finally, it is worth noting that, although mainly concerned with the impact of differences in social capital across Italian regions, Guiso et al. (2001) additionally present cross-country evidence in which enforcement (specifically, ICRG 'rule of law') and trust are included in regressions where several financial variables are explained: size of equity and debt markets, domestic listed firms, IPOs and proportion of publicly held companies. Enforcement was not significant in any of the regressions. It is plausible that this result may be driven by a possible correlation between enforcement and trust. Moreover, levels of enforcement may result from a combination of formal and informal mechanisms.

Financial markets and interaction variables
Table 7A.6 includes studies where the interaction of legal protection and enforcement is considered. The interactions capture the idea that legal effectiveness depends on the degree with which legal rules are enforced: high enforcement environments produce the results regulators expect; on the contrary, very little is achieved if institutions are weak. Rossi and Volpin (2001) show that the combination of rule of law and external finance protection increases the number of mergers and acquisitions (M&A). Interaction of minority shareholders' protection and rule of law fosters hostile takeover activity and cross-border M&A, and increases the takeover premium. Stephen and van Hemmen (2003) find that La Porta et al.'s shareholder protection variables only have an effect on stock market

capitalization when enforcement is at least moderate.[16] Similarly, these authors find that the size of the credit market is only affected by improving secured lenders' rights when enforcement is at least moderate.[17] However, they find that the size of the credit market responds positively to the degree of enforcement, independently of creditor protection rules. [18]

Working with a sample of mainly large firms in East Asia (Hong Kong, Indonesia, Japan, Korea, Malaysia, Philippines, Singapore, Taiwan and Thailand), Claessens et al. (2003) find that courts are more frequently used in insolvency if both laws and the judicial system protect creditors.[19] This result is not reported in Table 7A.6 because the model combines firm- and country-specific variables, and tables only include cross-country analysis. With the exception of Johnson et al. (2000), who do not find any interaction effect in explaining the loss of stock value during the Asian crisis, the studies show that formal mechanisms and institutions are more effective in countries where rule of law is high. Interestingly, Calderón et al. (2002) find that 'Rule of law * Trust' is negatively related to financial development (not reported in Table 7A.6). Although both rule of law and trust affect financial markets positively, the impact of trust (that is, informal institutions) is less important in high-enforcement countries, where the emphasis should be put on improving legal institutions.

3.2 Legal Institutions, Finance and Economic Growth

Although there are several empirical approaches to the role played by financial markets in fostering economic growth, our focus is limited to studies where this framework is tested at the cross-country level and whose concern is on the role played by financial laws and enforcement institutions.[20] Table 7A.7 reports 'law and finance' models where the existence of a causal link between finance and economic growth is tested. With regard to method, causality concerns have been addressed through instrumental variable regressions by using institutional variables as instruments for the size of financial markets; that is, by looking for variables which are connected with financial development, but are uncorrelated with economic growth beyond their link with financial development (Azfar and Matheson 2003; Levine 1998, 1999, 2002, 2003a).[21] Alternatively, these variables have been used to directly explain growth (Levine 1999, 2002). Also, a structural equations model has been tested in which legal rules and enforcement are modelled as the exogenous determinant of growth through the financial markets (Stephen and van Hemmen 2003).

In Levine (1998) (which deals with the importance of banks channelling funds to the productive sector) the component of banking development defined by creditor rights and enforcement is found to have a positive effect on different related economic development measures. Although with smaller coefficients, legal origin instruments produce similar results. On the other hand, Levine (2003a) finds the link of capital markets (value traded, capitalization and IPOs) and economic growth through the impact of accounting and minority shareholder rights.[22] Similar results are found when using legal origin as instruments: the exogenous component of equity that is explained by French legal origin shows a negative effect on growth.

In another paper, Levine (2002) jointly assesses the effect of both sources of external finance on growth. The author rejects the view that financial structure (that is, the relative weight of the banking and capital market) is relevant for economic growth, which leads him to perform similar tests to those in Levine (1998 and 2003), but now focusing on the overall size of the finance sector.[23] Concretely, three instrumental variables (shareholder protection, creditor protection and rule of law) are used to extract the component of overall financial development explained by legal environment (Levine 2002, p. 421). This component, it is shown, is strongly and positively linked to economic growth.

Azfar and Matheson (2003) show that an aggregate variable of both investor and creditor laws (that is, statutory external finance protection laws) together with enforcement have a significant and positive impact on per capita GDP growth through MMC. The right instrument here, Azfar and Matheson (2003) suggest, is commercial law, since enforcement may have an independent impact on growth (that is, an effect which is produced independently of financial markets).[24]

Stephen and van Hemmen (2003) find that bank credit and stock market capitalization are substitutes in the growth process. The model suggests that working through their effect on MMC, investor protection laws and giving priority to secured lenders have similar effects on growth. While Stephen and van Hemmen test the validity of the point made by Azfar and Matheson (2003) and Levine (2002), that debt and equity perform similar functions in the economic system (which supports aggregating bank and market development) and that what matters is the quality of legal and enforcement institutions, their model suggests instead that improving legal systems is only valid where laws are enforced at least moderately.[25]

Garretsen et al. (2003) show, however, that the effect of legal rules and enforcement may be conditioned by prevailing societal norms (which are measured through a factor that captures the joint contribution of the societal indicators obtained by Hofstede 1980). In particular, their results suggest that growth is not affected by the component of stock capitalization determined by formal and informal institutions, but that the exogenous part of bank credit actually is.

4 CONCLUSION

The literature on how legal rules protecting creditors and investors influence the size of an economy's financial markets which in turn influence economic development has been reviewed above. The studies discussed have used cross-country econometric analysis to test the influence of legal institutions protecting creditors and investors on the development of financial markets. Essentially we have dealt with studies in which the measures of creditor and investor protection first utilized by La Porta et al. (1997a, 1998) have been applied and further developed. After discussing the variables used by the various authors to measure (i) economic development, (ii) financial market development and (iii) legal rules and enforcement institutions, the results of econometric studies were discussed.

The legal institution rules which appear, typically, in this literature are those which it is argued protect creditors' (particularly secured creditors) and investors' (particularly minority shareholders) rights. Variables which are proxies for these rules appear individually or as cumulative indices as explanatory variables in regressions seeking to explain the size of credit markets and stock markets, respectively. Some of the studies in addition use measures of accounting standards. In many cases, measures of the efficiency of a country's legal system in enforcing legal rules are also used. In some studies these variables are seen as instruments to overcome the endogeneity of the financial market variables in explaining economic development. Legal origin variables have also been used to overcome problems of endogeneity. For some writers legal origin is seen as important as an explanatory variable in its own right.

However, others have cautioned against generalizing too much from the limited number of legal rule variables used in this literature. Those used deal almost exclusively with 'minimum requirements' of the law rather than those voluntarily adopted by companies to signal security to potential creditors or investors.

More recently there has been concern shown by a few authors that it is not 'laws on the books' or levels of enforcement that matter but the interaction between the two. It is a question of which laws *when enforced* encourage financial sector growth.

The results of a number of studies of the impact of legal rules and their enforcement on financial market development and economic growth are set out systematically in the appendix tables. The impact on both credit market and stock market size are discussed. Although a number of studies show that laws protecting secured creditors contribute to the explanation of cross-country variance in credit market size the result is sensitive to model specification. Furthermore, since it is mainly aggregated legal measures which appear significant it is not clear what the policy implications are. Finally the impact of these laws may be simply a result of legal origin. Further studies reported also find that stock market size is positively correlated with aggregate investor protection variables. However, some evidence suggests that this latter result may only be valid in certain legal environments.

Other studies reported in the tables find that measures of enforcement influence financial market development particularly for the credit market in civil law countries. However, studies which investigate the interaction of legal rules and levels of enforcement characteristics tend to show that at least a moderate level of enforcement is required for legal protection to have a positive effect on the size of financial markets.

Those studies which examine the impact of the financial sector on economic development tend to show a positive relationship. This indirectly reflects the influence of legal protection and enforcement variables on growth. However, one study suggests that since stock market and credit market growth are substitutes in the growth process, and the influence on each of the appropriate set of legal rules are also of the same magnitude, creditor and investor protection laws have a similar effect on growth. However, this result is only valid where the laws are at least moderately enforced.

Overall, the studies reviewed above suggest that there is a systematic relationship between the legal framework and the development of the financial sector. What remains contested is the nature of that relationship. This issue will only be resolved by further, careful, empirical research.

Weak institutions appear to cause less economic growth via the financial development channel. While the historically determined component of financial institutions has been isolated in the reviewed literature, crucial questions remain. The first one connects with the role of the IMF and World Bank: little is known as to whether these deep roots of development can successfully be changed through externally induced institutional reforms. Second, financial models (bank and market orientated) have been discussed in the past; now, *law and finance* theory and evidence suggests that emphasis should be put on the provision of sound regulations: methodological improvement is needed in order to show which specific laws have an impact on development. Third, if the effectiveness of laws depends on the degree of enforcement, more effort is needed to identify which formal (structure of the judicial system) and informal (levels of trust in the society) factors produce high enforcement.

Methodologically, since legal variables have been constructed for a limited number of countries (between 20 and 50), the evidence presented in this survey is largely provisional. Plausibly, the future will bring additional countries (transition economies, poorer countries) into the samples, which will offer the opportunity to check the robustness of the results.

APPENDIX 7A

Table 7A.1 *Dependent variable: size of credit market (normalized by GDP or GNP)*

Study[1]	Legal determinants	Sign (if significance is at least at 5%)
Panel A: Creditor protection laws		
La Porta et al. (1997a)	La Porta et al. creditors' protection *aggregated index*[2]	No effect[3]
Azfar and Matheson (2003)	COLLAW[4]	(+)
	La Porta et al. creditors' protection *decomposed variables*	No effect
Levine (1998)	COLLAW	(+)[5]
Levine (1999)	Automatic stay	(−)
	Management stays	(−)
	Secured creditors ranked first	(+)
	Accounting	(+)
Levine et al. (2000)	La Porta et al. creditors' protection *aggregated index*	(+)[6]
	Accounting	(+)
Pistor et al. (2000) (transition economies)[7]	Several creditor protection indices	No effect
Jappelli and Pagano (2002)	La Porta et al. creditors' protection *aggregated index*	(+)
Garretsen et al. (2003)	La Porta et al. creditors' protection *aggregated index*	No effect
Ergungor (2004)	COLLAW	(+)
Ergungor (2004) (only common law countries)	COLLAW	(+)
Ergungor (2004) (only civil law countries)	COLLAW	No effect
Panel B: Legal origin		
La Porta et al. (1997a)	(French, Scandinavian) legal origin	(−)
Levine (1998)	(German) legal origin	(+)
Jappelli and Pagano (2002)	(Scandinavian) legal origin	(−)

Table 7A.1 (continued)

Study[1]	Legal determinants	Sign (if significance is at least at 5%)
Calderón et al. (2002)	(French) legal origin	(−)
Beck et al. (2003a)	(French) legal origin	(−)
Beck et al. (2003b)	(French) legal origin	(−)

Notes
1. The dependent variable is defined in:
   - Levine (1998), Azfar and Matheson (2003), Garretsen et al. (2003): Credit by commercial and deposit-taking banks to private sector by GDP. Original source: IMF, *International Financial Statistics* (IFS). Secondary source: Levine and Zervos (1998); years 1976–93.
   - Ergungor (2004): Credit to the private sector by deposit money banks to GDP. Original source: *World Bank Financial Structure and Economic Development Database*. Secondary source: Levine et al. (2000); years 1960–95.
   - Jappelli and Pagano (2002): Bank claims on the private sector to GDP. Source: IFS; years 1994–95.
   - La Porta et al. (1997a), Pistor et al. (2000): Bank debt of private sector and outstanding non-financial bonds to GNP. Source: IMF, *World Bondmarket Factbook* (figure for year 1994) in La Porta et al.; *Business Environment and Enterprise Performance BEEPS survey* is also used in Pistor et al. (data for years 1997–98).
   - Calderón et al. (2002): Secondary source: Beck et al. (1999); years 1980–94.
   - Levine (1999): (i) credit allocated to the private sector divided by GDP, including credit initiatives and government subsidy programmes; (ii) ratio of credit allocated to the private sector to total domestic credit (excluding credit to banks); (iii) ratio of bank credit divided by bank credit plus central bank domestic assets; years 1960–89; see King and Levine (1993b) for original sources.
   - Levine et al. (2000): (i) Private credit (credit by deposit money banks and other financial institutions to the private sector divided by GDP, times 100); (ii) commercial–central bank (assets of deposit money banks divided by assets of deposit money banks plus central bank assets, times 100). Years: 1960–95. Original source: IFS.
   - Beck et al. (2003a,b): Credit by deposit money banks and other financial institutions to the private sector divided by GDP. Original sources: IFS and *World Development Indicators* (WDI); years 1990–95.
2. Index formed by variables referred to as Bankruptcy: Restrictions to reorganization + No automatic stay + Management does stay + Secured creditors paid first.
3. Significant at 10%.
4. COLLAW = Secured lenders paid first − Management stays − Automatic stay (is a La Porta et al.-based creditors' protection aggregated index).
5. Only Accounting is not significant with credit allocated to the private sector divided by GDP, including credit initiatives and government subsidy programmes. Results obtained using two-stage least squares, with legal origin dummy variables used as instruments.
6. Results are obtained by OLSs. When Income is controlled for, the regression shows no effect for creditors rights. Instrumental variables estimator using legal origin as instrument is also estimated; in this case, origin is taken as an instrument for LEGAL, which is the first standardized principal component of creditors' rights, enforcement and accounting. The exogenous component of LEGAL is positive and statistically significant.
7. Irrelevance of creditor rights is found on regressions on both market capitalization and external market capitalization (that is, correcting for ownership concentration).

Table 7A.2 *Dependent variable: size of capital market (normalized by GDP or GNP)*

Study[1]	Legal determinants	Sign (if significance is at least at 5%)
Panel A: Investor protection laws		
La Porta et al. (1997a)	Antidirector rights[2]	(+)
	One share–one vote	(+)
Azfar and Matheson (2003)	CORPLAW[3]	(+)
	La Porta et al. one share–one vote	(+)
	La Porta et al. oppressed minority	(+)
Pistor et al. (2000) (transition economies)	Several shareholder protection measures	No effect
Garretsen et al. (2003)	Shareholder rights[4]	(+)
Levine (2003a)	Antidirector rights	(+)
	Accounting[5]	(+)
Ergungor (2004)	Antidirector rights	(+)
Ergungor (2004) (only common law countries)	Antidirector rights	(+)
Ergungor (2004) (only civil law countries)	Antidirector rights	(+)
Panel B: Legal origin		
La Porta et al. (1997a)	(French, Scandinavian) legal origin	(−)
Beck et al. (2003a)	(French) legal origin	(−)
Beck et al. (2003b)	(French) legal origin	(−)

Notes
1. The dependent variable is defined in:
    - Levine (2003a), Garretsen et al. (2003), Pistor et al. (2000), Azfar and Matheson (2003): Value of listed domestic shares in domestic stock exchanges divided by GDP. Original source: IFC, *Emerging Markets Data Base* (electronic version) and IMF, *International Financial Statistics* (IFS). Secondary source: Levine and Zervos (1998).
    - Ergungor (2004): Value of listed shares divided by GDP. Original source: *World Bank Financial Structure and Economic Development Database*; years 1960–95.
    - La Porta et al. (1997a): Scaled by a measure of the fraction of the stock market held by outside investors. As a result the dependent variable is interpreted as the ratio of stock market capitalization held by minorities to gross national product (external capital). Original sources: Moody's International, CIFAR, EXTEL, Worldscope, 20-Fs, Price-Waterhouse, and various country sources; figure for year 1994.
    - Beck et al. (2003a,b): Value of outstanding shares divided by GDP. Original sources: IFS and World Bank International Finance Corporation; years 1990–95.
2. Formed by the following binary variables: Proxy vote allowed + No deposit of shares for shareholders' meeting + Cumulative voting allowed + Oppressed minorities mechanism + Percentage of shares for shareholders' meeting less than 10%.

Notes (continued)
3. It is a La Porta et al.-based capital investors protection aggregated index, CORPLAW = One share + Proxy + Legal recourse − Mandatory dividend.
4. Formed by the following binary variables: One share–one vote + No deposit of shares for shareholders' meeting + Cumulative voting allowed + Oppressed minorities mechanism + Preemptive rights to new issues + Percentage of shares for Shareholders' meeting less than 10%.
5. Comprehensiveness and quality of company reports as assessed by the Center for International Financial Analysis and Research.

Table 7A.3 Dependent variable: market mobilized capital (normalized by GDP or GNP)

Study	Legal determinants	Sign (if significance is at least at 5%)
Azfar and Matheson (2003)	COLLAW[1]	(+)
	Several La Porta et al.-based creditors' protection *decomposed variables*	No effect
	CORPLAW[2]	(+)
	La Porta et al. one share–one vote	(+)

Notes
1. A La Porta et al.-based creditors' protection aggregated index, COLLAW = Secured lenders − Management stays − Automatic stay.
2. A La Porta et al.-based capital investors protection aggregated index, CORPLAW = One share + Proxy + Legal recourse − Mandatory dividend.

Table 7A.4 Dependent variable: other financial system variables (explained by shareholder/creditor protection/legal origin)

Financial system dependent variable	Study	Legal determinants	Sign (if significance is at least at 5%)
Panel A: Characteristics of the credit market			
Liquid liabilities of the financial system[1]	Levine (1999)	Automatic stay	No effect
		Management stays	(−)
		Secured creditors ranked first	No effect
		Accounting	No effect
	Levine et al. (2000)	La Porta et al. creditors' protection *aggregated index*	(+)

Table 7A.4 (continued)

Financial system dependent variable	Study	Legal determinants	Sign (if significance is at least at 5%)
Government ownership of commercial banks[2]	La Porta Lopez and Shleifer (2002)	Accounting	No effect
		Business regulation index[3]	(−)
	La Porta Lopez and Shleifer (2002)	Government intervention in the banking sector[4]	(−)
	La Porta Lopez and Shleifer (2002)	Antidirector rights	No effect
	La Porta Lopez and Shleifer (2002)	Creditors' rights	No effect
Number of bankruptcies/ total number of firms	Claessens and Klapper (2002)	La Porta et al. creditors' protection *aggregated index*	No effect
Credit risk[5]	Jappelli and Pagano (2002)	La Porta et al. creditors' protection *aggregated index*	No effect
Existence of public credit register (Dummy)	Jappelli and Pagano (2002)	La Porta et al. creditors' protection *aggregated index*	(−)

Panel B: Characteristics of the equity market

IPOs/total population	La Porta et al. (1997a)	Antidirector rights	(+)
		One share–one vote	(+)
	Levine (2003a)	Antidirector rights	(+)
		Accounting	(+)
Number of domestic listed companies/ total population	La Porta et al. (1997a)	Antidirector rights	(+)
Turnover[6]	Levine (2003a)	Antidirector rights	No effect
		Accounting	(+)
Value traded[7]	Levine (2003a)	Antidirector rights	No effect
		Accounting	(+)

Table 7A.4 (continued)

Financial system dependent variable	Study	Legal determinants	Sign (if significance is at least at 5%)
Ownership concentration[8]	La Porta et al. (1998)	Antidirector rights	(−)
		One share–one vote	No effect
		Mandatory dividend	No effect[9]
		Creditor rights	No effect
		Legal reserve[10]	(−)
		Accounting[11]	No effect[12]
Ownership separation[13]	Roe (2003) (only OECD countries)	Antidirector rights	No effect
		Employee protection	(−)
Value of control-block votes to firm value	Nenova (2003)	Antidirector rights	No effect
		Takeover regulations[14]	No effect
		Charter provisions[15]	(−)
Aggregate earnings management measure[16]	Leuz et al. (2003)	Antidirector rights	(−)[17]
		Accrual rules	(−)[18]
Weight in US stock portfolio	Dahlquist et al. (2002)	Antidirector rights	No effect
Change in stock market value[19]	Johnson et al. (2000) (Emerging markets)	Corporate governance (Shareholder protection)[20]	(+)
Venture capital/ GDP	Allen and Song (2002) (Asian countries)	La Porta et al. creditors' protection *aggregated index*	(+)
New funds raised (total annual disbursements)[21]	Allen and Song (2002) (Asian countries)	La Porta et al. creditors' protection *aggregated index*	(+)
Panel C: Legal origin			
Bank liquid liabilities[22]	Calderón et al. (2002)	(French, British) legal origin	No effect
	Beck et al. (2000a)	(German) legal origin	(+)
Deposit money bank assets[22]	Calderón et al. (2002)	(British) legal origin	(−)

Table 7A.4 (continued)

Financial system dependent variable	Study	Legal determinants	Sign (if significance is at least at 5%)
Number of bankruptcies/ total number of firms	Claessens and Klapper (2002)	(French, German) legal origin (Scandinavian) legal origin	(−) (+)
Banks' overhead costs[22]	Calderón et al. (2002)	(French, British) legal origin	No effect
Banks' net interest margin[22]	Calderón et al. (2002)	(French) legal origin	(+)
Credit risk	Jappelli and Pagano (2002)	(German) legal origin	(−)
Existence of public credit register (Dummy)	Jappelli and Pagano (2002)	(French, German) legal origin	(+)
IPOs/total population	La Porta et al. (1997a)	(French, German) legal origin	(−)
Number of domestic listed companies/ total population	La Porta et al. (1997a)	(French, German, Scandinavian) legal origin	(−)
Turnover	Beck et al. (2000a)	(British) legal origin	(+)
Ownership concentration	La Porta et al. (1998)	(French) legal origin	(+)
Venture capital/ GDP	Allen and Song (2002) (Asian countries)	(German) legal origin	(−)
New funds raised (total annual disbursements)	Allen and Song (2002) (Asian countries)	(German) legal origin	(−)

Notes
1. Dependent variable: Currency plus demand and interest-bearing liabilities of banks and non-bank financial intermediaries divided by GDP. Results obtained using two-stage least squares, with legal origin dummy variables used as instruments. Years 1960–89 in Levine (1999); see King and Levine (1993b) for original sources. Years: 1960–95 in Levine et al. (2000); original source is IMF, *International Financial Statistics* (IFS).
2. Calculated as the share of the top ten banks in a given country owned by the government of that country in 1995. The percentage of the assets owned by the government is calculated by multiplying the share of each shareholder in that bank by the share the government owns in that shareholder, and then summing the resulting shares. It is obtained by author's calculations based on various sources (La Porta, Lopez and Shleifer 2002, p. 292).

Notes (continued)
3. Obtained from Holmes et al. (1997); an index of the regulation policies to opening a business and keeping open a business.
4. Obtained from Holmes et al. (1997); an index of the degree of openness of a country's banking system, and captures: how heavily regulated the banking system is; the degree of government influence over the allocation of credit; whether banks are free to provide customers with insurance, sell real estate, and invest in securities; and whether foreign banks are able to operate freely.
5. Survey-based measure; considered the most reliable available measure of the probability of default on bank loans. Source: *International Country Risk Guide Financial Indicator* (ICRGF).
6. Value of domestic shares traded on domestic exchanges divided by the value of listed shares. Years: 1976–93. Original source: IFC, *Emerging Markets Data Base* (electronic version) and IFS.
7. Total value of the trades of domestic stock on domestic stock exchanges divided by GDP; years: 1976–93. Original source: IFC, *Emerging Markets Data Base* (electronic version) and IFS.
8. Average of the ownership stake of three largest shareholders in the ten largest (by market capitalization) non-financial domestic totally private publicly traded companies. Original sources: Moody's International, CIFAR, EXTEL, Worldscope, 20-Fs, Price-Waterhouse, and various country sources.
9. Positive, significant only at 10% level.
10. The minimum percentage of total share capital mandated by corporate law to avoid the dissolution of an existing firm. It takes a value of zero for countries without such a restriction. Source: Company law or commercial code.
11. Comprehensiveness and quality of company reports as assessed by the Center for International Financial Analysis and Research.
12. The coefficient is significant and negative at 10%.
13. Indicates how many of the 20 firms with just above $500 million market value lack any stockholder owning 20% or more of the firms stock. Source: La Porta et al. (1999).
14. Sources: International Society of Securities Administrators, year 1997; and takeover code, company law, securities law, Economist Intelligence Unit, year 1997.
15. Sources: various company filings, stock exchange publications, Moody's.
16. Aggregate index which includes: two variables measuring income smoothing (variability of earnings related with variability of cash flows), one variable capturing the magnitude of accruals and another identifying the proportion of firms that avoid small losses. Computed for fiscal years 1990 to 1999, on financial accounting information by *Worldscope Database*.
17. These results are obtained through OLS; instrumental analysis suggests that this result is not driven by simultaneity bias (instruments: legal origin and country average per capita GDP). However, a loss of significance is shown when controlling for accrual rules.
18. Instrumental analysis (instruments: legal origin and country average per capita GDP) suggests, however, that accounting rules are endogenous.
19. Value of the IFC investable index, measured in US dollars, at its lowest point in 1998, taking the value of this index at the end of 1996 to equal 100.
20. Corporate governance as measured by Flemings Research in their *Global Emerging Markets* report, which is mainly concerned with capturing the extent of shareholder rights in practice.
21. Total capital raised (invested) from 1997 to 2000 as percentage of GDP. For Asian and European countries, the numbers include both venture capital and buyouts. For US, only venture capital is included. Sources: *Yearbook of National Venture Capital Association* (NVCA), *Guide to Venture Capital in Asia* (AVCJ) and European Private Equity and Venture Capital Association (EVCA).
22. Source: *Financial Structures Database* (World Bank); Beck et al. (1999).

Table 7A.5 Finance, enforcement and the judicial system

Financial system dependent variable	Study	Enforcement variable used	Sign (if significance is at least at 5%)
Panel A: Credit markets			
Size credit market	La Porta et al. (1997a)	ICRG rule of law[1]	(+)
	Levine (1998)	Average of ICRG rule of law and country risk[2]	(+)
	Levine (1999)	ICRG country risk	(+)
	Levine et al. (2000)	Average of ICRG rule of law and country risk	(+)
	Azfar and Matheson (2003)	Average of ICRG rule of law and country risk	(+)
	Jappelli and Pagano (2002)	ICRG rule of law	(+)
	Guiso et al. (2001)	ICRG rule of law	No effect
	Garretsen et al. (2003)	BIC efficiency of judicial system[3]	No effect
	Pistor et al. (2000) (transition economies)	CEER rule of law[4]	(+)
	Calderón et al. (2002)	ICRG rule of law	(+)
	Ergungor (2004)	Average of ICRG rule of law and country risk	No effect
	Ergungor (2004) (only common law countries)	Average of ICRG rule of law and country risk	No effect
	Ergungor (2004) (only civil law countries)	Average of ICRG rule of law and country risk	(+)
	Beck et al. (2003a)[5]	Case law	(+)
		Legal justification	(−)
		Tenure of Supreme Court judges	No effect
		Supreme Court power	No effect

Table 7A.5 (continued)

Financial system dependent variable	Study	Enforcement variable used	Sign (if significance is at least at 5%)
	Stephen and van Hemmen (2003)	Average of ICRG rule of law and country risk	(+)
Liquid liabilities of the financial system	Levine (1999)	ICRG country risk	No effect
	Levine et al.(2000)	Average of ICRG rule of law and country risk	(+)
Bank liquid liabilities	Calderón et al. (2002)	ICRG rule of law	(+)
Deposit money bank assets	Calderón et al. (2002)	ICRG rule of law	(+)
Government ownership of commercial banks	La Porta, Lopez and Shleifer (2002)	ICRG corruption	No effect
	La Porta, Lopez and Shleifer (2002)	Property rights[6]	(−)
	La Porta, Lopez and Shleifer (2002)	ICRG rule of law	No effect
	La Porta, Lopez and Shleifer (2002)	ICRG government repudiation of contracts	(−)
Number of bankruptcies/ total number of firms	Claessens and Klapper (2002)	ICRG rule of law[7]	(+)
Number of bankruptcies/ total number of firms (belonging to a sample of mainly large firms in East Asia)	Claessens et al. (2003)	JUD[8]	(+)
Banks' overhead costs	Calderón et al. (2002)	ICRG rule of law	No effect

Table 7A.5 (continued)

Financial system dependent variable	Study	Enforcement variable used	Sign (if significance is at least at 5%)
Banks' net interest margin	Calderón et al. (2002)	ICRG rule of law	(+)
Credit risk (survey based measure)	Jappelli and Pagano (2002)	ICRG rule of law	(−)
Existence of public credit register (Dummy)	Jappelli and Pagano (2002)	ICRG rule of law	No effect

Panel B: Capital markets

Size external capital market	La Porta et al. (1997a)	ICRG rule of law	(+)
	Azfar and Matheson (2003)	Average of ICRG rule of law and country risk	(+)
	Pistor et al. (2000) (transition economies)[9]	CEER rule of law	(+)
	Guiso et al. (2001)	ICRG rule of law	No effect
Size capital market	Garretsen et al. (2003)	BIC efficiency of judicial system	
	Pistor et al. (2000) (transition economies)	CEER rule of law	(+)
	Ergungor (2004)	Average of ICRG rule of law and country risk	(+)
	Ergungor (2004) (only common law countries)	Average of ICRG rule of law and country risk	No effect
	Ergungor (2004) (only civil law countries)	Average of ICRG rule of law and country risk	(+)
	Beck et al. (2003a)	Case law	(+)
		Legal justification	(−)
		Tenure of Supreme Court judges	No effect
		Supreme Court power	No effect

Table 7A.5 (continued)

Financial system dependent variable	Study	Enforcement variable used	Sign (if significance is at least at 5%)
	Stephen and van Hemmen (2003)	Average of ICRG rule of law and country risk	No effect
IPOs	La Porta et al. (1997a)	ICRG rule of law	(+)
	Guiso et al. (2001)	ICRG rule of law	No effect
Number of domestic listed companies/ total population	La Porta et al. (1997a)	ICRG rule of law	(+)
	Guiso et al. (2001)	ICRG rule of law	No effect
Percentage of companies publicly held[10]	Guiso et al. (2001)	ICRG rule of law	No effect
Value of control-block votes to firm value	Nenova (2003)	ICRG rule of law	No effect
Aggregate earnings management measure	Leuz et al. (2003)	ICRG rule of law	(−)
Weight in US stock portfolio[11]	Dahlquist et al. (2002)	BIC efficiency of judicial system	No effect
	Dahlquist et al. (2002)	ICRG corruption	No effect
	Dahlquist et al. (2002)	ICRG expropriation risk[12]	(+)
	Dahlquist et al. (2002)	Enforcement of insider trading laws[13]	(+)
Venture capital/ GDP	Allen and Song (2002) (Asian countries)	ICRG rule of law[14]	(−)
Number of M&A	Rossi and Volpin (2001)	Judiciary efficiency	(+)
Change in stock market value[15]	Johnson et al. (2000) (emerging markets)	BIC efficiency of judicial system	No effect

Table 7A.5 (continued)

Financial system dependent variable	Study	Enforcement variable used	Sign (if significance is at least at 5%)
		ICRG corruption index	(+)
		ICRG rule of law	(+)
Panel C: Market-mobilized capital			
Market-mobilized capital	Azfar and Matheson (2003)	Average of ICRG rule of law and country risk	(+)

Notes
1. Rule of law: Law and order tradition as assessed by *International Country Risk Guide*.
2. ICRG country risk: risk that a government will modify a contract after it has been signed (taking the form of a repudiation, postponement and so on).
3. Assessment by Business International Corporation (BIC) of the efficiency and integrity of the legal environment as it affects business.
4. Assessment by the Central European Economic Review.
5. Regressions estimated using instrumental variables two-stage least squares, where 2nd stage is Financial Development = α_1 [Political Indicator] + α_2 [Adaptability Indicator] + $\beta X + u$, and instruments for political and adaptability indicators are legal origin (and others which produce similar results). Adaptability indicators: Case law (judges base decisions on case law) and legal justification (judgments based on statutory law rather than on principles of equity). Political indicators: Tenure of Supreme Court and Supreme Court power. Sources: La Porta, Lopez-de-Silanes, Pop-Eleches and Shleifer (2002) for case law, tenure of Supreme Court judges and Supreme Court power; Djankov et al. (2003) for legal justification.
6. Index of the degree to which a government protects and enforces laws that protect private property, as assessed by Freedom in the World (1996).
7. For transition economies the index is taken from Pistor (2000).
8. Expense, difficulty, efficiency and speed of liquidating or restructuring an insolvent corporate borrower. Source: World Bank and Asian Development Bank (1999).
9. The authors also use alternative measures of enforcement (like the European Bank for Reconstruction and Development Legal Effectiveness index), which gives similar results (not reported).
10. Proportion of the largest companies that is not closely held, using 20% as a threshold (see La Porta et al. 1999).
11. Foreign country's share in the portfolio of stocks of US investors. Sources: *Report on US Holdings of Foreign Long-Term Investments* (US Department of Treasury), *Emerging Markets Fact Book* (International Finance Corporation, IFC), Fédération Internationale des Bourses de Valeurs (FIBV), World Bank and Salomon Guide to World Equities.
12. Higher values for less expropriation risk.
13. Taken from Bhattacharya and Daouk (2002).
14. Obtained from La Porta et al. (1998) except for China, which is from Allen et al. (2002).
15. Value of the IFC investable index, measured in US dollars, at its lowest point in 1998, taking the value of this index at the end of 1996 to equal 100.

Table 7A.6 Use of variables which result from the interaction of financial and enforcement variables

Study	Dependent variable	Explanatory variables	Sign (if significance is at least at 5%)
Rossi and Volpin (2001)	Number of M&A[1]	(Antidirector rights * Rule of law) / 10	(+)
		(Creditor rights * Rule of law) / 10	(+)
	Incidence of hostile takeovers[2]	(Antidirector rights * Rule of law) / 10	(+)
		(Creditor rights * Rule of law) / 10	No effect
	Frequency of cross-border M&A[3]	(Antidirector rights * Rule of law) / 10	(+)
		(Creditor rights * Rule of law) / 10	No effect
	Takeover premium[4]	(Antidirector rights * Rule of law) / 10	(+)
		(Creditor rights * Rule of law) / 10	No effect
Johnson et al. (2000) (emerging markets)	Change in stock market value[5]	Antidirector rights * Judicial efficiency	No effect[6]
		Antidirector rights * Corruption	No effect[6]
		Antidirector rights * Rule of law	No effect[6]
Stephen and van Hemmen (2003)	Size of credit market	SECLEND * (ENF)[7]	(+)
	Size of stock market	CORPLAW * (ENF)[8]	(+)

Notes
1. Number of M&A in the 1990s by target country/average population of firms. Sources: SDC Platinum (Thompson Financial Securities Data, and World Development Indicators).
2. Attempted hostile takeovers as a percentage of domestic traded companies. Source: SDC Platinum and World Development Indicators.
3. Number of cross-border deals as percentage of total completed deals. Source: SDC Platinum.
4. Logarithm of the ratio of the price paid and the closing price four weeks before the announcement of the deal. Source: SDC Platinum.
5. Value of the International Finance Corporation (IFC) investable index, measured in US dollars, at its lowest point in 1998, taking the value of this index at the end of 1996 to equal 100.

Notes (continued)
6. Not reported in their tables (see pp. 178 and 181).
7. SECLEND * (ENF) = (Secured lenders paid first * High enforcement) + (Secured lenders paid first * Moderate enforcement). This result is obtained both in OLS and in a structural equations system where bank lending is one of the three equations estimated (jointly with per capita growth and market capitalization). Enforcement is average of ICRG rule of law and country risk.
8. Enforcement variable is average of ICRG rule of law and country risk. CORPLAW * (ENF) = HIFONE + HIFPRO + HIFMIN − HIFMAND + MEDONE + MEDMIN − MEDMAND, where HIF indicates interaction with high enforcement (>8.00) and MED is interaction with moderate enforcement (between 8.00 and 6.00). This result is obtained both in OLS and in a structural equations system where market capitalization is one of the three equation system estimated (jointly with per capita growth and bank lending).

Table 7A.7 *Economic growth and financial institutions (laws and their enforcement)*

Study	Dependent variable	Explanatory variables	Sign and estimation method (in instrumental analysis, the sign and below 5% significance of the exogenous part of the instrumented variable is reported)	
Azfar and Matheson (2003)	Per capita GDP growth	COMMERCIAL LAW[1]	(+) (+)	OLS Instrumental variable estimation where COMMERCIAL LAW is instrument for MMC
		Average of ICRG rule of law and country risk	(+) (+)	OLS Instrumental variable estimation where COMMERCIAL LAW is instrument for MMC
Levine (2003a)	Per capita GDP growth	Accounting Antidirector rights	(+)	Instrumental variable estimation where antidirector rights and accounting are instruments for size of capital market (plus a conditioning information set)
		(French) legal origin	(−)	Instrumental variable estimation where legal origin dummy variables are instruments for size of capital market

Rule of law, finance and economic development 231

Table 7A.7 (continued)

Study	Dependent variable	Explanatory variables		Sign and estimation method (in instrumental analysis, the sign and below 5% significance of the exogenous part of the instrumented variable is reported) (plus a conditioning information set)
Levine (1998)	Per capita GDP growth	Creditor rights Average of ICRG rule of law and country risk	(+)	Instrumental variable estimation where creditor rights and enforcement are instruments for size of credit market (plus a conditioning information set)
		(German) legal origin	(+)	Instrumental variable estimation where legal origin dummy variables are instruments for size of credit market (plus a conditioning information set)
	Per capita capital stock growth	Creditor rights Average of ICRG rule of law and country risk	(+)	Instrumental variable estimation where creditor rights and enforcement are instruments for size of credit market (plus a conditioning information set)
		(German) legal origin	(+)	Instrumental variable estimation where legal origin dummy variables are instruments for size of credit market (plus a conditioning information set)
	Productivity growth	Creditor rights Average of ICRG rule of law and country risk	(+)	Instrumental variable estimation where creditor rights and enforcement are instruments for size of credit market (plus a conditioning information set)

Table 7A.7 (continued)

Study	Dependent variable	Explanatory variables	Sign and estimation method (in instrumental analysis, the sign and below 5% significance of the exogenous part of the instrumented variable is reported)	
		(German) legal origin	(+)	Instrumental variable estimation where legal origin dummy variables are instruments for size of credit market (plus a conditioning information set)
Levine (1999)	Per capita GDP growth[2]	Automatic stay Management stays Secured creditors ranked first Accounting ICRG country risk Legal origin	(+) (+)	Instrumental variable estimation where four variables (automatic stay, management stays, secured creditors ranked first, accounting and ICRG country risk) are used as instruments for the size of the financial intermediaries (plus a conditioning information set)[3] Alternatively, legal origin dummies have been taken as instruments for financial intermediaries size[4]
Levine et al. (2000)	Per capita GDP growth	Legal origin	(+)	Instrumental variable estimation where legal origin is used as instrument for financial intermediation variables[5]
Levine (2002)	Per capita GDP growth	Antidirector rights * Financial structure	No effect	OLS

Table 7A.7 (continued)

Study	Dependent variable	Explanatory variables	Sign and estimation method (in instrumental analysis, the sign and below 5% significance of the exogenous part of the instrumented variable is reported)	
		La Porta et al. rule of law * Financial structure	No effect	OLS
		Antidirector rights Creditor rights ICRG rule of law	(+)	Instrumental variable estimation where three variables (shareholder rights, creditor rights and rule of law) are used as instruments for the size of the overall financial sector (plus a conditioning information set). The same test is performed with these variables as instruments for activity and for efficiency (banking overhead costs)
Garretsen et al. (2003)	Per capita GDP growth	Aggregate index antidirector rights BIC efficiency of the judicial system	No effect	Three-stage least squares estimation system, where the exogenous part of size of capital market explains growth. Instruments include both formal (laws protecting minority shareholders and enforcement) and informal institutions (societal norms)
Garretsen et al. (2003)	Per capita GDP growth	Aggregate index creditor rights BIC efficiency of the judicial system	(+)	Three-stage least squares estimation system, where the exogenous part of size of credit market explains growth

Table 7A.7 (continued)

Study	Dependent variable	Explanatory variables		Sign and estimation method (in instrumental analysis, the sign and below 5% significance of the exogenous part of the instrumented variable is reported)
				Instruments include both formal (laws protecting minority shareholders and enforcement) and informal institutions (societal norms)
Stephen and van Hemmen (2003)	Per capita GDP growth	SECLEND * (ENF)[6] CORPLAW * (ENF)[7]	(+)	Structural equations system, with three equations where MMC explains growth as and endogenous variable, and where size of credit market and size of capital market are, respectively, explained by a set of legal institutional variables and enforcement. Coefficients of BPY and MCAP validly constrained to be equal (MMC = BPY + MCAP)

Notes
1. COMMERCIAL LAW = COLLAW + CORPLAW, where COLLAW = Secured Lenders − Management Stays − Automatic Stay and CORPLAW = One Share + Proxy + Legal Recourse − Mandatory Dividend.
2. Regressions are run for two different periods: (a) 1980–1989 (since legal and regulatory variables are measured over the 1980s); and (b) 1960–1989 (because the paper is concerned with long-run economic growth). Results remain virtually unchanged.
3. Financial system variables: (i) credit allocated to the private sector divided by GDP, including credit initiatives and government subsidy programmes; (ii) ratio of credit allocated to the private sector to total domestic credit (excluding credit to banks); (iii) ratio of bank credit divided by bank credit plus central bank domestic assets; and (iv) liquid liabilities of the financial system. When the exogenous component of liquid liabilities is considered, the accounting instrument does not enter the regression.
4. Only in the liquid liabilities variable is considered does the exogenous component of financial intermediaries not show significant effect on economic growth.

Notes (continued)
5. Financial intermediation variables are: (i) liquid liabilities of the financial system (currency plus demand and interest-bearing liabilities of banks and nonbank financial intermediaries) divided by GDP, times 100; (ii) assets of deposit money banks divided by assets of deposit money banks plus central bank assets, times 100; and (iii) credit by deposit money banks and other financial institutions to the private sector divided by GDP, times 100.
6. SECLEND * (ENF) = (Secured lenders paid first * High enforcement) + (Secured lenders paid first * Moderate enforcement). Validity of the constraint tested.
7. Based on Levine's (1998) antidirector and enforcement variables. CORPLAW * (ENF) = HIFONE + HIFPRO + HIFMIN − HIFMAND + MEDONE + MEDMIN − MEDMAND, where HIF indicates interaction with high enforcement (>8.00) and MED is interaction with moderate enforcement (between 8.00 and 6.00). Validity of the constraint tested.

NOTES

* This chapter has received financial support from DGICYT BEC2001-2552-C03-01; and from Consolidated Research Groups (Generalitat de Catalunya) 2000SRG00052.
1. Investor legal protection variables have been used in studies where other macroeconomic variables are explained, such as economic volatility, measured by the standard deviation of long-run real GDP per capita growth rate (Acemoglu et al. 2003), or currency depreciation during the Asian financial crisis (Johnson et al. 2000). The reason we do not review these results is that they do not explicitly seek to explain financial markets or economic development.
2. La Porta et al. (2000a) offer a first general perspective on the legal approach to finance and corporate governance. Other reviews of the law and finance theories of development can be found in Beck et al. (2001b) and Levine (2003b).
3. Levine (2002, pp. 400–401) classifies this 'law and finance' perspective on growth as a special case of the 'financial-services view', which is concerned with the creation of an environment in which intermediaries (whether banks or market agents) provide sound financial services.
4. Closely related to the size of credit market, this variable measures the size of financial intermediaries; Levine (1999, p. 12) acknowledges that it may not accurately measure the effectiveness of the financial system in intermediating resources and that it includes deposits by one intermediary in another (involving 'double counting'). As can be observed in the appendix, we have classified this measure in 'other financial system variables' (Table 7A.4).
5. It measures the degree to which commercial banks versus the central bank allocate credit; however, as Levine points out, it does not consider other financial intermediaries, and it does not exclude the credit that is provided by banks to government and public enterprises.
6. The variable is derived from the measures of banking sector development and stock market development used by Levine and Zervos (1998). Their data differ from La Porta et al. (1997a) in that they use 1976–93 averages of the financial market measures rather than the 1976–97 averages, and have a slightly different set of countries.
7. For these type of countries, Pistor et al. (2000, p. 8) take several rights into consideration: the right to challenge decisions taken by the shareholder meeting; cumulative voting rights; pre-emptive rights of current shareholders in the case of new issues; and a quorum requirement that makes binding decisions of at least 50 per cent in a shareholder meeting as well as put options for shareholders that have voted against major decisions affecting the current structure of the firm.
8. Aspects such as self-dealing, insider trading, the independence of a shareholder register, and the existence and formal independence of a supervising agency are covered.

9. Besides the ICRG Corruption index, in La Porta et al. (1999, p. 480) another source for corruption can be found: Transparency International. It is an average of up to ten independent surveys on businessmen's perception of the degree of corruption in a given country.
10. Note, however, that this variable is endogenous in Beck et al. (2001a), where a strong relation is found with legal origin.
11. Time-series research (Rousseau and Wachtel 2000) and panel data estimators are alternatively used to deal with endogeneity (see, for instance, Levine et al. 2000; Beck and Levine 2004; Arestis et al., 2001). Other benefits of this technique include incorporating the variability of the time-series dimension and controlling for unobserved country-specific effects (see Levine 2003b). However, there are no legal and institutional time-series data available (particularly survey-based measures) which reduces the benefit of the technique in testing law and finance theories of development. Consequently, the results obtained with this approach have not been surveyed here.
12. Note that Levine and Azfer and Matheson (2003) do not include La Porta et al's 'Restrictions to Reorganisation' feature in their aggregated creditors' index.
13. Scandinavian countries' debt to GDP is 0.57, close to the La Porta et al. sample average: 0.59.
14. When separating the sample in two subsamples by legal origin, Ergungor (2004) performs a Chow test which shows, however, that the coefficients might be significantly different, suggesting that the results obtained by other authors originate mainly in common law countries.
15. It is not constructed by analysing the text of the law but on the assessment of experts.
16. Table 7A.6 shows that an aggregate index that results from the interaction between CORPLAW and high–moderate enforcement is highly significant. When the four components of CORPLAW are interacted individually with high and moderate enforcement, we find that: 'High enforcement * One share–one vote', 'High enforcement * Oppressed minority' and 'Moderate enforcement * Oppressed minority' show positive and significant effects. An F-test for the restrictions suggests that it is the aggregate index which must be introduced in the regression.
17. An F-test on exclusion and equality restrictions indicates that the aggregate index is not justified for creditor protection.
18. With regard to the macroeconomic effects of enforcing shareholder rights, Johnson et al. (2000) also show that the interaction of different enforcement-related measures (judicial efficiency, corruption and rule of law) and minority shareholder rights results in relatively less depreciation in the crises which affected emerging markets (not reported in Table 7A.6).
19. The interaction variable, CREDIT-JUD, is shown to be positively related to the number of bankruptcies. CREDIT and JUD are indices of creditor rights and the efficiency of the judiciary system, respectively; they are constructed by the authors based on Asian Development Bank data. CREDIT includes binary variables: TIME (1 if timetable for rendering judgement is less than 90 days); MANAGER (1 if manager does not stay); STAY (1 if there is no automatic stay on assets); CREDITOR (1 if secured creditors are paid first).
20. Other approaches include panel data analysis and microeconomic studies (see Levine 2003b, for a recent review and Demigürç-Kunt and Levine 2002, for a general perspective).
21. For instance, Azfar and Matheson (2003) criticize King and Levine's (1993a) use of size of the banking sector to explain current and future growth, because of the effects that anticipated growth can have on investors' and entrepreneurs' propensity to lend, borrow and invest, rendering Granger causality arguments unpersuasive. With regard to stock market variables, Levine and Zervos' (1998) use of market capitalization is even more problematic, since it represents the present value of future earnings, as Azfar and Matheson (2003) point out, which would have a positive correlation with future economic performance.
22. Azfar and Matheson (2003) argue that some of Levine's models lack the inclusion of enforcement (that is, his results may be based on mis-specified equations), which

is found to have an independent and significant effect on growth: 'Growth equations without law enforcement variables on the right hand side may be mis-specified, and find significant effects of capital mobilisation through omitted variable bias' (1999, p. 4).
23. In Levine (2002) both shareholder rights and rule of law are interacted with the financial structure (activity, size and regulatory restrictions on commercial bank activities); the author aims to test whether countries select their financial structure depending on their level of institutional development. However, as reported in Table 7A.7, these interactions do not show any effect on economic growth.
24. Azfar and Matheson (2003) suggest that enforcement provides the social peace necessary for even production and exchange and allows private agents to write contracts for goods other than capital.
25. The panel data approach by Beck and Levine (2004) suggests, however, that it is not the size of the market that is relevant for economic development; rather, they find that what matters is the ability of economic agents to exchange ownership claims (turnover) in the stock market.

REFERENCES

Acemoglu, D., S. Johnson, J. Robinson and Y. Thaicharoen (2003), 'Institutional causes, macroeconomic symptoms: volatility, crises and growth', *Journal of Monetary Economics*, **50**, 49–123.
Allen, F., J. Qian and M. Qian (2002), 'Law, finance, and economic growth in China', Working Paper, University of Pennsylvania, Philadelphia, PA and Boston College, Chestnut Hill, MA.
Allen, F. and W. Song (2002), 'Venture capital and corporate governance', Wharton Financial Institutions Center WP 03–95, Philadelphia, PA.
Arestis, P., P.O. Demetriades and K.B. Luintel (2001), 'Financial development and economic growth: the role of stock markets', *Journal of Money, Credit, and Banking*, **33** (1), 16–41.
Azfar, O. and T. Matheson (2003), 'Market-mobilized capital', *Public Choice*, 117, 357–72.
Azfar, O., T. Matheson and M. Olson (1999), 'Market-mobilized capital', IRIS Center working paper no. 233, University of Maryland, College Park.
Barro, R. and X. Sala-i-Martin (1995), *Economic Growth*, New York: McGraw-Hill.
Beck, T. and R. Levine (2004), 'Stock markets, banks, and growth: panel evidence', *Journal of Banking and Finance*, **28** (3), 423–42.
Beck, T., A. Demirgüç-Kunt and R. Levine (1999), 'A new database on financial development and structure', World Bank policy research working paper no. 2146, Washington, DC.
Beck, T., A. Demirgüç-Kunt and R. Levine (2001a), 'Law, politics and finance', World Bank policy research working paper no. 2585.
Beck, T., A. Demirgüç-Kunt and R. Levine (2001b), 'Legal theories of financial development', *Oxford Review of Economic Policy*, **17** (4), 438–501.
Beck, T., A. Demirgüç-Kunt and R. Levine (2003a), 'Law and finance: why does legal origin matter?', *Journal of Comparative Economics*, **31** (4), 653–75.
Beck, T., A. Demirgüç-Kunt and R. Levine (2003b), 'Law, endowments and finance', *Journal of Financial Economics*, **70** (2), 137–81.
Berkowitz, D., K. Pistor and J.F. Richard (2003), 'Economic development, legality, and the transplant effect', *European Economic Review*, **47** (1), 165–95.

Bhattacharya, U. and H. Daouk (2002), 'The world price of insider trading', *Journal of Finance*, **57**, 75–108.
Calderón, C., A. Chong and A. Galindo (2002), 'Development and efficiency of the financial sector and links with trust: cross-country evidence', *Economic Development and Cultural Change*, **51** (1), 189–204.
Claessens, S. and L. Klapper (2002), 'Bankruptcy around the world: explanations of its relative use', World Bank policy research working paper series 2865, Washington, DC.
Claessens, S., S. Djankov and L. Klapper (2003), 'Resolution of corporate distress: evidence from East Asia's financial crisis', *Journal of Empirical Finance*, **10** (1–2), 199–216.
Coffee, J.C. (1999), 'The future as history: the prospects for global convergence in corporate governance and its implications', *Northwestern University Law Review*, **93** (2), 631–707.
Dahlquist, M., L. Pinkowitz, R. Stulz and R. Williamson (2003), 'Corporate governance and the home bias', *Journal of Financial and Quantitative Analysis*, **38**, 87–110.
Davis, L.E. and D.C. North (1971), *Institutional Change and American Growth*, Cambridge: Cambridge University Press.
Demirgüç-Kunt, A. and R. Levine (2002), *Financial Structure and Economic Growth: A Cross-Country Comparison of Banks, Markets and Development*, Cambridge, MA and London: MIT Press.
Demirgüç-Kunt, A. and V. Maksimovic (1998), 'Law, finance, and firm growth', *Journal of Finance*, **53**, 2107–37.
Djankov, S., R. La Porta, F. Lopez-de-Silanes and A. Shleifer (2003), 'Courts', *Quarterly Journal of Economics*, **118** (2), 453–517.
Dyck, A. and L. Zingales (2004), 'Private benefits of control: an international comparison', *Journal of Finance*, **59** (2), 537–600.
Easterly, W. and R. Levine (2003), 'Tropics, germs and crops: how endowments influence economic development', *Journal of Monetary Economics*, **50** (1), 3–39.
Eberhart, A., W. Moore and R. Roenfeldt (1990), 'Security pricing and deviations from the absolute priority rule in bankruptcy proceedings', *Journal of Finance*, **45** (5), 1457–69.
Ergungor, O.E. (2004), 'Market- vs. bank-based financial systems: do rights and regulations really matter?', *Journal of Banking and Finance*, **28** (12), 2869–87.
Esty, B.C. and W.L. Megginson (2003), 'Creditor rights, enforcement, and debt ownership structure: evidence from the global syndicated loan market', *Journal of Financial and Quantitative Analysis*, **38** (1), 37–59.
Freedom in the World (1996), *Freedom in the World: The Annual Survey of Political Rights and Civil Liberties 1995–1996*, Freedom House, New Brunswick, NY.
Garretsen, H., R. Lensink and E. Sterken (2003), 'Growth, financial development, societal norms and legal institutions', CCSO working paper no Z00210, University of Groningen.
Guiso, L., P. Sapienza and L. Zingales (2001), 'The role of societal capital in financial development', mimeo, University of Chicago.
Hansen, L.P. (1982), 'Large sample properties of generalized method of moments estimators', *Econometrica*, **50** (4), 1029–54.
Harris, M. and A. Raviv (1991), 'The theory of capital structure', *Journal of Finance*, **46** (1) (March), 297–355.

Himmelberg, C.P., R.G. Hubbard and I. Love (2002), 'Investor protection, ownership, and the cost of capital', World Bank working paper no. 2834.

Hofstede, G. (1980), *Culture's Consequences: International Differences in Work-Related Values*, Beverly Hills, CA: Sage.

Holmes, K.R., B.T. Johnson and M. Kirkpatrick (eds) (1997), *1997 Index of Economic Freedom*, Washington, DC: The Heritage Foundation and New York: Dow Jones & Company.

Hung, M. (2001), 'Accounting standards and the value relevance of financial statements: an international analysis', *Journal of Accounting and Economics*, **30**, 401–20.

Jappelli, T. and M. Pagano (2002), 'Information sharing, lending and defaults: cross-country evidence', *Journal of Banking and Finance*, **26** (10), 2017–45.

Johnson S., P. Boone, A. Breach and E. Friedman (2000), 'Corporate governance in the Asian financial crisis', *Journal of Financial Economics*, **58**, 141–86.

King, R.G. and R. Levine (1993a), 'Finance and growth: Schumpeter might be right', *Quarterly Journal of Economics*, **108** (3), 717–38.

King, R.G. and R. Levine (1993b), 'Finance, entrepreneurship, and growth: theory and evidence', *Journal of Monetary Economics*, **32**, 513–42.

La Porta, R., F. Lopez-de-Silanes and A. Shleifer (1999), 'Corporate ownership around the world', *Journal of Finance*, **54**, 471–517.

La Porta, R., F. Lopez-de-Silanes, C. Pop-Eleches and A. Shleifer (2002), 'The guarantees of freedom', Unpublished working paper, Harvard University, Cambridge, MA.

La Porta, R., F. Lopez-de-Silanes and A. Shleifer (2002), 'Government ownership of banks', *Journal of Finance*, **57**, 265–301.

La Porta, R., F. Lopez-de-Silanes, A. Shleifer and R.W. Vishny (1997a), 'Legal determinants of external finance', *Journal of Finance*, **52**, 1131–50.

La Porta, R., F. Lopez-de-Silanes, A. Shleifer and R.W. Vishny (1997b), 'Trust in large organizations', *American Economic Review: Papers and Proceedings*, **87**, pp. 333–8.

La Porta, R., F. Lopez-de-Silanes, A. Shleifer and R.W. Vishny (1998), 'Law and finance', *Journal of Political Economy*, **106**, 1113–54.

La Porta, R., F. Lopez-de-Silanes, A. Shleifer and W. Vishny (1999a), 'Investor protection: origins, consequences, reform', mimeo.

La Porta, R., F. Lopez-de-Silanes, A. Shleifer and W. Vishny (1999b), 'The quality of government', *Journal of Law, Economics and Organization*, **15** (1), 222–79.

La Porta, R., F. Lopez-de-Silanes, A. Shleifer and W. Vishny (2000a), 'Investor protection and corporate governance', *Journal of Financial Economics*, **58**, 3–27.

La Porta, R., F. Lopez-de-Silanes, A. Shleifer and W. Vishny (2000b), 'Agency problems and dividend policies around the world', *Journal of Finance*, **55** (1), 1–33.

La Porta, R., F. Lopez-de-Silanes, A. Shleifer and W. Vishny (2002), 'Investor protection and corporate valuation', *Journal of Finance*, **57** (3), 1147–70.

Leuz, C., D. Nanda and P.D. Wysocki (2003), 'Earnings management and investor protection: an international comparison', *Journal of Financial Economics*, **69**, 505–27.

Levine, R. (1998), 'The legal environment, banks, and long run economic growth', *Journal of Money, Credit, and Banking*, **30** (3), 596–613.

Levine, R. (1999), 'Law, finance and economic growth', *Journal of Financial Intermediation*, **8**, 8–35.

Levine, R. (2002), 'Bank-based or market-based financial systems: which is better?', *Journal of Financial Intermediation*, **11**, 398–428.

Levine, R. (2003a), 'Napoleon, bourses, and growth, with a focus on Latin America', in O. Azfar and C.A. Cadwell (eds), *Market-Augmenting Government: The Institutional Foundations of Prosperity*, Ann Arbor, MI: University of Michigan Press, pp. 49–85.

Levine, R. (2003b), 'More on finance and growth: more finance more growth?', Federal Reserve Bank of Saint Louis Review, **85** (4) (July/August), 31–46.

Levine, R., N. Loayza and T. Beck (2000), 'Financial intermediation and growth: causality and causes', *Journal of Monetary Economics*, **46**, 31–77.

Levine, R. and S. Zervos (1998), 'Stock markets, banks and economic growth', *American Economic Review*, **88**, 537–58.

Modigliani, F. and M. Miller (1958), 'The cost of capital, corporation finance and the theory of investment', *American Economic Review*, **48**, 261–97.

Nenova, T. (2003), 'The value of corporate voting rights and control: a cross-country analysis', *Journal of Financial Economics*, **68**, 325–51.

North, D.C. (1981), *Structure and Change in Economic History*, New York: Norton.

North, D.C. (1990), *Institutions, Institutional Change and Economic Performance*, New York: Cambridge University Press.

North, D.C. and B.R. Weingast (1989), 'Constitutions and commitment: the evolution of institutions governing public choice in seventeenth-century England', *Journal of Economic History*, **64**, 803–32.

Pistor, K. (2000), 'Patterns of legal change: shareholder and creditor rights in transition economies', *European Business Organisation Law Review*, **1** (1), 59–108.

Pistor, K., M. Raiser and S. Gelfer (2000), 'Law and finance in transition economies', European Bank for Reconstruction and Development, mimeo.

Rajan, R. and L. Zingales (1998), 'Financial dependence and growth', *American Economic Review*, **88**, 559–86.

Reynolds, T.H. and A.A. Flores (1996), *Foreign Law: Current Sources of Codes and Basic Legislation in Jurisdictions of the World*, Littleton, CO: Fred B. Rothman.

Rodrik, D., A. Subramanian and F. Trebbi (2004), 'Institutions rule: the primacy of institutions over geography and integration in economic development', *Journal of Economic Growth*, **9** (2), 131–65.

Roe, M.J. (2003), 'Institutional foundations for securities markets in the west', Keynote lecture given at European Association of Law and Economics Annual Conference, Nancy, France, September, http://www.univ-nancy2.fr/RECHERCHE/EcoDroit/DOWNLOAD/EALE/ROElecture.pdf.

Rossi, S. and P. Volpin (2001), 'Cross-country determinants of mergers and acquisitions', Finance Working Paper no 25/2003, European Corporate Governance Institute.

Rousseau, P.L. and P. Wachtel (2000), 'Equity markets and growth: cross-country evidence on timing and outcomes, 1980–1995', *Journal of Banking and Finance*, **24** (12), 1933–57.

Shleifer, A. and R. Vishny (1997), 'A survey of corporate governance', *Journal of Finance*, **52** (2) June, 737–83.

Stephen, F. and S. van Hemmen (2003), 'Legal rules and the development of financial systems', Paper presented at European Association of Law and Economics Annual Conference, Nancy, France September.

Utrero, N. (2002), 'Legal environment, capital structure and firm growth: international evidence from industry data', Paper presented at European Financial

Management Association 2002 London meetings and European Financial Association 2002 Berlin meetings.

Warner, J. (1977), 'Bankruptcy, absolute priority, and the pricing of risky debt claims', *Journal of Financial Economics*, **4**, 239–76.

Williamson, O.E. (2000), 'The new institutional economics: taking stock, looking ahead', *Journal of Economic Literature*, **38**, September, 593–613.

8. Judicial independence as a necessary component of the rule of law: preliminary insights and economic consequences
Stefan Voigt*

1 INTRODUCTION

In recent years, it has become almost commonplace to turn to institutional variables for explaining differential growth rates. The ensuing debate on 'good governance' focuses primarily on institutional factors among which the 'rule of law' occupies a prominent place. In this debate, judicial independence (JI) has always fared prominently.

If the judiciary is independent from pressures by the other government branches, this will make the promises of the other branches – for example, with regard to the protection of property rights – more credible. In the long run, even the other branches which are constrained by an independent judiciary will be better off: if promises are attributed higher credibility, this will lead to additional investment which will, in turn, lead not only to higher income and growth but also to higher tax receipts of the state. Yet, an independent judiciary that constrains government action can be costly in the short run and there is always the danger that factual independence is lower than the degree of independence found in legal documents.

In this chapter, one indicator for measuring formal as well as factual JI is introduced. There have been some attempts to estimate the degree to which the rule of law is realized in different countries. The data published by the International Country Risk Guide (ICRG; see, for example, Knack and Keefer 1995) is one such example. These are data used by foreign investors in order to assess country-specific risks. Use of these data has led to interesting results: Knack and Keefer show that the ICRG Index is correlated with economic growth in a statistically significant way. Yet, these data are subjective. They are generated by letting country experts evaluate the situation in the respective countries. Thus, nobody answering to these polls has a complete picture of all the countries surveyed. The grades attributed to the countries depend on the expectations one has with regard to them. These will be influenced by the home countries of those being polled and by what those being polled have already heard about the country.

Although many of the attempts to measure JI have been somehow related with the World Bank, there are critical voices with regard to their hitherto existing success. On the web pages of the World Bank, one can read (Stephenson 2000): 'Although many attempts have been made to assess how "independent" the judiciary is in different countries, most have not been terribly successful'. And in another World Bank publication (Messick 1999, 122): 'The proxies for judicial system performance are often questionable, and there are problems with the endogeneity of the independent variables'. There is thus considerable discontent with the existing indicators, and enough of a challenge to propose new ones. The two indicators introduced here are based on the premise that they should be as objective as possible. Somebody else using the same criteria should thus arrive at identical results.

Before presenting our approach on how to measure both *de jure* and *de facto* JI, we shall deal more systematically with the relationship between JI and the rule of law as well as their possible consequences on economic growth (Section 2). The presentation of the two indicators (Section 3) is followed by some checks on the plausibility of the new indicators as well as some first econometric estimates (Section 4). Section 5 concludes.

2 ON THE RELATIONSHIP BETWEEN THE RULE OF LAW AND JUDICIAL INDEPENDENCE

The concept of the rule of law has been traced back all the way to the Greek philosopher and scientist, Aristotle (1959). Others point to Montesquieu ([1748] 1989) and the close relationship the concept bears with the notion of the separation of powers (Shklar 1998 describes these two thinkers as representing quite distinct archetypes of the concept). During its history, more and more proponents have turned from a purely formal to a substantive approach of the concept, the experiences with totalitarian regimes in the first half of the twentieth century being the events that triggered change in the ways the rule of law was conceived. Still others have pointed out that various states contributed different aspects to what is today called the rule of law: for modernity, Friedrich von Hayek (1960) describes a British, an American, a French and a German contribution to the concept. Yet, the development in these states not only led to different contributions to the concept of the rule of law, it also led to quite diverse approaches towards implementing what is now known as 'rule of law', '*Rechtsstaat*' or '*État de Droit*' in these four states (Grothe 1999 is a more recent comparison).

This chapter will not attempt to give yet another scholarly overview of these developments. Instead, it will focus on two specific points: first, the hypothesis that JI is a necessary component in any concept of the rule of law and second, the hypothesis that JI as such is *not* a proxy for the rule of law, that is, that there are a host of other variables that need to be taken into account. In order to get to grips with the concept, we propose to draw on the concept as developed by Immanuel Kant and Hayek (1960). This might seem to be a partisan approach. It is chosen because these thinkers clearly remain within the formal approach towards the rule of law; Hayek, moreover, provides his readers with a thorough overview over the development of the concept.

The rule of law is often contrasted to the rule of man. It is also called government under the law because the law is to be applied equally to all persons (*isonomia*), government leaders included. According to the rule of law, no power used by government is arbitrary, all power is limited. Drawing on Kant ([1797] 1995), laws should fulfil the criterion of *universalizability*, which has been interpreted to mean that the law be *general*, that is, applicable to an unforeseeable number of persons and circumstances; *abstract*, that is, not prescribing a certain behaviour but simply proscribing a finite number of actions to be; *certain*, that is, anyone interested in discovering whether a certain behaviour will be legal can do so with a fairly high chance of being correct and can furthermore expect that today's rules will also be tomorrow's rules; and that the law be *justifiable* via rational discourse *vis-à-vis* anybody.

There are a number of institutional provisions regularly used in order to maintain the rule of law. Among the most important ones are the separation of powers and the closely connected judicial review, the prohibition of retroactive legislation, the prohibition of expropriation without just compensation, habeas corpus, trial by jury, and other procedural devices such as protection of confidence, the principle of the least possible intervention, the principle of proportionality and the like. Empirically, a 'perfect' or 'complete' rule of law has probably never been realized: men and women have been treated differently just as members of different races have been. Successful rent seeking that leads to tax exemptions or the payment of subsidies is not in conformity with a perfect rule of law either, because it is equivalent to treating people differently. The rule of law should therefore rather be understood as an ideal type in the sense of Max Weber ([1922] 1947). Realized types can be compared with each other.

By necessity, the rule of law implies a market economy since decisions by the government of who is to produce what in which quantities and so on cannot be subsumed under general rules but imply the arbitrary discrimination between persons (Hayek 1960, 227). Individual liberty will only be exempt from arbitrary interference by government – or other powerful groups – if it is secured by an effectively enforced rule of law. Closely related to the rule of law is the concept of constitutionalism which has been developed primarily by settlers in the British colonies of North America. It links the rule of law with the notion of a written constitution in which the basic procedures that government is to use are laid down. Logically, a rule of law constitution does not imply that the political system is democratic. Since we are here interested in identifying preconditions for maintaining the rule of law, no particular assumption concerning the political system will be made.

Before dealing with the crucial importance of JI for the rule of law, we need to propose a definition of judicial independence. This implies that judges can expect their decisions to be implemented regardless of whether they are in the (short-term) interest of other government branches upon whom implementation depends. It would further imply that judges – apart from their decisions not being implemented – do not have to anticipate negative consequences as the result of their decisions, such as (a) being expelled, (b) being paid less, or (c) being made less influential.

In cases of conflict between government and the citizens, the citizens are in need of an organization that can adjudicate who is right (who has acted according to the law) – the judiciary. This not only means ascertaining the constitutionality of newly passed legislation but also checking whether the representatives of the state have followed the procedural devices that are to safeguard the rule of law.[1] If the judiciary is not independent from executive and legislature, there will be a government of people – and not of the law. If the judiciary is not independent from executive and legislature, citizens will not trust in the existence of the rule of law.

An independent judiciary is also relevant for settling conflicts between various government branches. In the absence of an impartial arbiter, conflicts between government branches are most likely to develop into simple power games. An independent judiciary can keep them within the rules laid out in the constitution.

Among the many functions of legislation, the reduction of uncertainty is certainly of paramount importance. But the law will only reduce uncertainty if the citizens can expect the letter of the law to be followed by government representatives. An independent judiciary could thus also be interpreted as a device to turn promises – for example, to respect property rights and abstain from expropriation – into credible commitments. If it functions like this, we can expect citizens to work harder, to develop a longer time horizon, and to invest more. In short, an independent judiciary is not only of overwhelming importance for the rule of law, we also expect it to be conducive to economic growth.

Of course, the judiciary should not be unconstrained. It needs incentives to interpret the law and not to make new law itself. It needs to be accountable, like the other branches of government. Elsewhere, I have shown that factually, the judiciary is never entirely independent from the other branches. Indeed, the interactions of the various branches can be modelled as a strategic game. If we assume that the judiciary is interested in getting its sentences implemented, it has incentives to take the preferences of the other actors explicitly into account (Voigt 1999).

In their treatise on the separation of powers and the competencies that should be given to the various government branches, the authors of the *Federalist Papers* note that in hereditary monarchies the executive would be the most powerful – and the most dangerous – branch. In democracies, this could well be the legislature, having access to the purse (papers 48 and 51). In 'Federalist paper 78', Alexander Hamilton makes the famous assessment of the judiciary being the least dangerous branch.[2] In this chapter, however, the primary focus is not with normative issues, that is, we are here not interested in an 'optimal' degree of judicial independence. Rather, we are interested in measuring the various degrees of JI found in different countries. And this section has argued that an independent judiciary is indeed a necessary component of the rule of law.

On the other hand, JI is not sufficient for the rule of law. The reason for this should be apparent once all the components of the rule of law provided above are taken into consideration: that laws need to be general, abstract and certain, procedural safeguards such as the prohibition of retroactive legislation, habeas corpus, proportionality and the like need to be in place. If all this is not the case, even a factually independent judiciary will not turn an arbitrary regime into one belonging to the family of rule of law regimes.

3 INTRODUCING TWO NEW INDICATORS FOR JUDICIAL INDEPENDENCE

3.1 Introductory Remarks

In this chapter, two objective indicators are introduced. They are based on verifiable facts and not on subjective evaluations. Anybody interested in recalculating them should, in principle, arrive at identical values. The components making up our indicator of judicial independence reflect the major aspects that are conventionally in mind when we talk about these concepts. We are interested in a measure of the independence of an entire government branch. In many states, this branch is made up of thousands of decision makers. Often, there is an elaborate division of labour between specialized courts. In federal states, there is usually a state judiciary, which is separate from the federal one. In short, complexity needs to be radically reduced. We therefore propose to focus on just one court for every country, namely its highest court.[3] Regardless of whether it deals exclusively with constitutional issues (as, for example, the German Constitutional Court) or whether it is the Supreme Court for all areas of law (as, for example, the US Supreme Court), it will deal with interpreting the constitution. If the constitution is viewed as the most basic rule set of a state, its interpretation will be of great importance. The court system is organized hierarchically, with the higher courts being able to overrule the sentences of the lower courts. It is therefore the independence of the highest court that is important for the degree of judicial independence observed in a polity.[4]

3.2 A *De Jure* Indicator for Measuring Judicial Independence

This measure is based solely on the legal foundations as found in legal documents. The possibility that the law of the books does not reflect legal reality will be considered in Section 3.3, in which a *de facto* indicator is proposed.

There does not seem to be one single proxy which would reflect all relevant aspects of JI. We therefore draw on a number of characteristics – 23 grouped into 12 variables – in order to assess it. Each of the 12 variables can take on values between 0 and 1 where greater values indicate a higher degree of JI. A country with a maximum degree of JI could thus get a total of 12. Unfortunately, for some of the countries included in this sample, we were not able to get data for all 12 variables. In order to include countries even if information on some variables is lacking, the sum of the coded variables was divided by the actual number of variables for which data were available. The indicator can thus take on any value between 0 and 1.

Information was obtained by country experts via a questionnaire that was e-mailed to them jointly with a short paper explaining the purpose and hypotheses of the enterprise. To complete the questionnaire, the country experts did not have to make a personal evaluation of the situation in the country, but were asked to simply give information concerning the legal structure of the judiciary. Among these experts are former Supreme Court judges, law professors, lawyers but also activists from organizations such as Transparency International. We also attempted to obtain at least two questionnaires from each country in order to increase our confidence in the quality of the data. If the information contained in the two questionnaires was contradictory, we sought clarification from the informants. We now turn to discuss the 12 variables that are to proxy for JI and their underlying rationale in some detail.

The independence of judges is dependent upon the stability of the set of institutional arrangements within which they operate. Formally, the stability of the powers and procedures of the court depend on how difficult it is to change them. If they are specified in the constitution itself, we expect a greater degree of independence than in cases where these arrangements are fixed by ordinary law. This does only hold, however, if a majority is needed to change the constitution which is more inclusive than that which is needed to pass ordinary legislation.

We therefore asked (1) whether the highest court is anchored in the constitution and (2) how difficult it is to amend the constitution. The codings for 'yes' answers are given in parentheses. The hypothesis behind the coding is that mention of the highest court is of overwhelming importance whereas the regulation of specific aspects is much less relevant. The reasoning behind the coding of the second variable is straightforward: the higher the number of 'chambers' that have to agree to amend the constitution, the less likely such amendments are to occur and the more stable the institutional foundations on which judges operate.[5] The answer 'one' ('two' or 'three') is coded with 1/4 (1/2 or 3/4, respectively) under the condition that 2a is answered in the affirmative. The last 1/4 can be obtained if the amendment process previews a cool-off period because that will also make amendments less likely.

1. Is the highest court anchored in the constitution? (1/2)
    a. Are its competencies enumerated in the constitution? (1/8)
    b. Are its procedures specified in the constitution? (1/8)
    c. Is its accessibility specified in the constitution? (1/8)
    d. Are the arrangements concerning the members of the highest court enumerated in the constitution?
        aa. Is the term length specified in the constitution? (1/16)
        bb. Is the number of judges specified in the constitution? (1/16)
2. How difficult is it to amend the constitution?
    a. Is a majority necessary that is above that necessary for changing ordinary legislation?
    b. How many chambers of government have to agree?
    c. Are majority decisions necessary at different points in time?

Note that the numerical coding shown in parentheses is given if the question is answered in the affirmative.

The appointment procedure of the judges may have a notable effect on the independence of the court. As it is *inter alia* supposed to protect citizens from illegitimate use of powers by the authorities as well as to settle disputes between the branches of government, it ought to be as independent as possible from the other branches. We hypothesize that the most independent procedure for judicial appointment is by professionals (other judges or jurists).[6] The least independent method is appointment by one powerful politician (for example, prime minister or a minister of justice).

3. Taking into consideration that nomination and election (or appointment) competencies do not have to be unified, a large number of possible procedures emerges. Assuming that in principle representatives of every government branch could have the competence of nomination as well as that of appointment, we obtain a 3×3 matrix:

		Competence to elect/appoint members of highest court		
		Executive	Legislature	Judiciary
Competence to nominate members of highest court	Executive	0	1/3	2/3
	Legislature	1/3	0	2/3
	Judiciary	2/3	2/3	1

The hypothesis underlying the coding is that JI from other government branches would be highest if the other branches did not have any say in the appointment process (1). If they do, any kind of influence of the judiciary is positively evaluated, that is, a combination of one of the other two branches with the judiciary scores 2/3 whereas a combination of executive and legislature only scores 1/3 and a monopoly in the process of either the executive or the legislature is coded 0. What the matrix does not cover is the involvement of all three branches in the process; this is also coded 1 in the indicator.[7]

It is, of course, possible to argue that the proposed coding is problematic because it ignores – maybe naïvely – some ugly possibilities. For example, members of the judiciary, on average, could be more conservative than society as a whole. In that case, appointment by cooptation might indicate not only the independence of the judiciary but also its ability to preserve a conservative bias quasi indefinitely. An alternative way to think of the possible consequences of the nomination and appointment procedures on JI is to assume that 'independence' is closely correlated with something like 'public reputation for integrity'; then procedures which make appointment contingent on the consensus of all three branches might be considered as being conducive to a higher degree of independence. On the other hand, a high number of veto players in the appointment process could also have entirely different consequences. It could, for example, lead to the appointment of streamlined middle-of-the-road candidates. Alternatively, it could lead to package deals (one rightist and one leftist candidate are appointed at the same time) and so on.

Judicial tenure will be crucial for the independence of the judiciary. We assume that judges are most independent if they are appointed for life (or up to a mandatory retirement age) and cannot be removed from office, save by legal procedure. Judges are less independent if terms are renewable because they have an incentive to please those who can reappoint them.

Further, if the members of one of the other government branches determine their salaries, this raises incentives to take the preferences of these members explicitly into account. General rules that their salary cannot be reduced increase, in turn, the independence of the judiciary. The level of income is assumed to be an additional component of the independence of a judge. A (very) low income could, for example, force a judge to spend some of his/her time on making a second living and in turn make him/her spend less time for the preparation of decisions. The level of income also contains a signal concerning the attractiveness of judgeships and, hence, the probability that bright people will be attracted into becoming judges. Comparing absolute income levels across countries makes little sense. This is why we decided to compare the incomes of judges with other occupations or positions, which highly qualified lawyers might also choose to pursue, namely (i) university professor, (ii) private lawyer, or (iii) the minister of justice.

It could be argued that it is not income alone which makes an occupation interesting, but also the prestige that is connected with it. Lower monetary income could well be compensated for by high prestige as seems to be the case in many Anglo-Saxon countries. A partner of a law firm might be willing to accept a substantial cut in salary in order to enjoy the high prestige of a judgeship. In such a case, a low income would even imply a *high* degree of JI, as judges whose independence is at risk can credibly threaten to leave since they have an excellent outside option at their disposal.[8] But, there is a counter-argument: if there is indeed an excellent outside option, judges might not mind leaving if government members put pressure on them. This would mean that politicians would be more successful in undermining JI in such a situation.[9]

The following questions were asked:

4. What is the legal term length of the judges in the highest court?
5. Can judges be re-elected/reappointed? (0)

6. How can judges be removed from office?
   a. only by judicial procedure (1)
   b. by decision of one or more members of the executive (0)
   c. by decision of parliament (or a committee thereof) (0)
   d. by joint decision of one or more members of the executive and of parliament (or a committee thereof) (1/2)
7. Is there a measure against income reduction of judges? (1)
8. Are judges adequately paid?
   a. Are they paid more than university professors? (1/3)
   b. Are they paid more than an average private lawyer? (1/3)
   c. Are they paid as well as the minister of justice? (1/3)

Concerning legal term length, emphasis in the institutional arrangement is usually either on a specification in number of years or on a fixed retirement age. Therefore two term of office (too) coding scales are required. First:

Term of office	Coding
• 12 years	1.0
• $10 \leq \text{too} < 12$	0.8
• $8 \leq \text{too} < 10$	0.6
• $6 \leq \text{too} < 8$	0.4
• $4 \leq \text{too} < 6$	0.2
• $4 > \text{too}$	0.0

Second, judges are often appointed rather late in their careers. Early and mandatory retirement is hypothesized to constrain JI because judges could be less daring during their first couple of years in office:

Term of office	Coding
• for life	1.0
• mandatory retirement (mr) ≥ 75 years	1.0
• $65 \leq \text{mr} < 75$	0.8
• $65 > \text{mr}$	0.6

Concerning possible answers to question 6, only one of the answers offered was possible whereas with regard to question 8, all three parts could in principle be answered in the affirmative. Here, the sum of the three parts of the variable was entered into the indicator.

Another component of judicial independence is the accessibility of the court and its ability to initiate proceedings. A court which is accessible only by a certain number of members of parliament or other officials will be less effective in constraining government *vis-à-vis* its citizens than a court which is accessible by every citizen who claims that his or her rights are violated.

9. Who can access the highest court?
   a. individuals in any case relevant to the constitution and with which they are personally concerned (1)
   b. individuals, but only in a subset of cases relevant to the constitution (such as human rights) (1/2)
   c. only other government branches (0)

If the allocation of cases to the various members of the court is at the discretion of the chief justice, his/her influence will be substantially greater than that of the other members of the court. It follows that in such an institutional environment, it could be interesting to try to 'buy' just the chief justice. We expect independence to be greater if there is a general rule according to which cases are allocated the responsibility of single members of the court (see Salzberger 1993).

10. Is there a general rule allocating the responsibility concerning incoming cases to specific judges? (1)

The competencies assigned to the constitutional court do not bear directly on its independence. Yet, highest courts must have certain competencies in order to be able to check the behaviour of the other government branches. If the constitution is interpreted as the most basic formal layer of rules that is to restrain (and to enable) government, then the competence of the court to check whether legislation is in conformity with the constitution is crucial.

11. Does the constitution (or the law establishing the highest court) preview the power of constitutional review? (1)

If courts have to publish their decisions, others can scrutinize them and the reasoning can become subject to public debate. This can be interpreted as making it more difficult for representatives of the other government branches to have irrelevant considerations influence their decisions. The transparency will be even higher if the courts publish dissenting opinions.

12. Does the highest court have to publish
    a. the main reasons for a decision? (1/3)
    b. an extended proof? (1/3)
    c. are dissenting opinions published regularly? (1/3)

The indicator has been calculated for 101 countries (plus the EU). The choice of countries could be called 'biased random' due to a number of factors: contacts with legal experts are not spread equally around the world, and nor is the use of e-mail as a distribution channel. But cultural factors might also play a part. The Middle East and Africa are clearly underrepresented in our study.

In Table 8.1, the results are presented in the rank order that emerged as a result of the coding described above. The ranking contains more than one surprise: among the ten top-scoring countries, there is not one single OECD member. Long-established democracies with affluent economies such as the United States or Switzerland fare rather badly: the United States is ranked 35th, Switzerland at 88th even belongs to the lowest-ranked quintile. However, this ranking only reflects JI as it is written down in various legal documents. Politicians all over the world have incentives to promise their citizens that the judiciary will be independent. Most of the top-ranked countries have close ties with the United States and US legal thinking which emphasizes the importance of judicial independence.[10] For example, law professors from the Chicago Law School drafted large parts of Georgia's constitution. It is not surprising that they put heavy emphasis on the formal independence of the judiciary. What will be interesting now is whether the *de facto* indicator will lead to a similar ranking or whether the two indicators radically diverge. To determine this, we shall now examine the *de facto* indicator.

3.3 A *De Facto* Measure for Judicial Independence

We now turn to possible ways of measuring JI not as it is written down in legal documents but as it is factually implemented. As with the *de jure* indicator, no one single proxy adequately reflects all relevant aspects of JI. To assess *de facto* JI, eight variables have been used. Again, each of the eight variables can take on values between 0 and 1 where greater values indicate a higher degree of JI.

The *de jure* indicator is based on various legal documents. Even if they are changed frequently, exact values can be calculated for every instance, depending on the formal validity of the respective documents. This does not hold for *de facto* JI. The factual term length of highest court judges cannot be calculated right after a new constitution has been passed but will be the result of years of living with the legal documents. We therefore tried to base the *de facto* indicator on quite a long period, namely that between 1960 and 2000. This means, of course, that the indicator will be very sticky in comparison to the *de jure* indicator. Some respondents simply did not answer the second part of the questionnaire because they believed it did not apply to their country. The countries of Central and Eastern Europe are a case in point here: all of them passed new constitutions after 1990. According to the

Table 8.1 Ranking and scores according to the de jure indicator

Rank	Country	Score	# VAR	Rank	Country	Score	# VAR
1	Colombia	0.939	12	42	Paraguay	0.658	10
2	Philippines	0.909	10	43	Venezuela	0.650	12
3	Brazil	0.907	12	44	Bahamas	0.646	12
4	Georgia	0.893	12	45	Estonia	0.641	11
5	Slovenia	0.869	12	46	France	0.634	11
6	Singapore	0.851	12	47	Uganda	0.632	12
7	Russia	0.845	11	48	Netherlands	0.631	12
8	Botswana	0.841	12	49	Armenia	0.629	12
9	Dominic Rep	0.839	10	50	India	0.629	12
10	Ecuador	0.835	12	51	Hungary	0.628	12
11	Greece	0.833	10	52	England and Wales	0.626	9
12	Belgium	0.825	10				
13	Australia	0.817	11	53	Japan	0.622	12
14	Cyprus	0.817	12	54	Yemen	0.617	11
15	Mexico	0.804	12	55	European Union	0.612	11
16	Nepal	0.799	12				
17	Mauritius	0.797	11	56	Korea, South	0.607	12
18	Italy	0.793	12	57	Sweden	0.605	10
19	Denmark	0.779	11	58	Trinidad/Tobago	0.596	10
20	Chile	0.778	9				
21	Turkey	0.774	12	59	Bosnia-Herceg	0.590	11
22	Pakistan	0.765	12				
23	Czech Republic	0.761	12	60	New Zealand	0.587	11
				61	Bangladesh	0.587	11
24	Austria	0.733	11	62	Uruguay	0.577	11
25	Germany	0.729	12	63	Taiwan	0.575	12
26	Fiji Islands	0.729	11	64	Kuwait	0.574	10
27	Bolivia	0.726	12	65	Jordan	0.573	11
28	Zimbabwe	0.723	8	66	Panama	0.572	12
29	Kenya	0.709	12	67	Croatia	0.570	11
30	Egypt	0.708	12	68	Mauretania	0.569	12
31	Ukraine	0.703	11	69	Slovakia	0.569	12
32	Zambia	0.703	10	70	Senegal	0.567	11
33	Poland	0.693	11	71	Honduras	0.555	10
34	Benin	0.691	10	72	Iceland	0.554	12
35	USA	0.685	12	73	Nigeria	0.553	12
36	Costa Rica	0.685	12	74	Spain	0.551	12
37	Namibia	0.684	12	75	Romania	0.548	7
38	Canada	0.681	10	76	Finland	0.544	8
39	South Africa	0.681	12	77	Haiti	0.538	10
40	Argentina	0.665	12	78	Kazakhstan	0.538	11
41	Israel	0.663	12	79	Portugal	0.530	10

Table 8.1 (continued)

Rank	Country	Score	# VAR	Rank	Country	Score	# VAR
80	Ivory Coast	0.507	11	92	Niger	0.423	10
81	Guatemala	0.499	11	93	China	0.406	12
82	Peru	0.485	11	94	Bulgaria	0.397	12
83	Sri Lanka	0.476	12	95	Vanuatu	0.377	10
84	Norway	0.468	12	96	Nicaragua	0.357	12
85	Madagascar	0.468	11	97	Cambodia	0.341	11
86	Montenegro	0.465	11	98	Malaysia	0.313	8
87	Ghana	0.464	7	99	Indonesia	0.300	8
88	Switzerland	0.459	12	100	Morocco	0.275	5
89	Azerbaijan	0.451	10	101	Tanzania	0.265	12
90	Lithuania	0.447	11	102	Vietnam	0.159	12
91	Mozambique	0.441	12				

Note: $N = 102$; mean = 0.621; standard deviation = 0.158.

time span proposed by our indicator, the treatment of the judiciary by socialist regimes still weighs heavily on today's *de facto* values. We chose this approach because we think the past matters for how JI is evaluated by citizens and other potential investors. A government – or more broadly, a regime – will not be able to build up a reputation as law abiding or JI respecting overnight.[11]

The eight variables and the reasoning used for coding them follow. The literature on central bank independence has focused on one single such indicator, namely the 'turnover rate of central bank governors' (TOR) (Cukierman 1992; de Haan and Kooi 1999). The same criterion could be applied to the highest court. For coding, we simply multiplied the effective average term length in years by 0.05. In other words: a country gets the highest possible rating if the average term length is 20 years (or more). If the actual term length and the one to be expected on the basis of the legal foundations deviate, the country is coded 0 in variable 14. Removing a judge before the end of term is a serious breach of JI. Whenever this has occurred at least once, the country is coded 0 for that variable.

13. What has been the effective average term length of judges since the respective legal foundations were passed?[12]
14. Does the effective average term length deviate from the average term length to be expected by the legal foundations? (0)
15. How many judges have been removed from office before end of term? (0)

The influence of a judge depends on the number of other judges who are members of the same court. By increasing the number of judges, the weight of those judges who do not decide along the lines of the preferences of the median members of the other branches can supposedly be diminished. This is exactly what President Roosevelt had in mind with his plan to 'pack' the Supreme Court. We thus asked:

16. How many times has the number of judges been changed since 1960?

The answers were coded as follows:

Number of changes	Coding
• 0	1.0;
• 1–2	0.8;
• 3–4	0.6;
• 5–6	0.4;
• 7–8	0.2;
• more	0.0.

Of course, there might be reasons entirely unrelated to the independence of the judiciary which can lead the legislature to increase the number of judges, for example, reducing the time-lag until a decision is taken on a case. This can even be interpreted as an increase of legal certainty or – more broadly – the rule of law. But trying to ascertain the motives behind the changes would have introduced an element of subjectivity. We thus refrained from doing so and simply counted how many times the number of judges had been changed since 1960.

The importance of an adequate income has already been discussed with regard to the *de jure* indicator. With regard to the *de facto* situation, we are interested to learn whether the income of judges has at least remained constant in real terms. But the efficacy of courts depends not only on the income level of judges but also on the number of clerks employed, the size of the library, the availability of modern computer equipment and so on. We captured this aspect by asking about the development of the court's budget as an organization.[13]

17. Has the income of judges remained at least constant in real terms since 1960? (1)
18. Has the budget of the highest court remained at least constant in real terms since 1960? (1)

Any change in the basis of the legal foundation of the highest court will increase uncertainty among its potential users, that is, will be counter to one of the most fundamental functions of the law. Frequent changes of the respective legal rules are here interpreted as an indicator for low *de facto* independence.

19. How often have the relevant articles of the constitution (or the law on which the highest court is based) been changed since 1960?

The answers were coded using the matrix also used for coding variable 16. Implicitly, we have thus assumed that changes are always for the worse. Besides being very conservative, this ignores the possibility that changes might indeed improve things, that is, increase the independence of the judiciary. It is likely that this has, indeed, happened in a number of countries, for example, in Central and Eastern Europe. But again, we have refrained from asking whether changes were motivated by 'good' or 'bad' reasons as this would have introduced an element of subjectivity into the indicator.

The *de facto* degree of judicial independence is low if decisions of the highest court, in order to be implemented, depend on some action of one (or both) of the other branches of government and this cooperation is not granted.

20. In how many cases has one of the other government branches remained inactive when its action was necessary for a decision to become effective?

Again, coding was done as before. It was suggested that this should be called the 'effectiveness' of the judiciary rather than its independence. But according to our definition of JI provided above, one aspect of JI is that judges can expect their decisions to be implemented regardless of whether these are in the (short-term) interest of the other government branches. It is exactly this aspect which this variable aims to capture. Admittedly, answers to this question introduce a subjective element as it is a matter of personal evaluation whether a government branch has remained inactive.

Table 8.2 shows the results of the coding, presented in rank order. Getting data for the *de facto* indicator is more difficult than for the *de jure* indicator. In order to ensure a minimum amount of accuracy, countries were ranked only if a minimum of three variables could be coded. This explains the lower number of countries ranked here.

Some of the results are unexpected: the good results for Armenia and Kuwait can probably be explained by the low number of variables used (namely, three), but this does not explain the high ranking of, say, Turkey (six variables) or Taiwan (eight). On the other hand, the high ranking of Switzerland is reassuring as is the fact that among the lowest quintile there is no EU member state and only one OECD member (the Czech Republic which has been a member since 1995), but there are some of the

Table 8.2 Ranking and scores according to the de facto indicator

Rank	Country	Score	# VAR	Rank	Country	Score	# VAR
1	Armenia	1.000	3	41	Ukraine	0.543	7
2	Kuwait	1.000	3	42	Colombia	0.529	7
3	Switzerland	0.943	7	42	Guatemala	0.529	7
4	Costa Rica	0.920	5	44	Pakistan	0.525	8
5	Norway	0.901	7	45	Mozambique	0.520	5
6	Austria	0.900	4	45	Nepal	0.520	5
7	Japan	0.900	4	47	Greece	0.500	4
8	Taiwan	0.863	8	48	Brazil	0.494	8
9	Israel	0.860	5	49	Paraguay	0.490	5
10	Italy	0.858	6	50	Netherlands	0.467	3
11	Georgia	0.850	6	51	Uruguay	0.450	7
12	EU	0.845	6	52	Bahamas	0.450	4
13	England and Wales	0.830	4	52	Finland	0.450	4
				54	Fiji Islands	0.436	7
14	South Africa	0.825	8	55	Ivory Coast	0.433	3
15	Hungary	0.821	8	55	Lithuania	0.433	6
16	Australia	0.819	8	57	Slovenia	0.431	8
17	Sri Lanka	0.813	7	58	Bangladesh	0.429	7
18	Denmark	0.813	6	59	Singapore	0.421	7
19	Belgium	0.806	8	60	Botswana	0.414	7
20	Madagascar	0.800	5	61	Venezuela	0.400	4
21	Germany	0.800	6	61	Yemen	0.400	5
21	Turkey	0.800	6	63	Ecuador	0.388	8
23	France	0.786	5	63	Trinidad/Tobago	0.388	4
24	New Zealand	0.783	3				
25	Spain	0.750	8	65	Panama	0.388	8
26	Cyprus	0.743	7	66	China	0.370	5
27	Philippines	0.731	8	67	Argentina	0.333	6
28	India	0.708	6	68	Nicaragua	0.320	8
29	Mexico	0.707	7	68	Vanuatu	0.320	5
30	Portugal	0.706	8	70	Slovakia	0.319	8
31	Estonia	0.700	8	71	Ghana	0.300	3
31	Sweden	0.700	5	72	Malaysia	0.270	5
33	Iceland	0.675	8	73	Uganda	0.250	4
34	Croatia	0.657	7	74	Nigeria	0.243	7
35	Mauretania	0.600	7	75	Egypt	0.240	5
36	USA	0.592	6	76	Cambodia	0.200	3
37	Korea, South	0.588	8	76	Jordan	0.200	7
38	Chile	0.575	4	78	Kenya	0.175	6
39	Bolivia	0.560	5	79	Czech Republic	0.167	3
40	Benin	0.550	3				

Table 8.2 (continued)

Rank	Country	Score	# VAR	Rank	Country	Score	# VAR
80	Peru	0.160	5	84	Montenegro	0.100	4
81	Bulgaria	0.133	6	85	Zambia	0.100	7
81	Russia	0.133	6	86	Niger	0.080	5
83	Zimbabwe	0.131	8				

Note: $N = 82$; mean = 0.547; standard deviation = 0.250.

East European and African states that one would intuitively expect to fare badly.

It cannot be completely excluded that some respondents pursue their own agenda and have an incentive to make reality fit to their agenda: a loyal citizen could try to make his/her country look better than it really is, whereas a political activist striving for improvement might try to make his/her country look worse than it really is.

In principle, a judiciary that scrupulously follows the wishes of, say, the executive, could score very well in the *de facto* indicator: dictators could nominate their family and friends as judges; as long as these judges conformed to the dictator's wishes, there would be no incentive to remove them from office, to reduce their salary or the budget of the court and so on. This can indeed not be entirely excluded. The question would be what aspects could be checked to ensure that this is not the case. The number of laws rejected by the highest court as unconstitutional (possibly as a proportion of all laws passed) is not a good proxy for a number of reasons: (i) often, the highest court does not have the competency to initiate a constitutional review; it thus depends on others initiating this process; (ii) the legislature will not naïvely maximize the utility of its median member but will try to anticipate the position of the court and will subsequently adjust its own position in order not to be called back by the court. In that sense, every time a law is rejected by the court, this is an expression of faulty expectations concerning jurisdiction by the majority of the legislature.

The level of corruption within the judiciary is another potentially important aspect. It would, of course, be nice to take explicitly into account how corrupt the judges are. Being corrupt supposedly means that decisions can be bought and that judges are not entirely neutral with regard to the disputing parties. This would translate into a lower degree of independence. It would indeed be interesting to integrate this aspect. However, for lack of reliable and comparable data we refrained from doing so.

4 FIRST EMPIRICAL RESULTS

4.1 Comparing *De Jure* and *De Facto* Independence

Abstracting from the specific characteristics of the two indicators just presented, it could be argued that the difference between them should optimally be zero because this would indicate a high congruence between *de jure* and *de facto* JI which appears normatively desirable. This is, however, premature because the difference between them could also be zero if both *de jure* and *de facto* indicators take on low values. However, taking the specific characteristics of the two indicators into consideration, their subtraction does not make sense because they are based on different variables. The *de facto* indicator needs some *de jure* base (variable 13, for example) but many of the other variables do not overlap which means that subtracting data does not make sense.

We now turn to a first comparison of the *de jure* and the *de facto* indicators, which will be little more than a first glance at the data. Above, it was pointed out that potentially, everybody could be made better off if politicians were able to make promises credible. Rational politicians will therefore at least try to let the judiciary appear independent. We would expect this to be reflected in the respective legal documents. *De facto* JI will not necessarily be closely correlated with *de jure* JI. We should therefore expect

$$\text{mean } dj > \text{mean } df\ (0.621 > 0.547),$$

which is indeed the case as the actual values in parentheses indicate. Similarly, we would expect the standard deviation of the *de jure* indicator to be lower than that of the *de facto* indicator, which is also the case:

$$\text{standard deviation } dj < \text{standard deviation } df\ (0.158 < 0.250).$$

We can now compare various country groups. Here, the countries of Central and Eastern Europe are of special interest. They have all changed their legal foundations recently and should rank fairly high in the *de jure* indicator. As discussed in the last section, their *de facto* values should be considerably lower due to the stickiness of the indicator. We propose to compare the values with those of the countries of the European Union before enlargement in May 2004. We have at our disposal data from 13 member states. If we compare the data, we see that the difference in the mean values concerning *de jure* JI is not that great (0.628 and 0.678). Yet, the mean for the Central and Eastern European countries is below the mean of the entire sample which is unexpected.

Concerning the *de facto* indicator, we would expect the countries of Central and Eastern Europe (i) to do worse than those of the European Union and (ii) to display a greater standard deviation:

$$\text{mean } df_{\text{CEE13}} < \text{mean } df_{\text{EU13}} \ (0.482 < 0.733)$$

$$\text{standard deviation } df_{\text{CEE13}} > \text{standard deviation } df_{\text{EU13}} \ (0.292 > 0.162)$$

These considerations can also be interpreted as a check concerning the plausibility of the indicators. We now turn to discussing the correlation with various indicators that serve similar, yet not identical purposes. Remember that it was argued in section 2 that JI is a necessary but not a sufficient component for the Rule of Law. Table 8.3 is a correlation matrix between the two indicators here introduced and some other indicators.

The ICRG data have already been mentioned above. Respondents to the survey were asked to code countries on 'Rule of Law: Legal Institutions Supportive of the Principles of Rule of Law, and Access to a Non-discriminatory Judiciary'.[14] It is still astonishing that the correlation with our *de jure* indicator does not even have the correct sign; this is the case with the correlation between our *de facto* indicator and the ICRG data but it is only modest even then. A possible reason for the rather modest correlation is, of course, not only that different things were measured but also that different techniques for measuring them were used: whereas our approach was as objective as possible, theirs is based on a survey approach which means that subjective evaluations were asked for.

Something similar happens with the data provided by the Economist Intelligence Unit (EIU) that are supposed to proxy for the transparency and accountability of the legal systems of 60 countries. Again, correlations are far from perfect with *de facto* correlation faring better than *de jure* correlation. Freedom House represents civil liberties on a scale between 1 and 7 where 1 represents the best possible value. Note that a negative sign with the other indicators stands for a positive correlation. Again, JI is a necessary condition for a high degree of civil liberties in a society, yet it is in no way sufficient. The Freedom House indicator is thus more encompassing than the two indicators introduced here. As with the first two indicators discussed here, the correlation is far from perfect and partial correlation with our *de jure* indicator is higher than with the *de facto* indicator.

Heritage/*Wall Street Journal* is another index of economic freedom. The variable used here is the one on property rights, which are on a scale between 1 and 5 where 1 stands for the highest possible value (correlations with our indicators should thus have a negative sign). Again, it can be

Table 8.3 Correlation matrix of the indicators of judicial independence with other indicators

	De jure	De facto	ICRG	EIU	Freedom House	Heritage/Wall Street Journal
De jure	1					
De facto	0.199	1				
ICRG	–0.045	0.387	1			
EIU	0.113	0.580	0.648	1		
Freedom House	–0.226	–0.446	–0.541	–0.786	1	
Heritage/ Wall Street	–0.253	–0.490	–0.655	–0.848	0.758	1

Notes:
ICRG is the variable 'rule of law' as used in the Economic Freedom Index (Gwartney et al. 2000); EIU is an index on the basis of data provided by the Economist Intelligence Unit on transparency and accountability of the legal systems; Freedom House represents the civil liberties on a scale between 1 and 7 where 1 represents the best possible value. Note that a negative sign with the other indicators stands for a positive correlation. Heritage/*Wall Street Journal* is another index of economic freedom. The variable used here is the one on property rights. The rights are on a scale between 1 and 5 where 1 stands for the highest possible value (correlations should thus have a negative sign except for the one with the Freedom House data).

argued that JI is a necessary condition for secure property rights, but it is in no way a sufficient condition. As before, the correlation with our *de facto* indicator is higher than with the *de jure* indicator. (See Table 8.3.)

Many correlation coefficients are very low which at first glance is disquieting. However, the various indicators measure different things. We believe that a major advantage of our indicator is that it can be replicated by anybody interested in doing so. This is clearly not the case for ICRG, Freedom House and the Heritage Foundation/Wall Street Journal indicators. Moreover, we believe that the components used here to measure JI reflect all the major aspects that are generally considered when talking about these concepts. Therefore, if regression of economic variables on these indicators shows little correlation, it would mean that the relationship is not as straightforward as is sometimes assumed. This is already a result in its own right. More research inquiring into the intricate relationships between JI, on the one hand, and civil liberties, the security of property rights, the transparency and accountability of legal systems and the rule of law in its entirety, on the other, is thus needed. But the data can also be used to examine whether JI is conducive to economic growth. First estimates are reported in the next subsection.

4.2 Econometric Estimates

In a first study based on the indicators presented here, Feld and Voigt (2003) find that *de jure* JI does not have any consequences for economic growth. But they do find that on the basis of 56 countries, *de facto* JI does indeed lead to economic growth. This result is quite robust: *de facto* JI remains a significant explanatory variable for explaining economic growth even after controlling for a host of other political and legal variables such as government consumption, openness, population growth, average inflation, but also the origin of the legal system, political stability, and the age of the constitution. The authors conclude that higher degrees of *de facto* JI are conducive to economic growth.

Feld and Voigt (2006) is based on a larger and – we hope – more precise dataset. The authors find their earlier results confirmed: *de facto* JI is a highly significant variable for explaining per capita GDP growth between 1980 and 1998. In addition to the variables recognized in their earlier paper, they ask whether the kind of highest court has any effect on growth rates. Distinguishing between constitutional courts and all other courts, they find that this variable does not have additional explanatory power. Two other variables do, however: the higher the level of realized checks and balances in a country, the higher is, *ceteris paribus*, per capita income growth. Concerning parliamentary versus presidential systems, the former seem to be connected with higher growth rates. The interaction effect between parliamentary systems and *de facto* JI leads to an interesting effect, however. Given a high degree of *de facto* JI, growth rates are higher in *presidential* systems!

The next logical step consists in asking how the difference between *de jure* and *de facto* independence can be explained. JI is thus no longer assumed to be exogenous but is endogenized. Table 8.3 shows that the correlation coefficient between the *de jure* and the *de facto* index is (a low) 0.199. *De jure* JI is thus an unreliable predictor of the factually realized degree of JI in a specific country. In a first attempt to explain *de facto* JI, Hayo and Voigt (2003) distinguish between explanatory variables that can be manipulated in the short run and variables that are exempt from deliberate change – at least in the short run. Examples of the first type of variable are the number of veto players in a political system, the question whether the political system is federal or unitary and how the court system of a country is organized. Examples of the second type are the ethnolinguistic heterogeneity of a country, the religious traditions followed by its members, and its legal tradition. The authors chose such a separation of variables in order to be able to answer the question whether societies do have the capacity to construct their political systems in ways that are likely to lead to factually independent judiciaries.

Using a rigorous reduction algorithm, five variables seem to be particularly relevant in order to explain the factually realized degree of JI. According to this estimate, the following factors are conducive to a high degree of *de facto* JI: (1) a high degree of *de jure* independence; (2) a high per capita income; (3) trust of the population in the legal system of its country; (4) political instability (!); and (5) parliamentary (as opposed to presidential) systems. These results should, however, be interpreted with care. For some of the variables mentioned, data were available only for a small number of countries. More complete datasets are therefore definitely a desideratum.

5 CONCLUSION AND OUTLOOK

In this chapter, we have not only presented two new indicators for measuring judicial independence but have also inquired into the relationships between judicial independence and the rule of law. It was hypothesized that JI is a necessary but not a sufficient component of the rule of law. The correlation coefficients offered in Section 4 seem to support this point: the coefficients between our indicators and other, related, indicators such as property rights, specific aspects of the rule of law, or civil liberties in their entirety are not very high. Therefore, their relationships should be examined in a more systematic way.

It seems plausible to assume that organizations that are related to the judiciary should also have some consequences on the degree of rule of law realized in a country – as well as on economic growth. In many instances, the judiciary does not have the competence to initiate proceedings but depends on the actions of other state organs such as state prosecutors. Aaken et al. (2004) argue that the way prosecutorial agencies are organized could be an important variable for determining the number of criminal acts committed by politicians in a given country. If, for example, ministers of justice have the competence to give orders to prosecutors, it cannot be excluded that criminal acts committed by politicians will be prosecuted less forcefully than if the prosecutorial agencies were independent.

NOTES

* The author would like to thank Anne van Aaken, Ivan Baron Adamovich, Helge Berger, Reiner Eichenberger, James Gwartney, Bernd Hayo, Witold Henisz, Gerald Hosp, Bruno Jeitziner, Wolfgang Kasper, Phil Keefer, Henner Kleinewefers, Robert Nef, Philip Pettit, Eli Salzberger, Oliver Volckart, and Zane Spindler for valuable comments. The German Agency for Technical Cooperation in Development (GTZ) supported the project with additional country information. Their help is gratefully acknowledged. Research assistance by Anja Sokolow and Lorena Jaume-Palasí often went far beyond what was required. Country-specific information was provided by the following and is likewise gratefully acknowledged: Angela Baronin Adamovich (Croatia); Terman Akumal (Turkey); Christian Alsøe (Denmark); Carlos Amayo O. (Colombia); Beth Aub (Jamaica); Thompson Ayodele (Nigeria); Adrian Baboi-Stroe (Romania); Maja Bacovic (Montenegro); Roberto Dala Barba Filho (Brazil); Abdel Azuz Bari (Malaysia); Maria Isabel Bonilla (Guatemala); Gyimah Boadi (Ghana); Boudewijn Bouckaert (Belgium); Nathan Brown (Egypt and Kuwait); Katja Chammas (Lebanon); Alfred W. Chanda (Zambia); Giovanni Cordini (Italy); Bibek Debroy (India); Jacques Dinan (Mauritius); Alaa Elemary (Egypt); Vladan Djuranovic (Montenegro); Fredrik Erixon (Sweden); Aissata Fall Bagnan (Niger); Charles Fornbad (Botswana); Marie-Noëlle Ferrieux Patterson (Vanuatu); Diogo de Figueiredo Moreira Neto (Brazil); R. Fischer (Chile); Ricardo Flores (Venezuela); Tamás Földi (Hungary); Pedro Galilea (Spain); Thomas Ginsburg (USA); Docent Jaan Ginter (Estonia); John Githongo (Kenya); Jorge Hernandez (Peru); Benedikte Holberg (Denmark); Stephan Hulka (Czech Republic); Robert Jagtenberg (Netherlands); Ikbal Janif (Fiji); Jae Ho Chung (South Korea); Akritas Kaidatzis (Greece); Hein Kiessling (Pakistan); Gia Kiknadze (Georgia); Sa'eda Kilani (Jordan); Victor Kimesera (Tanzania); Wolfgang Kleine (Namibia); Amalia Kostanyan (Armenia); Peter Kurrild-Klitgaard (Denmark); Andreas Kyriacou (Cyprus); Claudia Lange (South Africa); Toh Han Li (Singapore); Elena A. Lisovskaya (Russia); Cathrin Loffreda (European Union); Kalle Määttä (Finland); Elisio Macamo (Mozambique); Arne Mavcic (Slovenia); Andrés Mejía-Vergnaud (Colombia); Irena Mladenova (Bulgaria); Fouzi Mourji (Morocco); Robert Nef (Switzerland); Marassulov Nurgalim (Kazakhstan); Joachim Nyemeck Binam (Ivory Coast); Dagmer Oberlies (Cambodia); Krysztof Pawlowski (Poland); Nassef Perdomo (Dominican Republic); Vytautas Piesliakas (Lithuania); Joseph Pini (France); Jean-Eric Rakotoarisoa (Madagascar); Suri Ratnapala (Australia); Clara Elena Reales (Colombia); Boyd Reid (Trinidad and Tobago); Rena Safaraliyeva (Azerbaijan); Jorge Silvero Salgueiro (Paraguay); Frieder von Sass (Tanzania); Anja Schoeller-Schletter (Paraguay); Claudia Schönbohm (Bolivia); John T. Shieh (Taiwan); Pavel Skoda (Slovakia); Ricardo Ernesto Soto Barrios (Panama); Zane Spindler (Canada); Thomas Stauffer (Switzerland); Rigoberto Steward (Costa Rica); Neal Tate (Philippines); Jürgen Theres (Mauretania); Joan Thompson (Bahamas); Sübidey Togan (Turkey); Mamadou Traoré (Ivory Coast); Xiomara Vallesteros (Nicaragua); Artur Victoria (Portugal); Veselin Vukotic (Montenegro); Wolfgang Weigel (Austria); Omri Yadlin (Israel). The usual disclaimer applies.

1. Alexander Hamilton has put this succinctly in Federalist Paper 78 (Hamilton et al. 1788 [1961], 466): 'The complete independence of the courts of justice is peculiarly essential in a limited Constitution. By a limited Constitution, I understand one which contains certain specified exceptions to the legislative authority; such, for instance, as that it shall pass no bills of attainder, no ex post facto laws, and the like. Limitations of this kind can be preserved in practice no other way than through the medium of courts of justice, whose duty it must be to declare all acts contrary to the manifest tenor of the Constitution void. Without this, all the reservations of particular rights or privileges would amount to nothing'. Montesquieu (1748 [1989]) is also very outspoken: 'there is no liberty, if the judiciary power be not separated from the legislative and executive. Were it joined with the legislative, the life and liberty of the subject would be exposed to arbitrary control; for the judge would be then the legislator. Were it joined to the executive power, the judge might behave with violence and oppression'.

2. Hamilton (Hamilton et al. 1788 [1961], 465) writes: 'Whoever attentively considers the different departments of power must perceive that, in a government in which they are separated from each other, the judiciary, from the nature of its functions, will always be the least dangerous to the political rights of the Constitution; because it will be least in a capacity to annoy or injure them. The executive not only dispenses the honors but holds the sword of the community. The legislature not only commands the purse but prescribes

the rules by which the duties and rights of every citizen are to be regulated. The judiciary, on the contrary, has no influence over either the sword or the purse; no direction either of the strength or of the wealth of the society, and can take no active resolution whatever. It may truly be said to have neither FORCE nor WILL but merely judgment; and must ultimately depend upon the aid of the executive arm even for the efficacy of its judgments'.

3. Strictly speaking, none of the courts of the member states of the European Union warrants inclusion because their highest court is the European Court of Justice in Luxemburg. This has been the case since the ECJ has decided that (i) EU law is directly applicable in the member states and (ii) it has precedence over national law. This is why the independence of the ECJ is reported in this survey.

4. It can, of course, be argued that private law courts are more relevant for the security of property rights and investment behaviour than constitutional courts. For a follow-up study, it would thus be interesting to measure the independence of private law courts and compare it with the indicators presented here.

5. Chambers is written in inverted commas because we really mean independent decision-making units: in the United States, for example, not only the House and the Senate would have to agree to a constitutional amendment but also the president who would thus be counted as a third chamber; in Switzerland, constitutional amendments require the consent of the people in a referendum; and so on. What we are really interested in is thus what has been called the number of veto players or veto points (Beck et al. 1999; Hennisz 2000).

6. In Federalist Paper 51, James Madison (Hamilton et al. 1788 [1961], 321) writes: 'In order to lay a due foundation for that separate and distinct exercise of the different powers of government . . . it is evident that each department should have a will of its own; and consequently should be so constituted that the members of each should have as little agency as possible in the appointment of the members of the others'. On the same topic, Hamilton writes (ibid., 470f.): 'That inflexible and uniform adherence to the rights of the Constitution, and of individuals, which we perceive to be indispensable in the courts of justice, can certainly not be expected from judges who hold their offices by a temporary commission. Periodical appointments, however regulated, or by whomever made, would, in some way or other, be fatal to their necessary independence. If the power of making them was committed either to the executive or legislature there would be danger of an improper complaisance to the branch which possessed it; if to both, there would be an unwillingness to hazard the displeasure of either; if to the people, or to persons chosen by them for the special purpose, there would be too great a disposition to consult popularity to justify a reliance that nothing would be consulted by the Constitution and the laws'.

7. The number of institutional arrangements that are empirically used is astonishingly high: in Greece, for example, a number of judges are chosen randomly from the pool of law professors that formally qualify for the job. An astute observer remarked that nomination and appointment by the judiciary was only possible after a judiciary has been in place. In other words, there must be some first round in which members of the highest court could *not* be recruited by the sitting members. Although true, this issue will be ignored here.

8. I owe this consideration to Paul Mahoney.

9. In Feld and Voigt (2006), this variable has been moved to *de facto* JI, as it is the factual pay of judges that is under consideration.

10. These countries outrank the United States because some of the competencies that the US Supreme Court factually holds – such as constitutional review – only emerged over time but are not fixed in the constitution (variable 11). Most of the more recent constitutions incorporate this competence on the constitutional level.

11. See also Blinder (2000, 1427) who notes with regard to the credibility of central banks: 'In contrast to some naïve interpretations of rational expectations, in which credibility can be created or destroyed abruptly by, say, announcing or legislating an institutional change, our respondents believe that a consistent track record matters most for credibility'.

12. In coming up with the data, we relied not only on the questionnaires but also on Henisz (2000), which contains a list of 45 countries with average Supreme Court Justices' tenure for the period between 1960 and 1990. We did not correct for changes that could have occurred between 1990 and 2000 but simply adopted the Henisz figures.
13. It was suggested that we should also check whether the income of judges and the budget of the court have increased sharply, which could be interpreted as an attempt 'to buy the court'. We have not incorporated that suggestion because a substantial increase can also occur with the aim of making judges more independent. A potentially problematic implicit assumption of this variable is that the starting level in 1960 was the same everywhere: if it was inadequately low in 1960, it might still be (too) low although it has remained constant in real terms; if it was very high in 1960, it might still be (sufficiently) high although it has not remained constant in real terms.
14. I take them as they are reprinted by the authors of the Economic Freedom Index (Gwartney et al. 2000). Unfortunately, this means that they have already been corrected. Gwartney et al. (2000, 236) write: 'Because the ICRG ratings inexplicably increase from the mid-1990s to late 1990s, all ratings were adjusted using the maximum and minimum procedure used in other components in order to make the component consistent over time.' Additionally, ratings for some countries here rated were not provided for by ICRG: Estonia and Lithuania were rated on the basis of Poland and Russia, Slovenia on that of the Czech Republic and Slovakia. Another country for which we provide original data was scored according to the ratings of apparently similar countries, namely Mauritius on that of Botswana.

REFERENCES

Aaken, A.V., E. Salzberger and S. Voigt (2004), 'The prosecution of public figures and the separation of powers: confusion within the executive branch', *Constitutional Political Economy*, **15** (3): 261–80.

Aristotle (1959), *Politics*, ed., translated and with an introduction by John Warrington, London: Heron Books.

Beck, Th., G. Clarke, A. Groff, Ph. Keefer and P. Walsh (1999), 'New tools and new tests in comparative political economy: the database of political institutions', World Bank: Washington, DC.

Blinder, A. (2000), 'Central-bank credibility: why do we care? How do we build it?', *American Economic Review*, **90** (5): 1421–31.

Cukierman, A. (1992), *Central Bank Strategy, Credibility, and Independence*, Cambridge, MA: MIT Press.

de Haan, J. and W. Kooi (2000), 'Does central bank independence really matter? New evidence for developing countries using a new indicator', *Journal of Banking and Finance*, **4** (4): 643–64.

Feld, L. and S. Voigt (2003), 'Economic growth and judicial independence: cross country evidence using a new set of indicators', *European Journal of Political Economy*, **19** (3): 497–527.

Feld, L. and S. Voigt (2006), 'Making judges independent – some proposals regarding the judiciary', forthcoming in R. Congleton (ed.), *Democratic Constitutional Design and Public Policy – Analysis and Evidence*, Cambridge: MIT Press.

Grothe, R. (1999), 'Rule of law, Rechtsstaat and "Etat de droit"', in: Chr. Starck (ed.), *Constitutionalism, Universalism and Democracy: A Comparative Analysis*, Baden-Baden: Nomos, pp. 269–306.

Gwartney, J., R. Lawson and D. Samida (2000), *Economic Freedom of the World: 2000 Annual Report*, Vancouver: Fraser Institute.

Hamilton, A., J. Madison and J. Jay (1788), *Die Federalist-Artikel [The Federalist Papers]*, with an introduction by C. Rossiter (1961), New York: Mentor.

Hayek, F. (1960), *The Constitution of Liberty*, Chicago: University of Chicago Press.

Hayo, B. and S. Voigt (2003), 'Explaining de facto judicial independence', mimeo, Universities of Essen and Kassel, http://www.wirtschaft.uni-kassel/voigt.

Henisz, W. (2000), 'The institutional environment for economic growth', *Economics and Politics*, **12** (1): 1–31.

Kant, I. (1797), The Metaphysics of Morals, introduction, translation and notes by Mary Gregor (1995), Cambridge: Cambridge University Press.

Knack, St. and Ph. Keefer (1995), 'Institutions and economic performance: cross-country tests using alternative institutional measures', *Economics and Politics*, **7** (3): 207–27.

Messick, R. (1999), 'Judicial reform and economic development: a survey of the issues', *World Bank Research Observer*, **14** (1): 117–36.

Montesquieu, Charles L. de (1748), *The Spirit of the Laws*, book X1 §6, (Cambridge Texts in the History of Political Thought (1989)), Cambridge: Cambridge University Press.

Salzberger, Eli M. (1993), 'A positive analysis of the doctrine of separation of powers, or: why do we have an independent judiciary?', *International Review of Law and Economics*, **13**, 349–79.

Shklar, J. (1998), 'Political theory and the rule of law', in J. Shklar (ed.), *Political Thought and Political Thinkers*, Chicago: University of Chicago Press, pp. 21–37.

Stephenson, M. (2000), 'Judicial independence: what it is, how it can be measured, why it occurs', http://www.worldbank.org/publicsector/legal/judicial independence.htm, 13 December.

Voigt, S. (1999), 'Implicit constitutional change – changing the meaning of the constitution without changing the text of the document', *European Journal of Law and Economics*, **7** (3): 197–224.

Weber, M. (1922), *The Theory of Social and Economic Organization*, with an introduction by Talcott Persons (ed.) (1947), New York: The Free Press.

9. Democracy, citizens and judicial power: do judges contribute to democracy?
Sophie Harnay[*]

1 INTRODUCTION

A democracy can be defined as a regime in which citizens, because they are considered as the source and origin of power, choose more or less directly their representatives or public policies. Thus, in terms of agency theory, a democracy can be depicted as a regime in which the citizens, namely the principals, delegate tasks and responsibilities to some *elected* agents. An ongoing and important process of delegation of power has resulted in the increasing role that non-elected, also named non-majoritarian, institutions play in democratic regimes. In addition to positive justifications and explanations that it receives (see, for instance, Voigt and Salzberger 2002), such a phenomenon raises important normative questions. What is at stake here is the control of the behaviour of these non-elected and non-majoritarian 'agents' and the subsequent legitimacy of the decisions they make. If one takes into consideration that exit is a costly way to express oneself and voice (for instance, through vote) is ineffective on non-elected agents, the question is then how citizens give their consent to the decisions made by those non-elected agents?

The question has a particular flavour when it involves judges, who are, among the many groups of non-elected agents granted with a non-negligible rule-making power, the ones who create the biggest problems. This is clearly illustrated by the debates about the legitimacy of the choices made by the US Supreme Court or the European Court of Justice. Are the decisions these courts legitimate from the point of view of the citizens? Or, in other words, what makes judicial decisions more legitimate than political choices? As a corollary, one can ask whether the possible judicial review of political decisions makes any sense from a democracy based on citizenship. These questions can be answered in two alternative ways, which are derived from the analysis made by Ackerman (1998) to compare two –

monist and dualist[1] – forms of democracy. First, the answer given by monism refers to a definition of democracy as a regime in which power resides *where* there is political accountability, that is in an elected body. Therefore, the decisions made by judges have to be controlled by the elected agents of the citizens. The latter, to put it more precisely, must retain formal authority and be able to challenge judicial decisions. Judges are not independent from politicians. From this perspective, the possible judicial review of political decisions is considered as opposed to democracy – 'presumptively antidemocratic' (Ackerman 1998, p. 10). By contrast, dualism criticizes monism, stating that the possible political review of judicial choices gives politicians opportunities to escape from the effective control of the citizens and even leaves them uncontrolled. The institutions of democracy are thus criticized for allowing democratically chosen ministers and parliamentarians – more broadly, politicians – to give birth to rules favourable to the interests of pressure groups. In these regimes, law and public policies are governed by the preferences of political leaders, whose efforts are misdirected, as noted by Holcombe, 'toward predatory opportunities rather than toward productive ones' (2002, pp. 152–3). From this perspective, monist democracies, because of the emphasis they put upon political norms and the leaders in charge of their application, are particularly vulnerable to a coercive and arbitrary use of power. This shortcoming can be corrected in suppressing the hierarchy of norms upon which monist democracies rest. More prerogatives are then granted to non-elected institutions as a way to check and balance the power of elected agents. The separation of power among different competing institutions and the system of checks and balances are thus devices which ensure that rules not only constrain the citizens but also bind the government. More precisely, devices are adopted to achieve the requirements of the rule of law rather than to let the system depend upon the discretionary use of the political norm. It is thus guaranteed that, '[u]nder rule of law, government acts according to well-defined rules that apply *equally* to everyone' (Holcombe 2001, p. 44; emphasis added). Within this framework, the independence of the judiciary is necessary to ensure the correct functioning of the system. Therefore, judges granted with the right to review political decisions, and thus freed from political pressures, contribute to the cause of democracy in disallowing illegitimate decisions of politicians. Indeed, a dualist democracy ensures that the legal rule prevails over the political norm and, as a consequence, it prevents elected agents from using their institutional position to create rules. In other words, dualism is aimed at protecting citizens from the illegitimate non-democratic behaviours of politicians.

Although it is possible to demonstrate that no regime, monist or dualist, is immune from any form of manipulation, in this chapter, the focus is rather put upon the justification of the monist approach to democracy and judicial accountability. The argument will show that, in a monist institutional framework, even if judges are not independent, they nonetheless benefit from a certain amount of discretionary power which can be used to promote the interests of the citizens. In other words, the possible political review of judicial choices nonetheless leaves room for a certain amount of judicial discretionary power. Therefore, it will be shown that judicial discretionary power can be considered as a source of democracy. In order to illustrate this part of the argument, reference will be made to the French administrative system, which is one of the most typical examples of a monist democracy.

2 JUDICIAL ACCOUNTABILITY AND DEMOCRATIC CONTROL OF JUDICIAL DECISION MAKING

Judicial democratic accountability takes two main forms. First, judicial decision making takes place in a hierarchy of norms in which the higher norm is the political decision. Second, seizure rules give citizens the opportunity to take an active and direct part in the judicial procedure and prevent the judge from engaging in self-empowerment. Thus, the democratic control of the judicial decision entails both an *ex ante* and an *ex post* form.

2.1 The Democratic Constraint as a Hierarchy of Norms

If one accepts the idea that judges are in the situation of creating rules, and not only able to discover already existing rules, then the question raised by the necessary role of citizens in a democracy is that of possible conflicts between rules created by politicians (the elected agents of the citizens) and rules created by judges (non-elected 'agents'). As seen above, the issue of the organization of the relation between judges and the other law producers from the customary legal order perspective makes sense if and only if legal rules are created by judges. Then, the trade-off between these two kinds of rule has to be organized by a higher norm, namely the constitution. This implies that democracy is defined as a hierarchy of norms that explicitly provides a ranking for the decisions made by various institutional actors. From this – clearly Kelsenian – perspective, a rule is valid only if its content and the conditions of its production satisfy the dispositions established by higher norms. Kelsen envisages the hierarchical ordering of rules from the perspective of a democracy in which the agents of the citizens – namely politicians, ministers or elected representatives – have the last word. Thus, courts, as non-elected bodies, are not only without democratic support but also lack political legitimacy when they create legal rules or check whether the decisions made by elected agents are in conformity with alleged superior principles. In other words, the higher norm is the political norm.

This assumption does not deny the existence of a significant power of judicial challenge. Indeed, the control of the conformity of a rule with the higher rule nonetheless requires the intervention of a judicial authority (Kelsen [1934] 1962). This judicial power is defined by two rules: first, constitutional judges are granted with the right to reverse a decision made by elected politicians; second, a superior jurisdiction also exists with the right and responsibility to control decisions made by judges in the first instance. Within this legal framework, the decision of low-rank actors can be reversed and replaced by the decisions of the actors who have a higher position in the hierarchy. Thus, if we consider three types of agents who are respectively a first-rank judge, a second-rank judge (a judge of appeal, that is, some higher court or a constitutional court) and a political decision maker, it appears that a first-rank judge can have his/her decision reversed either by the second-rank judge or by the politician. In other words, a first-rank judge can have his/her decision vetoed either by a judicial or by a political agent. Thus, because of the existence of appeal and reversal mechanisms, some players in the judicial and political game benefit from a veto and counter-veto power.

However, in relation to the principles of the separation of powers and judicial independence, some restrictions apply to the issue of political reversal of a judicial decision. For instance, the French *Conseil Constitutionnel* (CC) provides that the legislative validation of decisions that have been cancelled by a court is an infringement upon judicial independence and must be restricted to very specific situations (CC, decisions 22 August 1980, 24 August 1985, 26 June 1987) (Chevallier 1994, p. 87).

2.2 Seizure by Litigants as Participation in the Judicial Process

Seizure rules provide another democratic control available to citizens when they decide whether to resort to the judiciary. When they choose not to enter into a litigation process, individuals deny courts the opportunity to consider particular issues. On the contrary, if they decide to litigate, rather than to settle a negotiated agreement, litigants thus play the role of a gatekeeper in the judicial process. Therefore, a judge is not allowed to issue a decision on a particular case when he/she has not been explicitly asked to do so by a litigant. The participation of a judge to the game is conditional on the action of litigants. Therefore, a democratic judicial system must guarantee that as many litigants as possible have access to the judicial system. This means that judicial services must be free or, at least, available to the litigant at a low cost. Mechanisms of *aide juridictionnelle* can thus be seen as attempts to guarantee that potential litigants will not be deprived of their judicial consumption due to the lack of resources and will be in a position to file a suit nonetheless. Legal provisions providing the distribution of judicial costs and fees among litigants play a similar function, as well as a range of other services aimed at facilitating judicial seizure by potential litigants (judicial advisers and experts, judicial professions, insurance companies, associations and so on) which are a way of limiting social and cultural inequalities in legal matters. *A contrario*, if seizure is legally impossible for a citizen, this can be interpreted as a lack of democratic accountability and openness in the judicial system. For instance, the fact that a French citizen cannot refer a case to the *Conseil Constitutionnel* directly clearly reveals the lack of democratic openness of the French higher court in constitutional matters.

3 STRATEGIC BEHAVIOURS, JUDICIAL DISCRETION AND SELF-RESTRAINT

3.1 The Model

To represent the democratic interactions among citizens, judges and politicians, we utilize a model in which there are four types of player: the citizens–potential litigants, the first- and second-rank judges and the politicians. The players decide on a policy issue that can be represented as a one-dimensional set of possible solutions (denoted Γ). The preferences of each player i on Γ are represented by a utility function U_i, $U_i = U_i(j)$. Preferences are assumed to be single-peaked. Let j be the decision of the i-player, $j \in \Gamma$, whose set of non-strictly-preferred points can be written

$$P_i^{ns}(j) = \{j' \, U_i(j') \geq U_i(j), \, j' \neq j, \, j' \in \Gamma\}.$$

The structure of the game and the players' preferences are common knowledge.

The democratic control of judicial decision making through a hierarchy of norms and the respect of seizure rules can be analysed within a four-step sequential game (see Figure 9.1). At the first step, a litigant may decide whether to file a suit. By doing so, he/she triggers the judicial process. On the contrary, if the litigant chooses not to file a suit, then the whole procedure is stopped from the very outset. Thus, the litigant can be considered as a gatekeeper in the game. Once the gate is open, and the suit filed, then,

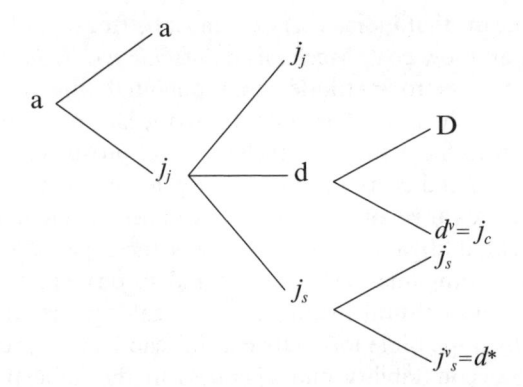

Figure 9.1 Four-step sequential game

at the second step, the first-rank judge enters the game. This judge makes a decision about a choice made by a public agent (a public bureaucracy), and can comfort either the plaintiff or the defendant, or neither of them. At the third stage of the game, one of the two other players, that is the appeal judge or the politician, may play. However, because of the sequential nature of the game, only one of them does play. The third-step player can choose to accept the decision made by the first-rank judge or reverse it and decide to substitute his/her own choice for the previous one. Let us note that when the political decision maker is the third-step player and if he/she rejects the decision rendered at the second stage of the game, then he/she will replace the judicial decision by a law. Finally, at the fourth stage of the game, the player who has not already participated joins in the game – depending on who played at the preceding step.

The four-step game can be depicted as a relationship in which first-rank judges are the agents of two principals, the politician and the second-rank judge. Each of these two principals is able to overrule the first-rank judge and therefore retain, to use the words of Aghion and Tirole (1997), 'formal' authority. Furthermore, it is important to note that the principals may not have full information about the agent's costs and actions but, at the same time, he/she ignores the possible or actual imperfections of information that can occur. It thus means that the game takes place in a full and complete information environment. This latter assumption is perfectly justified by the sequential nature of the game: the players cannot play simultaneously simply because a decision has to be issued for a counter-decision to exist. The sequential nature of the game gets its justification from the existence of a hierarchy of norms, thanks to which the third- and fourth-step players benefit from a veto power over the decisions made by the first-rank judge. The possibility thus granted to the two principals to reject decisions made in earlier stages of the game satisfies the democratic constraint. Indeed, that politicians can overrule legal decision makers means that these are the elected agents of the citizens who are in a position to control the behaviours of non-elected agents. Therefore, ministers and parliamentarians have the explicit power to rework the decisions made by first- or even second-rank judges.

Besides this *ex post* aspect, the hierarchy of norms also has an *ex ante* dimension. Indeed, players may behave strategically in order to avoid the reversal of their decisions. In this way, they conform by anticipation to the most preferred choices of the principal. Judicial discretion thus does not contradict democratic control. How these strategic behaviours develop is discussed in the next subsection.

3.2 Strategic Behaviours and Judicial Discretion

Let us start with the analysis of the consequences of the veto power granted to the political decision maker. If he/she plays at the fourth step of the game, the politician may accept the decision of the second-rank judge or choose to veto it and replace it by its most preferred point d^*. The second-rank judge is perfectly aware of the veto power of the political decision maker. If one assumes that the second-rank judge tries to achieve his/her most preferred point under the constraint of a possible reversal, he/she will choose to replace j_j by his/her own decision if and only if there exists a point j_s which satisfies both his/her own preferences (strictly) as well as those of the player granted with the veto power (non-strictly). One can write the set of the viable decisions that can be made by the higher-rank judge in the following way:

$$j_S \in P_P^{nS}(j_j) \cap P_{j_s}^{S}(j_j).$$

These decisions will not be reversed by the political decision maker because the latter prefers each point of this set to the decision made by the first-rank judge. In other words, unable to impose his/her most preferred point d^*, the political decision maker prefers to choose j_j to j_s.

Keeping the same objective in mind – namely to guarantee the survival of his/her decision – the first-rank judge may also decide to adopt a strategic behaviour. The judge is going to choose a viable or stable decision at the second step of the game, that is a decision that will not be reversed either by the judge of appeal or by the politician. Therefore, the final outcome made by the administrative first-rank court does not actually result from effective but simply from potential monitoring. Anticipating a

```
    d              j_j              j_s
    P_1
    |───────────────|────────────────|
         ←─────────────────────→
```

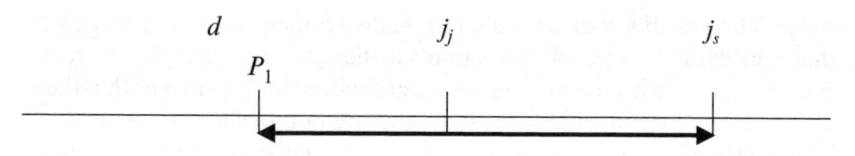

Figure 9.2 Set of structure-induced equilibria

'response' by one or the other principal, the agent chooses a point such as the set of solutions simultaneously preferred by both principals is empty. In other words, he/she chooses j_j as a structure-induced equilibrium (SIE):

$$j_j \in P_P^{ns}(j_j) \cap P_{J_s}^{s}(j_j) \text{ and } P_P^{ns}(j_j) \cap P_{J_s}^{s}(j_j) = \emptyset.$$

Graphically, the set of structure-induced equilibria is located on the segment $[d, j_s]$ (see Figure 9.2).

- When j_j is located within the interval $[d, j_s]$, the decision is stable. No political response is possible from either principal. Since any move in a direction or the other, towards d or j_s, would obviously harm either one principal or the other, any political intervention favouring one principal would be disfavoured by the other. No Pareto improvement is possible, the principals' capacity to react is neutralized. As they cannot agree on an alternative solution commonly preferred to the judicial decision, political decision makers cannot but recognize the agent's independence. From the standpoint of the agent, the interval $[d, j_s]$ represents the set of politically viable decisions.
- When j_j does not belong to the set of equilibrium compromises, it no longer represents a stable outcome. Pareto improvements are possible. The principals' response consists in overturning the judicial decision, so as to shift it within $[d, j_s]$. The new choice, now an SIE, will be closer to the preferences of both principals. Then, the two principals agree on the dependence of the first-rank court.

Such an institutional design enables the agent to engage in strategic behaviours. When his/her preferred point is located within the interval $[d, j_s]$, he/she can make a choice perfectly in accordance with his/her own preferences without provoking any political response. When the agent's preferred point is located outside $[d, j_s]$, he/she chooses either d or j_s, depending on which one is closer to j_j^*; d and j_s represent then a second-best solution, which will stand unchallenged. The agent anticipates possible bargaining between the principals, and will thus strategically locate his/her decision within $[d, j_s]$, in order to avoid a reversal of his/her decision. In other words, a 'feedback effect' promotes stability of choices and while it secures judicial independence, it also prevents judges from behaving as totally independent agents. Therefore, one can observe a twofold phenomenon: while there exists a certain amount of discretionary power, in spite of the absence of any provision to guarantee judicial independence, the decisions made by first- or second-rank judges are not so far from the most preferred points of the political principal. In other words, the choices made by judges fall within a set of choices designed as acceptable by the agents of the citizens.

We shall not discuss the nature of the preferences of the players in detail or their impact on the final decision. Suffice it to say that, even if the type of judge influences the decisions, it does not modify the fact that the set of potential decisions remains bounded by the preferences of the other players.[2] Therefore, judicial discretion does not necessarily mean a lack of democracy (as long as the political decision makers' preferences represent the preferences of the voters, and the preferences of the higher court are shaped by the constitution).

3.3 Litigants, Seizure Rules and the Control of Judicial Behaviour

As said earlier, the game is sequential and the first sequence depends on the decision of a citizen to initiate a legal procedure. Thus, one has necessarily to take into account the seizure strategy of a potential litigant. The latter, if dissatisfied with a decision he/she finds unacceptable, will sue before the first-rank court, and exert a democratic control over the behaviour of the administration. The choice to sue before an administrative court then depends on the expectations about the effect of the seizure and the knowledge of the preferences of the other players. More precisely, the potential litigant will balance the expected gains from triggering the judicial machinery with the satisfaction derived from the status quo. Since the potential litigant knows that any decision of the first-rank judge (j_j) is veto-proof when it belongs to $[d, j_s]$ and because he/she takes the future responses of the third- and fourth-step players into account, the potential litigant chooses to sue only when the expected j_j is closer to his/her most preferred point (a^*) than the actual decision made by the administration (a). On the contrary, whenever a is closer to a^* than the expected j_j, the citizen prefers not to sue.

As a consequence, the defendant, that is the administration whose decision is at stake, can act so as to make decision that the plaintiff is not induced to sue before the administrative court. When the decision preferred by the bureau belongs to $[d, j_s]$ and the decision preferred by the plaintiff does not, no suit can durably change the decision and the citizen can exert no judicial action in the situation. This raises the issue of the collusion between the administration and the administrative courts. However, any decision preferred by the administration which is not located between d and j_s is not an SIE. Therefore, a judicial action initiated by a plaintiff may succeed in overturning the administrative decision. In other words, even though the administration makes a decision which is d or j_s, according to whether his/her preferred point is located at the right or left of $[d, j_s]$, the plaintiff may keep an incentive to sue as long as he/she prefers a point located on the SIE segment but different from one of its extremities.

There is another situation in which the potential litigant has no incentive to refer his or her case to a court. It occurs when both the administration and the plaintiff share the same interest in the status quo, compared with the solution that would derive from a solution imposed on them by the higher ranks of the hierarchy of norms. In that case it is likely that the plaintiff and the defendant should negotiate rather than resort to the judicial system.

We shall provide an illustration of these results through the case of French administrative courts and show that in this case the delegation of the control of bureaucracies to a non-elected agent has not led to partial and dependent or 'political' decision making by the judges.

4 APPLICATION TO FRENCH ADMINISTRATIVE JUSTICE

4.1 Brief Description of the French System of Administrative Courts

Broadly defined, legal regimes can be divided into two categories, monist and dualist systems (Josselin and Marciano 1995), with their related conceptions of administrative law. On the one side, common law countries are based on monist systems. Within such regimes, a regular judge is in charge of the litigation involving public bureaucracies. Therefore, there are no separate administrative tribunals but merely 'regular courts'. These are 'control' systems, like the English one, in which administrative law is designed with the purpose of limiting the powers of government in order to protect the citizen. On the other side, alternative systems (of the instrumentalist type, like the French one) are based on the principle that the state and public administrations have to be judged in a separate or specific way. These systems are dualist in that they clearly define the domain of public affairs; the state has to be judged and controlled in a separate way. In these systems, administrative law is directed towards the functioning of the administration. The administrative judiciary controls the administration, on behalf of political decision makers.

The French legal system is a typical example of a dualist system, which is characterized by the fact that administrative judges belong to the administration and thus form a specific judiciary, apart from 'normal' judges. Such a structure seems to imply a lack of some traditional guarantees of independence. Indeed, even if French administrative judges enjoy obvious guarantees of structural independence, such as tenure and fixed monetary compensations, they are also part of a bureaucratic hierarchy and therefore subject to traditional bureaucratic incentives – of a budgetary nature, for instance. As a former prime minister once said, 'administrative judiciary does not exist, there is only an administrative staff in charge of judging' (Michel Debré, quoted in Lochak 1994, p. 61). In addition, the existence of administrative courts is not written into the constitution or the fact that high officials of the court frequently join ministerial teams and the cabinet. Finally, at least as far as their appointment and to some extent the monitoring mechanism are concerned (Lochak 1994; Chapus 1998), judges remain structurally dependent on political decision makers.

As a consequence, one might expect that the administrative judiciary controls the administration on behalf of the political decision makers – that is, that the administrative court really behaves as the agent of the politician. However, the independence of French administrative judges is rarely threatened by political interventions hence, the possible conclusion that 'the legislature and the executive allow a certain degree of judicial independence that exceeds the structural provisions' (Salzberger 1993, p. 353). Substantive independence seems to exceed structural independence (Salzberger 1993). Interestingly, Salzberger's statement is made in an analysis of monist legal regimes. Thus France, although being a typical example of a civil law country, provides an illustration of why a government might choose to leave its judges free of any control. In other words, the French administrative justice system shares the same characteristics as monist systems in terms of an independent judiciary. In the context of administrative justice, the question is all the more important since it suggests the possible independence of agents granted with the right to control the state. The effectiveness of judicial independence in the dualist French regime can be explained in practice by the existence of appeal mechanisms and the fact that the first-rank judge is not only the agent of the politician, but also the agent of a higher court. This can be inferred from the current practice of French administrative courts.

4.2 Current Practice

First, there seems to be no obvious tendency of the administrative courts to systematically make decisions in favour of the administration and such decisions to be accepted by the two principals. These decisions can be interpreted as being in the zone in which independent behaviours are consistent with the goals of the two principals. Thus, there is a wide agreement that the administrative judiciary has largely contributed to the French *État de droit* (rule of law). Note that the preferences of the administrative courts may exhibit increasing legal concerns rather than political ones, as emphasized for instance by the then minister of justice, Jean Foyer, who, according to Lochak (1994, p. 32), declared in 1963 that the administrative judiciary needed to be reformed so as to prevent judges from ignoring administrative and governmental realities and developing an 'abuse of legal mind, an abstract reasoning, a taste for deductive systems'.

Second, if it is correct that judges anticipate sanctions and decide accordingly, one should find very few illustrations of choices made outside the zone of stability. Indeed, relatively few crises have occurred, most of them during times of trouble, such as war or post-war periods: for instance, the purges that occurred in 1879 when the Republicans came to power; under the Vichy regime; after the Second World War; and more recently – perhaps more interestingly for our purpose since the structural conditions of judicial decision making are closer to current conditions – the famous Canal affair (1962) in which the French *Conseil d'Etat* (Council of State) invalidated a decision issued by the French President of the Republic allowing the creation of a specialized military court of justice, but was in turn reversed by a political intervention of both the French Government and Parliament. In that case, the council of state invalidated a decision issued by one of the principals, namely the French president, concerning the creation of a special court of justice. But the decision of the Council of State – that was located outside the SIE set, which made infringement upon the independence of the agent possible – was in its turn invalidated through a joint decision of the two principals.

All these cases share the common features of having occurred in troubled times during which the set of viable decisions is limited. In times of peace, the decisions made by administrative courts have very rarely been reversed by political decision makers. Thus, despite a lack of formal guarantees of independence, the administrative courts seem relatively 'free' to make decisions as long as these decisions do not contradict the political objectives too obviously (as in times of crisis). This not only corroborates the existence of judicial strategies of self-restraint but also shows that the decisions made by judges do not necessarily lead to decisions that are inconsistent with the interests of the citizens.

5 CONCLUSION

This chapter has shown that the political review of judicial decision making may be a source of rather than a limitation to democracy. The argumentation developed and the example of the French system of administrative justice is, of course, no definitive and formal proof. Nonetheless, it provides interesting elements of evidence to support this institutional explanation of judicial discretion and the practice of self-restraint by administrative judges.

NOTES

* A previous version of this text was presented at the European Law and Economics seminar in Erfurt (2003) and at the 4th Corsica Law and Economics Workshop (Reims, 2003). I would like to thank all the participants and, in particular, Jean-Michel Josselin and Alain Marciano for comments on previous versions of the chapter.
1. Note that monist and dualist political regimes as defined by Ackerman, differ from monist and dualist legal regimes as will be defined in Section 4. Therefore, there exist dualist political regimes characterized by monist legal systems (the United States, for instance), monist political regimes with monist legal systems (Great Britain) or monist political regimes with dualist legal systems (France).
2. It is possible to distinguish three main judicial types. The 'political' judge can be portrayed as systematically providing decisions in accordance with the preferences of the political decision maker. The 'legalist' judge makes decisions in accordance with the preferences of the higher courts. The 'independent-but-realistic' judge tries to impose his/her own preferences but under the constraint of the preferences of the other players.

REFERENCES

Ackerman, Bruce (1998), *We the People, vol 1: Foundations*, Cambridge, MA: Belknap Press.
Aghion, Philippe and Jean Tirole (1997), 'Formal and real authority in organizations', *Journal of Political Economy*, **105** (1), 1–29.
Chapus, R. (1998), *Droit du Contentieux Administratif [Administrative Litigation Law]*, Paris: Montchrestien.
Chevallier, Jacques (1994), *l'Etat de droit [The Rule of Law]*, 2nd edn, Paris: Montchrestien.
Holcombe, Randall G. (2001), 'Constitutions and democracy', *Economie Publique*, **7** (1), 43–58.
Holcombe, Randall G. (2002), 'Political entrepreneurship and the democratic allocation of economic resources', *Review of Austrian Economics*, **15** (2/3), 143–59.
Josselin, Jean-Michel and Alain Marciano (1995), 'Constitutionalism and common knowledge: assessment and application to the design of a future European constitution', *Public Choice*, **85**, 177–85.
Kelsen, Hans, (1934 [1962]), *Théorie Pure du Droit [Pure Theory of Law]*, Paris: Dalloz.

Lochak, Danielle (1994), *La Justice Administrative [Administrative Courts]*, Paris: Montchrestien.
Salzberger, Elie (1993), 'A positive analysis of the doctrine of separation of powers, or: why do we have an independent judiciary?', *International Review of Law and Economics*, **13**, 349–79.
Voigt, Stefan and Eli Salzberger (2002), 'Choosing not to choose: when politicians choose to delegate powers', *Kyklos*, **55** (2), 289–310.

10. Law, justice and republic: the French republican model of judicial regulation

Christian Barrère

1 INTRODUCTION

Judicial institutions have a growing role in our societies. In France, some scholars have even introduced the idea of a 'government of the judges'. However, while judicial institutions do not substitute for government and public administration they are becoming an important means of social regulation, perhaps the main one. In France, this tendency is not the result of desires within the judiciary to increase the power of magistrates, rather it arises from the social functions attributed to the judicial system by the French model of the republican law and justice.

The development of European judicial cooperation, the establishment of a 'European judicial area' and building of a new European judicial system demand cooperation and highlight areas of competition between different national models. Consequently, an evaluation of these models is necessary.

This chapter focuses on the structural logic of the French model. Starting from the standard analysis of judicial regulation (Section 2), I consider the basis of the model and the republican dualism (Section 3) to explain the present role of judicial regulation (Section 4).

2 THE STANDARD MODEL OF JUDICIAL REGULATION

A judicial system is necessary to enforce the law by monopolizing the power of constraint which obliges everyone to accept legal consequences. But the judicial system plays other roles in the application of the legal system. It is the arbiter of the law when there are different interpretations of it, and when opposite claims are advanced. Hence the judicial system is a system of legitimate interpretation and distribution of the concrete effects of law in a social context. The judicial system has two main types of effects on law: efficiency effects and distribution – equity – effects. This is true in the two great functions of the judicial system: the function of law enforcement (Subsection 2.1), and the function of law interpretation (Subsection 2.2).

2.1 Law Enforcement

An efficiency perspective

The need for an enforcement apparatus   A legal system without enforcement is no more efficient than a system without law. If the legal system is an efficient one, judicial enforcement is efficient. This is easily demonstrated through a game-theoretic presentation.

We use an evolutionary game approach because the problem is not only one of static equilibrium, but also one of evolution of strategic choices in a context of evolving conventions. This approach makes two interesting innovations in game theory. It requires players to have merely weak rationality. They observe the gains from the different strategies and choose the most profitable one whereas in classical games they must conceive their strategic planning for the whole game. It introduces the possibility of random strategy moves – for instance mutations – and of strategies which become winning because of imitation. It is assumed that the players gradually prefer winning strategies. A replication mechanism associates variations in the proportion of players using one strategy and the gap between the earnings of this strategy and the average gain of the other strategies.

Let us suppose that two persons or two groups are facing PR effects (for instance, when renting a flat). The contract gives each of them some rights and some obligations. If PRs are not monitored and enforced, they tend to renege on their obligations, as is typical in free-rider problems. If we use an evolutionary game, with pure or mixed strategies (belonging to an axis from absolutely no respect – NR – to strict respect –R– of PR organization), the payoffs are ordered so that $G(nr, R) > G(r, R) > G(nr, NR) > G(r, NR)$. $G(nr, R)$ represents the temptation to cheat because the opportunistic behaviour gives the greatest payoff when the other player observes the law; $G(r, R) > G(nr, NR)$ because the observance of law leads to cooperation, the result of which is better than a non-cooperative outcome; $G(r, NR)$ is the worst payoff. In all cases we have the following game matrix (on the left the game and on the right the normalized game):[1]

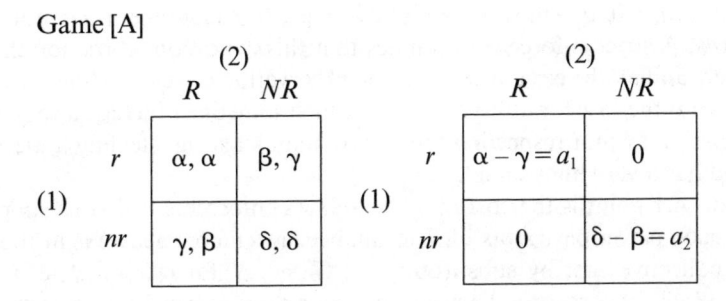

The French republican model of judicial regulation

Game [A]

	(2) R	(2) NR			(2) R	(2) NR
(1) r	α, α	β, γ	(1) r	$\alpha - \gamma = a_1$	0
(1) nr	γ, β	δ, δ	(1) nr	0	$\delta - \beta = a_2$

Figure 10.1

with $\gamma > \alpha > \delta > \beta$, so $a_1 < 0$ and $a_2 > 0$. The unique evolutionary stable equilibrium is a prisoners' dilemma equilibrium, *nr – NR*, suboptimal. No mutant strategy can invade the game, the *nr* strategy being a dominant strategy (a standard replicator, with *nr* the proportion of players using *nr*, gives $dnr/dt = nr \cdot [a_2(1-nr) \cdot nr - a_1(1-nr)^2]$, always >0).

A judicial system can be seen as a means to rule the *nr* strategy out of the strategy space, so as to impose a strategy of respect for the law and the associated high equilibrium *r, R* with the optimal outcome α, α. From an economic point of view the choice of players between *r* and *nr* strategies is a rational choice, based on costs and benefits (including non-monetary ones, such as time or ethics). Justice cannot get rid of *nr* strategies (or mixed strategies including *nr* actions) but only makes them costly. In the enforcement of law, justice is not only a coercive machine (all criminals are not arrested and punished, crime is not eradicated), but also an incentive mechanism.

A partial and unequal enforcement   If players are reasonable individuals who take into account costs and benefits, the enforcement of law needs efficient sanctions. In the new game:

Game [B]

	(2) R	(2) NR			(2) R	(2) NR
(1) r	α', α'	β', γ'	(1) r	$\alpha' - \gamma' = a_1$	0
(1) nr	γ', β'	δ', δ'	(1) nr	0	$\delta' - \beta' = a_2$

Figure 10.2

we need $a'_1 > 0$, $a'_2 > 0$, so $\alpha' > \gamma'$ and $\delta' > \beta'$, to encourage observation of the law. A strict enforcement implies that this condition is true for all the players and all the circumstances. The observation of reality shows us that this is not the case for utility functions which sometimes include a very high estimation for not respecting the law (if I am starving, stealing a piece of bread has a very high value).

Another point is the cost of judicial law's enforcement. Let us suppose that each player pays a tax of T to finance law enforcement. We introduce this collective cost by substituting α'', β'', γ'', δ'' for α', β', γ', δ' (with $\alpha'' = \alpha' - T$, and so on). Then the new cooperative outcome in game [C] may be, for the individual and for the collective, inferior to the old non-cooperative outcome of game [A]. It is the case if $\alpha'' < \delta$.

Game [A]

(2)

	R	NR
r	α, α	β, γ
nr	γ, β	δ, δ

(1)

Game [C]

(2)

	R	NR
r	α'', α''	β'', γ''
nr	γ'', β''	δ'', δ''

(1)

Figure 10.3

The enforcement of law is only partial, and it is relative to its cost. The cost itself, has two components.

The first one relates to the configuration of the instruments of enforcement. For instance, the enforcement of software or music files property rights can be achieved through public forms (courts impose sanction on the violations of rights) or private forms (producers introduce technical instruments as tools to protect their rights effectively). The question is how to achieve an efficient mix public enforcement (especially judicial enforcement) and private enforcement.

The second point is that judicial enforcement costs are not only of a direct nature (for example judges' salaries). To sue someone in court is costly, including monetary expenses and transaction costs (time, psychological costs and so on). Optimal enforcement policies have to include this problem.

If the law enforcement has a collective cost, arbitration is necessary between the benefit and the cost of protection. Some laws will be strictly enforced and others will not. And the extent of enforcement will change with enforcement cost and law respect benefits. It also depends strongly on the modalities of social advantages valuation.

Substitutes Justice changes the earnings of *r* and *nr* strategies and increases law observance. Some alternative means also have to be considered as producers of norms; these include ideology, ethics, deontology, religion, customs, culture, social conventions and so on. They can encourage conventions of respect for the law in place of law violation (Bradney and Cownie 2000; Ellickson 1991; Goh 2002; Posner 1980). They work, as in the substitution of game [B] to [A], by increasing the payoffs of the *r* strategy in relation to the *nr* strategy (for example, by excluding someone from the group for rule infraction, rewarding someone for loyalty, or reproving immoral actions).

These sets of norms may emerge from the repetition of inter-individual and group relations and are reinforced by it. Repetition, under different hypotheses of rational behaviours, allows the emergence of cooperation through reciprocity, and organization or reputation building (Hardin 1982; Fudenberg and Maskin 1990; Kreps 1990). These self-organized processes were formulated in repeated games terms (Axelrod 1984) and in evolutionary games terms (Bicchieri et al. 1997).

We can imagine, following Axelrod, that cooperative strategies emerge with the repetition of the game. Nevertheless, their ability to enforce law is doubtful. Repeated game theory has shown that strong and numerous conditions are necessary to support cooperation. Rules will be 'spontaneously' respected in small communities (as in a family or a bureau), between identified players, through repeated interactions, and under the possibility of retaliation. This is not the case when players are numerous, changing, unknown, in favour of different ideologies and ethics and so on. Moreover, in an evolutionary perspective, the unique evolutionary stable equilibrium is the dominant non-respect strategy. If any other strategy becomes the general one (for example, the respect strategy), a player choosing a non-respect strategy has a greater payoff; he/she is then mimicked by the others. Many examples of a progressive degradation of cooperation can be recalled. A historical perspective shows that small, closed stable societies, based on tradition, and with ideological enforcement (for example, the taboo system) develop cooperative behaviours (for example, through the means of gift relations). Large, open, unstable modern societies, with many fluctuating interactions, evolving norms, continuous refinement and increasing complexity of the rules and of the law system, on the other hand, need more explicit enforcement. Thus, the development of legal systems is accompanied by a development of a judicial enforcement.

Extension of competition When competition becomes tighter, spontaneous observance of law becomes less likely (Barrère 2001).

In Axelrod-type situations, spontaneous respect of law is likely[2] because, even if interests are not necessarily parallel, the individuals are only interested in their individual payoff, and not in others'. They are not 'jealous'. Obviously player (1) prefers outcome (5, 3) to outcome (3, 3) but is indifferent between outcome (5, 3) and outcome (5, 5). The profit of his/her partner is strictly immaterial to him/her. This assumption is appropriate in smooth and peaceful competition, but irrelevant in world of tight competition in unstable markets. To gain more than competitors can be decisive in upcoming battles; therefore, a player may prefer outcome (2, 0) to an outcome (3, 3). However, the solutions of the game are very sensitive to the levels of the payoffs.

Tight competition increases the risk incurred by cooperative players and use of opportunistic strategies with regard to observance of law. Players are intent on avoiding the disastrous situations (r, NR) and (nr, R) and prefer the more secure but suboptimal repeated outcome (nr_T, NR_T). The repetition of the game reinforces this tendency, because the 'repetition' is not in fact an identical repetition: the economic and competitive power of each player evolves according to the results of the previous rounds. The dynamic of the game widens the differences between the profits, which are used as additional weapons in competition, and may cause the elimination of some players. The introduction of additional players would make this threat even more poignant. The use of tit-for-tat or carrot-and-stick strategies is hardly likely. Then, the extension of competition needs a more explicit and powerful law enforcement system, which explains the growing power of judicial systems.

Enforcement as a public good and a club good   In enforcing law, a judge produces a public good. Even if the sentence of a court is particular and limited, it contributes to reinforcing the weight of the law system. It creates a working incentive system, which produces cooperation and wealth. Enforcement produces a public intermediate good (cooperation), which is the means of producing a public final good (to increase social wealth, to live in peace and so on). In addition to its static effect, enforcement has a dynamic effect, in increasing the stability, predictability and credibility of the law, and in providing a stable basis for expectations and a stable framework for investment. Law enforcement is an important means of reducing transaction costs.

With the supply of public goods, however, we meet a problem of free-riding. If the cost of law enforcement is generally higher than individual profit and lower than collective profit, it implies a collective procedure, based on a constructivist project or on self-organization processes. According to the dispersion of individual utilities of enforcement for some types of law (if I am a smoker, I do not have a great preoccupation with the enforcement of anti-tobacco regulations), enforcement may vary. It becomes a club good and many clubs can coexist. History shows many types of club institutions of justice, be they local or communitarian (fishermen), or temporary (as during medieval fairs). Today many private institutional systems work to enforce specific types of law (for example, to manage law on credit cards). Other organizations incorporate law enforcement: the main one is the firm because it is a local property rights enforcement system. Evolution affects the efficient configuration of these clubs, their number, types and sizes. The increasing complexity of the legal system implies more sophisticated and specialized clubs.

Law enforcement can use private means of enforcement. Nevertheless, law acts as a system, so enforcement has to be systemic. Enforcement requires coherence; and the power of sanctioning deviant behaviours must be founded on legal and public legitimacy. So, every enforcement apparatus ultimately needs public enforcement. Moreover, to be able to induce cooperation inside competition, this coherence must be particularly strong in market societies.

An equity perspective on law enforcement

Enforcement lovers and enforcement adverse people (the pros and cons of enforcement) As it enables the distribution of effective rights, powers and wealth to be modified, judicial enforcement does not represent a standard public good. Some individuals or groups may win with a strong system of law enforcement (obviously the owners); and some others with a weak system of enforcement (the robbers). Instead of the previous symmetrical game, with parallel interests, let us now consider game [D], characterized by non-symmetrical distributions in the symmetric outcomes. Suppose the collective surplus to be shared between the two players is 10, and the cost of cheating (loss of reputation, organization cost and so on) is 2. In the r, R outcome, player (2) is favoured when sharing the total surplus, while in the nr, NR outcome player (1) is favoured; for instance (1) performs better in illegal conditions, and (2) in legal ones. The cheat takes the whole surplus minus the cost of cheating, 2.

Game [D]   (2)

		R	NR
(1)	r	3, 7	0, 8
	nr	8, 0	5, 1

Figure 10.4

The equilibrium in dominant strategies is (*nr, NR*; 5, 1). Suppose that the court reverses the result, when one player does not respect the law, while the other one respects it. That leads to game [E]:

Game [E]

(2)

		R	NR
(1)	r	3, 7	8, 0
	nr	0, 8	5, 1

Figure 10.5

Equilibrium becomes (*r, R*; 3, 7). The collective surplus is increased; but while player (2) is in a better situation, player (1) is worse off. In this case, enforcement is not a common wish and needs an authority decision. Posner (1973) contests this point of view and argues that individuals are ready to accept a common law based on wealth maximization. In the long run they are most likely to profit from it, even if a particular application of the rule penalizes them at a given time. Nevertheless, there can be a permanent separation between a group with an interest in law enforcement and one against it. If so, public enforcement power becomes necessary (see the mafia's problems).

Another way to combine distribution effects and the acceptance of regulatory control can be demonstrated within an exchange framework. In order to increase social wealth, player (2) can propose that player (1) enforces law while modifying the shares. The non-cooperative outcome of game [D] works as a threat value (5, 1). So, every solution [*r, R*] with a redistribution of the type $(5+a, 1+2-a)$ with $0 < a < 2$ is acceptable and efficient. One can, for example, interpret in these terms the institutionalization of inequitable systems based on medieval law.

Unequal enforcement   Since justice enforces law, opportunistic behaviours are involved. Individuals demand strong enforcement of their rights and weak enforcement of their obligations. As a driver I prefer weak enforcement of the Highway Code, but as a pedestrian I want strong control. If individuals have moving positions within the law system, sometimes as drivers and sometimes as pedestrians, there are minimal consequences. On the other hand, if the roles in the division of labour and the roles in social organization are permanent and rigid, the consequences are more significant. Judicial strategies emerge and compete with one another. Being in a world of scarcity, justice can only use limited resources. The enforcement of law is never perfect. Justice has to decide priorities: to enforce strongly the protection of people, or ownership; to control compliance with fiscal duties; to enforce minor protection, or anti-sexism laws; to place less emphasis on enforcement of the Highway Code, fiscal evasion, prohibition of prostitution or financial delinquency. It can be more determined when enforcing workers' rights, or the property rights of managers, or of ownerships; or when deciding to enforce the rights of consumers over the rights of producers, and so on. Individuals and groups propose different priorities for judicial working. These strategies do not necessarily result from complex calculations, but can derive primarily from opposition to existing legislation, be it lax or rigorous. Moreover, they may oppose projects to redefine judicial priorities. These strategies express the defence of immediate interests, but may be the result of clever constructions. Some interest groups will be able to format them in a more coherent and more presentable way than others, and to lobby in the social field. Judicial strategies, relating to the 'imperfect' character of the justice system and judicial enforcement, are not mainly the inescapable ransom of imperfect human nature, but are the effect of scarcity's economic constraints.

This can also lead to lacunae between modifying the law and modifying law enforcement. For instance, 'society' may prefer to tolerate the personal consumption of marijuana without amending the law, instead of modifying it. So legal policies and strategies are accompanied by enforcement policies and strategies. In some areas of new law (tobacco regulation, sexist or racist practices, disability rights, prisoners' rights, and so on), the debate about legal intervention just begins. The second round involves fighting to enforce these regulations; an international comparison clearly highlights that the Highway Code is enforced to very different degrees across countries, even in those with a similar level of development.

Our modelling showed, from an economic point of view, that law enforcement implies two different logics, efficiency logic and equity logic. Judicial enforcement is an incentive by modifying the parameters of economic calculation, by reducing the effects of uncertainty on law and it increases the social welfare. At the same time, the distribution of wealth effects depends on the configuration of imperfect and unequal law enforcement. Justice is simultaneously producing efficiency effects and distribution effects.

2.2 Legal Interpretation

In order to become a concrete incentive, the legal system needs not only enforcement, but also interpretation. Justice appears as a referee among opposite pretensions. Different players, including government and state organizations, claim their entitlement to do something and dispute other players' rights to do the same.

The interpretation of the facts

The judge must connect the legal system with the facts related to a particular case. The judge's first task is to draw up an assessment of the facts, in the role of 'neutral' and 'independent' referee. The judge must establish the 'truth' and produce a legitimate reading of the facts, while the parties propose different versions according to their interests, their opportunism, even their bad faith.

The divergences between the pretensions are also related to cognitive reasons. Let us substitute the idea of limited or procedural rationality for that of substantive rationality. Individuals will then seek an average, subjective and approximate level of results, rather than the strict maximization of objective functions; they would look for 'justice' (reasonable compensation) rather than ask for maximum compensation. They use procedures, often organizational ones (the individual has to decide as a member of an organization, a company, a family and so on), conventions, references to norms, thinking frameworks, 'points of view'. As a consequence, different people, using different cognitive frameworks, may build different versions of the same reality. Contemporary sociology shows that social contexts influence the behaviours and lead to 'habitus', that is interiorized forms of behaviour related to the social status of the individuals. A professional litigant – say a lawyer or an insurance company – will not have the same type of behaviour or understanding of arbitration between costs and benefits as an occasional litigant. Rationalities become socio-historically situated.

At the same time, the referee is not generally limited to an 'objective' observation of facts (which corresponds more to the logic of the expert); on the contrary, the judge provides a specific interpretation of the facts and defines responsibilities and torts: are the damage and the law violation intentional or not?

Hence, to build this interpretation, judges have to be real and active producers. They base their findings on a specific mode of reading reality; they give more or less importance to particular type of consideration, to social logic, psychological logic or economic logic. Spatial comparisons show that, in the same legal area of jurisprudence, the same attacks against the law are judged and sanctioned in different ways. Moreover, the judge is not always a public judge. In some cases, conflicting parties agree about the choice of a specific referee in order to have a particular reading of the facts; for instance, firms will ask a private or a professional referee to intervene in a dispute, in anticipation of a decision based on economic criteria, whereas they fear that such criteria would be minimize by a public judge.

Legal interpretation

The legal system cannot be a perfect and complete system. It cannot specify all the legal rights and duties in every situation, according to every type of contract. And, within the legal system, some laws are very precise but some are vaguer ('human rights', privacy law and so on). Williamson (1985) distinguishes three types of law, corresponding to his three general categories of economic institutions:

- the 'classical law' for the market; the law strictly specifies and records the conditions of an instantaneous market transaction. Thus, it is simple and indisputable;
- the 'neoclassical law' for the contract, a hybrid form between market and hierarchy; it organizes a longer relation than the market one (for example, industrial cooperation contract or the franchising commercial contract). It is no more than a partial framework, because nobody can anticipate all future contexts; and
- the 'evolutionary law' for the hierarchy; it organizes a framework for managing changes (such as labour legislation, which allows under some conditions modifying the description of workers' jobs or their earnings).

From an economic point of view, it appears that the legal system enforces and implements a broad spectrum of rights. At one extreme, we have precise laws, the implementation of which has been envisaged by the parties (for instance, they signed a contract; therefore the role of the legal institution is to make them respect it). At the other end of the spectrum there are general rights, the concrete consequences of which are not well specified; for example, civil liability specifies only general duties (to behave like a good father), without saying precisely what it implies in any circumstance. Generally the law does not envisage all the specific cases but establishes principles, general rules. So, to enforce law, the legal institutions are not inclined to point out their obvious consequences. In many cases they must interpret general principles, and then draw a solution for a particular case. The degree of interpretation is variable, larger when the application of a general law is concerned, weaker but nevertheless not nil, when interpreting a precise law (for example, when the contract does not envisage everything or when it is necessary to appreciate the good will of the parties).

The judicial interpretation as transaction cost minimization

Transaction costs make it impossible to have a system of *complete* contracts. Therefore, the judicial system, through a legitimate interpretation, is again efficient when it succeeds in reducing the social costs of transaction;

the specialization of the judge and the economies of scale in the construction of a corps of specialized interpreters move in the same direction as the transaction costs reduction. And this reduction is more or less strong, depending on whether they are precise or general laws. Cooter and Ulen (1988), like Williamson, oppose the legal theory of contract, which refers to an area where transaction costs are weak, and the legal theory of liability which covers an area where transaction costs are high. Whereas in the first case the interpretative role of justice is limited (it has to interpret the contractual wishes and agreements of the contractors), in the second case the interpretative role is much more significant. This approach also explains the absence of monopoly of the judicial system as an interpreter of the law. In case of litigation, parties can agree on a compromise (the lawyers of both firms establish a private agreement), or call upon a third person (a mediator). The choice of procedures will be guided by the comparison of the transaction costs.

The judicial interpretation as formulation of the rules in an open society
In the Hayekian approach, rules are thought of as incomplete (all states of nature cannot be anticipated) and imperfect (the conditions of their application can contradict each other), because they are necessarily abstract. No rule or condition can fits the infinite number of possible situations; their adaptation to a particular situation is not immediate. Hayek (1973) refuses any legal scale of sanctions, any standard solution which would deny the specificity of cases and the need to appreciate comparative responsibilities. So, the judge is in an eminent position to interpret the legal system.

Judicial functioning results from a spontaneous self-organized process, through trials and errors and progressive selection. It does not consciously maximize welfare but achieves it through managing ignorance. Individuals are ignorant for three reasons:

- some information is missing before the action, for the future is always unknown, at least in part;
- some individuals may not know that some information exists; and
- some pieces of information, tacit or codified information, are only partially transferable, or not transferable at all.

In this context, the judicial system allows the socialization of the individual, by transforming a spontaneous disorder into a self-organized order. Therefore, the emergence of rules, through a spontaneous self-organized process, and their judicial consecration by the judge, allows uncertainty to be managed and reduced. Individuals can rest upon rules which carry information and underpin routines. Cooperation is helped by these rules, although they do not result from calculation or maximization. On the contrary, they are general, and abstract not finalized, rules. This guarantees their social efficiency and enables them to act as general and stable references for individual action.

The judge operates by formulating the implicit social rules on property. Thus, judicial formulation and interpretation is a central point for society. Rules generally emerge from complex self-organized processes in an implicit form. The first role of the judge is to make explicit the implicit rules, to clarify them so that everyone can know them and profit from them. In this way, the judge fulfils a function of information transmission of similar importance to that of the Walrasian 'auctioneer'. The judge formulates the implicit rules, but does not create the rule, because there is a guiding tradition, the legal inheritance, which carries the threat of the loss of legitimacy.

Thus, the interpreting role of the judge is also limited; being under the law the judge has to comply with it. A judge must not determine to producing a new or a finalized, thus arbitrary, rule. By interpreting laws, the judge reinforces its stability and makes the future decisions of courts more predictable, which minimizes excessive recourse to the courts.

The judicial interpretation of legal problems has a second important effect, in that it allows rules to evolve. The judge is confronted with problems which are unsolvable in the existing legal system. Pressures to modify the existing rule in the context of other laws which have been handed down by tradition can make changes in the rule while preserving the coherence of the legal order.

A transaction cost approach and the Hayekian approach provide interesting points of view. Nevertheless they fail to explain the role of the judicial system when interpreting the law and defining what is 'just'. The judge produces lawful and 'just' sentences. He/she defines not only what is legal but also what is just. The judge is not a legal scholar, but rather a creative producer; for the 'just' sentence has not, always, already been written in the law. He/she is not only a communicator of laws but also a provider of justice. And this function is a complex one in the French republican model of law because it gives system of justice a dual foundation.

3   THE REPUBLICAN DUALISM

The standard economic analysis of law supposes that market logic, founded on the pursuit of efficiency, can be contradicted or limited by ethics (for example, of slavery, of child labour or of trafficking in women and children). However, these limits and constraints have no particular coherence and do not express any specific logic. Therefore, the analysis of the law can be conduced according to efficiency criteria and be modified when external considerations (specifically ethical ones) intervene.

Our hypothesis is that, in the case of the French republican model, these 'values' express a specific order. This means that the problem of the judicial system is not only to modify, *post facto* and in a marginal way, market rules and outcomes, but also to organize the coexistence of two logics, the market logic and the republican logic. As each has its own coherence and they have to coexist, we confront a dualistic regulation, which characterizes the institutional and cultural French heritage.

3.1 Two Orders

The legal system and the judicial system do not constitute a homogeneous whole. On the contrary, history shows that these systems are heterogeneous ones. They are characterized by diversity (Arnaud 1991): diversity between countries (continental civil law based on Roman basis and common law), diversity between subjects (with heterogeneous foundations, for example, where civil and labour law are concerned). However historical analysis of the law shows that this diversity goes deeper: 'law' gives place to 'laws'. These come from different foundations linked to different orders: for instance, in the Middle Ages canonical law expressed religious order and power, while royal law expressed royal order and power.

This legal diversity explains why the legal and the judicial systems have often been 'torn' between different and competing orders. Each one of these orders wants to be dominant within the whole society, urged by the forces it favours; that is, it tends to subsume all social functioning to its own logic and to become hegemonic.

As our societies are mainly organized according to two different logics, a market logic with market societies, a republican logic with societies organized as republican democratic nations, our legal and judicial systems inherit a double foundation. So the definition of what is legal and what is just refers to heterogeneous standards, norms and criteria, some being the expression of the republican society and the others the expression of the market society.

The republican order imposed in France by the Revolution and widely diffused all over the world, rests upon old principles. They were elaborated and implemented centuries earlier, in the Greek democracies or in the Roman republic, and developed in the political philosophy of the seventeenth and eighteenth centuries with the concepts of *corps social*, of *contrat social* and of government according to the reason (*gouvernement de la raison*).

The republican order is founded on the identity of individuals considered as citizens and as having an equal status. It introduces democracy as a political link between citizens. Social cohesion is ensured through everybody's submission to the law. This order distinguishes between the private and the public, between individuals and the collective, between private, individual interests and the general interest. It allows the emergence and the institutionalization of a political dimension in a political space, with its own institutions and specific political public processes (elections, law, government and so on) no longer subject to the cabinet of the king, the court of the lord or the sovereignty of the prince). It sets up a new representation of society as a political entity, a community of citizens, and no longer as a '*Chrétienté*' or as the widened family of the prince. In this model, political institutions have the responsibility of organizing the pursuit of the general interest and of the common welfare. The political society is responsible for its own organization, for its own government and for its future.

The expression and the management of the general interest define the republic. The designs of the general interest and the methods of its management are eminently variable, from the personality of a leader, who is seen to guide the society, to pluralistic forms of democracy. Theoretically underpinned by the submission of everyone to the law, republican mechanisms place great emphasis on law and justice.

Critical analysis – from Marxism to the public choice school – has highlighted the obvious differences between formal conditions and the real conditions in the application of the republican principles. This does not mean that these principles are without effect, particularly in relation to the conditions of working of the market order. The public and egalitarian character of the republican order gives the individuals political rights, independently of their market rights; for instance, rights to enjoy privacy, to develop and express personal ideas, to demonstrate, to vote, and so on (Barrère 2001)[3]. The logic of these rights is different from the logic of economic property rights. Some personal rights are inalienable (I cannot sell my organs or my freedom or my public role); the principles of the distribution of rights are intangible, which contradicts the economic logic of the market, of generalized exchange and of standard efficiency.

As the difference between political equality (a person = a person) and market equality (a euro = a euro) shows, the relative heterogeneity of market order and republican order can provoke tensions between both modes of socialization. The legal and the judicial systems can only be partially coherent since they join together diverse heterogeneous principles. For justice, a key issue is to build a coherent vision of law and of reality but the sources of the law are heterogeneous and refer to different logics. Moreover, these logics may be competitive.

3.2 Republican Order and Rule of Law

Modern legal rule has an abstract character. The law is based on general principles ('legal principles', 'constitutional principles' and so on). As independent from the power, the wealth or the status of individuals, it has a general character. As in a constructivist approach it expresses the ambition of the state, a collective project to develop social objectives and welfare.

In this framework, the judge plays a limited role of the *bouche de la loi*, a communicator of laws. Surprisingly two opposite ideas reach a similar conclusion on limiting the judicial function. In the old republican conception, the judge has a limited function in pointing out the law which expresses collective preferences; in the liberal conception (Buchanan 1972; Hayek 1973; Posner 1973), the judge has a limited function in pointing out the law which expresses individual preferences. Besides this, the judge also has the role of a provider of justice.

In a society governed by a heteronomous order, in which law and justice are only transcriptions of intangible and revealed rules, as in the systems of divine law and ecclesiastic justice, a judicial system has as an essential role when applying the law, in noting the facts and pointing out the rules.

As far as Canon law is concerned, the law to be applied by the Catholic Church comes from the Gospel, and is therefore a priori fixed. Its application is based on the doctrines denoted by the authorities (that is, the representatives of the Revealed Word on earth) and excludes any different one; the right 'interpretation' is opposed to wrong interpretations. This kind of justice establishes what is just (penitence especially, because the price of sin has to be fixed within the framework of moral law), according to tradition. Any pluralism is rejected, there is only one law, one right interpretation, one right standard transmitted by the tradition starting from the revelation; anything that opposes the law is of a schismatic nature. As the use of religious practices (the *ordalie*) demonstrates, feudal justice, based on religion, is of this kind (Duby 1987). The authoritarian republican forms, through extending constructivism but denying pluralism, give law a significant role but give justice a marginal one, because the law does not allow interpretation; the legitimate application is the interpretation of the producers of law, that is, the politicians.[4] What is just is also supposed to be indisputable for it results from the will of the people through the state.

On the other hand, the recognition of diversity and pluralism logically results in giving the judicial institution an increased role. There are two main reasons for this. First, as law is based on general and rational principles it has to be specified and interpreted in order to be applied to each particular case. The judge not only has to apply a whole range of tariffs (robbery is worth the amputation of the hand, and so on), but he/she also has to produce an original solution, taking into account the specific personalities and the circumstances involved, according to general principles.

The second reason is that society recognizes that the state itself, far from being an impartial arbitrator at the pinnacle of a hierarchy or a genuine incarnation of the general will of society and its zealous executor, holds a special point of view, fights for particular interests and has to be subjected to the law. Therefore, law changes its status. It is no longer the product of the state. The legal system introduces the regime of the rule of law. It is up to the institutions of justice to judge the conformity of the state action to legal principles.

3.3 The Primacy of the Republican Order

The French cultural heritage leads to an affirmation of the primacy of the republican logic. Such a primacy does not mean that in all particular cases socio-political criteria must be determining and override economic criteria. A necessary but very expensive measure to remove a marginal inequality will not be ordered by the magistrate. The primacy of the republican order does not imply its hegemony. However, if market and republican logics are different and can be opposed, they are, at first, complementary in so far as society needs them both to organize itself. It can no more ignore the economic data given by the market than it can ignore the socio-political data that republican logic intends to manage. A judge must also take them both into account and define the articulation between them. But the primacy of the republican order means that republican logic is a starting point. This is demonstrated by the following assertions.

Republican logic is necessary to found market logic
This is to the very conditions of the market game. The market allocation of resources requires that the 'agents' of the exchange should be defined as subjects of the law, free and responsible, having the rights and capacities for signing contracts. These rights are inalienable, which is in opposition to the logic of the efficient generalized exchange.

Republican logic delimits the impact and the perimeter of market logic
If a legal intervention cannot be satisfied by legitimating market standards, it is also because the socio-political republican principles that it serves lead, in some situations, to limit the role of the market logic. Historically, the European cultural model has produced a legal model which moderates or

controls the market logic by the assertion of the pre-eminence of republican law. Market logic encourages the confrontation of interests. The legal core defines a legal structure which may encourage cooperating, to moderate competition, to limit it or, on the contrary, to make it easier to exacerbate it. However, because of the primacy of the republican logic, it has a role in limiting the intensity and the extension of the market logic: not everything can be left to the market (one cannot buy organs, blood, persons, some honours, and so on[5]); tendencies to competition have to be fought to avoid economic war and to allow the market to produce cooperative effects (prices of predation will be prohibited, opportunism moderated and so on). Thus the law contributes to a definition of the place of market regulation within wider social regulation, its extent and its limits.

Republican logic imposes extra requirements on market logic
For the traditional law and economics, a market transaction is supposed to be voluntary as soon as formal conditions have been observed. This rule is extended to any implicit transaction. Any contract, explicit or implicit, is consequently accepted as legal and efficient. The republican logic introduces principles of freedom and equality that are not directly comparable to the formal freedom and equality of the contract, implicit or explicit, and that lead to distinctions between constrained and free exchange, equal exchange and exchange within the framework of dominant positions.

The legal contract is not identified with the economic transaction as represented by economists. The institutionalization of some feudal rules is impossible within the republican order; there cannot be legal 'contracts' or 'exchanges' such as between a slave and a slave trader, between a prostitute and client, or minor and paedophile. For the judge, control of the application of the principle of the autonomy of a decision has a considerable potential impact.[6]

Republican logic can contest market values and criteria
The idea of a double foundation of our republican and market societies led to an insistance on the possible divergences between socio-political republican criteria and market criteria, and, beyond, between the logic of the republic and the logic of the market. Then, the question is how to weight the various types of criteria, the various systems of representation, values and social projects. The concrete management of the relation between the market and the republic is not obvious, because no simple criterion can determine 'the right proportion'; the image of the balance is insufficient to represent the difficulty of weighing qualitatively heterogeneous criteria.

4 THE JUDICIAL REGULATION: TO SAY WHAT IS 'JUST'

4.1 Defining Law and Defining Justice

The judge produces not only lawful sentences, but 'just' sentences, defining not only what is legal but also what is just. The judge is not a legal scholar, but rather a creative producer; for the 'just' sentence is not always already written in the law.

The judge evaluates the rights and claims; mediates between conflicting claims and opposed rights; delineates the perimeter of each right, what actions are exactly authorized by the law and up to what limit; balances damages and compensations. Justice embraces the symbols of the glaive (to impose law) and the balance (to determine what 'just'). It intervenes much more directly in social working than merely by enforcing and interpreting the law. Legal institutions hold the legal monopoly, determining the concrete consequences of law, in respect of the existing legal system.

To announce what is 'just' according to the legal system implies two judicial functions: the judge introduces a concrete judicial entitlement which is an allocation of precise rights; and to apply equity criteria the judge introduces a new process of allocation and valuation, before and alongside the market process.

4.2 To Define the Rights

The judge has to define the precise powers, rights and obligations given to the parties by their rights in a system of rights, in situations where there are opposite claims. It is the role of the judge to determine who has the right to do what and under which circumstances. Has the tenant the right to require the owner to maintain the building in which he or she lives, and if this is the case, to what extent?

The legal system is a system of *relative rights* (who has which rights, but also, which rights override which other rights), a system of *relative capacities to act* (who can force what, and up to what point), a system of *relative powers*, of *relative responsibilities* (which party has perpetrated the damage, which party should receive damage compensation). Justice is mainly concerned with dispute resolution. It has to decide between competing interests (Mercuro and Medema 1997, p. 115). As in the Hayekian framework, legal rules, and especially the legal system, constitute, with the market, the two main institutions for organizing inter-individual relations. But an institutionalist view highlights the diversity and the opposition of individuals' interests, representations and projects. If the market expresses competition, it includes a selection mechanism according to willingness to pay; law uses another mechanism, according to political logic and ethical criteria. So, the rule of law is not only a coordination mechanism, but also a social compromise; an organization of relative rights and powers.

Moreover, a right is generally a relative power, power for one agent and constraint for another one. It is very difficult to organize a system of rights, that is to say to combine everybody's rights,[7] to establish where the right of somebody ends and where somebody else's right begins: obviously in order to respect rights to sleep, noise at night must be prohibited; but what is the standard definition of 'noise'? Is it 60 decibels or 80 or what? Is it the same in Las Vegas and in a Maine village? In summer and in winter, on Saturday and on other days? And so on. The recognition of children's rights is a recent movement, but how does one combine children's and parents' rights? Combining all legal actions a priori is unimaginable, both because of the transaction costs, and because we are in an uncertain world.

The judge determines the boundaries of legal actions. For that judgment, equity criteria have to be introduced, because in most countries – if not all of them – the judge has to dispense justice, to determine what is 'just', that is, to apply both efficiency and equity criteria.

Let us consider an interesting case. In France, in March 2001, when the Court of Marseilles authorized two hundred squatters to remain in possession of their squat for a year, because they had suffered from 'collective deficiencies as regards to social housing', although the occupation of a building 'without right or title' violates the right of the owner and constitutes 'an obviously illicit disorder'.[8] This decision was taken in a 'legal vacuum': in this particular situation no legal text or jurisprudence gives the answer to the question of how to combine different and opposite claims, different and opposite law.

From an institutionalist point of view (Schmid 1989, 1994) this function of the judge has to be accepted. The judicial decision is the last means of resolving the conflict between the rights' holders and those who dispute their rights. The conflict between the parties can only be through the intervention of a third party, the judge, the official and legitimated producer of just decisions; the only individual to be entitled to that function by the law. Justice is the institution that makes law active. Instead of leaving it in a formal state it organizes a system of relative concrete law, a configuration of relative capacities to act, that is to say a system of mutual coercion, which is similar (but prior) to the other system of mutual coercion, the market.

4.3 The Judge Cannot Only Use Market and Efficiency Criteria

The institutionalist approach has shown that the efficiency criterion is not sufficient for two reasons.

The first is that any rights entitlement modifies relative rights, relative capacities and relative wealth and therefore has an economic effect, modifying prices, production and incomes. Hence, a specific efficiency solution generates consequences in terms of income/wealth distribution; efficiency can no longer be used as a criterion, independently from any judgment on the distribution.

The second reason is that judicial institutions should not be aligned with the working of the market. Market values, standards and norms cannot be used as normative references. Market standards are not comparable to equity standards, nor do they correspond to natural standards. As a result of market processes, they are dependent, on the one hand on the exchanges that have taken place, and on the other hand on the bargaining powers from which they are derived and on pre-established social positions on the market. Their legitimacy is debatable since it refers to the history of the markets and rests, generally, in fine, upon non-market forms of appropriation, the equitable character of which is doubtful (societal violence, war and spoils, theft, public monopolization and so on). Moreover, market standards can be refused for ethical or political reasons.

To accept the existing prices, to be a 'price-taker' is to be a 'rights-taker' and to accept the prevailing legal configuration as if its implication as regards fairness were acceptable. But equity itself is an element in the judicial process. If the judge based the entitlement of concrete rights only on market prices and rights, he/she would reason in a circle: market data themselves result from the system of pre-established rights,[9] which are disputable or even disputed. The market cannot constitute the fixed point since it supposes another fixed point, the legal one. This is why some authors insist on the necessary transparency of the judicial decision when equity considerations have to be introduced.

To specify the relation between entitlements and solutions with distribution effects, we can use a parabola; I call it the Titanic model. The shipwreck creates a strong scarcity of lifeboats, which are not enough to accommodate all passengers and crew. We are here in a typical situation of a lack of property rights, moreover of a lack of a legal system, on a resource becoming tragically scarce. We have to specify entitlements. The efficiency criterion is inoperative: whatever the legal allocation is, no more lifeboats are to be constructed. A wild conception of efficiency – to give the people with the highest earnings the seats – is questionable from an ethical point of view. A naïve conception of efficiency – to give the people with the highest individual preferences for life the seats – makes little sense. Surely, entitlements are a problem of equity and many solutions can be envisaged (and different conventions can exist): women and children first, drawing perhaps according to age, gender, hair colour, political preferences, nationality, physical strength and so on. This is an illustration of the 'arbitrariness of the rights': as in the critical philosophy and sociology of Bourdieu (1982) and Foucault (1976), every right is related to primary entitlements, through free exchanges or power relations; these entitlements are not the legal translation of some pre-existing standard of fairness, efficiency or equity, but a part of a specific system of rights among many potential systems. In the majority of situations efficiency has obviously to play a role but together with equity criterion. In the Coasian framework, when there are no (or few) transaction costs, entitlement is neutral for efficiency, so the judge may favour equity criterion (in the standard example of air pollution, he/she determines an entitlement to clean air, which means that he/she decides who pays for the anti-pollution filter). When there are transaction costs and when the law does not establish any order of precedence, the question is how to combine different types of criteria that lead to different outcomes. In these cases, the judge has to evaluate both types of criteria case by case.

In the same way, the republican logic affects the choice of the social level of law enforcement. Considering costs and benefits, judicial and political systems have to include collective interests and non-market values.

4.4 A Creative Producer

The judge has to say:

- how to combine the precise application of different laws, possibly partially contradictory; how to arbitrate between rights and in which proportion to make such or such right prevail; how to weigh the rights in both sides of the scales of justice; into what new complex of concrete rights translate the system of theoretical law;
- how to apply these laws and these rights in combination by taking into account the specific features of the situation and of the individuals' personalities; and
- how to apply them with reference to efficiency and equity. Judicial intervention is all the more necessary in so far as the market as an equity producer is disputed. Formal equality on the market can be accompanied by 'real' inequalities related to the preliminary distribution of rights.[10]

The judge is a creative producer because he or she does not mechanically apply standard formulae but must say how to apply a legal system of property rights in a global legal framework and a specific context. This includes consideration of all the effects in the efficiency field and in the equity field. Moreover, changes in the context can modify the consequences of the existing law as far as efficiency and equity are concerned (and frequently modify them in opposing ways). Sometimes, a decision is a choice among many, as is obvious in criminal law which envisages a range of sanctions. The judge or the jury decides among these possibilities, according to particular conditions, adjusts punishment to crime. This may be also true in civil law, for instance compensating decisions relating to oil spills. There is no standard for sanctions; no objective and indisputable sum for damages which will exactly compensate the injured parties. The judge has to make an evaluation, using different valuation systems; and different judges or courts may fix different amounts. No one can use indisputable norms or conventions, since explicit markets for such damages are missing. Moreover there is no clear *ex ante* delimitation of who is entitled to be considered as a victim. What would compensate for the disutility of oil wastes on the ocean? Will that take into account the contaminated birds? History shows that the logic of these decisions may change; and not only according to the changes in market prices.

In an analogy with market, the judge replaces the individuals, the inter-individual exchange or the market process to evaluate and compare rights and duties, to determine implicit prices (how much is an aggression 'worth', in terms of compensation for the victim and sanctions for the culprit? How much is damage 'worth'? What are their implicit 'prices'?). The judge introduces a process of judicial valuation into a world governed by market processes of valuation. It can only be legitimated when coming from 'wise persons, deciding in the name of the French people' (and not in the name of the market and according to the willingness to pay) and according to the legal and constitutional principles shared by the national community (freedom, equality, fraternity).

The judicial system introduces principles of evaluation which are not of a technical nature. In fact legal principles are insufficient to determine that the adultery of a man is less serious than that of a woman or that, in a divorce, children should rather be entrusted to their mother's care than to their father's according to the natural 'maternal instinct'. One could multiply ad infinitum examples which would testify to the simultaneous evolution of the dominant representations or of the various representations within society and legal institution.

The judge intervenes in the inter-individual relations, but does not exercise any arbitrary power. First, the judge acts within the legal framework, under legal and constitutional principles; and secondly, regulatory mechanisms, such as the possibility of appeal to higher courts and the hierarchical organization of judicial systems, have emerged to avoid arbitrary decisions.

The new relation which is established between real conditions and formal conditions, the passage according to Habermas (1996) of a paradigm of the formal law to a paradigm of the materialized law, is deeply influenced by the constructivist role of the state. The state enables a centralized system to monopolize coercion as a means of enforcing the law through public justice. It represents the organization of a law and an order which are imposed to everyone and which give law an essential role in the function of inter-individual relations, that is, of socialization. The modern republican order, coming from the American and French revolutions, bequeaths general foundational legal principles and elements of common ideology, which seem to result from a natural law ('human rights'). On these bases the political organizations that express the general will voluntarily build a complex legal order. Law appears as a substantive law, a self-made constructivist law, directly opposed to laws with heteronomous bases, should they make claims for custom or religion. The democratic forms further increase the central character of the law in the social system by allowing public discussion around the construction of the law, considered as a means of organizing the public sphere. The democratic forms of the republican logic admit the pluralism of interests and opinions. Therefore, the constructivist character of the law gives more weight to judicial intervention than would ever be the case in other modes.

4.5 The New Role of the Judge

This questions the function traditionally entrusted to the law to establish social standards. The legal standard is supposed to define what is just or not just, according to general principles which constitute for the citizens a guarantee against the risks of arbitrary decisions of judges. Therefore it has an absolute nature which radically opposes just situations to unjust situations. However, other social standards are tending to lose their absolute character and become increasingly contingent. These emerge from social relations, develop with them, and depend on negotiations and on bargaining powers. They are part of contracts, compromises, mediations, even when the state itself pushes them forward. Above all they are caught more and more between opposed constraints: some resulting from the market and others from the republic. This raises the question of how to weigh the different types of criteria, the different systems of representation, values and social projects. Judicial institutions are thus subjected to various pressures aiming at bending the hierarchy of social values towards such or such direction.

Consequently judicial intervention has to extend across new fields: appreciation of the legitimacy of strikes, contents of social plans, organization of audio-visual markets, evolution of medical treatments, procreation and bioethics. And beside the judicial institution, we observe the development of new legal forms and independent authorities. Judicial regulation partially supplants pure political regulation and pure economic regulation to become the main means of a more multidimensional regulation. The concrete management of the relation market and republic is not obvious because no simple criterion can determine 'the right proportion'. Wise people are coming back and the judges (public, independent or private) seem to be the best of the wise; their independence is foregrounded to justify their new function. If judicial institutions are today a central issue in debates and are subjected to pressure, it is because the task of establishing the balance between heterogeneous dimensions and criteria converges on it. More than firm or state, justice becomes the ultimate resort, the ultimate regulation for all that escapes the standards defined by the traditional ways of regulation. As the image of a government of the judges expresses it, it is transformed into a central institution for social regulation.

As judges introduce a process of judicial valuation there will be growing competition between market valuation and judicial regulation. We are only at the early stages of this competition, which will become more and more closely fought. Thus the increasing need for a stronger legitimation for the system of justice: in the republican model of judicial regulation, justice has to work as a public utility, for the people and not for professionals.

NOTES

1. The symmetrical structure of the game is not a restrictive hypothesis. The payoffs are utility indices and may be arbitrarily chosen as being equal in the same outcomes for each player. The important point is that, for everyone, $\gamma > \alpha > \delta > \beta$.
2. Optimal cooperative equilibrium is possible but the possible outcomes are infinite. Any system of identical strategies (to cooperate n times, not to cooperate m times, to cooperate n times . . .) constitutes a system of best responses and is a solution, according to the folk theorem, with the two extreme systems $n = 0$ (no-cooperation indefinitely repeated) and $m = 0$ (cooperation indefinitely repeated).
3. The idea of the autonomy of the political logic of law is sustained in the United States by the 'Modern Civic Republican Tradition School'; see Mercuro and Medema (1997, p. 97).
4. Interpretation for the French revolutionists is all the more limited that Reason makes it possible to produce rational and transparent laws. Moreover, as popular election is seen as the only right mechanism of revelation of the general will, justice cannot claim to express a different and unspecified popular will.
5. Personal rights are not legally defined as property rights. Nobody is the owner of his/her name, body or freedom. Their logic is not the logic of market property: one cannot give them up and they are not transferable.
6. That raises the frightening problem of defining or, at least, of considering what a voluntary or free transaction is. Is accepting clandestine work for miserable wages a real free act? Is for an Afghan woman, to get married in Kabul under Taliban law, as free an action as a free transaction? Today magistrates have to face this kind of problem (for

example, problems of obligations). In the United States, it was recently decided that in women's prisons, any sexual relations between a warder and a prisoner would be considered as a rape, whatever the formal appearances of the 'exchange' had been, because of the real inequality between the persons.
7. To enforce ownership and, so, to enforce some right, is, simultaneously, to prohibit a hypothetic right to steal. As for every monopoly power a right – except for public goods – is, at the same time, exclusion. Prohibition is the other face of freedom.
8. *Le Monde* 20 March 2001, p. 18.
9. 'The economy is a system of power, of mutual coercion, of reciprocal capacity to receive income and/or to shift injury – whose pattern or structure and consequences are at least partially a function of law'. (Samuels 1971, p. 440).
10. Further, unequal positions on the market can have a cumulative effect, as the debates on free exchange and protectionism in the case of young nations' industrialization showed.

REFERENCES

Arnaud, A.J. (1991), *Pour une pensée juridique européenne* [*For a Judicial European Thought*], Paris: PUF.
Axelrod, R. (1984), *The Evolution of Cooperation*, New York: Basic Books.
Barrère, C. (2001), 'Marchandisation et judiciarisation [Judicial growth and market expansion]', *Economie Appliquée*, **54** (3), September, 9–37.
Bicchieri, C., R. Jeffrey and B. Skyrms (1997), *The Dynamics of Norms*, Cambridge: Cambridge University Press.
Bourdieu, P. (1982), *Ce que parler veut dire. L'économie des échanges linguistiques* [*What is Meant by Discourse Analysis. The Economics of Linguistic Exchanges*], Paris: Fayard.
Bradney, A. and F. Cownie (2000), *Living without Law*, Aldershot: Ashgate.
Buchanan, J.M. (1972), 'Politics, property, and the law: an alternative interpretation of *Miller et al.* v. *Schoene*', *Journal of Law and Economics*, **40** (2), October, 439–52; republished in S. Pejovich (ed.) (2001), *The Economics of Property Rights, vol. I: Cultural, Legal and Philosophical Issues*, Cheltenham, UK and Northampton, MA, USA: Edward Elgar, pp. 362–75.
Duby, G. (1987), *Le Moyen Age* [*The Middle Ages*], Paris: Pluriel, Hachette.
Ellickson, R.C. (1991), *Order without Law*, Cambridge, MA: Harvard University Press.
Foucault, M. (1976), *La volonté de savoir* [*The Will to Know*], Paris: Gallimard.
Fudenberg, D. and E. Maskin (1990), 'Evolution and cooperation in noisy repeated games', *American Economic Review*, **80**, 274–9.
Goh, B.C. (2002), *Law without Lawyers, Justice without Courts*, Aldershot: Ashgate.
Habermas, J. (1996), *Between Facts and Norms*, Boston, MA: MIT Press.
Hardin, R. (1982), *Collective Action*, Baltimore, MD: Johns Hopkins University Press.
Hayek, F. (1973), *Law, Legislation and Liberty: A New Statement of the Liberal Principles of Justice and Political Economy*, vol. 1: *Rules and Order*, London: Routledge & Kegan Paul.
Kreps, D.M. (1990), *A Course in Microeconomic Theory*, Hemel Hempstead: Harvester Wheatsheaf.
Mercuro, N. and S.G. Medema (1997), *Economics and the Law: From Posner to Post-Modernism*, Princeton, NJ: Princeton University Press.

Pejovitch, S. (ed.) (2001), *The Economics of Property Rights*, vol. I: *Cultural, Legal and Philosophical Issues*, vol. II: *Property Rights and Economic Performance*, Cheltenham, UK and Northampton, MA, USA: Edward Elgar.
Posner, R.A. (1973), *Economic Analysis of the Law*, Boston, MA: Little, Brown.
Posner, R.A. (1980), 'A theory of primitive society with special reference to law', *Journal of Law and Economics*, **23** (1), April, 1–53.
Samuels, W.J. (1971), 'Interrelations between legal and economic processes', *Journal of Law and Economics*, **14** (2), October, 435–50.
Schmid, A. Allan (1989), 'Law and economics: an institutional perspective', in N. Mercuro (ed.), *Law and Economics*, Boston, MA: Kluwer, pp. 57–85.
Schmid, A. Allan (1994), 'Institutional law and economics', *European Journal of Law and Economics*, 1, March, 33–51.
Williamson, O.E. (1985), *The Economic Institutions of Captitalism: Firms, Markets and Relational Contracting*, New York and London: Free Press.

11. Should non-expert courts control expert administrations?
Georg von Wangenheim*

1 INTRODUCTION

In most modern democracies, administrative decisions are subject to judicial control. Citizens use their right to dispute decisions of public administrations in courts – in some countries extensively, in others to a lesser degree. Due to the wide range of decisions handed down by the public administration, courts are frequently concerned with cases and problems on which they have little expertise. Whenever the courts have less expertise than the administration which has handed down the original decision, the questions whether and why such non-expert control is socially valuable suggest themselves. This chapter investigates these questions. The answers will shed additional light on the discussion over judicial deference, that is, over the degree to which courts should accept administrative or political decisions.

Court control of administrative decision making may improve the latter for three reasons. First, and most simple, courts could simply hand down better decisions from a social point of view. This may be due to accidental higher expertise in the specific case or to procedural differences between administrative and judicial decision making which produce sufficiently more and better information in court procedures to offset any lack of expertise (for example, adversarial procedure with stronger effects of advocacy as stressed by Dewatripont and Tirole 1999). For example, Spiller and Talley (2000) base their argument on biased or non-biased review on such superiority of courts. They, and others, ignore the two further reasons.

Second, courts do not review a random selection of administrative decisions. Due to self-selection in the appeals process similar to the one described by Shavell (1995) for review of judicial decisions by higher courts, courts rather concentrate on cases which are more likely to be incorrect than the average administrative decision. Hence, court decisions only need to be better than this (negatively) biased sample of administrative decisions in order to improve the outcome of the overall decision-making procedure.

Third and finally, court review may induce administrators who dislike having their decisions overturned to exert more error-avoiding effort. Judicial review decisions then merely seem to serve as signals for the effort the administrator exerts to avoid making errors. Holmström (1979) has shown that incentive mechanisms based on any signal for the level of effort of agents may induce higher effort levels of the agent, as long as the signal reveals any information on the agent's effort. Courts who are more likely to hand down correct decisions than not (but not necessarily more likely than the reviewed administrators) provide such a signal (compare, for example, Kirstein 2002, whose analysis of incentives in banking explicitly relies on this point). Different from other signals for administrators' effort, court review necessarily combines its incentive effects with replacing the administrative decisions by possibly far poorer judicial decisions. Due to these additional costs of producing the signal, incentive mechanisms relying on court review deserve explicit discussion in this chapter.

I shall ignore the case that court control of administrative decisions is desirable because of the superiority of judicial decision making as trivial, and instead concentrate on the other two reasons. First, I shall adapt Shavell's (1995) model of the appeals process as a selection mechanism to judicial review of administrative decisions (Section 2). In an extension of the Shavellian model, I shall then show how only the interplay of three variables – quality of administrative information, quality of judicial information, and quality of information provided by the launching of an appeal – may decide on whether benevolent courts will adhere to judicial deference or will aggressively repeal administrative decisions (Section 3). I shall then discuss under what conditions court review may serve as a worthwhile signal for administrators' effort despite its deteriorating effect on the cases actually going through court review (Section 4). Section 5 concludes.

Before presenting the arguments, some definitions need clarification. Throughout the chapter, I shall assume that the aim of administrative law is to improve social welfare, which is defined as the difference between gains and harm resulting from all realized projects which are subject to regulation by administrative law. Administrative law may pursue this goal by an unambiguous definition of what projects from a certain field have to be approved and which ones have to be rejected. If such definition is clear enough, neither the administration nor the judiciary have any discretion to approve or reject a project, either by statutory interpretation or by exercising any discretion in choosing legal consequences for the circumstances of the specific case. Such clear and unambiguous regulation is rare and not the topic of this chapter. I rather concentrate on regulations which allow either for statutory interpretation or for some discretion in choosing legal consequences. Moreover, I deal only with the material side of administrative decisions. Procedural rules and their violation are left for future study.

I thus use the expressions 'legal', 'correct', and 'welfare improving' as synonyms. Accordingly, there is also no difference between the terms 'illegal', 'wrong', and 'welfare reducing'.[1] I also assume that all gains and harm resulting from projects are well defined and may be obeserved by some individuals at least after the project has been carried out.

Further, I use the term 'expertise' to denote the ability to separate welfare-improving from welfare-reducing projects. Hence an expert is more likely to find out correctly whether a specific project increases or reduces welfare than a non-expert. Expertise thus does not refer to superior knowledge on a subset of the qualities which influence the welfare effects of projects, but to the entirety of these qualities.

Finally, the 'owner' of a project is the individual who can carry out the project from a factual point of view and who will gain directly from the realization of the project. The owner may become an 'applicant' if he/she files for a public law permission for his/her project with the competent authorities and an 'appellant' if he/she appeals the rejection of his/her application by the administration. Opposed to the owner of the project are third parties who will only bear the costs (harm) from realization of the project. They can also become 'appellants' if they appeal the administrative approval of the project.

2 APPEALS PROCESS AS A SEPARATION DEVICE

An adaptation of Shavell's (1995) basic model of appeals of low court decisions serves as the starting point of the present discussion. Let there be two types of projects, one welfare increasing and legal and one welfare decreasing and illegal. The welfare effects of the projects are $w_h > 0$ for the legal project and $w_\ell < 0$ for the illegal one. Let the proportion of legal plans among the applications be given by f^o. Administrators have incomplete information about the legal merits of the projects brought before them. They investigate the cases to find out each project's true type, but they err with probability $q_A \in (0, 1/2)$. Judges decide similar to administrators: they investigate the cases which are appealed to find out each project's true type and err with probability $q_J \in (q_A, 1/2)$, that is, their error probability is larger than the administrators' error probability. This reflects their lacking expertise.

After the administration has handed down its decision on a project, both the applicant and third parties may appeal the administration's decision if it is to their disadvantage. The private costs of filing an appeal for the applicant and third parties include both the resources the appellant spends and the fees; they are denoted by $c_1 > 0$ and $c_3 > 0$ for the applicant and a third party, respectively. The corresponding social costs are $c_1^s > 0$ and $c_3^s > 0$. The gains from a successful appeal are $g_x = w_x + h_x > w_x$ for $x \in \{h, \ell\}$ for the applicant and $\lambda h_x = \lambda(g_x - w_x) > -\lambda w_x$ for $x \in \{h, \ell\}$ for the third party which is most affected and bears a fraction $\lambda \in (0,1)$ of the total harm.[2] Applicants and third parties perfectly know the values of g and h of the relevant project. Administrators and courts only know which values are possible and the probability f^o.

Applicants appeal an unfavourable decision on a legal project if and only if $c_1 < g_h(1 - q_J)$ and on an illegal project if and only if $c_1 < g_\ell q_J$. Similarly, third parties appeal a project-approving decision on an illegal project if and only if $c_3 < \lambda h_\ell(1 - q_J)$ and an approving decision on a legal project if and only if $c_3 < \lambda h_h q_J$.

Following Shavell, I call the appeals process 'perfectly separating' if all and only incorrect decisions of the administration are appealed. This is the case if

$$c_1 \in (g_\ell q_J, g_h(1 - q_J)) \quad \text{and} \quad c_3 \in (\lambda h_h q_J, \lambda h_\ell(1 - q_J)). \tag{11.1}$$

For the sake of the argument, assume that both intervals exist and that the appeals costs satisfy both parts of (11.1).[3]

Measure social welfare by the expected welfare effect per application net of the expected appeals costs. For the perfectly separating appeals process, that is, if all and only administrative errors are appealed, social welfare then is

$$W_{\text{perfect}} = f^o (1 - q_A q_J) w_h + (1 - f^o) q_A q_J w_\ell - q_A c^s \tag{11.2}$$

where $c^s = f^o c_1^s + (1 - f^o) c_3^s$ abbreviates for the average social costs of an appeal. It is easy to see that without any review, social welfare is $W_0 = f^o(1 - q_A) w_h + (1 - f^o) q_A w_\ell$. Then the following proposition is obvious:

Proposition 1 (Shavell 1995) *The perfectly separating appeals process is socially superior to the absence of any appeal if and only if*

$$c^s < (1 - q_J)[f^o w_h - (1 - f^o) w_\ell]. \tag{11.3}$$

Whether this condition is satisfied is independent of whether q_J is smaller or larger than q_A. Hence judicial review of administrative decisions are welfare improving as long as the review process does not consume too many resources. This results also holds true if courts are more likely to misjudge a case than the administration, and even if the court's decision is perfectly arbitrary ($q_J = 1/2$).

The intuition of this result is simple. Since perfect separation by the appeals process implies that courts deal only with cases which the administration has decided incorrectly. Hence every reversal of such decision is an improvement. The right-hand side of equation (11.3) is the product of the probability that the administrative decision becomes reversed in court and the average gain from each such reversal, hence it is the expected social gain from an appeal. Obviously, if the appeals process consumes fewer resources than this expected social gain, it is worthwhile for society. The probability q_A only determines how often an appeals process may realize these social net gains.[4]

3 USING THE INFORMATION FROM SEPARATION EFFECTS IN JUDICIAL DECISIONS

The argument of the previous sections was based on the assumption that courts infer no information from the fact that an appeal was lodged or from the decision of the administration. Shavell (1995: 393 and 412) justified this simplification by the problems of finding equilibria if courts infer information from the lodging of an appeal. His central argument was that this would imply reversing all appealed decisions and thus destroying the separating effect of the appeals process. He concludes that procedural rules should forbid courts from inferring information from the fact that an appeal was lodged.

However, Shavell's argument is too simple. First, even when courts reverse all appealed decisions, appeals costs may still be perfectly separating, namely if they are larger than the possible gains of the appellant whose appeal is unjustified and smaller than the possible gains of the appellant whose case is justified ($g_\ell < c_1 < g_h$ and $\lambda h_h < c_3 < \lambda h_\ell$ in the above notation). Second, even if the appeals process lost its separating property when courts reversed all appealed decisions ($c_1 < g_\ell$ and $c_3 < \lambda h_h$ or $g_\ell = g_h$ or $h_h = h_\ell$), the possibility of equilibria in mixed strategies, which Shavell neglects, may solve the problem. The structure of the problem is that of an enforcement game. Shavell is thus right in pointing out that an equilibrium in pure strategies fails to exist (since he starts from an assumption which is equivalent to $g_\ell = g_h$ and $h_h = h_\ell$). If the courts use the information that an appeal has been lodged, then, as Shavell rightly points out, no separation occurs, and all parties unhappy with the administration's decision will appeal. However, then the information on who lodged the appeal is worthless, the courts will not use this information but rely on their investigations. With optimal appeals costs, however, this implies that only incorrect administrative decisions are appealed, the courts' optimal reply is to rely on the information on who lodged the appeal.

The unique Nash equilibrium of this game is one in mixed strategies. The courts will rely on the information conveyed by the appeal in some cases and disregard this information in the other cases. They will rely on the information conveyed by the appeal in exactly the proportion of cases which makes parties whose case was rightly dismissed before the administration indifferent between lodging an appeal or not (note that this implies that all parties whose case was wrongly dismissed before the administration will appeal). On the other hand, all parties whose case was rightly dismissed before the administration will appeal with a probability which makes the courts indifferent between reliance on prior information (conveyed by the appeal) and investigation of all cases.

It is, however, doubtful whether such mixed strategy Nash equilibria may serve as a reasonable predictor of human – and specifically: judicial – behaviour. In addition, stability of such equilibria is highly debated (for example, Samuelson (1997: 27) or von Wangenheim (2004: ch. 2)). While the latter problem could be solved by assuming heterogeneous parties (heterogeneity may refer to appeals costs as suggested by Shavell or to the individual costs and benefits of the projects under scrutiny), the former remains valid as long as the courts may receive either one of two signals. I therefore refrain from discussing such an equilibrium in any detail. Instead I take the natural next step and allow for more than two signals which the court may receive. It then makes sense to rely on the concept of perfect Bayesian equilibrium instead of simple Nash equilibria, since this reduces the necessary assumptions on information sets.

To keep close to the model of the previous section I adapt only the following elements. While the administration errs with probability $q_A \in (0, 1/2)$ as in the previous section, the court's decision is now explicitly based on a signal $y \in \{a, r\}$ on whether the administrative decision was correct and should therefore be approved ($y = a$) or the administrative decision was incorrect and should therefore be reversed ($y = r$). The court observes both the content of the signal and its quality, which is high with probability τ and low with probability $1 - \tau$. The high quality signal is wrong with probability $\bar{q}_J \in (q_A, 1/2)$ and the low quality signal is wrong with probability $\underline{q}_J \in (\bar{q}_J, 1/2)$. The court knows $\bar{q}_J$ and $\underline{q}_J$. It forms beliefs $\hat{q}_{A1}$ and $\hat{q}_{A3}$ on the probabilities q_{A1} and q_{A3} that appeals are justified given that the applicant or a third party has appealed, respectively. The court also knows the welfare effects of legal and illegal projects (w_h and w_ℓ). Based on this information, the court aims at handing down decisions which maximize expected social welfare.[5]

Applicants and third parties form beliefs $\hat{p}_{kx}$ on the probabilities p_{kx} that an appellant for type $k \in \{1, 3\}$ prevails in court if the project is of type $x \in \{h, \ell\}$. They base their decision to file an appeal on these beliefs, on their gains from a successful appeal and on their individual costs c of filing an appeal. The costs of appeals are distributed according to the cumulative distribution functions $F_1(c)$ and $F_3(c)$ for applicants and third parties,

Table 11.1 Court's subjective probability that administration erred

Signal in favour of	Quality of signal	
	High	Low
Administration ($y=a$)	$\overline{\hat{q}^a_k} = \dfrac{\hat{q}_{Ak}\overline{q}_J}{\hat{q}_{Ak}\overline{q}_J + (1-\hat{q}_{Ak})(1-\overline{q}_J)}$	$\underline{\hat{q}^a_k} = \dfrac{\hat{q}_{Ak}\underline{q}_J}{\hat{q}_{Ak}\underline{q}_J + (1-\hat{q}_{Ak})(1-\underline{q}_J)}$
Appellant ($y=r$)	$\overline{\hat{q}^r_k} = \dfrac{\hat{q}_{Ak}(1-\overline{q}_J)}{\hat{q}_{Ak}(1-\overline{q}_J) + (1-\hat{q}_{Ak})\overline{q}_J}$	$\underline{\hat{q}^r_k} = \dfrac{\hat{q}_{Ak}(1-\underline{q}_J)}{\hat{q}_{Ak}(1-\underline{q}_J) + (1-\hat{q}_{Ak})\underline{q}_J}$

respectively. For simplicity, I assume $F_1(c) = F_3(c) = 0$ for all $c \leq 0$.[6] The game has reached its perfect Bayesian equilibrium, if beliefs and behaviour coincide, that is, if $\hat{q}_{Ak} = q_{Ak}$ and $\hat{p}_{kx} = p_{kx}$ for all $k \in \{1, 3\}$ and $x \in \{h, \ell\}$.

First consider how the true p_{kx} follow from the court's decision. Based on its beliefs $\hat{q}_{A1}$ and $\hat{q}_{A3}$, on its knowledge of $\overline{q}_J$ and $\underline{q}_J$ and on the signal it received, it will infer by Bayes's Theorem that the administration erred with the probabilities as shown in Table 11.1, where $k \in \{1,3\}$ denotes the type of the appellant.

The welfare-maximizing judge will reverse an administrative decision if the expected welfare effect of such reversal is strictly positive, given these subjective probabilities. He/she will confirm the administrative decision if the expected welfare effect of a reversal is strictly negative. If this welfare effect is zero, he/she may randomize. The welfare effect of reversing an administrative decision is $\hat{q}w_h + (1-\hat{q})w_\ell$ with $\hat{q} \in \{\overline{\hat{q}^a_1}, \underline{\hat{q}^a_1}, \overline{\hat{q}^r_1}, \underline{\hat{q}^r_1}\}$ if the applicant has filed the appeal and $-\hat{q}w_\ell - (1-\hat{q})w_h$ with $\hat{q} \in \{\overline{\hat{q}^a_3}, \underline{\hat{q}^a_3}, \overline{\hat{q}^r_3}, \underline{\hat{q}^r_3}\}$ if a third party has filed.

Denote the court's decision by $\overline{\delta}^y_k$ if it has received a high quality signal and by $\underline{\delta}^y_k$ if it has received a low quality signal, in both cases with $y \in \{a, r\}$ and $k \in \{1, 3\}$. One can then write the court's decision rule as follows:

For any pair $(\delta, \hat{q}) \in \{(\overline{\delta}^a_k, \overline{\hat{q}^a_k}), (\underline{\delta}^a_k, \underline{\hat{q}^a_k}), (\overline{\delta}^r_k, \overline{\hat{q}^r_k}), (\underline{\delta}^r_k, \underline{\hat{q}^r_k})\}$ choose

$$\delta \begin{cases} = 1 & \text{if } \hat{q}w_h + (1-\hat{q})w_\ell > 0 \\ \in [0,1] & \text{if } \hat{q}w_h + (1-\hat{q})w_\ell = 0 \quad \text{if } k=1 \\ = 0 & \text{if } \hat{q}w_h + (1-\hat{q})w_\ell < 0 \end{cases}$$

$$\delta \begin{cases} = 1 & \text{if } -\hat{q}w_\ell - (1-\hat{q})w_h > 0 \\ \in [0,1] & \text{if } -\hat{q}w_\ell - (1-\hat{q})w_h = 0 \quad \text{if } k=3. \\ = 0 & \text{if } -\hat{q}w_\ell - (1-\hat{q})w_h < 0 \end{cases}$$

(11.4)

Should non-expert courts control expert administrations? 317

This behaviour implies the following success probabilities of appellants. An applicant whose welfare-increasing project has been rejected by the administration wins in court with the probability

$$p_{1h} = \tau[(1-\overline{q}_J)\overline{\delta}_1^r + \overline{q}_J\overline{\delta}_1^a] + (1-\tau)[(1-\underline{q}_J)\underline{\delta}_1^r + \underline{q}_J\underline{\delta}_1^a]. \quad (11.5)$$

If his/her project is welfare decreasing, he/she wins with probability

$$p_{1\ell} = \tau[\overline{q}_J\overline{\delta}_1^r + (1-\overline{q}_J)\overline{\delta}_1^a] + (1-\tau)[\underline{q}_J\underline{\delta}_1^r + (1-\underline{q}_J)\underline{\delta}_1^a]. \quad (11.6)$$

If a third party files an appeal, he/she prevails in court with probability

$$p_{3h} = \tau[\overline{q}_J\overline{\delta}_3^r + (1-\overline{q}_J)\overline{\delta}_3^a] + (1-\tau)[\underline{q}_J\underline{\delta}_3^r + (1-\underline{q}_J)\underline{\delta}_3^a], \quad (11.7)$$

if the project he/she opposes is welfare increasing, and with probability

$$p_{3\ell} = \tau[(1-\overline{q}_J)\overline{\delta}_3^r + \overline{q}_J\overline{\delta}_3^a] + (1-\tau)[(1-\underline{q}_J)\underline{\delta}_3^r + \underline{q}_J\underline{\delta}_3^a], \quad (11.8)$$

if he/she opposes a welfare-decreasing project.

This discussion of the court's behaviour implies the following:

Lemma 1 *Each perfect Bayesian equilibrium of the interaction between appellants and courts satisfies the following properties for all $k \in \{1, 3\}$:*

1. $\overline{q}_k^a \times \hat{q}_k^a \times \hat{q}_k^r \times \overline{q}_k^r$,
2. $\overline{\delta}_k^a \leq \underline{\delta}_k^a \leq \underline{\delta}_k^r \leq \overline{\delta}_k^r$,
3. $\delta_k \in (0, 1)$ for at most one $\delta_k \in \{\overline{\delta}_k^r, \underline{\delta}_k^r, \underline{\delta}_k^a, \overline{\delta}_k^a\}$,
4. $p_{1h} > p_{1\ell}$ and $p_{3\ell} > p_{3h}$ for all $p_{kx} \in (0, 1)$ with $x \in \{h, \ell\}$.

Proof: Property 1 follows directly from the table defining the different values of $\hat{q}$ and $\overline{q}_J < \underline{q}_J < 1/2$. Then Property 2 is a direct consequence of the court's decision rule (11.4). Property 3 follows from the strictness of the inequality in Property 1 and the court's decision rule (11.4). Property 4 is obvious since $\overline{q}_J < \underline{q}_J < 1/2$ and due to Property 2. ∎

Now turn to the question how the appellants' beliefs translate into true appellant dependent error probabilities of the adminsitration. A utility-maximizing party whose project has been denied permission by the administration will file an appeal if and only if his/her belief-based expected gains outweigh his/her appeals costs, that is, if and only if $\hat{p}_{1x}g_x > c$ for applicants and $\hat{p}_{3x}h_x\lambda > c$ for third parties, where $x \in \{h, \ell\}$. Given the distributions $F_1(c)$ and $F_3(c)$, a permission-denying administrative decision will thus be appealed with probability $F_1(\hat{p}_{1\ell}g_\ell)$ if the rejection was justified and with probability $F_1(\hat{p}_{1h}g_h)$ if it was not. Similarly, a permission-granting administrative decision will be appealed with probability $F_3(\hat{p}_{3h}h_h\lambda)$ if the approval was justified and with probability $F_3(\hat{p}_{3\ell}h_\ell\lambda)$ if it was not.

By definition of $f°$ and q_A the administration rightly rejects a proportion $(1-f°)(1-q_A)$ of all projects and erroneously rejects a proportion $f°q_A$ of all projects. Simple use of Bayes's theorem then yields

$$q_{A1} = \frac{f°q_A F_1(\hat{p}_{1h}g_h)}{f°q_A F_1(\hat{p}_{1h}g_h) + (1-f°)(1-q_A)F_1(\hat{p}_{1\ell}g_\ell)} \quad (11.9)$$

as the probability that the administration erred given that the applicant filed an appeal. Similarly,

$$q_{A3} = \frac{(1-f°)q_A F_3(\hat{p}_{3\ell}h_\ell\lambda)}{(1-f°)q_A F_3(\hat{p}_{3\ell}h_\ell\lambda) + f°(1-\underline{q}_A)F_3(\hat{p}_{3h}h_h\lambda)} \quad (11.10)$$

is the probability that an appeal against an approving administrative decision is justified.

To find the perfect Bayesian equilibria of the game, one has to set $\hat{p}_{kx} = p_{kx}$ and $\hat{q}_{Ak} = q_{Ak}$ for all $k \in \{1, 3\}$ and $x \in \{h, \ell\}$ and solve the resulting equation system. Considering part 2 of Lemma 1, the number of perfect Bayesian equilibria in which courts never randomize is $5^2 = 25$. Since all these equilibria may be induced by choosing the appropriate parameters, a thorough discussion of all equilibrium behaviours of the courts would go beyond the scope of a single chapter and add little insight in addition to what one can acquire from a small number of archetypical equilibria. These archetypical equilibria are those in which judicial behaviour is symmetric in the sense that all δ are independent of the type of the appellant k. The following discussion thus concentrates on them. To simplify notation, it goes without saying that use of k without further qualification in the following discussion always means 'for all $k \in \{1,3\}$'.

Of the symmetric perfect Bayesian equilibria without judicial randomization one is of little interest: $\overline{\delta}_k^a = \underline{\delta}_k^a = \underline{\delta}_k^r = \overline{\delta}_k^r = 0$ rejects all appeals ($p_{k,h} = p_{k,\ell} = 0$) and deters all appeals ($F_k(0) = 0$), which implies that q_{A1} and q_{A3} are undetermined and thus every sufficiently small $\hat{q}_{A1}$ and $\hat{q}_{A3}$ constitute perfect Bayesian equilibria. Hence the welfare effect of the appeals process is zero. Uninteresting as this equilibrium may be, it is important to note that by choosing $\overline{\delta}_k^a = \underline{\delta}_k^a = \underline{\delta}_k^r = \overline{\delta}_k^r = 0$, courts can always achieve a zero welfare effect of the appeals process independently of how potential appellants behave.

Among the remaining four symmetric perfect Bayesian equilibria without judicial randomization, three are of major interest. Before discussing these equilibria, let me introduce a numerical example by which I can show that all three of these equlibria may exist and which clarifies some of the following arguments.

Example 1 Suppose $f^\circ w_h + (1-f^\circ)w_\ell = 0$, that is, the proportion of legal plans among all applications is such that information prior to any further signal on a particular case is useless in as much as any decisions based purely on this prior information has zero expected effect on social welfare. As a numerical example, take $g_h = h_\ell = 2, g_\ell = h_h = 1$, and $f^\circ = 1/2$ and let the two signal qualities be equally likely ($\tau = 1/2$). In addition, let the negative externality of all projects be concentrated on one individual ($\lambda = 1$).[7] Further, let $q_A = 0.2, \bar{q}_J = 0.3$, and $\underline{q}_J = 0.4$. In words, administrators are less error prone than courts, even if the latter receive the high quality signal. Finally, let the costs of appeals for applicants and third parties be distributed according to a beta distribution[8] with variance 0.02 and mean 0.2, 0.45 and 0.82 to induce the three different symmetric perfect Bayesian equilibria.[9]

1. *Judicial deference* $\bar{\delta}_k^a = \underline{\delta}_k^a = \underline{\delta}_k^r = 0 < \bar{\delta}_k^r = 1$. Such behaviour of the court is a perfect Bayesian equilibrium if the administrative decision is more informative than the appellant's decision to file an appeal and a weak signal of the court. Only if the court receives a strong signal that the administration's decision was wrong does the court reverse it. The numerical example produces this equilibrium if the mean of the beta distribution is close to 0.2.[10]
2. *Judicial self-reliance* $\bar{\delta}_k^a = \underline{\delta}_k^a = 0 < \underline{\delta}_k^r = \bar{\delta}_k^r = 1$. Courts rely exclusively on their own information (as Shavell required it on the basis of his simple model) in the[11] perfect Bayesian equilibrium if the information conveyed by the fact of there being an appeal is not substantially more or less reliable than the countervailing information from the content of the administrative decision. Then even a weak signal is sufficient to tip the court's decision in accordance with the signal. In the numerical example, this equilibrium results if the mean of the beta distribution is close to 0.45.[12]
3. *Extra-critical courts* $\bar{\delta}_k^a = 0 < \underline{\delta}_k^a = \underline{\delta}_k^r = \bar{\delta}_k^r = 1$. Courts will reverse all administrative decisions unless they get a strong signal in favour of the administration's case, if the information they can infer from the fact that an appeal has been filed is very reliable as compared to the information included in the administrative decision. In the numerical example, this situation emerges as perfect Bayesian equilibrium, if the mean of the beta distribution is close to 0.82.[13]

The last symmetric perfect Bayesian equilibrium without judicial randomization drives the case of judicial deference to appellants to its extreme: all appealed administrative decisions are reversed: $\overline{\delta}_k^a = \underline{\delta}_k^a = \underline{\delta}_k^r = \overline{\delta}_k^r = 1$. In the numerical example, this case cannot occur since the gains from a successful appeal are at least as large as the costs of filing an appeal for every applicant and for every third party. Hence, all administrative decisions would be appealled against and thus the fact of there being an appeal conveys no information. Thus courts never have information which induces them to disregard their signal when it favours the administrative decision.

However, if one considers other distributions with larger support, appeals costs may be large enough to deter (nearly) all unjustified appeals even if the success probability is unity. This effect would then make the information included in the filing of an appeal strong enough to allow for extra-critical courts.

The symmetric perfect Bayesian equilibria without judicial randomization already allow to draw an important conclusion:

Proposition 2 *Depending on*

1. *how error prone the administration is,*
2. *how well the appeals costs separate justified from frivolous appeals,*
3. *how reliable the courts' own information is, and*
4. *how large the ratio of welfare gains to welfare losses would be without regulation,*

courts will either defer to the administration (follow it unless a court receives a strong signal against the administration), rely completely on their own signals, or be extra-critical (reverse the administration's decision unless a court receives a strong signal supporting it).

Besides these five symmetric perfect Bayesian equilibria without judicial randomization, asymmetric equilibria or equilibria in which courts randomize may occur, depending on the parameters and the exact shape of the distributions of appeals costs. Randomization suffers from exactly the problems which have been brought forward against the mixed strategy equilibrium in the simple Shavellian setting. However, when allowing for more different qualities of the courts' signals, randomization as equilibrium behaviour becomes less and less likely – if one drives the number of different signal qualities to the extreme, the likelihood of randomization as equilibrium behaviour vanishes. I therefore ignore randomization by courts in what follows. Asymmetric equilibria may be interpreted as one of the courts' behaviours described in Proposition 2 with a bias in favour of the applicant or third parties. Hence they do not require a thorough discussion either.

Since judges have been assumed to maximize social welfare in their decision making, Proposition 2 is most relevant for an evaluation of the appeals process from a welfare point of view:

Proposition 3 *The influence of judicial review of administrative decisions on social welfare is negative whenever courts fail to follow strong signals against the administration with certainty. If the social costs of running the appeals process are small enough, the influence of judicial review of administrative decisions on social welfare is positive, when courts follow strong signals against the administration with certainty.*

The reason for the condition of courts following strong signals against the administration in the proposition is simple. Suppose courts randomize after receiving a strong signal against the administration ($\bar{\delta}_k^r \in (0,1)$). Then the expected welfare effect of reversing the administrative decision after a strong signal against the administration must be zero, or courts would not randomize. By parts 2 and 3 of Lemma 1, the courts will then defer to the administration after having received a weak signal against the administration or a signal in favour of the administration ($\underline{\delta}_k^r = \underline{\delta}_k^a = \bar{\delta}_k^a = 0$). Hence, the courts' behaviour either interferes with the administrative decisions but with an expected welfare effect of zero, or leaves them unaffected. The courts' behaviour thus never has a positive influence on social welfare, but consumes resources – the total welfare effect of the appeals process is negative. Only if the courts reverse the administrative decision for at least one signal with a strictly positive expected welfare effect (hence with certainty), then the overall welfare effect of the appeals process may be positive. One should note that this result holds for any number of different signal qualities.

Before turning to the legal interpretation of Proposition 2 let me stress that heterogeneity of applicants and third parties need not be restricted to the appeals costs. In the same vein, one could also argue that both legal and illegal projects differ with respect to their benefits for the applicant and the costs for third parties. If the administration and the courts only receive stochastic signals on the costs and benefits of a project, appeals procedures may run very much along the lines I discussed for heterogeneous appeals costs. Due to the larger number of heterogeneous variables and possible signals, the formal discussion would require far more space, but the result would still be the same: depending on the four aspects enumerated in Proposition 2, courts will defer, or rely on their own information, or be extra-critical – in other words, courts will follow the doctrine of judicial deference, will ignore it, or will reverse it into its opposite.

This may explain why courts seem to be not very consistent in their reliance on the doctrine. When the parties self-select according to the merits of their cases but it is hard for the administration (and the courts) to find evidence on the social merits of the project, then the fact that an appeal has been lodged may be strong and decisive information for the courts. They will not grant any discretionary range to the administration and thus discard the doctrine of deference. Conversely, if administrators can easily observe gains and harms accruing from a project, the courts will take the administrative decisions as hard information and thus follow the doctrine of deference, that is, grant the administration a wide range of discretion in which the courts' own information will not be sufficient to overturn the administrative decisions.

This line of argument also concords with the dividing line between *unbestimmte Rechtsbegriffe* (unclear legal terms) and *Ermessensspielräume* (discretionary ranges) in German administrative law. In both cases, the wording of the law leaves space for interpretation. When the parties can more easily determine than the administration whether their case is justified and when they can thus easily determine their chances in a court appeal, the law is interpreted as including unclear legal terms – administrative decisions are subject to full (and sometimes very critical) review by courts. When, on the other hand, the administration is as able as, or even more able than, the parties to estimate gains and harm of a project, German law is interpreted as granting discretionary ranges to the administration, courts follow a doctrine similar to judicial deference.

I have shown in this section that both reference to, and rejection of the doctrine of judicial deference may maximize social welfare. Which one is better depends not only on the courts' expertise relative to the administration's, but equally on how separating the appeals process is and even the expected welfare effect of abolishing any regulation plays a role. In the following section, I shall discuss an alternative argument in favour of judicial review of administrative decisions despite the larger expertise of the administration.

4 INCENTIVE EFFECTS

This section deals with two questions: (i) Is it possible that the incentive effect makes judicial review of administrative decisions socially valuable even if courts are more error prone than administrators? (ii) If the incentive effect alone may justify judicial review, does social welfare increase if random selection of cases for review is replaced by an appeals process?

To isolate the incentives effect of judicial review, assume for the moment that court review is not triggered by appeals but by random selection of a subset of the administrative decisions. Let e_A denote the representative administrator's effort to avoid errors and $q_A(e_A)$ his/her consequential error probability, with the properties $q_A(0) \leq 1/2$, $\lim_{e_A \to \infty} q_A(e_A) = 0$, $q'_A < 0$, and $q''_A > 0$. For simplicity, assume that the courts' error probability remains exogenously given as q_J. To describe relative expertise of the administrators, assume $q_J \in [q_A(e_A^o), 1/2]$ where e_A^o is the effort a representative administrator exerts in the absence of court review and corresponding incentives.

To derive the representative administrator's effort, assume that his/her effort is determined by some intrinsic motivation to decide correctly,[14] an 'extrinsic' motivation to avoid court reversals,[15] and the negative of his/her disutility of effort. In particular, assume his/her expected utility per case decided is given by:

$$EU_{stoch} = -rs_x\{q_A(e_A)(1 - q_J) + [1 - q_A(e_A)]q_J\} \\ + s_i\{f^o[1 - q_A(e_A)]w_h + (1 - f^o)q_A(e_A)w_\ell\} - u(e_A) + \omega \quad (11.11)$$

where r is the review probability, s_x is the sanction describing the 'extrinsic' motivation, s_i is the sanction describing the 'intrinsic' motivation, $u(e_A)$ is disutility of effort, and ω is the wage he/she receives per case decided.[16]

Taking the derivative of the expected utility EU_{stoch} with respect to the administrator's effort e_A, setting the result equal to zero, and abbreviating $\tilde{w} = f^o w_h - (1 - f^o)w_\ell > 0$ yields the first-order condition

$$\frac{dEU_{stoch}}{de_A} = -[s_i\tilde{w} + rs_x(1 - 2q_J)]q'_A(e_A) - u'(e_A) = 0 \quad (11.12)$$

to determine the administrator's optimal effort e_A^*. The second-order condition is satisfied by the assumptions on $q_A(\cdot)$ and $u(\cdot)$. Taking the total derivative of condition (11.12) and interpreting e_A^* as a function of $r \cdot s_x$ yields

$$\frac{de_A^*(rs_x)}{d(rs_x)} = \frac{-(1 - 2q_J)q'_A(e_A^*)}{[s_i\tilde{w} + rs_x(1 - 2q_J)]q''_A(e_A^*) + u''(e_A^*)} \quad (11.13)$$

which is strictly positive. One should note that the only way in which r and s_x influence the effort of the representative administrator is by their product. As a consequence, with sufficiently large sanctions s_x, an arbitrarily small r may induce every effort level and thus every error probability. Of course, all caveats against high sanctions with low enforcement probabilities in criminal law and economics[17] apply here as well.

Increasing external incentives for administrators has four effects on social welfare: (i) the replacement of administrative decisions by court decisions, (ii) the resources consumed for court review, (iii) the desired improvement in administrative decisions, and (iv) the administrators' utility loss resulting from higher incentives. The last of these effects is relevant directly only if administrators extract a rent from occupying this role. Otherwise, they have to be compensated for this loss or they will quit the job. This differentiation need not be followed any further, since the compensation has to exactly offset the loss and thus is the same from a social point of view. The following welfare function embraces the three elements:

$$W_{stoch} = (1-r)\{f^o[1 - q_A(e_A^*(rs_x))]w_h + (1-f^o)q_A(e_A^*(rs_x))w_\ell\}$$
$$+ r[f^o(1-q_J)w_h + (1-f^o)q_Jw_\ell - c^s] + EU_{stoch}(e_A^*(rs_x)) \quad (11.14)$$

Taking the first derivative of this welfare function with respect to the review probability r yields

$$\frac{dW_{stoch}}{dr} = [q_A(e_A^*(rs_x)) - q_J]\tilde{w} - c^s - (1-r)\tilde{w}q_A'(e_A^*(rs_x))\frac{de_A^*(rs_x)}{d(rs_x)}s_x$$
$$- \{q_A(e_A^*(rs_x))(1-q_J) + [1 - q_A(e_A^*(rs_x))]q_J\}s_x, \quad (11.15)$$

which states the welfare effects of additional random review in the same order as introduced above. Note that the marginal effect on the representative administrator's utility reduces to the term in the second line of the equation by the envelope theorem.

Since dW_{stoch}/dr is strictly negative at $r=1$, the welfare-maximizing level of review r^* is in the interior of the unit interval if $dW_{stoch}/dr > 0$ at $r=0$. This is the case if

$$\tilde{w}q_A'(e_A^o)\frac{de_A^*(rs_x)}{d(rs_x)}\bigg|_{r=0} > q_A(e_A^o)(1-q_J) + [1 - q_A(e_A^o)]q_J \quad (11.16)$$

and s_x is sufficiently large so that the last two terms in equation (11.15) outweigh the first two terms which are strictly negative. Condition (11.16) tends to be violated if due to strong internal motivation (large s_i) administrators' behaviour is already little error prone: with small q_{ae}^o the absolute value of $q_A'(e_A^o)$ becomes arbitrarily small and further increases in the administrators' incentives have little effect on their effort (that is, $[de_A^*(rs_x)/d(rs_x)]|_{r=0}$ is small, too) while the right-hand side of condition (11.16) tends towards $q_J > 0$.

Satisfaction of condition (11.16) is sufficient for a strictly positive welfare-maximizing level of r but not necessary. Since the second line of equation (11.15) grows in r, the derivative may turn positive for strictly positive r even if condition (11.16) is violated. Then at least one local maximum for some larger r must exist due to $(dW_{stoch}/dr)|_{r=1} < 0$. If this maximum (or one of these maxima) is global, the socially optimal review frequency r^* again is strictly positive.

I summarize the results of this discussion in the following:

Proposition 4 *Incentive effects alone may thus justify judicial review of administrative decisions even if courts are more error prone than the administration. Whether they actually do justify judicial review depends on the specifics of how administrators' effort affects their error probability and their utility as well as on the strength of internal and external motivation.*

I now turn to the question how incentive effects of judicial review and the separation effect of the appeals process interact. I restrict the discussion to the basic model of the appeals process in which courts decide on the basis of a binary signal. The arguments extend in a natural way to the model with more signals.

If one includes the incentives effect in a model of perfect appeals, the resulting social welfare effect will be strictly larger than without the incentive effect. I shall show, however, that replacing random selection of cases for review by an appeals process may reduce social welfare, if this implies an increase in the number of cases reviewed.

With a perfect appeals process and the incentives effect, the administrators' expected utility becomes

$$EU_{p\&i} = -s_x q_A(e_A)(1 - q_J) \\ + s_i\{f^\circ[1 - q_A(e_A)]w_h + (1 - f^\circ)q_A(e_A)w_\ell\} - u(e_A) + \omega \quad (11.17)$$

since the review probability of correct administrative decisions is zero and the review probability of incorrect decisions is one. The administrators' optimality condition then becomes

$$\frac{dEU_{p\&i}}{de_A} = -\{s_i[f^\circ w_h - (1 - f^\circ)w_\ell] + s_x(1 - q_J)\}q_A'(e_A) - u'(e_A) \stackrel{!}{=} 0.$$

As one can easily see, the resulting optimal effort $e_A^{**}(s_x)$ of the administrator increases in s_x and is strictly larger than with random selection of cases for review since the cofactor of $q_A'(e_A)$ becomes larger in absolute terms due to $s_x(1 - q_J) > rs_x(1 - 2q_J)$.

Social welfare with a perfectly separating appeals process and a positive incentives effect ($W_{p\&i}$) is the same as in equation (11.2) with q_A replaced by $q_A(e_A^{**}(s_x))$. Obviously, social welfare increases in s_x since $q_A'(\cdot) < 0$ and $dW_{p\&i}/q_A < 0$. Hence, one gets the following:

Proposition 5 *The social welfare effect of appeals triggered review is larger if an incentive effect exists than if it does not.*

However, social welfare with appeals triggered review is unambiguously larger than with stochastic review, *only* if the number of appeals is not larger than the number of random reviews (that is, $q_A(e_A^{**}(s_x)) \leq r$). Otherwise, the second term of the difference

$$W_{p\&i} - W_{stoch} = (1-r)q_A(e_A^*(rs_x))[f^\circ w_h - (1-f^\circ)w_\ell]$$
$$+ [r - q_A(e_A^{**}(s_x))]\{c^s + q_J[f^\circ w_h - (1-f^\circ)w_\ell]\} \quad (11.18)$$

is negative and may outweigh the first term. A numerical example shows that the difference may become negative. With the values

$$\left.\begin{array}{l} r = 0.01,\ f^\circ = 0.5,\ w_h = 1,\ w_\ell = -1,\ q_J = 0.29,\ c^s = 0.8 \\ q_A(e_A^{**}(s_x)) = 0.26,\ q_A(e_A^*(rs_x)) = 0.27,\ q_A(e_A^*(0)) = 0.28 \end{array}\right\} \quad (11.19)$$

one gets

$$W_{stoch} = 0.2218 > W_o = 0.22 > W_{p\&i} = 0.2166 > W_{perfect} = 0.1948. \quad (11.20)$$

Here, stochastic review is the optimal solution while perfectly separating appeals as a trigger for review is the worst approach. Of course, perfectly separating appeals as a trigger for review with incentives effects is better, but still worse than no review at all.

The intuition is straightforward. With stochastic review of one per cent of all decisions, one can induce a reduction of the error probability of one per cent for all other decisions at the cost of one per cent additional error probability for the one per cent of reviewed cases. The effect on the average error probability is thus a reduction by 0.98 per cent. For this reduction, society has to incur the resource costs of reviews of one per cent of all cases. With appeals as a trigger for reviews instead of random selection, all 26 per cent of false decisions are reviewed, the resources society spends on review are thus 26 times as high. The error probability of the entire process, however, declines only from $(1-r)q_A(e_A^*(rs_x)) + rq_J = 0.2702$ to $q_A(e_A^{**}(s_x))q_J = 0.0754$, that is, by 0.1948. This reduction is less than 26 times the error reduction of 0.0098 induced by the transition from no review to stochastic review. Hence, the resources which have to be spent for court reviews may be justified by stochastic review with a small review probability but not by appeals triggered review.

One should note, however, that the result changes, if one leaves the number of reviews unchanged, that is, if one assumes that not all false decisions of the administration are reviewed but only a proportion thereof which results in the same total number of reviews as under stochastic review. Then the administrators' expected utility becomes

$$EU_{P\&i\&r_a} = -s_x r_a q_A(e_A)(1-q_J)$$
$$+ s_i\{f^\circ[1-q_A(e_A)]w_h + (1-f^\circ)q_A(e_A)w_\ell\} - u(e_A) + \omega \quad (11.21)$$

where $r_a = r/q_A(e_A^*(rs_x))$ is the review probability of stochastic review divided by the error probability of the administrator, that is, the probability that appealed decisions are reviewed. Note that if the administrator includes this dependence into his/her optimization, then he/she knows that, for example, one per cent of his/her decisions will be reviewed and that all these decisions are false (assuming that he/she will not be able to achieve a lower error probability with reasonable effort), and hence that the size of the sanctions he/she faces when his/her decisions are reversed by the courts is independent of his/her effort level. The administrator will thus exert as little effort as without any extrinsic incentives effect. If, however, the administrator takes the review probability of his/her false decisions as given and independent of his/her own error probability, then his/her optimization condition becomes

$$\frac{dEU_{p\&i\&r_a}}{de_A} = -\{s_i[f^\circ w_h - (1-f^\circ)w_\ell] + r_a s_x(1-q_J)\}q_A'(e_A) - u'(e_A) \stackrel{!}{=} 0.$$

Comparing this condition to the earlier optimality conditions shows that the resulting effort $e_A^{***}(s_x r_a)$ is less than the effort with review of all appeals in a perfectly separating appeals process $e_A^{**}(s_x)$ but more than the effort with strictly stochastic review $e_A^*(rs_x)$.

Social welfare with this limited appeals triggered review is

$$W_{p\&i\&r_a} = f^\circ\{1 - q_A(e_A^{***}(s_x r_a))[1 - r_a(1-q_J)]\}w_h$$
$$+ (1-f^\circ)q_A(e_A^{***}(s_x r_a))[1 - r_a(1-q_J)]w_\ell - q_A(e_A^{***}(s_x r_a))r_A c^s.$$

Since $r_A = r/q_A(e_A^*(rs_x))$ by definition, the difference

$$W_{p\&i\&r_a} - W_{stoch} = \{r[1 - q_A(e_A^*(rs_x))] + q_A(e_A^*(rs_x))$$
$$- q_A(e_A^{***}(s_x r_a))\cdot[f^\circ w_h - (1-f^\circ)w_\ell]$$

is strictly positive due to $q_A(e_A^*(rs_x)) > q_A(e_A^{***}(s_x r_a))$. The intuition is obvious: with an appeals-based review under which the same number of cases are reviewed as under the stochastic review, the courts cost the same amount of resources, but may only correct false decisions or leave them unchanged while under the stochastic review process they may also reverse correct decisions.

Thus appeals processes with perfectly separating appeals but only partial judicial review of appealed decisions may be the optimal decision. A proposition summarizes the results of the last step of the argument in this section:

Proposition 6 *If the incentive effect is sufficient to justify random review of administrative decisions by non-expert courts, then replacing random selection by an appeals process unambiguously increases social welfare, if the number of reviewed cases remains constant.*

5 CONCLUSIONS

In this chapter, I have shown that judicial control of administrative decisions may be welfare improving even if courts are substantially more likely to approve welfare-reducing projects and reject welfare-enhancing projects than administrators. In this sense, non-expert judicial control of expert administrative decisions may be worthwhile. I extended the basic framework to a situation in which the courts may receive high and low quality signals on the merits of an appeal. This allowed me to discuss how the courts' willingness to approve projects depends on the prior administrative decisions. It turned out that courts which are benevolent with respect to the content of their decisions follow the doctrine of judicial deference if and only if appellants are clearly less self-selecting than the administrative decisions are reliable. In the reverse case, courts will reverse administrative decisions unless their signals strongly support the administrative decision. Only if the appellants' self-selection and the administrative decisions are equally informative, will courts strictly follow their own signals.

This chapter thus implies two additional arguments for the discussion whether courts should defer to administrative decision making due to their lacking expertise in many cases. First, the information which courts can infer from the fact that and by whom an appeal has been lodged may partly offset their lack of own expertise, but only if parties can better judge the legal merits of their projects than administrators. Second, even if the single decision becomes more error prone as a result of judicial review, the incentives resulting for administrators from judicial review for all cases on which administrators have to decide may result in a positive welfare gain.

The approach still leaves open a bundle of variations of the model which may be worthwhile to investigate more closely. With more than two types of projects, one could assume that courts are informed not only about the binary value of the administrative decision, but also on the administration's findings on the costs and benefits underlying its decision. Again, the central arguments would not change: whether the courts grant discretionary ranges to the administration or repeal administrative decisions in the case of unclear court signals still depends on the relative quality of the information the courts can infer from the administrative decision and the fact that one party appealed that decision. Only the set of judicial signals which cast sufficient doubt on their reliability may vary with the absolute size of the difference between the administrator's estimates of gains and harm.

Finally, variations concerning the benevolence of administrators and judges with respect to the content of the decisions might change the results substantially. If lacking expertise not only results in higher error probabilities but also in biased error probabilities, non-expert control may reinforce the problem of imperfect administrators at least in so far as the argument rests on the incentives effect.

NOTES

* I am indebted to the many helpful comments of the participants of the fourth Corsica Law and Economics Workshop at Reims and in particular to Stefan Voight's comments. All remaining errors are, of course, mine.
1. Obviously when I allow court decisions to be 'illegal', this conflicts with Holmes's (1897) definition of law as 'the prophecy of what the courts will do in fact'.
2. Keeping λ fixed is a crude simplification. I conjecture that this simplification does not substantially affect the results.
3. Note that at least one of the intervals must exist due to $1 - q_J > q_J$ and $w_\ell = g_\ell - h_\ell < w_h = g_h - h_h$ which implies $h_h - h_\ell < g_h - g_\ell$ so that either $g_h > g_\ell$ or $h_\ell > h_h$ or both.
4. Of course this intuition does not imply that there should be as many appeals as possible (q_A should be as large as possible), since these net gains are only possible because a larger social loss results from administrative errors.
5. Alternatively, one could assume that the court forms beliefs for the probabilities that the administration erred given the content and the quality of the signal the court receives. The court may then be ignorant of $\bar{q}_J$ and q_J, and only has to know w_h and w_ℓ to maximize social welfare. While the results would be the same, more formalism would be needed to derive the perfect Bayesian equilibrium. I therefore remain with the version presented in the text.
6. This simplification excludes the possibility to gain from filing an appeal even if it will be rejected with certainty. Allowing for such a possibility may be interesting for cases of frivolous litigation, but would not contribute to the arguments brought forward in this chapter.
7. This simpification is not particularly intuitive, but eases the argument. Smaller λ combined with larger expected welfare effects yield the same results but imply formal complications.
8. Restricting the domain of the appeals cost distribution to the entire unit interval implies that an appeal will be lodged in all cases if and only if $\bar{\delta}_k^a = \underline{\delta}_k^a = \underline{\delta}_k^r = \bar{\delta}_k^r = 1$.

9. Writing the beta distribution as $F'(p) = [\Gamma(\alpha + \beta)/\Gamma(\alpha)\Gamma(\beta)]p^{\alpha-1}(1-p)^{\beta-1}$ these means together with variance 0.02 imply $(\alpha, \beta) \in \{(1.4, 5.6), (5.11875, 6.25625), (5.2316, 1.1484)\}$.
10. The resulting equilibrium values of the other endogenous variables are the following: success probabilities of appeals: $p_{1h} = p_{3\ell} = 0.35$, $p_{3h} = p_{1\ell} = 0.15$; probability that an erroneous administrative decision is appealed: $F_1(p_{1h}g_h) = F_3(p_{3\ell}h_\ell\lambda) \approx 0.998$; probability that a correct administrative decision is appealed: $F_1(p_{1\ell}g_\ell) = F_3(p_{3h}h_h\lambda) \approx 0.441$; probabilities that appeals are justified prior to the court's signal: $q_{A1} = q_{A3} \approx 0.361$; same probabilities after court's signal and expected welfare effect of reversal of administrative decision: $\hat{q}_k^a \approx 0.195 \Rightarrow E(w|\text{reversal}) \approx -0.61, \hat{q}_k^a \approx 0.274 \Rightarrow E(w|\text{reversal}) \approx -0.452, \hat{q}_k^r \approx 0.459 \Rightarrow E(w|\text{reversal}) \approx -0.082$, and $\overline{\hat{q}}_k^r \approx 0.569 \Rightarrow E(w|\text{reversal}) \approx 0.138$.
11. Uniqueness of the equilibrium is due to the specific shape of the distribution of appeals costs.
12. Again, I provide the resulting equilibrium values of the other endogenous variables: $p_{1h} = 0.65$; $p_{1\ell} = 0.35$; $F_1(p_{1h}g_h) = 1$; $F_1(p_{1\ell}g_\ell) \approx 0.255$; and $q_{A1} \approx 0.495$. Due to symmetry, I now omit the corresponding variables for third-party appeals. The probabilities that appeals are justified after the court's signal and the consequential expected welfare effect of reversal of administrative decision become: $\hat{q}_k^a \approx 0.296 \Rightarrow E(w|\text{reversal}) \approx -0.408$; $\hat{q}_k^a \approx 0.395 \Rightarrow E(w|\text{reversal}) \approx -0.209$; $\hat{q}_k^r \approx 0.595 \Rightarrow E(w|\text{reversal}) \approx 0.191$; and $\overline{\hat{q}}_k^r \approx 0.696 \Rightarrow E(w|\text{reversal}) \approx 0.392$.
13. Once more the resulting equilibrium values of the other endogenous variables: $p_{1h} = 0.85$; $p_{1\ell} = 0.65$; $F_1(p_{1h}g_h) = 1$; $F_1(p_{1\ell}g_\ell) \approx 0.13$; and $q_{A1} \approx 0.659$. Again, the corresponding variables for third-party appeals follow from symmetry. The probabilities that appeals are justified after the court's signal and the consequential expected welfare effect of reversal of administrative decision now become: $\hat{q}_k^a \approx 0.452 \Rightarrow E(w|\text{reversal}) \approx -0.095$; $\hat{q}_k^a \approx 0.562 \Rightarrow E(w|\text{reversal}) \approx 0.125$; $\hat{q}_k^r \approx 0.743 \Rightarrow E(w|\text{reversal}) \approx 0.486$; and $\overline{\hat{q}}_k^r \approx 0.818 \Rightarrow E(w|\text{reversal}) \approx 0.636$.
14. Note that the motivation to decide correctly instead of a motivation to have a good outcome of the overall decision process avoids the problem discussed in Aghion and Tirole (1997: 10), who argue that the principal's (that is, court's) additional effort to produce, and decide on the basis of, reliable information may reduce the agent's (that is, administrator's) effort to produce reliable information because the final decision depends less on the agent's decisions; in the extreme case (replacement of all administrative decisions by courts), administrators had no motivation to exert effort at all because their information would not influence the final decision. Also note that the label 'intrinsic' is an abbreviation for all incentives which are not influenced by judicial review of the decision.
15. The 'extrinsic' motivation may be due to sanctions, for example, of superiors in the form of promotion probabilities or of social sanctions from peers but may also be due to a simple dislike of having a decision reversed, that is, a sanction which is not extrinsic in a strict sense.
16. The number of cases on which the administrator has to decide is assumed to be constant in this chapter. So the assumption of a wage per case merely simplifies notation.
17. See Polinsky and Shavell (2000) for an overview.

REFERENCES

Aghion, Philippe and Jean Tirole (1997), 'Formal and real authority in organizations', *Journal of Political Economy* **105**, 1–29.

Dewatripont, Matthias and Jean Tirole (1999), 'Advocats', *Journal of Political Economy* **107**, 1–39.

Holmes, Oliver W. (1897), 'The path of the law', *Harvard Law Review* **10**, 457–78.

Holmström, Bengt (1979), 'Moral hazard and observability', *Bell Journal of Economics* **10**, 74–91.

Kirstein, Roland (2002), 'The new Basle Accord, internal rankings, and the incentives of banks', *International Review of Law and Economics* **21**, 393–412.

Polinsky, A. Mitchell and Steven Shavell (2000) 'Public enforcement of law', in Boudewijn Bouckaert and Gerrit De Geest (eds), *Encyclopedia of Law and Economics*, Vol. V, Cheltenham, UK and Northampton, MA, USA: Edward Elgar, 307–44.

Samuelson, Larry (1997), *Evolutionary Games and Equilibrium Selection*, Cambridge, MA: MIT Press.

Shavell, Steven (1995), 'The appeals process as a means of error correction', *Journal of Legal Studies* **24**, 379–426.

Spiller, Matt and Eric Talley (2000), 'Judicial auditing', *Journal of Legal Studies* **29**, 649–83.

von Wangenheim, Georg (2004), *Games and Public Administration: The Law and Economics of Regulation and Licensing*, Cheltenham, UK and Northampton, MA, USA: Edward Elgar.

PART III

The state at work: regulation and public policies under informational and legal constraints

PART II

12. *Pelle sub agnina latitat mens saepe lupina*: copyright in the marketplace
Giovanni B. Ramello

1 INTRODUCTION

The question of intellectual property and incentives for invention and creation is one that has arisen repeatedly in the history of economic thought.[1] However, in recent decades it has developed in new directions that have attracted particular attention. More specifically, the formulation of the concept of innovation as a public good, introduced by Schumpeter (1943) and supported by the empirical findings of Solow (1957), launched a flourishing body of literature that has sought to justify intellectual property rights as an essential – though admittedly imperfect (Arrow 1962) – tool for stimulating technological progress. The present contribution focuses on one specific type of intellectual property right, namely author's right or copyright (the two terms will here be used synonymously[2]), which has today taken on a primary role in economic systems.[3]

Nevertheless the application of economic analysis to copyright is important not just for the purposes of measuring economic flows, but also for evaluating how the right can influence the structure of the market, the behaviours adopted by economic agents and the resultant competitive outcomes. This, essentially, is the approach that has been taken in this chapter.

In the following sections we shall focus in particular on the relationship between the right's aims of providing an incentive for creative activities, and the overall efficiency. It can in fact be shown that, even if the commodification of intellectual works by means of copyright does provide some incentive for creative activities, this benefit is offset by certain 'side-effects' on the diversity and quality of the ideas produced, and interference with access to information and the incremental process of creation. All of which, if duly taken into account, can seriously call into question the overall balance of efficiency.

In the present-day debate, the justifications given for copyright and author's rights invoke both considerations of economic efficiency, as well as ethics and rhetoric. However such arguments fail to factor in the social costs, thus portraying in false light an institution that has, in practice, often served private interests very distant from its purported aims, injecting a significant amount of inefficiency into the economic system. This state of affairs can therefore be aptly summed up by the Latin adage of the title: 'a wolf often lies concealed in the skin of a lamb'.

Nevertheless, the objections raised thus far in the literature on the economic analysis of intellectual property rights, have inevitably resorted to the contraposition of extra-economic values, such as equity and justice, against those of economic efficiency. In the present discussion we shall seek to reconcile these two sides, showing how, under an expanded analytical perspective with respect to costs and benefits, and taking into consideration additional elements, copyright proves to be fundamentally inefficient even from a strictly economic standpoint, and that this will only be aggravated by technological progress.[4] We shall therefore demonstrate that an examination of the dynamics of the right within the market and society can seriously call into question, or even entirely overturn, the traditional economic arguments in favour of copyright.

2 THE TRADITIONAL LAW AND ECONOMICS ANALYSIS

The standard justification for copyright (and intellectual property rights in general) is based essentially on the hypothesis that the legal institution emerged in response to a market failure, because in the absence of such a right, individuals would not have an adequate incentive to undertake the creation of new (expressions of) ideas.[5] The argument goes back to the theory of public goods and externalities, which Coase (1960) resolved through the attribution of property rights to individuals. These, as the outcome of a negotiation between economic agents (and in the absence of subsequent public intervention) make it possible, at least in the original model, to achieve an optimal equilibrium in the Paretian sense.[6]

The central assumption behind this approach is therefore that an appropriability problem exists which, in the absence of an adequate system of incentives, would result in a suboptimal level of new ideas being produced.[7] In other words, the non-rival consumption and low marginal costs of dissemination/reproduction of copyrighted works, set against their high fixed production costs, leads to free-riding behaviours that have a negative impact on investments. Therefore, in the absence of an appropriate mechanism – that is, provision for adequate incentives – the above-described situation can, in the extreme case, produce adverse selection phenomena and drastically reduce the number of those who undertake creative activities.[8]

The above is not a universally accepted view, and has been repeatedly challenged by various authors.[9] However, this dissent has by and large been suppressed by the vigorous lobbying of copyright stakeholders – first and foremost among these the content-producing multinationals – which has today prevailed in shaping the law-making process (Christie 1995; Ryan 1998).

In the final analysis, therefore, the most substantiated arguments in favour of intellectual property rights rest on the twofold thesis of a legal monopoly as an 'incentive to create' and/or as an 'incentive to disclose'.

In the first case, the monopoly profits secured through the exclusive right are necessary for fuelling creative activities. In the second case, the temporary revenues from the exclusive right help stimulate the disclosure of new ideas that would otherwise, due to disinterest or fear of appropriation by others, fail to be disclosed (Audretsch 1997). The static inefficiency arising from the intellectual property right monopolies is thus remedied through a dynamic efficiency, that is, the creation of an optimal level of new copyrightable works over time.[10] We note, however, that the public objective is not merely to promote the production of new expressions of ideas, but rather to attain a general enrichment of knowledge – which is by nature collective and public. And for this reason copyright is not an absolute right, but on the contrary limited in duration, and in certain cases subject to derogation (Gordon and Bone 1999; Bently and Sherman 2001).

The above-described position relies heavily on the assumption that intellectual property rights have virtuous effects on scientific and cultural development, but fails to consider that 'the familiar devices for protection of intellectual property are known to have a variety of untoward side-effects that may distort and even impede the progress of technology' (David 1993, p. 17).[11] These side-effects in fact influence the dynamic efficiency and substantially alter the final balance, as we shall see below.

For now, it should be clear that the underlying premise invoked by supporters of intellectual property rights is that this system can achieve the goal of maximizing the net social surplus, to produce an optimal quantity and quality of information. This point is crucial for the economic analysis of copyright.

3 INCENTIVES AND VALUE

Upholders of intellectual property thus resolve the problem of the optimal production of a public good (information and knowledge in general) through its *ex lege* transformation into a private good. This solution effectively rests upon the (by no means obvious) assumption that it is possible to reconcile the often dialectically opposed camps of private and public interests. Only a careful and detailed analysis can reveal, for each particular case, whether these two spheres share any common ground that might enable them to enter into a virtuous relationship.

3.1 Ideas and Externalities

From this perspective, the first question to address hinges on the conversion of intellectual works into commodities, that is, their transfer from the cultural to the commercial sphere, a metamorphosis that underpins the functioning of the market. However this transition implies a difficult reconciliation between the 'use-value' that society attributes to cultural products[12] and their 'exchange-value' as defined by the market.[13] This rift, which naturally also applies to objects other than ideas, becomes especially significant in the case of copyrightable works which, by virtue of belonging to the knowledge and information sphere, are inherently appurtenant to collective contexts. An idea cannot be attributed an exchange-value if it is devoid of use-value for a community; and, an anthropologist would say, it will have use-value for a community as a consequence of its close interrelationship with the system of values and beliefs that generated it.[14]

The peculiarity of intellectual property, as compared with conventional property, lies precisely in the fact that categories of the physical, measurable and divisible world are applied to the sphere of culture and knowledge, where boundaries and quantities are to some extent a legal artifice, and hence open to discussion. In fact, the margin of separation between one copyrightable work and another (unlike that separating tangible objects), is fuzzy and arbitrary; already in the nineteenth century, the English scholar Augustine Birrell noted that, while it is easy to draw the boundaries of a physical asset, it is altogether more arduous to determine how much a book truly belongs to an author, because any creative endeavour contracts a significant and indissoluble debt with its precursors, and with the context in which it is generated (Goldstein 1994).

The use-value of an intellectual work is inevitably based on its semiotic content, which in its turn is inherently social in character:[15] the form of the idea, that is, its fixing in a tangible medium, will have an exchange-value due to the fact that it conveys shared symbols, in other words a use-value. And in fact the institution of the right by the political authorities is motivated by use-value: the recurrent refrain being that ideas are socially desirable, but that in the absence of copyright they would be created – and disclosed – in suboptimal quantities, to the detriment of society.

However it is the exchange-value that underpins the incentive, and makes the attribution of exclusive economic exploitation rights attractive to an individual: in the marketplace, ownership of an idea is meaningful only when its exchange-value is high, that is, when the legal monopoly translates into (or approximates) an economic monopoly.[16] So, the theory of intellectual property rights implicitly assumes that exchange-value – whose sphere of action is the market – can provide an incentive for the creation of use-value – whose sphere of action is society. This is patently not a neutral assumption, unless one admits an equivalence or perfect correlation between the use-value and exchange-value of an idea, which is by no means true in practice.

An additional consideration on this point: from an economist's perspective the situation described is particularly convenient if production of use-values is viewed as a positive externality, with respect to the output of a production process, which in our case is the exchange-value. Now the dilemma of policy makers lies precisely in the peculiarity that the objective being targeted is the externality, whereas the stimulus is exerted on the output, which in the intellectual property right model furnishes the sole effective incentive for creators. Therefore, if we assume a highly variable distribution of externalities between different copyrightable works, the incentive for any one particular output does not guarantee that an optimal amount of externalities will nevertheless be produced.[17] On the other hand it can be dangerous to rely on the market for the stimulation and selection of ideas, because this entrusts the incentive exclusively to profit – that is, to a purely economic dimension that precludes any broader set of values. A mechanism of this type, which is only weakly aligned with its general objectives, can therefore produce results very much at odds with those for which the right was originally instituted.

In the case of patents, one can sometimes posit a degree of correlation between profits and the social value of ideas. However, the claim that a particular development is the one that produces maximum welfare remains unproven, because there is generally no opportunity to make comparisons between alternative paths. On the contrary, a rich body of literature has shown that successful ideas can crowd out others due to the so-called 'increasing returns of adoption' (Arthur 1988, 1989), which tend to direct the course of subsequent developments (Foray 1989). And in cases where a comparison can be made, it emerges that the outcome of the innovation race is not always the best one, because historical accident, demand-side network externalities, issues of compatibility with preceding standards and path-dependence can ordain the success of ideas that are actually inferior to competing ones (David 1985; Arthur 1988).

In the case of copyrightable works, the question is even more vexed because their cultural and social value hinges on complex phenomena, in which the role of the market is relatively recent and not yet fully understood. We can be justified in saying, though, that its pure profit orientation makes the market ill-equipped to handle non-economic variables connected with the wider social context – unless one is prepared to accept a questionable equivalence between market and society. Therefore, the only guaranteed effect of the monopoly created by copyright is that it attributes an exchange-value to the intellectual work, that is, assigns it a market price. However, this market price may be only marginally correlated with its possibly high use-value, or diverge from it completely.

3.2 Effects on Creative Activities

What can happen, on the other hand, is that the economic nature of the marketplace will mainly stimulate the creation of ideas geared to the profit-maximization objective, that is, those with a high exchange-value, even if their use-value is questionable, while neglecting those ideas whose use-value cannot be fully 'comprehended' by the exchange-value. The proliferation of websites that distribute pornographic material on the Internet is one instance of the above mechanism.[18]

What is more, the commercial rationale that favours the types of product most successful on the market will drive creative activities to converge towards the subset of ideas that promise greatest profits, with a general impoverishment of knowledge also in terms of diversity. It has already been documented, in the field of technological innovation, that from a social standpoint there is an excess of correlation between different research and development policies (Bhattacharya and Mookherjee 1986).

In the case of copyright, to borrow a definition from communication theory, we can speak of 'semiological reduction' (Baudrillard 1972): the processes set in motion by the market trigger a dynamic which favours the emergence of particular types of ideas, that is, those that are better equipped to answer the economic objectives. For example, a strategy of risk minimization will tend to move in this direction, because the uncertainty associated with preferences, and therefore with demand, will favour the production of similar ideas, that is, those clustered around the taste currently in vogue.

Once again, the thesis is corroborated by the sociological literature which, starting with the seminal work of Adorno and Horkheimer (1947), in fact denounces the products of cultural industries, pointing out their tendency to flatten out knowledge, creating a sort of pseudo-individuality which, behind an outward façade of minimal originality, in reality only bolsters conformity.

It is also reasonable to assume that, with respect to their use-value, intellectual works answer purposes that are not exclusively economic, but which fulfil the personal and collective utility functions of both their consumers and creators in a variety of ways.[19] As a consequence, the implicit assumption that individuals undertake the creation of ideas primarily to secure revenues is not only unproven, but widely contradicted by the anthropological, ethnographic, historical and even scientific literature (Dasgupta and David 1994). In fact the arts, in their most disparate forms, have always existed in a variety of cultural contexts (David and Foray 2002). This might prompt the objection that, precisely because creative activities are so deeply rooted in human nature and collective contexts, the continued creation of ideas with high use-value would nevertheless be assured, irrespective of the positive or negative effects of the market.

In response to this it should be pointed out that, over the long term, copyright mechanisms will have an impact even in this sphere. In fact, by favouring ideas that maximize expected profits, and transforming their beneficiaries into consumers, the right will also tend to alter the behaviours of both creators and consumers. As the market comes to prevail, the former may become more aware of, and influenced by, financial considerations, while the latter, continually exposed to market signals expounding the importance of intellectual works with high use-value, might alter their preferences accordingly.[20] This question has been explicitly investigated in the social sciences, where individuals have repeatedly been shown to be culturally 'malleable' (Mauss 1979).

Consumers might also interpret the market success of products with high exchange-value as an indication of their high use-value, thereby generating a sort of *ex post* equilibrium in which use-value and exchange-value coincide: however this is really only a consequence of the conditions artificially created by copyright. The described dynamic can ultimately lead to an opposite selection to that feared by supporters of intellectual property rights: only ideas with a high exchange-value are created, and these crowd out traditional preferences through the above-described mechanism.

4 AUTHORS VERSUS OWNERS: THE METAMORPHOSIS OF THE INCENTIVE

Another peculiar attribute of copyright that sets it apart from other intellectual property rights, concerns the separation between the sphere of authorship, which defines creative proprietorship, and that of ownership, which defines economic proprietorship. This (by no means self-evident) distinction injects ambiguity into the market of copyrighted works, by casting doubt, as we shall see, not just on the efficiency of the right, but also (once again) on the consistency between its stated ends and the means of achieving them.

The above distinction occurs in every copyright law, where all the national variants (though admittedly with differences in interpretation from country to country) break up the right into two components, moral rights and economic rights, which are treated as distinct entities and applied in different contexts (Metaxas-Maranghidis 1995; Bently and Sherman 2001).

The standard explanation for this division states that the purpose of moral rights is to protect authorship, that is to say the intimate bond between an author and his/her work, as a result of which they fall under the scope of natural rights, which are inalienable.[21] By so doing the legislators have sought to acknowledge and protect the extra-economic significance of creative activities. Pecuniary rights, on the other hand, protect ownership, that is, the rights of economic exploitation of an intellectual work, and are perfectly alienable.[22]

Note that the intention of the legislation is that moral rights should temper the exploitation of pecuniary rights, in order to safeguard aspects that the latter are unable to protect. This implicitly accepts the thesis that creative activities extend into spheres that the market is not always able to reach.

In any case, there is lively debate in the juridical literature on the role and applications of these two components of copyright, with no shortage of cases in which theoretical contradictions abound.[23] Although these aspects are marginal for the purposes of this analysis, they contain an interesting parallel with the previously mentioned causal relation of exchange-value to use-value. In fact here we have ownership (which gives the owner, or licence holder, the exclusive right to duplicate and sell the intellectual work) being granted to stimulate authorship. In other words, although the economic activity hinges on ownership, the profits which it secures for the holder of the right are intended to stimulate the creation of new copyrightable works – in essence, new authorships.

So once again we see that the economic and creative dimensions, though theoretically distinct, are in practice placed on an equal footing, with the former being causal to the second. There have already been doubts expressed as to the validity of this position. But even setting this ambivalence aside, and assuming the incentive to be valid, the possibility of alienating economic rights raises serious questions as to the robustness of the mechanism: if authors, for whatever reason, are not the beneficiaries of the profits derived from the exploitation of their ideas, the incentive provided by copyright might not work.

Now it is reasonable to assume that creators generally operate outside the market, or at any rate that they are not perfectly informed about it, whereas their opposite numbers (publishers, record labels and so on) are as a rule better informed about the economic mechanisms, and therefore able to assign a specific probability distribution to the eventual 'success' of an intellectual work. What emerges, therefore, is a situation of asymmetric information, with creators at a disadvantage, that could potentially compromise the correct functioning of the incentive. In fact, because creators lack the adequate analytical tools, they are not in a position to calculate the real profits and might consequently undersell their rights. In such a case, the reward mechanism of copyright would fail to function (or do so in a distorted manner, attributing the profits to the wrong subjects), with the social costs of the monopoly still being incurred despite the prior alienation of the economic rights. Nor can we attribute any great significance to the inalienability and perpetual ownership of moral rights, because these cannot bring in economic benefits under the law.

It would therefore seem more logical, in pursuing the institutional objectives of intellectual property rights under conditions of uncertainty, to strengthen the position of authors – who are the weaker party in the negotiation – for example by allowing for the periodic renegotiation of transferred economic rights, which are the primary incentive of copyright. Such a clause might help correct the informational asymmetry that currently favours licence-holders, ensuring that more incentive-producing revenues reach creators, who in many cases are not the subjects truly rewarded by copyright.[24]

The above is indirectly backed up by the historical record: copyright and author's right were originally instituted for a very different purpose from the encouragement of creativity, namely to protect the right to duplicate and sell copies of an idea, under a 'utilitarian calculus that balances the needs of copyright producers [that is, the publishers] against the needs of copyright consumers, a calculus that appears to leave authors at the margins of its equation' (Goldstein 1996, pp. 168–9).[25]

The present-day reappraisal of moral rights, which on the one hand offers a more solemn and almost ethical justification for copyright (all to the benefit of stakeholders, and very rarely of the authors), on the other hand reflects a certain reluctance, on the part of legislators, to treat copyright as a purely economic matter.[26] In any case, the fact that the moral rights of authors (or their heirs) are exercised chiefly outside the market – because monetary claims cannot be advanced on the basis of moral rights – puts their effectiveness and, as mentioned previously, their true significance, very much in doubt.

5 THE RIGHT AND THE MARKET: A DIALECTICAL RELATIONSHIP

A rapid overview of the competitive dynamics can further contribute to an economic analysis of copyright, its workings on the market and the outcomes in terms of efficiency. In effect, the majority of the literature on this subject focuses on a static analysis of the market of ideas, and therefore treats the right as an instrument 'within the market': given a particular set of initial conditions, either with or without an *ex lege* monopoly, equilibria are identified and the outcomes in terms of welfare are compared. This exercise in comparative statics therefore assumes that there exists an unchanging market to which the different systems can be applied, in order to add up the various profits and consumer surpluses and compute the resultant social welfare outcomes (Landes and Posner 1989).

It does not, however, take into account the dynamic effects of the right on the behaviours of economic agents and on the market structure itself, and the not negligible fact that it gradually alters the scenario under study.

5.1 Market Structure and Rational Behaviours

The effects of copyright are not limited, *ceteris paribus*, to averting market failure, because it also progressively alters the structure of the market and behaviours, producing outcomes that are inconsistent, and often widely at variance, with its purported aims. For example, some observers (Fels 1994; OECD 1995) have noted that, in the recording, publishing and software industries (but also in chemicals and pharmaceuticals), firms have repeatedly leveraged their exclusive intellectual property rights to elevate trade barriers against parallel imports, with the clear aim of pursuing international price discrimination. In the case in point it was observed that (OECD 1995, paras 5 and 2). 'the copyright law goes further than correcting that market failure in also restricting the distribution of a copyrighted product, validly on the market consistent with copyright law in its country of origin' and there are 'two possible explanations for this state of affairs, that regulation [in imports] is in the public interest or that legislature has been "captured" by producers of copyrighted material'.

In the above-described situation intellectual property rights have thus been shown to promote anti-competitive behaviours, with the obvious negative repercussions on collective welfare. This is on no account a paradoxical phenomenon, and has a very simple explanation: because copyright attributes *de facto* market power, it is rational for owners to seek to exploit this to the full, for example by practising international price discrimination designed to extract maximum surpluses from consumers, even if this clearly undermines the welfare-enhancing purpose of the law. And yet in economic terms, from the perspective of the copyright owner, such behaviours are perfectly rational – and in the majority of cases legitimate (Ramello 2003).

What is more, the economic theory of rent-seeking tells us that incumbent monopoly-holders will generally have a rational tendency to make unproductive investments directed at maintaining their dominant position: an activity that 'destroys value by wasting valuable resources' (Tollison and Congleton 1995, p. xii). The limiting case, in this respect, would be that where the rent-seeker dissipates all the monopoly revenues.[27] Such an outcome is clearly at odds with the efficiency objectives of the intellectual property legislation.

5.2 The Dilemma of Competition

The points described thus far paint an ambiguous picture: because copyright is an exclusive right, it injects a monopolistic drift into the market that will be more or less pronounced depending on the market power that the owner is able to command (Ramello 2003). This drift may blur the existing margins between competitive and anticompetitive behaviours, and is clearly a source of inefficiency.

The analysis takes its cue from the controversial Magill case, and from the more recent International Marketing Services Health Inc. case.[28] In both suits, the exclusive rights granted under copyright were in fact judged to be illegitimate under the antitrust laws, because they had the effect of barring potential competitors from the market. Now, from an economic perspective the question is contradictory: if we accept the rationality hypothesis, then within any given regulatory framework behaviours will be consistent with the profit-maximization objective. Therefore, if an individual is granted a legal monopoly, it is perfectly rational for him/her to seek to translate it into an economic monopoly, and to endeavour to retain it. This behaviour will be anticompetitive only to the same extent that the copyright law itself is – in practice, albeit not in its original intention – anticompetitive. For goods that are sufficiently differentiated and poorly interchangeable (such as ideas), ownership of an exclusive right does in fact result in a monopoly, because it restricts access to a fundamental input. It would therefore be irrational to expect copyright holders to behave in a manner inconsistent with this framework.

And in fact, if we can say that copyrightable works in many cases have a naturally imperfect interchangeability (because every idea is in some way different from the others), it becomes rational for owners to pursue a strategy of accentuating this attribute, by widening the real or perceived distinction between competing products. This approach, of shifting competition to non-price elements, is manifestly aimed at attenuating price competition, and will have a correspondingly anticompetitive effect, with the attendant inefficiency.[29]

The tools for pursuing the above strategy are provided by the mass media, which are able at the same time to reach vast audiences, repeatedly exposing ideas until they become universal signs, and to make every cultural product unique and non-interchangeable. Through the combined workings of these economic and technological mechanisms, the uptake of an idea becomes increasingly equated with its market success. Thus, thanks to the communication media, exchange-value becomes causal with respect to use-value.

In other words, the market success and relentless media exposure of an idea trigger a self-enforcing mechanism that tends to augment its uniqueness and desirability. The result is a sort of 'perceived quality' or 'perceived uniqueness' in the eyes of consumers, that increases roughly in direct proportion with notoriety and success.

So that, ultimately, the logic of the market drives towards ever-increasing (unproductive) investments aimed at affecting this factor: for example, high expenditure on marketing and special effects, huge sums paid to artists, entertainers, actors and so on. All this can increase the quality and uniqueness perceived by consumers, the rigidity of demand and, ultimately, the volume of revenues. However, these types of investment are a move in the direction of rent-seeking behaviours, which makes them, at least to some extent, anticompetitive and inefficient.

The competitive game between copyrighted works is essentially played out on the definition of their quality and uniqueness as it is perceived by consumers, which can at times be artificially enhanced or even artificially constructed. This sets in motion a sort of recursive, positive-feedback mechanism between exchange-value and use-value that ultimately serves to maximize the profits of producers, with the additional consequence of aggravating the net loss due to monopoly (Silva and Ramello 2000).

What is more, this mechanism shifts the industrial configuration toward a so-called 'winner-takes-all' market model (Frank and Cook 1995): the investments sunk for differentiating products become more and more like purchasing a lottery ticket, with an increasingly slender chance of winning an ever bigger jackpot.[30]

We therefore have, on the one hand, high expected profits for a few players which tend to skew expectations, attracting an above-optimal number of individuals and investments, with a resultant waste of resources; and on the other hand a rewards system that marks a sharp division between winners and losers, where in reality a continuous quality spectrum exists (Frank and Cook 1995). So that, as a result of this market structure, ideas that are only marginally inferior to the winners in terms of quality will fail to succeed.

A dynamic such as this impoverishes both society and cultural diversity. And most importantly, it by no means guarantees the correct functioning of the incentive to create: 'in an economy permeated by these markets, there can be no general presumption that private market incentives translate self-interested behaviour into socially efficient outcomes' (ibid., p. 20).

This once again confirms the hypothesis of the dynamic effects of the right on the market structure. The lottery logic in fact drives incumbents to pursue behaviours aimed at increasing their likelihood of winning, by elevating barriers to entry that limit the number of possible competitors–winners and acquiring a large number of 'tickets'. Both behaviours are essentially an updated version of the dissipation of monopoly quasi-rents. In the first case, there is an endogenous escalation of certain costs (for example, marketing, distribution and even production expenditure, as in the case of expensive special effects or high salaries for actors and so on), which become the focal point of competition, restricting the field of competitors to only those able to sustain such costs.[31]

In the second case, high diversification and the accumulation of large catalogues of copyrighted works increase the likelihood of winning, under the rationale of minimizing risk (Ramello 2003). Overall, however, the described dynamic consolidates the position of incumbents and further restricts competition, gradually increasing the concentration of industries, as has been confirmed by surveys of specific sectors.[32]

The situation therefore favours the emergence of players with strong market power, further enhanced through the continual acquisition of complementary sectors in the fields of information, entertainment and communication. The optimal strategy has been eloquently described by the former president of a large industrial conglomerate: 'When power is moving between different bits of the value chain, you need to own the whole chain' (Anonymous 1998).

6 STRUCTURE OF COPYRIGHT AND ITS OBJECTIVES

To further evaluate the impact of copyright on the market, it is necessary to analyse its structure: in fact, an efficient incentive needs to have a particular architecture. In the case in point, this requires proper handling of the instrumental variables involved: deciding what to protect (the 'scope' of the right) and for how long to protect it (the 'duration' of the right) are fundamental decisions in the design of the incentive mechanism. An exaggerated level of protection could cause excessive losses in terms of social welfare, and even compromise innovation by blocking the cumulative creation process (David 1993; Scotchmer 1998). On the other hand, a form of protection that is too weak, according to the standard approach, could lead to market failure.

6.1 Consistency of the Incentive

The reference value, as emerges from the economic literature on patents, is the costs that are incurred in creation: because the incentive is necessary for recouping these costs, it must be calibrated on this basis (Scotchmer 1998). Assuming therefore that a creator acts as an agent of the society, the incentive will have to satisfy the usual participation and compatibility constraints, which are strictly dependent upon costs.[33] However copyright fails to take these aspects into account, and provides structurally equivalent protection to a multitude of different ideas that all have different creation costs. As a consequence, it seems doubtful that it can correctly function as an incentive.

A much more likely situation in this scenario is that some producers of inefficient ideas will nevertheless receive an incentive, but that (because only successful copyrighted works cover the costs incurred) negative expectations will arise, leading to subsequently lower investments on the part of those who fail to achieve market success after a certain amount of time.[34] This could be equally detrimental to those creative activities that require a longer time period to become successful.

Finally, only a right that is diversified according to creative domains and types of ideas can efficiently balance the needs of creators, who are given an incentive by the right, with those of consumers, who are rationed by the right.[35] However, in the domain of copyright, equal protection is given to a vast assortment of ideas which do not all, or not in equal measure, contribute to the welfare function. We are therefore justified in asking, once again, to what extent such a blind mechanism is effectively able to protect collective interests.

6.2 Scope

Looking at the individual instrumental variables, the scope and duration of the right, there are other questions that arise. It is a commonly held view that in the case of copyright, the first variable is negligible, because – it is claimed – the right does not protect ideas in the abstract but only their expression, that is, fixing in a tangible medium, and hence the scope is determined by this same fixing.[36]

In reality, this assertion can be challenged in a number of ways and takes a rather short-sighted view of creative processes. Some authors (Jones 1990, p. 552) argue that the conceptual dichotomy may be sterile: ' no "expressionless idea" exists' because 'any "idea" must necessarily have an expression'. In addition, the 'distinction between the terms "idea" and "expression" cannot serve as a fundamental determinant for deciding what is protectible under copyright law' (ibid.). And, in fact, the scope depends on the law which defines what constitutes the subject matter. Consider in this respect the case of a musical piece: legislators generally give most importance to the melody, permitting third parties to imitate the orchestration, arrangements and so forth, even though these are clearly identifiable elements that account for a substantial – or even prominent – part of the compositional effort.[37] Strictly speaking, in fact, the decision to protect one specific element rather than another will have consequences on what is created, due to the clear demarcation that is made between what can and cannot be copied.

Another aspect also needs to be considered: the extension of copyright to the most disparate contexts has, in terms of competition, had a similar effect to the extension of scope in the domain of patents. If the incentive of a patent depends on what is understood by the definition of 'idea' – which delimits the bounds of the monopoly[38] – the incentive of copyright depends on what we accept to be an 'expression of an idea'. In the above-mentioned Magill and IMS cases, for example, the extension of copyright to objects that have little or no bearing on creativity, such as a television listing or a database, while it might provide a perhaps modest incentive to create, also encourages behaviours detrimental to competition.

6.3 Duration

An examination of the second instrumental variable, the duration of the right raises further questions as to the efficiency of the institution. Even if we accept, for simplicity's sake, that scope is of little importance in the copyright case, this is all the more reason for duration to become the crucial variable through which legislators balance out the trade-off between private incentive and collective welfare.

A correct duration, under the logic of incentive, is that which grants creators revenues at least equal to the costs incurred, and this value needs to be determined on a case-by-case basis. In general, though, the time horizon should always be defined in a manner that permits calculation of the correct expected profits, while the attribution of a long *post-mortem autoris* term (PMA), which shifts the duration well beyond the lifetime of the creator, remains a dubious proposition.

In effect in the European Union the duration can be as high as a 70-year PMA (Duration Directive 93/98/EEC) – exceeding the already substantial 50-year term set by the Berne Convention – while in the United States the Copyright Term Extension Act (CTEA, 1998) has extended the duration to 70 years for private individuals, or to 95 years if the owner of the right is a firm. Now these durations make it rather difficult to compute the expected benefits, so there is a danger of merely extending the quasi-rents to the detriment of market efficiency. In particular, there is the risk of hampering incremental creative activities whose access to knowledge will be rationed by a very long duration,[39] whereas accomplishing the ultimate aim of copyright – namely, the creation of new knowledge accessible to society through provision of a temporary private benefit – would require minimizing this exclusion effect which should certainly not extend beyond the creator's lifetime.

Moreover, the trivial assertion that 'a longer term of protection is necessary for them [copyright owners] to recoup their original financial outlay' (Antill and Coles 1996, p. 380) is unacceptable, because firms and managers rarely calculate even their longest-term investments over such extended time horizons.

In short, the necessity of assuring revenues over such a protracted time period (nearly perpetual from the perspective of economic agents) finds no support in economic theory, but can instead be plausibly explained as a successful capture of law-making processes by economic interest groups, who have in this way, aided and abetted by the authorities, effected a fully-fledged and permanent expropriation of public goods (that is, knowledge) from society, with the ill-concealed aim of creating solid intangible assets for themselves (Ryan 1998; David 2000). The clear consequences of this operation, which has little to do with the authors themselves (or with their heirs), are an increased cost to society, wasted resources (through the dissipation of quasi-rents) that could otherwise be used elsewhere, restriction of access to information, and impoverishment of the cultural domain.

7 REGULATORY PROCESS AND 'CAPTURE'

The issue of interference on the part of economic stakeholders requires at least a brief digression. The ostensible goal of copyright and author's right is to increase knowledge by providing an incentive to creators. From a historical perspective, though, we find that the sources of the laws are very different: the right originated as a privilege granted to publishers, and was often used by governments as a tool for controlling what was published (Patterson 1968; Goldstein 1994). Subsequently, various attempts were made to introduce corrections favouring authors, but powerful interest groups have continued to exert considerable influence over its evolution.

Moving on to recent times, we find that the national and international law-making processes have been at the very least distorted, if not steered wholesale, by intensive lobbying campaigns of economic interest groups and the resultant political pressures exerted by certain governments. The most active nation in this respect has been the United States (the leading exporter of intellectual property), which through its US trade representative has, beginning in the mid-1980s, insisted on incorporating into GATT (the General Agreement on Tariffs and Trade) specific agreements relating to intellectual property (Ryan 1998). In this connection, Christie (1995, p. 527) asserts in no uncertain terms that 'the US obsession with obtaining "international harmonisation" of intellectual property laws . . . in real terms means the adoption of law satisfactory to the interests of US enterprises'.

Irrespective of opinion on this matter, the pressures exerted led to the 1994 drafting and ratification, in Marrakesh, of the Agreement on Trade-Related Aspects of Intellectual Property Rights (TRIPs). This has had a considerable impact on the national laws, first and foremost among these those of the European Community, further stimulated by the concomitant pressures of economic interest groups. Antill and Coles (1996, p. 379) have underlined its role:

> A protracted period of lobbying and industry investigation culminated on 20 November 1995 with the laying before Parliament of a draft Statutory Instrument entitled 'The Duration of Copyright and Rights in Performances Regulations 1995'. This Statutory Instrument amends the existing Copyright, Designs and Patents Act 1988 ('CDPA') and implements into national law the EC Directive 93/98 EEC, colloquially known as the 'Duration Directive'.

What emerges, therefore, is a clear impression, backed by a growing number of observers (Christie 1995; Altbach 1996; Ryan 1998; Lessig 2001), that the evolution of copyright laws is today determined by a complex dynamic, in which the pressures of special interest groups play a significant and prominent role. So it is unlikely that the development of these laws, driven by political negotiation, can best serve the public objectives of the right, and the goal of efficiency.

8 CONCLUSIONS

The stated objective of copyright relates to the public domain: the production of new knowledge through the private stimulation of creativity. Even if the resultant commodification of ideas, bolstered by the *ex lege* monopolies, does encourage creative activities, it also has various other consequences. First of all, it can influence the types of ideas that are produced, and limit their diversity. Second, it can favour rent-seeking economic behaviours which have a negative impact on efficiency. Finally, due to its peculiar structure, it does not fully answer the logic of incentive and can produce results very different from those intended, and which are not necessarily efficient.

Copyright does have the obvious but crucial effect of rationing demand, so that a considerable portion of potential consumers are excluded through price selection, with a detrimental effect on incremental knowledge creation. This exclusion effect should in theory be minimal – only in order to give a reward to creators for their contribution to society – whereas under the present structure of the right it is excessive. And the current regulatory trend is towards further augmenting it. In fact, the recent history of copyright protection laws has shown that this often indiscriminate extension is a response to powerful lobbying forces, which by their very nature serve private interests.

What is more, sector surveys have detected, over the past few decades, an increasing concentration of intangible assets in the hands of a limited number of subjects, who are gaining more and more control over creative activities and the dissemination of knowledge. This concentration, as we know from industrial economics, can interfere both with competition and with innovative processes.

Summing up, therefore, copyright today does not seem able to pursue the public goals that justify its existence, although it certainly does succeed in serving private interests. The former are, at best, manipulated in order to achieve the latter. This, essentially, is the message of the Latin motto of the title.

NOTES

1. See, for example, Goldstein (1994) and Ramello (2004).
2. The discussion that follows applies without distinction to both the *copyright* of common law systems and to *author's rights and neighbouring rights*, its juridical equivalent in civil law systems. Although not all observers agree in considering these two legal institutions to be equivalent, the generalization does not invalidate the arguments for this economic analysis. And it is also true that the various national laws have been tending to significantly converge, under the thrust of endogenous market forces – that is, growing internationalization and integration (see Goldstein 1994; Monopolies and Mergers Commission 1994). Strowel draws an interesting critical parallel (1993, p. 658), which underlines the evolutionary dialectic between these two juridical systems and notes how elements of each can be detected in the other.
3. Since 1996, for example, the category of copyright-protected goods occupies first place in the US balance of trade (see <http://www.iipa.com/> and Siwek 2002).
4. This does not, of course, rule out any extra-economic reasons.
5. We recall that copyright does not protect ideas in the abstract, but only their fixing in a tangible medium, in other words the 'expression of an idea' (see Bently and Sherman 2001). This peculiarity will be examined subsequently; whereas for the purposes of the present economic discussion, the term 'ideas' will be understood to also denote their expressions.
6. Note how this is not the only possible solution for overcoming the market failure in the case of public goods. For an overview of the alternatives, see, for example, Jha (1998, ch. 4).

7. See among many others, Arrow (1962), Landes and Posner (1989) and, for a rapid overview, Audretsch (1997).
8. However this hypothesis is not substantiated. And on the contrary, experimental economics has found that, in many cases, public goods are produced even where the predictions of non-cooperative equilibrium would indicate the opposite (Isaac and Walker 1998).
9. See, for example, Levin et al. (1987, p. 816).
10. However the hypothesis has not been clearly verified.
11. Scotchmer (1998, p. 273) also maintains that 'patents are a very crude incentive mechanism with many pernicious side effects'.
12. Communication theorists would more correctly replace the term 'use-value' with 'symbolic exchange-value', when speaking of the dynamics of social relationships (Baudrillard 1972). For the sake of simplicity, we shall here continue to define use-value as denoting all those socially and individually determined values that cannot be described in purely monetary terms.
13. The dichotomy between these values, which has inspired impassioned pages in the history of economic thought, can be traced back to the classical tradition, which we shall not be discussing here. The central idea, already put forward by both Karl Marx and Carl Menger (see Hong 2000), is that value is not a natural property of goods, but rather exists in the social domain, in the sense that it is defined by relationships between human beings. Now, such relationships can be economic, in which case they generate an exchange-value, but they can also extend far beyond the purely economic sphere (and in this, for example, we diverge from the strict Marxian interpretation). In the cultural sphere at least, and with all due respect to absolute proponents of neoclassical positions, the existence of values that are not purely economic has been verified by anthropological and sociological studies (beginning with Boas 1938).
14. On the shared and social nature of knowledge, see Geertz (1973).
15. Geertz (1973, p.11) asserts that 'culture is public because meaning is'.
16. See Ramello (2003).
17. To further clarify this idea, consider the possibility of producing electrical energy using either a green technology or a highly polluting but cheaper method. An entrepreneur faced with a long-term decision will obviously not consider the negative externalities, and prefer the more profitable but polluting technology, unless of course the structure of private costs is altered by some form of public intervention.
18. It is no coincidence that one of the first cases of on-line copyright protection arose precisely in this sphere: *Playboy Enters* v. *Chuckleberry Publ., Inc.* 939 F. Supp. 1032 (S.D.N.Y. 1996), *recons. Denied*, 1996 U.S. Dist. LEXIS 9865 (S.D.N.Y. 1996).
19. This can be said to apply, for example, in the Western scientific community, in which fame, the respect of colleagues and so forth often take precedence over financial considerations, in the utility functions of academics (Dasgupta and David 1994).
20. In point of fact, the tastes and preferences of individuals are not exogenous, as neoclassical theory would frequently have it, but endogenous (Hodgson 1988, pp. 13ff.).
21. Moral rights, which originated in civil law jurisprudence, have today also been incorporated into common law systems. They protect the right of publication, the right of integrity and the right of paternity (Bently and Sherman 2001).
22. They take the form of a bundle of rights for each possible form of economic exploitation (right of reproduction, right of distribution and so on; Bently and Sherman 2001).
23. See, for example, Strowel (1993) and Rushton (1998). In the US doctrine of work-made-for-hire, for example, the employer is considered to be the author and hence acquires all the rights, in defiance of the concept of an intimate bond between creator and work.
24. This observation is borne out by empirical evidence (see Towse 1996, 1999).
25. The same opinion is expressed in David (1993) and Strowel (1993).
26. On the possibility of undue manipulation of authorship, see Strowel (1993, p. 668: 'it is well-known that, under the banner of author's rights, publishers have from the outset sought to pursue their own interests, with increasing success the more they are able

27. David (1993) concurs with this view, for the case of patent.
28. Magill case, *Radio Telefis Eireann (RTE)* v. *Commission of the European Communities* (C-241/91 P e C-242/91P, 6 April 1995); *IMS Health* v. *NDC Health*, European Commission, 3/7/2001, COMP D3/38.O44.
29. For an in-depth discussion see Silva and Ramello (2000) and Ramello (2003).
30. This is borne out by empirical surveys on copyright revenues (Towse 1996, 1999).
31. As we can see, therefore, certain investments have the twofold consequence of reducing the replaceability of certain ideas while at the same time elevating barriers to entry.
32. See, for example, Marvasti (2000) for the film industry and Silva and Ramello (2000) for the recording industry.
33. For a presentation of the principal–agent model, see Varian (1992, ch. 25).
34. See Scotchmer (1998).
35. Altbach (1996, p.18) indirectly responds to this question: 'It is time to take a step back from rampant commercialism to examine the complex world of copyright and the distribution of knowledge. There is, in reality, a difference between a Mickey Mouse watch, a Hollywood film, or even a computer software program, on the one hand, and a scientific treatise, on the other . . . Those who control the distribution of knowledge treat all intellectual property equally and are perfectly happy to deny access to anyone who cannot pay'.
36. For example, Besen (1998, p. 479) says: 'The fixation requirement serves the obvious purpose of defining the scope of the claimed protection in objective terms'.
37. Confirming this, the American musicologist Paul Griffiths (1994, p. 9) speaking of the French composer Claude Debussy, said: 'As for colour, Debussy was a master of delicate orchestral shadings, and pioneer in consistently *making instrumentation an essential feature of composition* . . . Thus the orchestration has its part in establishing both ideas and structure; it's more than an ornament or a means for enhancing rhetoric' (added italics).
38. It is one thing to grant a patent to an electrical lighting system, but a very different one to say instead that the patent protects the idea of a light bulb, or of a carbon filament light bulb and so on. Clearly, the scope sets the bounds of competition.
39. Considering that an intellectual work is created *in vita*, its total revenues (*in vita* + *post mortem*) will have a duration of at least 100 years.

REFERENCES

Adorno, T. and M. Horkheimer ([1947] 1979), *Dialectic of Enlightenment*, London: Verso.

Altbach, P.G. (1996), 'The subtle inequalities of copyright', *The Acquisitions Librarian*, **15**, 17–26.

Anonymous (1998), 'Wheel of fortune. A survey of technology and entertainment', *The Economist*, 21 November, 1–21.

Antill, J. and P. Coles (1996), 'Copyright duration: the European Community adopts "Three score years and ten"', *European Intellectual Property Review*, **18**, 379–83.

Arrow, K.J. (1962), 'Economic welfare and the allocation of resources for invention', in R.R. Nelson (ed.), *The Rate and Direction of Inventive Activity*, Princeton, NJ: Princeton University Press, pp. 609–24.

Arthur, W.B. (1988), 'Competing technologies: an overview', in G. Dosi, C. Freeman, R. Nelson, G. Silverberg and L. Soete (eds), *Technical Change and Economic Theory*, London: Frances Pinter, pp. 590–607.

Arthur, W.B. (1989), 'Competing technologies, increasing returns and lock-in by historical events', *Economic Journal*, **99**, 116–31.

Audretsch, D.B. (1997), 'Technological regimes, industrial demography and the evolution of industrial structures', *Industrial and Corporate Change*, **6** (1), 49–81.

Baudrillard, J. (1972), *Pour une critique de l'économie politique du signe* [*For a Critique of Sign Political Economy*], Paris: Gallimard.

Bently, L. and B. Sherman (2001), *Intellectual Property Law*, Oxford: Oxford University Press.

Besen, S.M. (1998), 'Intellectual property', in P. Newman (ed.), *The New Palgrave Dictionary of Economics and the Law*, vol. 2, London: Macmillan, pp. 348–52.

Bhattacharya, S. and D. Mookherjee (1986), 'Portfolio choice in research and development', *Rand Journal of Economics*, **17**, 594–605.

Boas, F. (1938), *The Mind of Primitive Man*, New York: Macmillan.

Christie, A. (1995), 'Reconceptualising copyright in the digital era', *European Intellectual Property Review*, **11**, 522–30.

Coase, R. (1960), 'The problem of social cost', *Journal of Law and Economics*, **3**, 1–44.

Dasgupta, P. and P. David (1994), 'Towards a new economics of science', *Research Policy*, **23**, 487–532.

David, P. (1985), 'Clio and the economics of QWERTY', *American Economic Review*, **75** (2), 332–7.

David, P. (1993), 'Intellectual property institutions and the panda's thumb: patents, copyrights and trade secrets in economic theory and history', in M.B. Wallerstein, M.E. Mogee and R.A. Schoen (eds), *Global Dimensions of Intellectual Property Rights in Science and Technology*, Washington, DC: National Academy Press, pp. 19–62.

David, P.A. (2000), 'The digital technology boomerang: new intellectual property rights threaten "open science"', proceedings of the World Bank Conference on Development Economics.

David, P.A. and D. Foray (2002), 'An introduction to the economy of the knowledge society', *International Social Science Journal*, **54** (171), 9–23.

Fels, A. (1994), 'Compact discs. Intellectual property rights and competition policy', DAFFE/CLP(94)18, Paris: OECD.

Foray, D. (1989), 'Les modéles de compétition technologique: une revue de la litterature [The models of technological competition: a survey]', *Revue d'économie industrielle*, **48**, 16–34.

Frank, R.H. and P.J. Cook (1995), *The Winner-take-all Society*, New York: Free Press.

Geertz, C. (1973), *The Interpretation of Cultures*, New York: Basic Books.

Goldstein, P. (1994), *Copyright's Highway*, New York: Hill & Wang.

Gordon, W.J. and R.G. Bone (1999), 'Copyright', in B. Bouckaert and G. De Geest (eds), *Encyclopedia of Law and Economics*, Cheltenham, UK and Northampton, MA, USA: Edward Elgar, pp. 189–215.

Griffiths, P. (1994), *Modern Music: A Concise History*, London: Thames & Hudson.

Hodgson, G.M. (1988), *Economics and Institutions*, Cambridge: Polity Press.

Hong, H. (2000), 'Marx and Menger on value: as many similarities as difference', *Cambridge Journal of Economics*, **24**, 87–105.

Isaac, R.M. and J.M. Walker (1998), 'Nash as an organizing principle in the voluntary provision of public goods: experimental evidence', *Experimental Economics*, **1**, 191–206.

Jha, R. (1998), *Modern Public Economics*, London: Routledge.
Jones, R.H. (1990), 'The myth of the idea/expression dichotomy in copyright law', *Pace Law Review*, **10** (3), 551–607.
Landes, W.M. and R.A. Posner (1989), 'An economic analysis of copyright law', *Journal of Legal Studies*, **18**, 325.
Lessig, L. (2001), *The Future of Ideas*, New York: Random House.
Levin, R.C., A.K. Klevorick, R.R. Nelson and S.G. Winter (1987), 'Appropriating the returns from industrial research and development', *Brookings Papers on Economic Activity*, **3**, 783–820.
Marvasti, A. (2000), 'Motion picture industry: economies of scale and trade', *International Journal of the Economics of Business*, **7** (1), 99–114.
Mauss, M. (1979), *Sociology and Psychology*, London: Routledge & Kegan Paul.
Metaxas-Maranghidis, G. (ed.) (1995), *Intellectual Property Laws of Europe*, Chichester: Wiley.
Monopolies and Mergers Commission (1994), *The Supply of Recorded Music*, London: HMSO.
Organization for Economic Cooperation and Development (OECD) (1995), 'Annex to the Summary Record of the 66th Meeting of the Committee on Competition Law and Policy', Mini Roundtable on Compact Disks, Intellectual Property Rights and Competition Policy, DAFFE/CLP/M(94)2/ANN2, Paris: OECD.
Patterson, L.R. (1968), *Copyright in Historical Perspective*, Nashville, TN: Vanderbilt University Press.
Ramello, G.B. (2003), 'Copyright and antitrust issues', in W.E Gordon and R. Watt (eds), *The Economics of Copyright: Developments in Research and Analysis*, Cheltenham, UK and Northampton, MA, USA: Edward Elgar, pp. 118–47.
Ramello, G.B. (2004 forthcoming), 'Intellectual property and the market of ideas', in J. Backhaus (ed.), *Elgar Companion in Law and Economics*, 2nd edn, Cheltenham, UK and Northampton, MA, USA: Edward Elgar.
Rushton, M. (1998), 'The moral rights of artists: droit moral ou droit pécuniare?', *Journal of Cultural Economics*, **22**, 15–32.
Ryan, M.P. (1998), *Knowledge Diplomacy: Global Competition and the Politics of Intellectual Property*, Washington, DC: Brookings Institution Press.
Scotchmer, S. (1998), 'Incentives to innovate', in P. Newman (ed.), *The New Palgrave Dictionary of Economics and the Law*, vol. 2, London: Macmillan, pp. 273–7.
Schumpeter, J. (1943), *Capitalism, Socialism and Democracy*, London: Unwin.
Silva, F. and G. B. Ramello (eds) (1999), *Dal vinile a Internet: Economia della Musica tra Tecnologia e Diritti [From the Vinyl to the Internet. Studying Economics of Music Between Technology and Rights]*, Turin: Fondazione Giovanni Agnelli.
Silva, F. and G. B. Ramello (2000), 'Sound recording market: the ambiguous case of copyright and piracy', *Industrial and Corporate Change*, **9** (3), 415–42.
Siwek, S.E. (2002), *Copyright Industries in the U.S. Economy. The 2002 Report*, Washington, DC: International Intellectual Property Alliance.
Solow, R. (1957), 'Technical change and the aggregate production function', *Review of Economics and Statistics*, **39**, 312–20.
Strowel, A. (1993), *Droit d'auteur et copyright [Author's Right and Copyright]*, Brussels; Bruylant and Paris: L.G.D.J.
Tollison, R.D. and R.D. Congleton (eds) (1995), *The Economic Analysis of Rent Seeking*, Aldershot: Edward Elgar.

Towse, R. (1996), *Economics of Artists' Labour Markets*, ACE Research, Report no 3, Arts Council of England, London.

Towse, R. (1999), 'Incentivi e redditi degli artisti derivanti dal diritto d'autore e diritti connessi nell'industria musicale [Copyright incentives and incomes of artists in the music industry]', in Silva and Ramello (eds).

Varian, H.R. (1992), *Microeconomic Analysis*, 3rd edn, New York: W.W. Norton.

13. Competition in banking: switching costs and the limits of antitrust enforcement

Donatella Porrini and Giovanni B. Ramello[*]

1 INTRODUCTION

A recurring theme in the analysis of competition in the banking sector is the problem of stability, and the regulatory constraints that are consequently imposed on economic agents operating in this particular market.

Generally speaking, antitrust intervention in the banking is heavily influenced by considerations of stability, because although competitive processes are inherently selective, and presuppose the possible exit from the market of inefficient competitors, this is precisely the eventuality that economic policy decisions seek to avert. Therefore, as discussed in more detail in the paragraphs below, the regulation has historically given precedence to the stability objective, relegating competition to second place. This is borne out by the many structural and operational constraints imposed on the authorities and laws that ought to safeguard competition, and the elevation of administrative barriers to entry.

Under a law and economics perspective, regulatory intervention in the market is justified as a means of counteracting the emergence of inefficiencies, and so we can apply this same justification to the banking sector, where a specific inefficiency arises from the macroeconomic and systemic repercussions of the normal workings of the competitive process. The central problem, in this case, is entrepreneurial risk, which must necessarily exist in any competitive market, and plays a decisive role in ordaining the entry and exit of competitors. However, in the specific case of banks, price competition tends to encourage overly speculative behaviours, which essentially entail acceptance of excessive risk, with a resultant volatility that could potentially harm depositors, and ultimately compromise the stability of the economic system as a whole.

From the perspective of economic policy, this eventuality translates into a natural friction between stability and competition, which cannot always be overcome without penalizing one of the two, and which in the particular sector under study is resolved at the expense of competition.

The consequence of this approach is that the banking market becomes extremely rigid on the supply side and structurally not equipped for a competitive orientation, and banks come to occupy a privileged position *vis-à-vis* governments that – to a greater or lesser extent, depending on the countries and the situations – enables them to sidestep the antitrust authorities.

In such a scenario, the trade-off between stability and competition cannot be totally resolved through traditional antitrust actions, which are sometimes at odds with the stability objective and hampered by the constraints of the previously defined regulatory framework. On the other hand, the supply-side approach which characterizes a great deal of the scientific literature on competition policy appears unable to pursue one objective without penalizing the other.

It is precisely these considerations, found in a significant portion of the literature, which provide the starting base for the hypothesis of this work – described more in depth in the second section of this chapter – namely, the proposal of a novel demand-side perspective, that is, one which focuses on the central role of consumers in the competitive process. If intervention on the supply side is hampered a priori by the regulatory framework, it is nevertheless possible to implement pro-competition actions on the demand side, for example by enhancing the ability of consumers to change from one provider to the other without impacting on the market structure. In operational terms, the proposed approach is to leverage consumer mobility in order to stimulate the currently weakened competition between firms. This would make it possible to pursue the traditional antitrust objectives of efficiency and welfare maximization, without necessarily impacting on stability.

In the sector under study there is a simple solution for implementing such a strategy, which is to reduce the switching costs that currently restrict the mobility of consumers between different banks, with an obvious impact on competition. These policy implications will be presented in the final two paragraphs of this chapter.

2 RELATIONSHIP BETWEEN COMPETITION POLICY AND THE STABILITY OBJECTIVE

If stability is a crucial objective common to all banking and financial systems, control of competition policy is a fundamental tool for pursuing such a goal. In fact, an unrestricted competitive mechanism, with the attendant risk of entry–exit of firms from the market, clearly leaves open the possibility of bank failures: the risk that inefficient firms might fail is in fact a necessary condition for the existence of a competitive market. However, in the particular case of banking, because of the ties generally linking this sector to the rest of industry, failure of one firm is liable to trigger a contagion or domino effect, causing other banks and financial institutions to fail in their turn, and culminating in the collapse of the entire market, with very serious repercussions on the economic system as a whole, at both the national and, ever more frequently, international level (De Bandt and Hartmann 2002).

Confirming the above is the fact that, in most industrialized countries, the stability objective was first enshrined in regulations issued in the aftermath of the 1930s as a reaction to the Great Depression, that is, the most serious instance of market failure in modern history (Minervini and Onado 2000). Therefore, even though the national regulations for the safeguard of stability developed independently, under separate institutional frameworks and market regulation authorities, all systems nevertheless exhibit common traits. In fact, the various national frameworks embody certain shared assumptions that can be summarized as follows: (i) the risk of failure within the banking system, with the attendant danger of systemic repercussions on the economy as a whole, requires special treatment; (ii) depositors, in their role as producers of savings, should be protected; and (iii) competition in this specific sector has the effect of increasing risk and must therefore be controlled.

Associated with this is the idea that guaranteeing market power to banks will help attenuate the risks to which they are exposed, thereby furthering the goal of stability, as expressed in the so-called theory of 'charter value'.[1]

The stability objective thus becomes a real hindrance to competition policy and antitrust enforcement, due to the many special measures and exceptions that it causes to be imposed (though here again with national variants), for example with respect to mergers, supervision and so on.

In recent years the trend has been towards a partial restoration of market competition, while at the same time seeking to safeguard – or at least avoid significantly compromising – the stability objective.[2]

It thus remains an open question whether competition and stability are necessarily in opposition, or whether it is instead possible to pursue the one without necessarily compromising the other. The conventional result which emerges from the literature is that resolution of the conflict through regulation is generally the optimal solution. However, the new industrial economics, as we discuss below, provides a means for reconciling this position with (at least) a partial safeguard of competition.

3 REGULATION AS A CONSTRAINT ON COMPETITION POLICY

Generally speaking, regulation is the practical means by which competition is restricted and the stability objective pursued. But it can also sometimes be deployed to support competition, which places them in a sort of no-man's-land that effectively renews the dilemma of stability versus competition.[3] On the one hand, regulation restricts competition *ex ante*, creating a safety net to guard against bank failures, as well as providing for discretionary *ex post* interventions, through the monetary authorities, to rescue banks that run into difficulty. But on the other hand, regulation also seeks to uphold competition through *ad hoc* market interventions in specific situations, for the most part in the case of mergers. This is a source of further ambiguity, because in certain countries the activities of the central bank will then overlap with those of the antitrust authority, generating what is in essence a conflict, as will be clarified below (OECD 1998, 2000).

Each national situation is therefore characterized by its own set of regulatory measures, such as prohibitions on listing in the stock exchange, limits on diversification into non-banking products, barriers to entry of foreign banks, restrictions on branching, controls on interest rate levels, and capital requirements.

However, there is a particular distinction when it comes to the divide between depositors and investors. For the former, the most important thing is stability, whereas the latter are mainly interested in transparency and complete information. Therefore, the banking and financial markets have different needs which call for distinct regulatory frameworks. In this connection, we can identify two main lines of approach adopted by the various countries. At one end of the spectrum are nations whose regulatory frameworks make a distinction between banking and financial market operators, such as the United States, where the Banking Law and Securities and Exchange Act were enacted almost simultaneously, but as completely separate legislations. And at the other end are countries such as Italy, where banks function both as collectors of savings in the form of deposits and as financial intermediaries for investors, characterized by a unified banking law strongly conditioned by the stability objective, which takes precedence over transparency.

But even within the banking market, regulatory actions can be further subclassified as a function of the relevant market, identified through application of three criteria, of which two are borrowed from antitrust practice while one is specific to the sector under study: (i) the geographical market, which in this case is delimited by national and regional borders; (ii) the product market, expressing the substitutability of products as perceived by consumers; and, finally, (iii) the nature of the market players, which distinguishes between saving banks, and private, cooperative or state-owned banks (Amel and Starr-McCluer 2001).[4]

With regard to the second criterion, the European Commission provides clear guidelines for identifying markets, at least for those relating to traditional banking products:[5]

1. retail banking, which comprises the various groups of individual products and services that banks offer to households (current accounts, savings accounts, bonds, pension funds, short- and long-term loans, mortgages);[6]
2. corporate banking, which comprises services aimed at businesses (domestic corporate banking, public sector banking, international credits to public companies);[7] and
3. the financial market sector, which comprises services relating to government securities and capital markets (trading equities, bonds and derivatives, foreign exchange and money markets).[8]

These three product categories are seen as giving rise to distinct markets, due to differences in both the composition of demand and the nature of the offerings, which are provided through different channels. And, according to antitrust practice, each individual product category can then be further broken down into a series of separate product markets – known as sub-markets – corresponding, for example, to different categories of clients, distinguished according to the characteristics of their demand.[9]

Naturally, in defining relevant markets it is also necessary to carefully consider the ongoing evolution of the Internet and electronic commerce, which may introduce new classifications. In fact, the future prospect of electronic banking, with no need for physical branch banks, would entail a relaxation of the geographical constraint and a general increase in competition. However this prospective development is not considered in the present work, nor in the cited literature, because it is still poorly defined, and in any case negligible compared with the other activities. In the current scenario, the uptake of e-banking is still hampered by a variety of constraints, arising from the need to obtain information about clients, the substantial advertising investments required to establish a new product, and the difficulty of stipulating contracts on-line (Group of Ten 2001).

The three banking markets listed above have different attributes from a regulatory and competition-policy perspective. This work proposes to look more in depth at the retail market, that is, the specific market of products offered by banking institutions to households, examining its characteristics from the competitive standpoint. The analysis will illustrate how, from a supply-side perspective, the regulatory framework is a major obstacle to the development of policies for competition in this market. These limitations are discussed in more detail in the paragraphs that follow.

4 COMPETITION IN BANKING LAW AND PRACTICE

Competition policy in banking is different from competition policy in any other market. This peculiarity of banking policy can be traced back to the special charters granted to banks, and has been perpetuated to this day by a continuing friction between the need to guarantee stability on the one hand, and to sustain entrepreneurial opportunity and productive efficiency on the other.

Bank competition policy arose simultaneously with the birth of the banking market itself, and therefore long predates the advent of national antitrust laws. However, after the 1930s such policies were everywhere affected by a growing tension between the competition objective and the need to protect the national economic system as a whole from the risk of bank failure

As a result of this, the national banking laws placed very little emphasis on the safeguard of competition. In the United States, this historical bias was corrected after the Second World War, with the integration of antitrust and banking law, which marked a move towards upholding competition in banking after a period of anti-competitive restrictions imposed by the government (Shull 1996). In fact, even though the United States introduced a general competition law very early on (the Sherman Act was enacted in 1890 and the Clayton Act in 1914), a specific competition law for banking dates back only to the 1960s (the Bank Holding Act was enacted in 1957, the Bank Merger Act in 1960).

Similarly, in the case of Europe:

> For a long time, banking in many countries was exempted from the reach of competition law and subjected to regulation only. As a consequence of deregulation, this is different today. For example on the matter of mergers, banks in the EU are fully subjected to EU competition law. In this way, competition policy and regulatory interests can become intertwined and enter into conflict. (Canoy et al. 2001, p. 31)

However, since the 1980s, there has been a general reassessment of public policy in banking, with pro-competition policies emerging in the wake of structural, behavioural and technical developments, and changes to the banking law. In recent times, the banking market has felt the effects of novel trends, such as the relaxation of geographical constraints and the lifting of restrictions on the scope of activity, an unprecedented movement towards bank mergers, a sharp decline in the number of banking institutions, and the advent of secondary markets and new systems of payment – all of which presage a fundamental transformation in the industry.

Beginning in the 1980s, the European Commission and the national governments initiated a so-called 'competitive deregulation' process, embodied in the banking directives (first 77/780 and second 89/646) as well as the own funds (89/299 and 91/633) and solvency ratio (89/647 and 94/7) directives. This opened the way to the abolition of restrictions within the European common market, under the principle of mutual recognition. At the same time, however, the Basle Committee on Banking Supervision began formulating a series of capital adequacy requirements, starting from the agreement of 1988.

Despite the recent thrust towards increased competitiveness, competition policy in banking remains atypical due to the issue of financial market stability. This subordination of competition to stability continues to dictate the adoption of supervision mechanisms for ascertaining and limiting the risks to which banks are exposed.

Generally speaking, in the banking sector national antitrust authorities are confronted not so much with cases of abuse of dominant position, but rather with cases of cartels and especially mergers, resulting from the concentration process that has in recent years characterized, and continues to strongly characterize, this sector (Carletti and Hartmann 2003). The specific case of mergers and acquisitions is an interesting example of the peculiar manner in which competition, and the authorities charged with upholding it, are dealt with in the banking sector.

Merger and acquisition operations unite two formerly independent firms into a single entity, and are generally forbidden if they result in a dominant position that can in some way impair and/or restrict competition (Hovenkamp 1994). Or, alternatively, the operation may be authorized on condition that certain correctives are applied to neutralize its anticompetitive effects. However, in banking, all these decisions, and the manner in which they are taken, are once again influenced by the implicit or explicit consideration of a trade-off between stability and competition.

There is, first of all, a widespread belief that larger-sized banks, with the resultant attenuation of competition, can help protect against systemic instability, and this view to some extent prejudices the decisions. This position is also consistent with the theory of scale and scope economies, according to which organizational fixed costs imply economies of scale while the joint provision of deposit and credit activities can produce important scope economies (Porrini 1994, 1996).

A further indication of the special status granted to this market is the peculiar attribution of competencies over competition to institutions different from the antitrust authorities. Despite differences between countries attributable to historical legacies not directly linked to the efficiency-stability paradigm, and to varying preferences accorded to the authorities responsible for bank competition and financial stability, we can none the less say that the banking market everywhere enjoys a privileged status.

Looking, for example, at the situation in certain European nations, it should first of all be borne in mind that, in the European Union, national institutions are competent to decide on mergers below 'community dimension', whereas the Merger Task Force of the European Commission (DG Competition) handles those which exceed this dimension.[10]

In France, the body responsible for reviewing bank mergers is the 'Comité des établissements de credit et des entreprises d'investissement', one of the committees in charge of prudential supervision in the financial sector, headed by the governor of the Banque de France. The criteria applied by the Comité are not those defined in general competition law, but rather those defined in banking law, where the stability objective strongly prevails over competition.

In Germany, the Federal Cartel Office is entitled to issue a first opinion on bank mergers, based principally on the application of competition law. However, before a merger can be blocked it is also necessary to have the approval of the Federal Supervisory Office, which examines the case from the perspective of banking law, thereby also taking into account considerations of stability. Moreover, if the opinions of the cartel and supervisory offices are not in agreement, bank mergers can be submitted for political review to the Federal Minister for Economics, who issues a decision based upon macroeconomic and common welfare considerations.

In the United Kingdom, bank mergers are reviewed through the application of competition law, in the same way as any industry. Only in cases of particular importance is a report from the Office of Fair Trading also requested. So, although the Financial Services Authority and the Bank of England are consulted during the process, considerations of stability are comparatively less influential (see OECD 1998, 2000).

In Italy, the primacy of the stability objective over competition has led to responsibility for competition policy being transferred from the antitrust authority (Autorità Garante della Concorrenza e del Mercato) to the banking market supervision authority, the Banca d'Italia, which also handles antitrust issues and therefore any conflicts arising from the application of the two. This is true across the board for mergers, while in general antitrust practice there is an occasional overlapping of competencies, which is a feature peculiar to the Italian financial system (Di Giorgio and

Di Noia 2001). In fact, although Law 287 of 1990 which instituted the Autorità does include credit institutions under the scope of application of antitrust discipline, treating them in the same way as any other business, it also assigns enforcement of this discipline to the Banca d'Italia.[11]

Bank mergers which exceed the community dimension are examined by the Merger Task Force of the European Commission, which applies the EC Merger Regulation, as for any industry. However, in its process for examining mergers, the Commission requests all the necessary information from the competent national authorities, so that in countries such as France and Italy, central banks can still raise concerns over stability. Having said that, in its activities as a whole the Commission generally tends to emphasize competition aspects.

Ultimately, despite the fact that the community approach to mergers of community dimension is strongly competition-orientated in theory, there is no specific community-wide supervision authority, so European nations retain a certain degree of discretion in practice, through the involvement of their national supervisors who look at mergers from a prudential perspective (Carletti and Hartmann 2003).

Therefore, in the decision making on mergers at both the national and community levels, we once again detect a friction between stability and competition, and here again banking emerges as a peculiar market heavily influenced by monetary and financial policies, and generally by the views of central banks and other member state authorities charged with financial stability.

5 DEMAND AS A PRO-COMPETITIVE DEVICE: CONSIDERATIONS DRAWN FROM THE NEW INDUSTRIAL ECONOMICS

The analysis so far has repeatedly highlighted the conflict between regulation considered necessary for assuring the stability of national and international economic systems, and antitrust laws, which instead appear necessary for assuring market efficiency. The recurring theme, therefore, is that regulation is the inefficient but necessary solution by which competition is sacrificed to serve the 'greater good' of economic stability. In the paragraphs that follow we shall propose an alternative means of resolving this dilemma, based on the new industrial economics.

The central idea of this alternative solution is encapsulated in the following general principle, which has been emerging in the industrial economics literature: when competition is limited for whatever reason on the supply side, it can be at least partially stimulated on the demand side, provided that sufficient consumer mobility can be induced (Waterson 2002). In certain industries, for example, competition may be restricted or impeded due to structural reasons. Within such contexts, antitrust enforcement is largely irrelevant because it is barred from removing the cause of inefficiency, and in any case can only be applied sporadically. However in certain situations this rigidity can be sidestepped, by approaching the analysis from the consumer's perspective, if there are elements that, for whatever reason, work on demand to confer *de facto* market power to the firms. In such circumstances, these same elements can be leveraged to pursue a pro-competitive policy. However such actions lie outside the province of conventional antitrust practice, which generally looks only at the supply side, so that a novel approach is called for.

One situation where the above approach could be applied is the case of lock-ins, which prevent consumer mobility from one product to the other. This is an issue that has been widely debated in the technology sector, where incompatibility between different technical components can attribute market power to a particular firm. The precedent-setting case on this matter was that of photocopy machines and their spare parts,[12] so the literature in question generally makes reference to markets for durable goods and their related markets, which are termed 'aftermarkets' (Hovenkamp 1994). It is still possible, in some cases, for antitrust authorities to take direct action against firms that pursue allegedly abusive strategies and, in such circumstances, the remedies will be the traditional ones. But even when such conventional remedies are impracticable, competition can still be promoted through policies that enable consumers to choose alternative products.

Looking now specifically at the banking sector, we find certain significant affinities with the situation described above: this is in effect a market where repetitive consumption over time presents analogies with the previous representation, with the opening of an account or acquisition of a service constituting the primary market, while the continuation of this relationship in subsequent years generates the aftermarkets. In other words, for reasons connected with the cost of switching, consumers face a problem of compatibility between their initial purchase and successive purchases, and this locks them into the original provider, conferring market power to that firm.

Therefore, the existence of competition at an initial time t does not guarantee that competition will continue to exist in subsequent periods, with the paradoxical outcome that even a firm with no apparent market power when competing for new clients might nevertheless exert market power over its acquired consumers, who in a sense constitute a specific relevant market.[13]

One likely explanation for the persistency of consumption is hence the existence of switching costs, whose origins can be either structural, that is, relating to certain exogenous attributes of the sector, or strategic, that is, endogenously determined by the firms in order to create market power. But irrespective of their cause, the important point is that these costs lock consumers into their initial purchase, thereby conferring a certain degree of market power to the original provider.

In the case of exogenously determined switching costs, the level of market competition can be elevated through additional regulatory intervention, and this – at least in Europe – falls outside the remit of the antitrust legislation and authorities. In the case of switching costs that are endogenously determined, that is, for the explicit purpose of acquiring market power, antitrust enforcement could theoretically be applied, though this proves difficult in practice because the judgment will inevitably have an arbitrary component, requiring application of a 'rule of reason' on a case-by-case basis.[14] And such a judgment becomes even more difficult where there are *ex ante* reasons for restricting antitrust actions, as is the case in the banking sector.

6 DEMAND-SIDE RESTRICTIONS ON COMPETITION: SWITCHING COSTS

Promoting competition on the demand side should not be seen as a universal alternative applicable to every market structure, but rather as a remedy geared to specific markets where certain peculiar features characterize the relationship between consumers and firms: namely the existence of switching costs, which are exploited to secure market power over particular segments of demand, thereby restricting competition. The following subsections will first of all describe the nature of such costs and their workings in the market, before proceeding to identify the specific types of switching costs found in the banking industry. This with a view to formulating policy indications that are specific to that context, but extensible (and have in part already been applied, though not systematically) to other markets as well.

6.1 The Nature of Switching Costs

Switching costs can emerge in markets that are characterized by repeated consumption. Within such markets, consumers who initially purchase a good or service from a firm will remain 'loyal' to that firm in order to avoid incurring these costs again at a later date. This has the effect of weakening the substitutability between (even identical) products, once the initial act of consumption has been made.

So even if price competition exists at an initial time t, when firms are attracting new consumers, this tends to diminish in following periods, when consumers must repeat the purchase, due to the effect of switching costs.[15] We can therefore say, in this scenario, that at a time $t + n$ (where $n = 1, 2, \ldots$) the existence of switching costs can transform the relationship between firm and consumer in the relevant market. This in itself clearly complicates the antitrust analysis, because the implied dynamic perspective creates more scope for ambiguity, unless – as we saw earlier – concrete reasons exist for attributing the emergence of switching costs to clearly abusive behaviours.

There is a vast body of literature in economic theory devoted to switching costs, in which their impact on competition is examined from a variety of starting assumptions, such as whether consumers have perfect information (Klemperer 1995). Although no univocal conclusion exists, as a general principle (setting aside special cases in which switching costs do not compromise competition) we can say that such costs generally confer a certain amount of market power to firms, precisely by virtue of the exclusive tie which they create (or which is purposely created) between consumers and the firm. This is indirectly confirmed, for example, by the structural persistence of above-marginal cost pricing, even where there is apparent competition for the capture of new consumers, and by the emergence of multiproduct firms not attributable to scope economies, but rather to forms of scale economies on the demand side, deriving precisely from a consumer's desire to amortise switching costs.[16]

The balance of collective welfare which results is usually negative, because 'switching costs generally raise prices and create deadweight losses of the usual kind ... and may also discourage new entry and so further reduce the market competitiveness' (Klemperer 1995, p. 536).[17]

The conventional representation of switching costs is as a sunk investment (effective or perceived) made by consumers, which creates a certain inertia in the choice between apparently identical alternatives (Bruzzone and Polo 2000).

Such an investment can be 'real', for example connected with issues of technical compatibility, as in the case of a decoder for a particular pay-TV system, which would need to be replaced if the consumer switched to a new provider. Or it can be 'perceived', for example connected with the effort expended by the user to research a particular purchase, which would have to be repeated to select an alternative, or the time invested in becoming proficient with a new system, which creates a path-dependence, as in the learning curves confronted by computer users. It can also take the form of transaction costs, in situations where migrating from one product or service to another incurs added intermediation charges. And finally, there are also switching costs associated with the emotional sphere, when the user's familiarity with a particular product or service engenders a sort of affective dependency. This is in fact one of the mechanisms at the root of brand loyalty, and of course the effect can also be enhanced by artificial means, through commercial initiatives such as cumulative discount schemes (for example, airline 'frequent flyer' programmes), or coupon promotions.

It should be emphasized that the existence of switching costs does not in itself imply behaviours in violation of the antitrust laws. Nevertheless, as mentioned previously, from the standpoint of firms, switching costs do help create market power, and thus have a beneficial effect on profits, especially if price discrimination can be practised between old and new consumers. The monopoly pockets thus created will naturally have the side-effect of rationing demand. The cost of switching might prompt certain individuals not to consume at all, with a distorting effect on the allocation of resources. Further distorting the market structure is the emergence of multiproduct firms. In fact, if switching costs encourage consumers to source a variety of products or services from the same firm, by the same token they encourage firms to diversify into a variety of products and services, even inefficiently, exploiting the fact that consumers have already been 'captured' by their original purchase.

This mechanism can in its turn constitute a form of market foreclosure against potential competitors who are able to efficiently produce only a single product or service (Klemperer 1995). However, although it is fairly straightforward to describe the anticompetitive effect of switching costs, it is rather more difficult to identify behaviours that are clearly anticompetitive, and therefore punishable by the authorities. In other words, because switching costs can arise for so many different reasons, it can sometimes be difficult to determine their causes and judge whether they are explicitly anticompetitive. As a general principle, switching costs can be likened to a product differentiation strategy, so that although the underlying rent-seeking logic is quite clear, a univocal antitrust interpretation is more difficult: in the same way that a promotional campaign causes two objectively identical products to become differentiated in the eyes of consumers (we speak in this case of perceived differentiation), switching costs introduce an *ex post* differentiation between products that were substitutable *ex ante*.

Ultimately, the crux of the antitrust enforcement is the nature of the costs, which can be simultaneously exogenous, that is, arising from structural features of the market and/or technology in question, or endogenous, that is, arising from strategic policy decisions taken by firms to create market power, in much the same way as with product differentiation. It is only in rare cases that unequivocally abusive behaviours will emerge, although switching costs always create some amount of market power, and must thus have a correspondingly anticompetitive effect.

6.2 Switching Costs and the Banking Industry

In the discussion so far we have already mentioned the peculiar structure of the banking market, characterized by considerable rigidity on the supply side (largely a result of the regulation) and by high switching costs associated with repeated consumption and various endogenous and exogenous traits of this sector, such as multiproduct supply, market power over consumers and so on (Kiser 2002; Shy 2002). For example, the discrepancy between the interest rates offered to savers and those earned by banks on their investments, which in a perfectly competitive market ought to coincide (minus the operating intermediation costs), is a sign of market power which can be accounted for by the existence of switching costs (Sharpe 1997).

A growing body of literature supports the key role played by switching costs in the banking sector, although few studies have as yet attempted to define the magnitude of this effect, or to examine possible policy indications from an antitrust perspective (Bruzzone and Polo 2000; Kim et al. 2001; Kiser 2002; Shy 2002; Waterson 2002). In any case, the costs in question are sufficiently high to discourage movement of consumers from one bank to another, even where there are large differences in charges and interest rates, making them a significant constituent of banks profits.[18]

Switching costs appear in a variety of forms and can also be added together, thereby reinforcing their overall effect. The following paragraphs provide a brief, and by no means exhaustive, taxonomy specific to the banking sector. One category of switching costs are those relating to direct debit payments from a customer's bank account for utilities and other bills, for example phone, gas, electricity, credit cards and so forth. And of course a similar consideration applies to credit transfer operations into the account, such as the payment of salaries or other remunerations, dividends and so forth. On closing the account the customer would have to transfer all the aforementioned credit and debit operations to his/her new account, thereby incurring significant transaction costs.[19] Further compounding these are costs relating to uncertainty, due to the possibility of oversights or errors occurring during the transfer (Shy 2001).

The transfer times themselves are highly variable, and generally take longer than theoretically necessary, suggesting possible strategic behaviours pursued by the originator banks expressly to increase the cost of switching.[20]

Surveys of Italian operators have found that banks explicitly take such costs into account, and generally advise their staff to activate as many services as possible when a customer opens an account.[21] A similar conclusion was reached in the UK by the Competition Commission (2001, sect. 1.6 and 1.8) which found that personal current accounts 'the core product in personal banking . . . also serve as a "gateway" through which suppliers can sell other financial products, such as credit cards and personal loans', thus raising the overall switching costs.[22]

A similar trend exists in the United States, where competition in banking is increasingly centred not so much on individual products as on the provision of bundles of services (Biehl 2002).

Then there are additional switching costs associated with the information that consumers need to collect when deciding to open an account, and with the fixed fee normally charged for opening the account: both these elements fall under the category of start-up costs, that is, those costs that are unavoidably incurred when entering into a relationship with a bank, and which must be repeated whenever the individual starts again with a different supplier.[23]

Finally there is a category of switching costs associated with the bank's direct knowledge of the customer and, conversely, the latter's familiarity with the bank. This makes many operations quicker and easier, because the bank staff are directly acquainted with the customer and his/her history of solvency/insolvency and so forth. In the transfer to a new bank, all this accumulated background information will be lost. The bank customer, on his/her part, is likewise facilitated by familiarity with the procedures and staff, making it more convenient to continue with the existing bank rather than have to get used to a new one (Bruzzone and Polo 2000; Shy 2001).

It is important to remember that, taken individually, each of the switching costs listed so far can be relatively small, and not bring much market power by itself. Nevertheless, through the cumulative effect of various costs, it is possible to achieve considerable market power in practice.

Some authors have pointed out that this mechanism is offset by an implicit trade-off in the exploitation of switching costs, because the exercise of market power must be weighed against competitiveness in attracting new consumers. However in this particular sector, as mentioned previously, such costs appear to have a significant impact on the profits of banks (Bruzzone and Polo 2000; Shy 2001).

There is some fragmented evidence in support of this in the literature. For example, a study of the Norwegian mortgage market found that 25 per cent of the marginal profit of banks (that is, the profit arising from each additional borrower) could essentially be ascribed to the lock-in effect, with the bank–client relationship lasting on average 13.5 years (Kim et al. 2001). This span of time is consistent with the values found in both the European and US markets (Shy 2001). This confirms, at least in part, that the market power deriving from switching costs is being exploited, and does have an impact on competitive mechanisms and market outcomes. Many other signs further corroborate this assertion. For example, the phenomenon of diminishing interest rates on bank accounts – whereby higher rates are offered on opening the account and then gradually decreased – would seem consistent with the hypothesis that, as the relationship is prolonged in time, and the switching costs consequently increase, a lower remuneration is needed to retain the consumer.

A corollary to the above assertions is the empirical fact that the principal reason for which consumers switch banks is when they move house – in other words a drastic event that incurs very high overall transaction costs, which far exceed the switching costs themselves.[24]

All this is not to suggest, however, that the banking industry is pervaded by systematically abusive behaviours. Such an interpretation is unjustified because the behaviours are to some extent structurally determined by the particular conditions in which competition is played out, which are largely defined *ex lege*. In a sense, switching costs are built into the peculiar relationship between customer and bank, so that the market configuration makes them inevitable in the current context. What is more, the related observation – that firms strive to increase these costs to secure new pockets of monopoly – is also open to ambiguous interpretations, because this is in effect a competitive strategy in the particular market structure.

Irrespective of the market, any practice that shifts competition to non-price elements has the aim of attenuating price competition, and in this sense must have a corresponding anticompetitive effect. In the banking industry such practices are a rational and competitive course of action for firms operating in a peculiar market structure. They constitute rent-seeking behaviours only to the same extent as does advertising or product differentiation, and so are not punishable on this count by the antitrust authority.

We note also that when antitrust enforcement falls outside the price competition paradigm, and unless there is clear circumstantial evidence of infractions, it faces increasing difficulties because the analytical tools available are to some extent obsolete, and referred chiefly to static price-based competitive paradigms which are not very useful in complex contexts.[25]

7 POLICY INDICATIONS

The conventional analysis framework has accustomed us to look at competition from the supply side and to approach its stimulation from the perspective of firms. In this chapter we have instead shown how, in the banking market, competition on the supply side is institutionally restricted by the imperative of ensuring the stability of the banking system, and the economic system as a whole.

This creates a significant problem for the application of antitrust law, because it interferes substantially with regulatory activity. For example, if we accept the antitrust approach which interprets competition laws as tools 'for prohibiting bigness or facilitating ease of entry for small businesses' (Hovenkamp 1994, p. 275), the natural result is a profound ambiguity. The obvious solution would in fact be, as Justice Brandeis said in a celebrated US case, to punish practices that 'destroy' competition.[26] However in our particular case this route is precluded by definition, and what is more the practices in question are (ambiguously) competitive in the banking sector, due to the context created by the regulation.

This last observation once again raises the conventional antitrust dilemma of *per se* rules versus rules of reason. Application of the latter criterion, with the attendant connotations of political motivation and expediency, will tend to make decisions appear less absolute and objective, more open to question.[27] With, in this case, the aggravating factor that the underlying assumptions of the regulation have the practical effect of blocking any form of antitrust application.

For these reasons, there seems to be very little scope, overall, for increasing competition through traditional antitrust interventions directed at behaviours on the supply side.

But by turning to a different antitrust tradition – namely that which pursues the objective of maximizing consumer welfare – it is possible to map out an alternative strategy of demand-side interventions, as has in fact already been done in some other markets, though not in any systematic manner.

The idea is to precisely pinpoint and remove the elements that inhibit competition, not by altering the competitive scenario as such, but simply by operating in the sphere of consumers. In the case in point, if switching costs (coupled with the effects of national regulations) are one of the main sources of market power for firms, a competitive equilibrium may be approached by taking explicit actions to reduce such costs (Waterson 2002).

Such a strategy has already been successfully deployed to increase competition in certain other sectors. In the telephone industry, for example, liberalization of the so-called 'last mile' has enabled many countries to introduce competition into a sector that appeared locked into monopoly positions arising from historical inertia. Something similar has occurred in the sector of car liability insurance, through the introduction of a more effective system based on the portability of the insured party's risk status, and efforts to combat fraudulent practices. So taking precisely this insurance market as a model, one could envisage applying a similar system to the banking industry as well. The relationship between a customer and bank, much like that between insurance companies and their clients, is one of long standing that involves collection of a large data set, and is generally characterized by high transaction costs.

But notwithstanding these similarities, the sector of car liability insurance has seen a gradual reduction in its switching costs: contracts are generally annual and renewable, and customers are able to switch between different companies without loss of data, thanks to a standardized procedure that guarantees the accuracy of the information received by the new company, and retains any benefits (such as no-claims bonuses) matured with the original insurer.

A similar strategy could be deployed within the banking sector, in order to promote increased competition without compromising the overall market structure, and so preserving stability.

Some cautious moves in this direction have recently been attempted, though as yet not backed by an explicit theoretical position or clear economic policy. In a recent case of a proposed merger between two British banks, Lloyds TSB and Abbey National, the Competition Commission (2001, sect. 1.11) notes, for example:

> steps are being taken to improve the process of switching personal current accounts between banks. This is important in creating conditions for the market to become more competitive . . . The current project to automate the necessary exchanges of information must be completed and effectively implemented without delay and the process must be speeded up.

In the same market, a slightly earlier study underlined the need to ensure greater transparency and, most importantly, greater representativeness to consumers (Cruickshank 2000).

So an added advantage of the proposed solution is that, because it still passes through regulatory channels, unified control of the market can be retained. The market structure is ultimately not altered in any way and can continue to be defined in agreement with the stability objective. The increased mobility of consumers between the various banks on the market will simply have the primary effect of reducing the market power that each firm exerts over its locked consumers (arising from the switching costs). However, the resultant increase in competition and efficiency will only minimally impact upon the likelihood of failure and subsequent contagion, because both entry and exit remain regulated, and the banks are diversified into other submarkets such as financial products sold to large firms, wholesale banking and so on.

8 CONCLUDING REMARKS

This contribution has addressed the central dilemma of the banking sector, that of stability versus competition, and attempted to identify a novel solution. In fact, the prevailing idea, in the abundant literature on the subject, is that a trade-off exists between these two objectives, and that competition must largely be sacrificed to the greater good of economic stability. The result is an inevitable antagonism between regulatory activities and those which promote competition.

The thesis presented in this work does not attempt to refute this antagonism, but more simply leverages unexplored market resources in order to obtain an alternative competition strategy that sidesteps the problem. The proposed solution involves increasing the mobility of consumers, without any significant alteration to the regulated supply. More specifically, the existence of exogenous and endogenous switching costs makes it possible to pursue pro-competition policies that do not require imposition of penalties or changes to the market structure, but focus instead on eliminating the lock-in mechanisms, and hence the market power and inefficiencies associated with them. Although the described solution is undoubtedly a second-best alternative, it nevertheless makes it possible to pursue the goal of consumer welfare maximization, which is one of the stated aims of antitrust policies.

An analysis of the specific competitive attributes of the banking market – equally found in other markets – also indicates that there is an entire area as yet unexplored by antitrust practice, which could be exploited to at least partially pursue the efficiency objective, in contexts where competition appears to be structurally ruled out. In particular, such a solution could provide a new and alternative route for stimulating competition in sectors that are regulated, or whose market structure cannot be drastically altered.

NOTES

* We are greatly indebted for comments and suggestions to the participants to the 4th Corsica Law and Economics Workshop, to Francesco Denozza, Federico Ghezzi and Donato Masciandaro. The usual disclaimer applies.
1. A typical argument found in the literature is that a highly concentrated banking sector will be generally less susceptible to crisis. Naturally this thesis has both its supporters (Allen and Gale 2004) and detractors (Mishkin 1999). The relevant point, for the purposes of this chapter, is that the general predominance of the former view has prompted specific economic policy measures which effectively restrict competition. For an overview, see Carletti and Hartmann (2003).
2. The Italian experience provides an interesting example. Historically, the stability objective took precedence over competition, as one can see from the Italian banking law of

1936, enacted in the aftermath of the Great Depression of the 1930s. It is only recently, in the 1990s, that the competition objective has been formalized in Italy through the consolidation Act on Banking (Testo Unico) and the law instituting the antitrust authority. With these two legislations the country began placing greater emphasis on competition, relying on instruments such as risk ratios and deposit insurance to counter the risk of instability (Ciocca 1998).
3. For a description of the peculiarity of banking systems from a stability perspective, see Goodhart (1987).
4. For a more in-depth discussion of the first two, see also Hovenkamp (1994).
5. Dec. 25/11/1993, Fortis/Cger, in EECM.C. Rep., p. 1241. Naturally, the present-day dynamics are in part changing the market, for example with the advent of e-banking, so that the listed taxonomy may well need to be extended, as discussed in the following paragraphs.
6. Dec. 13/6/1994, Banco Santander/Banesto, in EECM.C. Rep., p. 1471.
7. Dec. 10/12/1997, Merita/Nordbanken, in CELEX, n. 397M1029.
8. Dec. 10/12/1997, Merita/Nordbanken, in CELEX, n. 397M1029.
9. For the European Union, see EC Commission, XXIII Report of the Commission on Competition Policy, COM(94) 161 def., 1994; for the United States, see 2A Antitrust Law par. 533 (2nd edn 1995). For a general discussion of submarkets as a relevant market, see Hovenkamp (1994).
10. Since a 1997 amendment of the EC Merger Regulation, income figures are used as a measure. So the 'Community dimension' is reached when: (i) the aggregate worldwide income of the merging banks exceeds €5,000 million; and (ii) the aggregate community-wide income of each of the merging banks exceeds €250 million.
11. This approach is perhaps a legacy of the pro-competitive function carried out by the Banca d'Italia before the enactment of the 'latecomer' Law 287 of 1990. See Ghezzi and Magnani (1999).
12. *Eastman Kodak. Co. v. Image Technical Services, Inc.*, US, 112 S.Ct. 2072, 1992.
13. This should naturally be taken into account when defining the relevant market where, as we have said, market power plays a central role.
14. It is also possible for switching costs to be partly endogenous and partly exogenous. The highly diverse nature of switching costs, which can originate from a multiplicity of sources, as discussed later in the text, makes distinguishing between these two components by no means a trivial matter.
15. Unless consumers have perfect information and are able to exactly calculate the costs for all periods, in which case competition would be preserved. But the hypothesis is nevertheless debatable, and the situation not likely in practice.
16. These are the so-called 'purchasing economies of scope' which make it more worthwhile for consumers to purchase n different products from the same firm. See Panzar and Willig (1981). See also Klemperer (1995); Kiser (2002); Shy (2002).
17. Note, however, that the overall competitive picture can be quite complex, with incumbent or dominant firms that impose higher switching costs on consumers, and newcomer or fringe firms which instead limit these costs as a strategy for attracting new consumers. See Shy (2002).
18. In the former case 'it has been widely observed that consumers refrain from switching between banks even when they are fully informed of large differences in bank services fees. The main (perhaps the only) explanation for this consumer behaviour is the existence of switching costs that are encountered by consumers each time they terminate services with one bank and switch to a competing bank' (Shy 2001, p. 188). The British Competition Commission (2001, sect. 1.8) confirms that 'consumers tend to see switching between banks as a difficult and unrewarding process, and the rate of switching is very low'.
19. In general, the existence of transaction costs in the banking sector is also taken into account for the purposes of defining the relevant market: 'Since the Supreme Court ruling in the Philadelphia National Bank case of 1963 [*US* v. *Philadelphia National*

Bank, et al., 374 U.S. 321] ... [t]ransaction costs were seen to limit a consumer's choice to a set of financial institutions that were within some relatively small distance of his or her home or work' (Biehl 2002, p. 91). As a result, the relevant market could be defined in geographical terms. The interpretation of switching costs as transaction costs that significantly alter the substitutability of products in the eyes of consumers could further call into question, at least in certain cases, the definition of the relevant market.

20. In the English market the average delay for the four leading banks in May 2001 was 11–13 days, but a process of slow deterioration could extend this period to up to six weeks (Competition Commission 2001).
21. From private communication to the authors in April 2003.
22. On this point, see also Competition Commission (2001, sect. 2.36 and after).
23. It is possible for different switching costs to coexist at the same time. Consider, for example, the process of applying for a credit card: as a rule there are certain *start-up costs*, largely deriving from the initial commission for opening the card account, in addition to switching costs relating to all the necessary paperwork, and others still arising from the possible inconvenience, when changing banks, of having to temporarily return the card and wait for a new one to be issued.
24. There appears to be a consensus among authors on this matter. Among these, see Sharpe (1997) and Kiser (2002).
25. In this sense, see Ramello (2003).
26. *Board of Trade* v. *U.S.*, 246 U.S. 231, 238, 38 S.Ct. 242, 244 (1918).
27. If, for example, a bank dynamites a competitor, the abusive behaviour is clearly punishable by a '*per se* rule', because the violation is manifest and, moreover, extends beyond the bounds of competition protection. But if a bank raises its switching costs (for example, through bundling, which has the effect of tightening the bonds between the firm and consumers), deciding whether such a practice is anticompetitive relies essentially on a 'rule of reason' that is inevitably characterized by an ideological component, or at least by an explicit scientific stance, and these are also susceptible to change over the years following new developments in economic theory, as evinced by over a century of US antitrust activity (Hovenkamp 1994; Ramello 2003).

REFERENCES

Allen, F. and D. Gale (2004), 'Competition and financial stability', *Journal of Money, Credit, and Banking*, **36** (3) (June), 453–80.

Amel, D. and M. Starr-McCluer (2001), 'Market definition in banking', Working Paper, Board of Governors of the Federal Reserve Board, Washington, DC.

Biehl, A.R. (2002), 'The extent of the market for retail banking deposits', *Antitrust Bulletin*, Spring, 91–106.

Bruzzone, G. and M. Polo (2000), 'Fonti di potere di mercato nel settore bancario: teoria e implicazioni per l'analisi antitrust [Sources of market power in banking: theory and implications for anti-trust analysis]', in Polo (ed.), *Industria bancaria e concorrenza*, Bologna: Il Mulino, pp. 533–96.

Canoy, M., M. van Dijk, J. Lemmen, R. de Mooij and J. Weigand (2001), 'Competitional and stability in banking', Central Planbureau – Netherlands document, no. 15, December.

Carletti, E. and P. Hartmann (2003), 'Competition and stability: what's special about banking?', in P. Mizen (ed.), *Monetary History, Exchange Rates and Financial Markets: Essays in Honour of Charles Goodhart*, vol. 2, Cheltenham, UK and Northampton, MA, USA: Edward Elgar, pp. 202–29.

Ciocca, P. (1998), *Concorrenza e concentrazione nel sistema bancario italiano* [*Competition and Integration in the Italian Banking System*], Rome: Banca d'Italia.
Competition Commission (2001), 'Lloyds TSB Group plc and Abbey National plc: a report on the proposed merger', Series CM 5208, 10/7/2001, www.Competition-Commission.org.uk.
Cruickshank, D. (2000), *Competition in UK Banking: A Report to the Chancellor of the Exchequer*, London: The Stationery Office.
De Bandt, O. and P. Hartmann (2002), 'Systemic risk in banking: a survey', in C. Goodhart and G. Illing (eds), *Financial Crises, Contagion, and the Lender of Last Resort*, Oxford: Oxford University Press, pp. 249–98.
Di Giorgio, G. and C. Di Noia (2001), 'L'impatto della tecnologia sulla regolamentazione finanziaria: il caso italiano [The influence of technology and financial regulation: the Italian case]', in D. Masciandaro and G. Bracchi (eds), *Dalla banca all'eurob@nk: nuovi mercati e nuove regole*, vol. 2, Rome: Edibank, pp. 145–71.
Ghezzi, F. and P. Magnani (1999), *Banche e concorrenza – Riflessioni sull'esperienza statunitense, comunitaria e italiana* [Banks and Competition – Considerations on US, EC and Italian Experiences], Milan: EGEA.
Goodhart, C. (1987), *The Central Bank and the Financial System*, London: Macmillan.
Group of Ten (2001), 'Report on consolidation in the financial sector', summary report, 25 January, 2001 www.imf.org>.
Hovenkamp, H. (1994), *Federal Antitrust Policy: The Law of Competition and Its Practice*, St. Paul, MN: West Publishing.
Kim, M., D. Kliger and B. Vale (2001), 'Estimating switching costs: the case of banking', *Journal of Financial Intermediation*, **12**, 25–56.
Kiser, E.K. (2002), 'Predicting household switching behavior and switching costs at depository institutions', *Review of Industrial Organisation*, **20**, 349–65.
Klemperer, P. (1995), 'Competition when consumers have switching costs: an overview with applications to industrial organization, macroeconomics and international trade', *Review of Economic Studies*, **62**, 515–39.
Minervini, G. and M. Onado (2000), 'Efficienza dei sistemi finanziari e tutela del risparmio: disciplina o deregolamentazione? [Financial systems efficiency and savings protection: rules or deregulation?]', in G. Tesauro and M. D'Alberti (eds), *Regolazione e Concorrenza*, Bologna: Il Mulino, pp. 103–27.
Mishkin, F.S. (1999), 'Financial consolidation: dangers and opportunities', *Journal of Banking and Finance*, **23**, 675–91.
Organization for Economic Cooperation and Development (OECD) (1998), *Enhancing the Role of Competition in Bank Regulation*, DAFFE/CLP/ (98)16, Paris: OECD.
Organization for Economic Cooperation and Development (OECD) (2000), *Mergers in Financial Services*, DAFFE/CLP/ (2000)17, Paris: OECD.
Panzar, J.C. and R.D. Willig (1981), 'Economies of scope', *American Economic Review*, **71**, 268–72.
Polo, M. (ed.) (2000), *Industria bancaria e concorrenza* [*Bank Industry and Competition*], Bologna: Il Mulino.
Porrini, D. (1994), 'Economie di scopo e sistema bancario italiano: alcuni spunti teorici ed un tentativo di verifica empirica ['Scope economies and the Italian banking system: a theoretical contribution and an attempt of empirical analysis']', *Economia Internazionale*, **47**, 3–22.

Porrini, D. (1996), 'La diversificazione produttiva nelle banche: definizione, applicazione e stima delle "economie di scopo" ['Product differentiation in banks: definition, enforcement and empirical evidence of the "scope economics"']', *Il Risparmio*, **4–5**, 789–816.

Ramello, G.B. (2003), 'Copyright and antitrust issues', in W. Gordon and R. Watt (eds), *The Economics of Copyright: Developments in Research and Analysis*, Cheltenham, UK and Northampton, MA, USA: Edward Elgar, pp. 118–47.

Sharpe, S.A. (1997), 'The effect of consumer switching costs on prices: a theory and its application to the bank deposit market', *Review of Industrial Organisation*, **12**, 79–94.

Shull, B. (1996), 'The origins of antitrust in banking: an historical perspective', *Antitrust Bulletin*, **41**, 255–88

Shy, O. (2001), *The Economics of Network Industries*, Cambridge: Cambridge University Press.

Shy, O. (2002), 'A quick-and-easy method for estimating switching costs', *International Journal of Industrial Organization*, **20**, 71–87.

Waterson, M. (2002), 'The role of consumers in competition and competition policy', *International Journal of Industrial Organization*, **21**, 129–50.

14. Old Master paintings: price formation and public policy implications

Paolo Figini and Laura Onofri

1 INTRODUCTION

The puzzle of price formation in the art market, and for paintings in particular, stems from the difficulty of applying the Marshallian theory of value to this particular market configuration. On one side, marginal utility – and thus demand factors – are not sufficient to define the equilibrium price of paintings; production costs, on the other side, are not able to settle any *natural value* underlying a painting.

In the literature, two alternative positions on price determination coexist. The first one states that 'the demand fluctuates widely, following collectors' fads and manias and paintings' prices are therefore inherently unpredictable' (Baumol 1986, p. 10): no fundamental value can therefore be identified for paintings. The opposite view assumes that although a natural price linked to production costs does not exist for paintings, market forces determine prices for art objects, as for any other economic good (Frey and Pommerehne 1989).

Following this second approach, the literature has recently focused on the mechanisms of price formation in the art market. The heterogeneity of works of art, the monopolistic power held by the owner of the painting, the infrequency of trading, and the existence of different segments in the art market constitute specific and problematic issues, linked to the determination and to the measurement of prices, the research has to deal with. The first necessary step to evaluate the profitability of investment in art, as compared to other financial assets, is to come up with some price indices; at least four approaches have been developed[1]: (i) indices which reflect experts' personal judgements (such as the Sotheby's Art Index); (ii) indices based on repeat sales regressions (see, among others, Locatelli-Bley and Zanola 1999; Pesando and Shum 1999; Mei and Moses 2003); (iii) indices based on the average painting methodology, with its refinement of the representative painting (see Candela and Scorcu 1997; Candela et al. 2005); (iv) indices based on hedonic regressions (see, among others, Buelens and Ginsburgh 1993; Chanel 1995; Agnello 2002).

In this chapter, we focus on two related questions. First, by using the hedonic methodology, we attempt to identify the elements that determine the painting price, particularly with respect to Italian Old Masters. Such methodology has the obvious advantage of allowing for the estimation of a given painting's value by adding the shadow prices of its characteristics. Second, in such a way, it is possible to derive further information from an institutional perspective and inquire whether the policy maker might elicit useful insights for the targeting of policies and the design of proper rules in the art market.

Following the literature of hedonic regressions, in the present work, along with usual painting-specific characteristics such as materials used, dimension support (that is, canvas, panel and so on), and subject, information on the level of attribution of the painting and on the school the artist belongs to is also included. Information about the sale, such as the auction date, auction house and marketplace and the order of sale in the sequential auction, which are likely to affect the auction price, are also considered.

Moreover, our econometric exercise aims at the explanation of the formation of the Old Master (OM) market price and not only at the definition of price indices; therefore, a distinct feature of our approach, with respect to previous hedonic literature, is the inclusion in the regressions of variables concerning the market performance of the artist, such as the artist's price index (as computed by Candela et al. 2005) and the percentage of paintings sold, as well as some macroeconomic variables such as the exchange rate, the growth rate and the indices of financial market performance.

This chapter has a twofold 'institutional' objective. First, understanding OM price formation is important in order to better understand the way art markets work. Second, understanding the market mechanism is a useful exercise in order to design proper institutional rules.

The chapter is structured as follows. Section 2 introduces the data and the methodology used while Section 3 presents some of the main results. Section 4 discusses the findings from an institutional perspective. Section 5 concludes and paves the way for further research.

2 DATA AND METHODOLOGY

2.1 Data

The structure of the art market is rather complex. A first problem is related to the different organization of the three main segments of the market.

The primary market deals with the artist who personally sells his/her work to buyers, mainly art dealers. In the secondary market, art dealers exchange paintings with collectors, mainly through galleries. Finally, the tertiary market is composed of auctions. These last transactions are organized as sequential English auctions, where the item is sold to the highest bidder. The importance of the tertiary market is twofold. On one hand, this is the only segment for which we have an information structure that (partially) overcomes the typical problem of incomplete and asymmetric information. On the other hand, the share of the total market arising from auctions, data availability and reliability, and the evidence that this segment leads the secondary one (Candela and Scorcu 2001) make the price of this segment the benchmark for testing price structure and dynamics. The chapter follows such considerations by examining only auction data, with the most important ones being analysed from an institutional perspective.

Several papers on hedonic price use quite specific data sets, often selected according to subjective selection procedures in order to control or reduce a very large heterogeneity and variability in the observations.[2] In this study we use a database provided by a Milan-based company, Gabrius S.p.A.[3] which has made available almost 400,000 observations of art objects auctioned worldwide since 1990, of which more than 100,000 are Old Masters.

For each observation the database includes, among other variables, name and code of the artist, his/her nationality and period, title and code of the painting, date, city and auction house where the item was auctioned, auction price (when the painting has been sold), dimensions (in terms of length and height), lot number, genre, subject, material, support and level of attribution of the painting.[4] For a complete statistical description of the database, see Candela et al. (2002). Moreover, the database includes information about whether the painting was recorded in the artistic literature, or was exhibited; whether the OM comes from a private collection or whether it has any kind of certificate issued by experts or critics.

We augment the original Gabrius database with two additional pieces of information; the first includes art market variables as computed by Candela et al. (2005); the second includes some macroeconomic variables. The former group of variables gathers information on the annual and artist-specific percentage of sold paintings and on the behaviour over time of the artists' price indices. The latter group includes CPI indices, short- and long-term interest rates, stock market indices, per capita income growth rates and exchange rates.[5]

From an artistic point of view, the most important problem in considering such a database relates to the fact that the OM database includes very different artistic periods and schools, ranging from Italian painters of the fourteenth century to English painters of the eighteenth century. Identifying artistic schools and assigning each painter to one school is a difficult task. For the sake of simplicity, and without losing in generality, a first rough identification of the artistic schools is made by matching the (artistic) nationality of the painter with his/her period of life. Using these criteria we are able to split the data into 42 different artistic schools; the present work considers only Italian OMs up to the eighteenth century.

Descriptive statistics of the subsample used are reported in Tables 14.1–5. The artistic classification by subject, material and support is taken from the original Gabrius database.

Table 14.1 *Frequency distribution by material*

Material	Observations	Frequency
Oil	18,251	92.15
Tempera	729	3.68
Other	846	4.98
Total	19,806	100.00

Source: Own elaboration on Gabrius S.p.A. database.

Table 14.2 *Frequency distribution by subject*

Subject	Observation	Frequency
Allegory	530	2.67
Architecture	833	4.20
Biblical	1,159	5.85
Figure	806	4.07
General scene	913	4.61
History	420	2.12
Landscape	1,577	7.96
Mythological	1,237	6.24
Portrait	1,462	7.38
Religious	6,501	32.80
Still life	1,998	10.08
View	1,155	5.83
Other	1,801	7.07
Total	19,823	100.00

Source: Own elaboration on Gabrius S.p.A. database.

Table 14.3   Frequency distribution by support

Support	Frequency	Percent
Canvas	15,268	77.02
Panel	3,249	16.39
Other	1,307	6.59
Total	19,824	100.00

Source: Own elaboration on Gabrius S.p.A. database.

Table 14.4   Frequency distribution by auction house name

Name	Frequency	Percent
Christie's	7,012	35.37
Dorotheum	1,139	5.75
Finarte	2,180	11.00
Phillips	1,178	5.94
Sotheby's	6,958	35.10
Tajan	520	2.62
Other	837	4.23
Total	19,824	100.00

Source: Own elaboration on Gabrius S.p.A. database.

Table 14.5   Frequency distribution by auction market

City	Frequency	Percent
Netherlands	175	0.88
USA	4,608	23.25
Italy	3,941	19.88
Germany	313	1.58
Switzerland	187	0.94
France	1,001	5.05
Sweden	73	0.37
Austria	1,139	5.75
UK	8,769	44.23
Total	19,824	100.00

Source: Own elaboration on Gabrius S.p.A. database.

2.2 Methodology

Whereas the use of hedonic models dates back to Court (1941), Lancaster (1971) and Griliches (1971), this methodology was used to analyse qualitative characteristics in the art market only recently by Frey and Pommerehne (1989), Buelens and Ginsburgh (1993), Agnello and Pierce (1996), Chanel et al. (1996) and Agnello (2002), among others. The intuition behind the hedonic approach is that the (logged) price of an item can be decomposed into the price of an 'average' item with average characteristics plus the prices of the deviations of the item characteristics from their respective averages. Thus the price may be described by a simple linear regression such as:

$$\ln p_{i,k,t} = \alpha_0 + \sum_{j=1}^{J} \alpha_j x_{j,k,t} + \beta_t + \varepsilon_{i,k,t} \qquad (14.1)$$

where $\ln p_{i,k,t}$ is the logarithm of the price of the painting i; $i = 1, 2, \ldots, N$ of painter k; $k = 1, 2, \ldots, K$ sold at time t; $t = 1, 2, \ldots, T$; $x_{j,k,t}$ is the jth (possibly qualitative) characteristics of the painting i (which may or may not depend on t, the year in which the painting is sold); $\varepsilon_{i,k,t}$ is an error term; and α_j and β_t are parameters. Obviously, within the same framework, a more complex, non-linear model might be considered. In equation (14.1) β_t represents the exponential trend, which can be interpreted as the annual return of the generic item.

To compute annual price indices (and returns), regression (14.1) can be modified as follows:

$$\ln p_{k,t} = \alpha_0 + \sum_{j=1}^{J} \alpha_j x_{j,k,t} + \sum_{t=1}^{T} \beta_t z_t + \varepsilon_{i,k,t} \qquad (14.2)$$

where z_t is a dummy variable taking the value of 1 if the painting is sold in year t and 0 otherwise.

After adjusting for the heterogeneity by considering artists – and paintings – specific variables, average prices are explained solely by the time. This allows the computation of price indices and rates of return from investment in art which are built on the β_t coefficients. However, this chapter does not focus on price indices, but rather attempts to explain the price of each art object. Therefore, as it appears a priori unlikely that all relevant information is reflected in the usual variables that appear in the auction catalogue, we consider other elements, possibly crucial in the analysis of the price structure and its evolution over time;[6] in addition to the effect caused by heterogeneous or idiosyncratic characteristics, we include in the regression the price dynamics of the artist and of the art market and several proxies of the macroeconomic climate.

After several checks on various specifications, the basic regression model of equation (14.2) selected to run on each artistic school presents $\ln p_{i,k,t}$ (the logged price of painting i of artist k sold at time t) as the dependent variable; on the right-hand side of the equation we include dummy variables for the marketplace, auction house, support, material, subject and the logged dimension of the painting. Moreover, dummy variables for the artistic literature, presence in exhibitions, the previous ownership and the presence of specific reports by art experts are added to the regression.

With respect to market variables, we include the percentage of paintings sold by the artist in year t,[7] a dummy for each artist, to capture the artist's specific effect; a dummy for the artist market index, as computed by Candela et al. (2005) to capture the evolution of the economic performance of the artist over time; a dummy for the sale year; and a dummy for the sale month.

Finally, the macroeconomic variables included in the regression are the US long-term interest rate, the Dow Jones index, a weighted index of the exchange rate, and the per capita growth rate. $\varepsilon_{i,k,t}$ is an error term with the usual properties.

It is important to highlight that two different price structures are identifiable in the database, according to the level of attribution for each painting. Therefore, each school has been split into two subschools, the first one including only those art objects for which the attribution to the artist is beyond any doubt; the second one including paintings of uncertain attribution. In this case, a different dummy variable for each level of attribution (studio of, circle of, after, manner of, school of) is included in the regression.

3 RESULTS

The main estimation results are reported in Tables 14.6 and 14.7. The following considerations can be highlighted:

- The regression for every subschool suggests that the auction price was strongly affected by the particular artist and by the level of attribution attached to each item. The effect is so strong that, as suggested above, there are in fact two different price structures, one for the paintings for which attribution to the author has been unequivocal beyond any doubt and the other for those paintings for which the level of attribution is classified ranking from the closest to the farthest to certainty.

Table 14.6 *Italian school, pre-Renaissance (pre-sixteenth century) and sixteenth century*

Variable	Pre-16th uncertain	Pre-16th certain	16th uncertain	16th certain
Constant	8.409***	9.327***	5.457***	8.493***
Christie's	base	base	base	base
Phillips	−0.613***	–	−0.357***	−0.457***
Circle of	−0.424***	–	−0.446***	–
After	−1.415***	–	−0.937***	–
Manner of	−1.161***	–	−0.907***	–
School of	−0.813***	–	−0.606***	–
Canvas	base	base	base	base
Panel	0.208**	0.735***	0.278***	0.215***
Paper	–	–	1.473***	–
Copper	–	–	–	0.809***
Other	0.639***	0.469***	1.654**	0.340***
Oil	base	base	base	base
Tempera	0.372***	–	–	–
Gilding	0.416**	–	–	–
Ink	–	–	−2.205**	–
Pen	–	–	−1.450**	–
Watercolour	–	–	−0.858**	–
Sanguigna	–	–	–	3.023***
Other	–	–	−1.756***	–
ln*dim*	0.121***	0.252***	0.259***	0.324***
lotpos	−0.965***	–	−0.682***	−0.839***
lot^2	–	–	0.429***	–
quota	0.192**	–	−0.129***	–
Religious	base	base	base	base
Decorative	–	−2.568***	–	–
Figure	–	−0.536**	0.259***	–
Allegory	–	–	0.371***	–
General scene	–	–	0.221***	–
Mythological	–	–	0.377***	0.266***
Portrait	–	–	0.169***	–
Animals	–	–	–	3.728***
January	base	base	base	base
February	−0.393***	−1.280***	−0.393***	−1.380***
March	–	−1.121***	–	−0.427***
April	–	−0.790***	–	−0.507***

Table 14.6 (continued)

Variable	Pre-16th uncertain	Pre-16th certain	16th uncertain	16th certain
May	−0.191***	−0.364**	−0.191***	−0.317***
June	–	−0.499**	–	−0.441***
July	–	−0.399**	−0.380**	−0.320***
September	−0.470***	–	−0.470***	–
October	−0.288***	−1.106***	−0.288***	−0.643***
November	−0.344	−0.483***	−0.344***	−0.629***
December	0.532***	−0.532***	–	−0.428***
Exhibition	–	0.3657***	0.305***	0.550***
Literature	0.400***	0.348***	0.337***	0.664***
Expertise	–	–	0.133***	–
Provenance	–	–	0.191***	0.342***
us_inf_r	0.380***	0.185**	–	0.218***
ami_r_us_r	–	–	–	0.252***
us_reer	–	–	–	−0.218***
R^2	0.84	0.77	0.64	0.68
F	4.81	5.65	8.92	6.36
N	884	549	2116	1651

Notes:
*** = coefficient significant at the 5% confidence level; ** = coefficient significant at the 10% confidence level.

- Such a model specification in which different subschools are run separately allows us to identify a more sophisticated structure of relations between variables than a pooled regression in which every available observation is included. As the impact of each variable on the auction price can be different according to the school and to the level of attribution considered, by running only one pooled regression these specific effects would be lost.
- The specification presented in this chapter offers satisfying predictions for a group of artistic schools. The regressions are always significant, as measured by the F-statistics, while the R^2 varies from 0.60 for the seventeenth century (uncertain) to 0.84 for the pre-sixteenth century (uncertain).
- The modeling of a macroeconomic framework does not lead to robust empirical results: estimated macroeconomic coefficients differ in sign and significance according to the school considered.[8] Therefore, further inquiry is needed to highlight this particular issue.

Table 14.7 *Italian school, seventeenth and eighteenth centuries*

Variable	17th uncertain	17th certain	18th uncertain	18th certain
Constant	4.956***	7.790***	7.056***	4.862***
Christie's	base	base	base	base
Phillips	−0.483***	−0.527***	−0.584***	−0.197***
Finarte	–	0.122***	–	0.238**
Studio of	−0.171***	–	−0.183***	–
Circle of	−0.385***	–	−0.343***	–
After	−0.913***	–	−1.014***	–
Manner of	−0.818***	–	−1.044***	–
School of	−0.588***	–	−0.646***	–
Canvas	base	base	base	base
Panel	–	0.269***	–	–
Paper	–	–	–	–
Copper	0.957***	0.799***	–	–
Stone	0.707***	0.639***	–	–
Board	–	−1.454***	–	–
Other	0.442***	0.551***	0.369***	–
Oil	base	base	base	base
Ink	–	–	–	−2.029***
Pen	–	−2.043***	–	–
Watercolour	0.728***	−0.926***	−0.749**	−0.997***
Sanguigna	–	–	–	−2.776***
Pastels	–	–	–	0.751***
Other	–	–	–	−0.776***
ln*dim*	0.371***	0.386***	0.306***	0.299***
lotpos	−0.541***	−0.475***	−0.116***	–
*lot*²	0.452***	0.321**	0.927***	–
quota	–	0.069**	–	–
Religious	base	base	base	base
Decorative	–	–	–	−1.366**
Figure	–	0.273***	–	0.273***
Allegory	0.284***	0.436***	–	0.411***
General scene	–	0.260***	0.339***	–
Mythological	0.269***	–	−0.195**	0.319***
Battle	0.493***	0.334***	–	0.379**
Portrait	0.194***	0.156***	–	0.173***
Landscape	0.127***	0.226***	0.361***	0.238***
Animals	0.335**	0.631***	–	0.433***
Still life	0.594***	0.748***	0.544***	0.603***
Study	−0.405***	–	–	–
View	–	–	0.910***	0.881***

Table 14.7 (continued)

Variable	17th uncertain	17th certain	18th uncertain	18th certain
January	base	base	base	base
February	−0.463**	−0.569***	−0.263***	−0.381***
March	−0.310***	−0.275***	–	−0.330***
April	−0.320***	−0.441***	–	−0.346***
May	−0.327***	−0.331***	–	−0.157***
June	−0.367***	−0.174***	–	−0.360***
July	−0.242**	−0.187***	–	−0.227***
September	−0.807***	−0.910***	–	−0.875***
October	−0.441***	−0.593***	–	−0.507***
November	−0.346***	−0.353***	–	−0.404***
December	−0.277***	−0.200***	–	−0.172***
Exhibition	0.379***	–	0.226***	–
Literature	0.322***	0.348***	0.450***	0.431***
Expertise	–	0.226***	–	–
Provenance	0.189***	0.145***	0.374***	0.219***
1991	–	−0.457**	–	0.742***
1992	0.247***	–	–	0.254***
1993	–	−0.346***	–	–
1995	–	−0.352***	–	0.205**
1997	–	0.437***	–	–
1998	–	0.588***	0.415***	–
1999	–	0.486***	–	–
us_inf_r	0.102***	0.741**	–	0.095***
ami_r_us_r	1.136**	–	–	–
us_ltr	0.605**	–	–	–
R^2	0.61	0.66	0.63	0.77
F	8.80	12.72	8.48	24.21
N	3124	4177	2042	3771

Notes:
*** = coefficient significant at the 5% confidence level; ** = coefficient significant at the 10% confidence level.

- Almost all the coefficients of auction houses are negative, and often significant, compared to Christie's; this is particularly true for Phillips.
- The month when the painting is sold affects the hammered price: the highest prices, *ceteris paribus*, are found in the month of January.
- Positive and significant coefficients are estimated for the dimension; more is paid for large paintings than for small ones, but the increase is less than proportional in absolute terms.

- There seems to be an order of sale effect, which is not linear. The majority of school regressions return negative and positive signs for the coefficients of lot position (*lotpos*) and the squared lot position (*lot*^{2}), respectively.
- With respect to the group of market variables, there is no significant effect stemming from a measure of liquidity of the artist, such as the percentage of items sold in auctions. Moreover, there is much heterogeneity in the significance of the coefficients of the artist indices, which are not reported in Tables 14.6 and 14.7 for space reasons. However, this group of variables allows the explanatory power of regression to be improved markedly, highlighting the importance of idiosyncratic effects due to single artists and due to their market performance, as measured by artist indices computed by Candela et al. (2005).
- The idiosyncratic characteristics of the considered paintings, subject, support and material, also affect the OM hammered price. In the OM data set, most of the works are oil painted on canvas. The effect played by other types of support or material is different. Copper and panel, for instance, have positive coefficients compared to canvas. Watercolours have negative coefficients compared to oil.
- With respect to the represented subject, the estimated coefficient signs change with the school; this simply attests the transformation of art over time. For example, in the case of OMs for the sixteenth century with uncertain attribution, and seventeenth and eighteenth centuries with certain attribution, almost all estimated coefficients are positive compared to the religious subject. On the contrary, for OMPs from the pre-sixteenth century school with certain attribution, we obtain negative estimated coefficients compared to the religious subject. For OMs from the pre-sixteenth century school with uncertain attribution, we do not obtain statistically significant coefficients.
- Another set of important variables includes those such as 'literature', 'exhibition', 'expertise' and 'provenance' which represent and capture the prestige, importance and popularity of the artist and the painting. The estimated coefficients are positive and statistically significant for almost all schools.

4 EMPIRICAL RESULTS AND POLICY PERSPECTIVE: OM 'BLACK MARKETS'

Understanding OM price formation is important in order to better understand the way art markets work and art collectors behave. Understanding the market mechanism is a useful exercise in order to design institutional rules and to derive important information that can affect the definition and enforcement of legal provisions.

The core of our empirical analysis is that OM auctioned prices are affected by two main sets of variables:

1. variables that signal the authenticity of the object, which significantly increase the price;
2. idiosyncratic characteristics that reflect the high heterogeneity in the database and that can catch the bidder's taste.

The used econometric model, however, only partially explains OM price formation; there is 'something missing'. Therefore, we suggest that the rules regulating national and international OM trade might affect price formation (and this legal effect is not captured by our estimated model).

If we consider the Italian case, for instance, the legislator sets a veto for the export of a particular OM (notified OM[9]). When a notified OM is sold at auction, an odd legal situation might arise: the buyer acquires the art work ownership, but not its possession, if the export veto applies. To be more concrete: if a German citizen buys a notified OM in Milan, he/she will become its owner. However, if the veto applies, the German citizen will never be able to export it from Italy. This ambiguous situation might discourage foreign purchasers from attending Italian auctions. More generally, a strict regulation might affect the trade and therefore the price formation of Old Masters.

In this study, the policy perspective analysis focuses on the formation and existence of an illegal OM market, for the understanding of which our empirical results might be helpful. OM illegal markets ('black markets') are markets where two particular types of demand and supply meet and interact. On the demand side, art collectors with a very price inelastic demand function, flexible budget constraint and well-defined preferences demand a product that is outside the legal market. The main driving force for OM purchasers in black markets is 'taste', the pleasure of owning an important work of art or the work of an important and well-considered painter. However, OM purchasers must be willing to consider the purchase as an investment.[10]

The existence of black markets is easily understandable when we look at our empirical results. Collectors have firm tastes and preferences. They buy what they like; the OM characteristics (whether a religious subject or a board support) and the well-known name of the painter (the regression for every subschool suggests a strong effect on the auction price played by the artist and by the level of attribution attached to each item) affect the OM purchase decision. If collectors cannot find what they are looking for in the legal market, they will search for the OM in illegal markets.

If the hedonic characteristics, the fame of the artist and the certainty of attribution mostly 'make the price', then potential buyers might be discouraged by the regulatory burden that affects the purchase and property of an Old Master. Therefore, they might be willing to buy in illegal markets because they want to own it for their own pleasure, disregarding the investment aspect.

On the supply side, the sellers are mostly private collectors. However, sellers can also be traders who directly commission the stealing of art masterpieces from museums, or churches, or indirectly find our about stolen art objects. Other private collectors[11] can be OM suppliers too.

Auction houses and fine-art dealers work as demand and supply 'matchmakers'. They own private information about private collectors' willingness to purchase and to sell and pass it on to the potential OM traders. Auction houses and fine-art dealers have a strong monetary incentive to trade in black markets, because they receive a payment that represents a percentage on the OM sale price. Given that, most of the time, seller and buyer never meet; the intermediaries can benefit from their informative advantages and extract a rent from the sale.

In economic terms, OM illegal markets are efficient institutions for several reasons. First, they allow a reduction in the transaction costs that occur when the transaction is concluded on legal markets. In Italy, for instance, the trading of fine-art objects is mostly regulated by law 1939/1089. This law was eventually modified and finally revised by law 1998/88. When fine-art objects are particularly relevant, the Italian government imposes a 'notification'. This means that private collectors are entitled to own fine-art objects, but they have to notify the competent authority and list the object in a particular register. When the owner of a notified object wants to sell it, he/she has to inform the authorities about this intention. The Italian government has a period (normally 60 days) to decide whether to purchase the fine-art object. This is an exclusive pre-emption right because the government has first right of purchase. When the fine-art object is sold in an auction house, the notification procedure can occur in the period between the pre-auction exhibition and the start of the auction. The legislation also regulates the export of notified fine-art objects. In general, this is not allowed. However, there are several exceptions (for instance, export is allowed in order to 'lend' the objects to other museums for temporary exhibitions). The various procedures provided for by the law all increase the transaction costs.

Second, black markets allow the sale contract parties to implement a win–win strategy. The buyers can purchase the Old Masters they want for their private collection and for which they are willing to pay. Sellers can offer their Old Master and sell it with fewer transaction costs involved.[12] Therefore, in an efficient perspective, black markets are transaction-cost minimizing institutions, for the implementation of which, procedures and art market regulation represent legal barriers.

Besides these benefits, the main cost associated with black markets is a loss for society; loss in terms of a decrease in cultural offerings. The illegal markets, in fact, allow that goods characterized by non-excludability and non-rivalry in consumption, become excludable and rival.

It is very difficult to suggest, design and implement policy solutions to OM black markets. One possible solution could be in opening up more markets to competitive dynamics. Whenever possible, the policy maker should design less onerous trading procedures or allow more Old Masters to enter the free market and, thereby, increase OM supply. By rendering the trade easier and (sometimes) feasible and the markets less regulated, the black-market agents could come out into the open, and the volume of transactions could increase. The latter effect might also decrease OM prices.

5 CONCLUDING REMARKS

In this chapter, we used the hedonic methodology to explain the market price structure of works of art. Using about 20,000 observations of Italian Old Masters auctioned worldwide in the 1990–2002 period, we grouped individual data into pre-sixteenth-, sixteenth-, seventeenth- and eighteenth-century schools. Those groups were further subdivided in order to distinguish the level of attribution. Hedonic regressions were run, in which the (logged) hammered price depended on a set of selected regressors, representing the painting's characteristics (subject, material, artist, support and dimension), macroeconomic variables and market information.

Empirical results for every school (and subschool) suggest that the auction price was strongly affected by the artist, the level of attribution attached to each item and other information related to the quality of the painting.

The chapter then discussed the empirical results in an institutional perspective. In particular, the policy perspective analysis focused on the formation and existence of illegal OM markets, whose existence might be better understood in the light of our empirical results. Collectors have clear tastes and preferences. They buy what they like; the OM characteristics (whether a religious subject or a board support) and the well-known name of the painter (the regression for every subschool suggests a strong effect on the auction price played by the artist and by the level of attribution attached to each item) do affect the OM purchase decision. If collectors cannot find what they are looking for in the legal market, they will search in illegal markets. We suggest that policy solutions to oppose OM black markets should be orientated towards opening up to competitive dynamics and weakening OM market regulation.

The way legal provisions affect OM hammered price in auctions and the link between prices and institutions are challenging and fascinating topics. Further research should focus on an empirical investigation into how national legislations, which forbid or constrain any Old Masters sold at auction from being exported outside the national territory, affect the hammered prices in auctions.

NOTES

1. For a survey, see Frey and Eichenberger (1995), Burton and Jacobsen (1999) and Ashenfelter and Graddy (2002).
2. For example, Ginsburgh and Jeanfils (1995) run hedonic regressions on a group of 82 Impressionist, Modern and Contemporary European painters and on a group of 139 contemporary American painters. Other well-known data sets, such as Reitlinger (1963 and 1970), suffer significant distortions. On this point, see Guerzoni (1995).
3. For more information, see www.gabrius.com.
4. In the database, only the items whose price is greater than $2,500, at 1990 prices are included. The database, moreover, includes auctions held by the major international auction houses in the last 12 years. This selection should enable us to reduce the weight of the marginal transactions that do not constitute the 'core' of the market.
5. An obvious problem arises concerning the imputation of the proper time- and country-specific rate to each observation, since no information about where the buyer's business is located. With respect to time, we consider contemporaneous variables although there can be short-run delays in the causal link between financial and art market indicators (see Chanel 1995). With respect to the marketplace, we use the US variables (Dow Jones, US CPI (Consumer Price Index) and long-term US interest rate).
6. The omission of relevant variables biases the estimated coefficients of the included variables, unless there is zero correlation between the two groups.
7. For this and other variables the problem of whether to include present or lagged variables arises. For yearly variables, the choice depends on the moment when the transaction takes place. Lagged values are to be considered if the transaction takes place at the beginning of the year, current values are to be considered if the transaction takes place around the end of the year. The latter is the assumption made in this chapter. For monthly variables, current values are to be preferred, since no intuitive lag-structure seems to arise.
8. The only robust result can be highlighted for the inflation rate. The estimated coefficients are almost always positive and statistically significant for all considered schools, suggesting that an increase in the US inflation rate causes an increase in the OM hammered price.
9. Notified Old Masters are pieces of art, which are owned by private collectors and which are subject to particular regulation. They are listed in a particular public register. The trade of such Old Masters is not regulated by free market dynamics but pursues particular procedures, set by the law. See further, note 11.

10. The United States represents 40 per cent of world demand for art masterpieces stolen in Italy (http://portal.unesco.org/culture).
11. Experience in Italy, for instance, has shown that criminal organizations are involved with the illicit trade. Antiquities leave Italy by road, perhaps in refrigerated trucks which are not carefully checked, or hidden in shipments of modern replicas. Some Swiss towns, for example Geneva, are important places of distribution where Italian antiquities enter the international market. Archaeologists inadvertently help the trade by acquiring works of uncertain provenance for museum and university collections and by authenticating pieces. In 1969, a department for the protection of cultural heritage was set up, and specialist *carabinieri* units are sent to areas at risk of looting. They patrol their relevant jurisdictions and monitor the market for stolen material. Over the years the *carabinieri* have recovered about 326,000 archaeological items from illegal excavations. Over the past five years 99,970 were recovered in Italy and 1,297 abroad. At the G8 Conference held in Bonn in 1999 it was decided to consider crimes against the cultural heritage alongside the traffic in drugs, human body parts and weapons, and money laundering (see www.mcdonald.cam.ac.uk).
12. Often OM sellers in black markets are paid cash. No transaction is registered, no bank is involved and, generally, the sale is not declared for fiscal purposes, thus avoiding tax obligations.

REFERENCES

Agnello, R.J. (2002), 'Returns and risk for art: findings from auctions of American paintings differentiated by artist, genre and quality', Mimeo, University of Delaware.

Agnello, R.J. and R. Pierce (1996), 'Financial returns, price determinants and genre effects in American art investment', *Journal of Cultural Economics*, **20** (4): 359–83.

Ashenfelter, O.C. and K. Graddy (2002), 'Art auctions: a survey of empirical studies', CEPR Discussion Paper, No. 3387, Centre for Economic Policy Research, London.

Baumol, W.J. (1986), 'Unnatural value: art as investment as a floating crop game', *American Economic Review*, **76**: 10–14.

Buelens, N. and V. Ginsburgh (1993), 'Revisiting Baumol's unnatural value, or art as investment as a floating crop game', *European Economic Review*, **37**: 1351–71.

Burton, B.J. and J.P. Jacobsen (1999), 'Measuring returns on investments in collectibles', *Journal of Economic Perspectives*, **13** (14): 193–212.

Candela, G., P. Figini and A. Scorcu (2002), 'Hedonic prices in the art market: a reassessment', paper presented at Association of Cultural Economics international conference, Rotterdam, 13–15 June.

Candela, G., P. Figini and A.E. Scorcu (2005), 'Price indices for artists – a proposal', *Journal of Cultural Economics*, forthcoming.

Candela, G. and A.E. Scorcu (1997), 'A price index for art market auctions', *Journal of Cultural Economics*, **21**: 175–96.

Candela, G. and A.E. Scorcu (2001), 'In search of stylized facts on art market prices: evidence from the secondary market for prints and drawings in Italy', *Journal of Cultural Economics*, **25**: 219–31.

Chanel, O. (1995), 'Is the art market behaviour predictable?', *European Economic Review*, **39**: 519–27.

Chanel, O., L.A. Gerard-Varet and V. Ginsburgh (1996), 'The relevance of hedonic price indices: the case of paintings', *Journal of Cultural Economics*, **20** (1): 1–24.

Coase, R. (1937), 'The nature of the firm', *Economica*, **4**, November: 386–405.
Court, L. (1941), 'Entrepreneurial and consumer demand theories for commodities spectra', *Econometrica*, **9**: 135–62 and 241–97.
Frey, B.S. and R. Eichenberger (1995), 'On the rate of return in the art market: survey and evaluation', *European Economic Review*, **39**: 528–37.
Frey, B.S. and W.W. Pommerehne (1989), *Muses and Markets: Explorations in the Economics of the Arts*, Oxford: Basil Blackwell.
Ginsburgh, V. and P. Jeanfils (1995), 'Long-term comovements in international market for paintings', *European Economic Review*, **39**: 538–48.
Griliches, Z. (1971), *Price Indexes and Quality Changes: Studies in New Methods of Measurement*, Cambridge: Cambridge University Press.
Guerzoni, G. (1995), 'Reflections on historical series of art prices. Reitlinger's data revised', *Journal of Cultural Economics*, **19**: 251–60.
Lancaster, K. (1971), *Consumer Demand: A New Approach*, New York: Columbia University Press.
Locatelli-Bley, M. and R. Zanola (1999), 'Investment in painting: a short-run price index', *Journal of Cultural Economics*, **23** (3), 209–19.
Mei, J. and M. Moses (2003), 'Art as investment and the underperformance of masterpieces: evidence from 1875–2002', *American Economic Review*, **92**: 1656–68.
Pesando, J.E. and P.M. Shum (1999), 'The returns to Picasso's prints and to traditional financial assets, 1977 to 1996', *Journal of Cultural Economics*, **23**: 182–92.
Reitlinger, G. (1963), *The Economics of Taste, Vol. I: The Rise and Fall of the Picture Market, 1760–1963*, New York: Holt, Rinehart & Winston.
Reitlinger, G. (1970), *The Economics of Taste, Vol. III: The Art Market in the 1960s*, New York: Holt, Rinehart & Winston.

15. Living it off or living it down: the economics of disinvestments
Jürgen Backhaus

1 DESCRIBING THE PHENOMENON

Are costs decreasing with scale? And if the costs do not give, let us increase the scale.

In 1989, shortly before the Berlin wall came down, heavy equipment stood ready to demolish the Andreas quarter in Erfurt, the historic centre of the free state of Thuringia. Earlier, an entire baroque quarter had been erased, making room for a set of pre-assembled skyscraper units, of which the Erfurt production unit was proud, as their purpose in the COMECON production effort was to erect as many living quarters in all the comrade socialist countries as possible. Hence, engineering skills combined the gravel of Thuringia and other necessary ingredients, and transported and reconstructed the resulting units throughout the former COMECON empire. We can see exactly the same units in Bucharest, Kiev and many points east and the prototypes in Erfurt, of course. In Erfurt, after the razing of the historic quarters and the erection of those towers, poor air circulation prevented the smoke from the many brown coal-heated households from leaving the valley, creating a highly polluted atmosphere. It is here where my tale begins.

1.1 A Point of Theory

After the enormous effort that had gone into organizing an unprepared for war after 1914, those who had organized it (not those who fought it) thought in terms of economies of scale. In the process it was discovered that medium-sized companies could not deliver the enormous quantities of goods now required. However, large-scale production not only allowed for the necessary output, but also could produce it at lower cost – giving rise to the miracle of decreasing costs to scale. This experience, in the aftermath of the war, led to the notion in the commission on socialization that a concentration of industry resulting in a further reduction in costs due to economies of scale might be the answer to the burden of reparations. This notion, at the time, was widely held, but survived primarily in communist economic thinking. Obviously, a country cartelizing its major industry is doomed to suffer from a lack of technical and technological progress. However, once such an idea has been enshrined in courses of indoctrination, many city managers can be trained pursue it too. Let us explain the issue with a simple example.

1.2 A Simple Example

Consider one thousand families living in well-maintained quarters, some of which may nevertheless still bear the signs of war damage or long neglect (due to a shortage of building materials or for other reasons). Consider now the decision opportunity of a city planner who wants to provide every citizen with heat. Historically, heat has been provided from stoves, fuelled with coal that has to be transported to individual homes. I have observed the practice of large amounts of coal being dumped on the wayside next to a particular house at a particular (perhaps inopportune) time and the householders hurrying to shovel it in, as the resource was scarce and difficult to protect from thievery.

Now, if you believe in economies of scale and production, would there not be a point in centralizing the heating system? Easy enough, you can centralize the heating in new buildings. So you create a heating source near to a railroad link, where the coal can be unloaded in a secure area, and the heat can be dispersed from there. Now that the heating source is there, given the amount of coal that is available, allocated per person in the community, the cheapest way to deliver the heat from this coal is to centralize the consumption. How can that be accomplished?

1.3 An Approach at Accomplishment

Consider a city which dates back to 752, which has its first highpoint in the Middle Ages and then another one during the Napoleonic wars. It consists of a historical architectural landscape unscathed by war. As a consequence of relocation, many citizens are sheltered in overcrowded homes. As a consequence of the raids after 1945, either the owners were killed or they left, and the question of ownership hangs in the air, with no maintenance ensuing. In due course, the city and the adjacent district find their new role in the COMECON and are given the task of producing housing for the entire communist economic community. Thuringian gravel and engineering skills allow for the production of prototypes that can be put on railroad cars and shipped to wherever the destination may be. The prototypes have to be erected in the town, so as to be inspected. Here we have a large number of dwellers in historic downtown buildings, who demand coal to heat their dwellings. Would it not be easier to connect them to a central heating device, thus burning the coal more efficiently, and remove them from their historic dwellings?

This city is full of historic buildings and more churches than anyone can count. There can be no doubt that the same number of citizens can be heated more efficiently in newly built houses a little way from the centre. In this sense, planning economic theory prevailed. Heating works were established at the city limits, and heating was provided at those points. In a pre-1989 scenario, the issue is simple. New living quarters are provided and can be furnished with lower energy costs due to economies of scale. However, the old people continued to demand their ration of coal for their inefficient heating devices in their inefficient (medieval) homes. What could be done? The obvious answer for the planners was to erase the entire district of medieval and historic houses and thereby force the inhabitants into new prototype high-rise housing, of which Erfurt and its industry was proud. Tram links were established and happy inaugurations were celebrated. Did you miss the point of the theory? Here it is. By destroying the historic dwellings the demand for the new dwelling is pushed outwards.

How did the push come about, however? It came about first, by creating a housing shortage and a limit on rents. This allows for political discretion. Hence, it was possible to allow the available living space to be allocated among those favoured by the decision makers. Since a more widespread system was intended, you would reach deeper into the bag of tricks. First, you move less-favoured applicants into the upper level of traditional large buildings. This is with the understanding that roofs will not be maintained because the policy is of 'down-living' (*ab- oder runterwohnen*). Clearly, after the roof begins to leak too badly, people will want to move down. At some point, the building becomes uninhabitable, and can therefore be demolished. This allows the demand to be moved forward for public housing in public energy consumption. From the point of view of the energy planner it makes plenty of sense, since inefficient users, that is, those outside the system, will join the more efficient system that is characterized by economies of scale. In the process it would make sense to demolish the entire historic city and provide energy to the prototype high-rise buildings of which the Erfurt building industry can actually be proud, even today.

Living it down is an interesting concept.

2 ANALYSIS

In the context of a modern market economy, the concept of real-estate use in terms of living it down from the top floor to the bottom in order to ultimately vacate a dwelling is totally inexplicable. Even for a planned economy, the obvious waste involved is surprising. For its explanation, the analysis requires several mutually reinforcing elements.

The first element is the dilution of property rights in real estate. Since 1945, the original owners have gradually lost their property rights in a process of outright expropriation and rent control. The rental income would not be sufficient for the upkeep of the properties and property taxes, which led many property owners to abandon the property, if they did not use it themselves. Only in the case of own use was there an incentive to maintain the property, and the phenomenon of living it down cannot be observed as a rule.

The dilution of property rights involved all three aspects, the use, the fruit of the use, and the abuse. Use was regulated by rental administration, tenants were selected by a city agency, and inputs and outputs were thoroughly controlled, since maintenance and repairs required the administrative allocation of material and labour, an allocation accomplished through an administrative process. Through the system of strict rent controls, fruits from the property could not be enjoyed. The only alternative left was the right to abuse in the most literal sense: to abandon the building or let it decay.

At the same time, the state had no effective system of using the abandoned property in an efficient way. Even if state entities held the title to the property, Marxist economic theory did not yield shadow prices with which to determine an optimal allocation of resources effectively. The value of the site of a particular piece of property is typically determined through the land rent. Marxist economic theory contained only a physical notion of land rent, land rent I and land rent II, the only difference being the agricultural melioration of a particular piece of land (type II), while the value of the site was not assessed at all.[1]

In addition, Marxist economic theory as taught and practised in the GDR had no concept of opportunity costs whatsoever. The value of the travelling time between the home and the place of work could not show up in any economically relevant decision. Apartments were allocated according to objectivized criteria (political reliability, number of children and so on) and in terms of plan fulfilment. In order to accomplish plan fulfilment measured in heatable residential cubic metres, large conglomerates of prefabricated concrete high risers were a technically efficient solution, if technical efficiency depended on the planning objective just described.

Finally, let us look at the incentives faced by the manager of the socialist housing firm applying an economic theory that lacks property, land rent and opportunity costs. This manager maximizes his/her leverage by maximizing the number of residents under his/her control subject to the budget constraint imposed by the plan. It is readily apparent that property management in terms of this maximization objective is easier in modern high-rise compact schematic constructions than the management of people living in many small buildings from many different centuries. When property has no shadow price, land rents do not figure in the plan, and opportunity costs are not assessed in the planning process, destroying the technically less-efficient property holding becomes an attractive option. Plan-fulfilment figures are in terms of newly completed entities uncorrected for those neglected and lost. In this sense, destroying housing stock by negligence is an attractive strategy to the socialist housing manager.

3 CONCLUSION

In this short chapter, the remarkable phenomenon of real property destruction under German state socialism is described and analysed. Part I offers a description of the phenomenon of living down real estate, and I try to capture the sense of astonishment with which the uninitiated visitor reacts when first confronted with it. Part II contains the analysis. The economic analysis of property rights, land rents and opportunity costs are all needed in order to render an explanation of the phenomenon.

NOTE

1. The German term is *Differentialrente*. See Willy Ehlert (ed.), *Lexikon der Wirtschaft: Finanzen*, [*Encyclopedia of Economics: Finances*], Berlin: Verlag Die Wirtschaft, 1986, p. 199.

Index

Aaken, A. van 264
Abadie, A. 147
accessibility of judicial system
  and democracy 272–3
  and judicial independence 251–2
accountability, judicial 271–3
accounting regulation 196
Ackerman, B. 8, 269–70
Act of Creation, The 113
Address to the Electors of Bristol 75
adjudication function of the state
  79–80, 82–5
administration function of the state
  79–80, 82–5
administrations, political role 11–13
administrative decisions, judicial
  control 310–29
Adorno, T. 340
agencies, separation of 80–85
agency costs of government
  impact of cyberspace 71
  and separation of agencies 84
aggregate evaluation, terrorism policies
  155–62
Aghion, P. 274
Agreement on Trade-Related Aspects
  of Intellectual Property Rights
  (TRIPS) 351
Akerlof, G.A. 39, 41
Aldy, J.E. 166
Allen, F. 208, 211
Altbach, P.G. 354
Animal Farm 124
Antill, J. 350, 351
antitrust rules
  banking 14, 358–76
  and switching costs 368–75
appeals process as separation device
  312–14
appointment of judges, effect on court
  independence 248–50
arbitrariness of the rights 304

Arrow, K.J. 37
art market 15, 381–96
  black market 393–5
  structure 382–3
Ash, T.G. 122, 125, 126, 130–31, 138
Austrian economics, political opinion
  formation 43–7
authors and copyright 341–3
averting behaviour approach, terrorism
  measurement 149–52
Azfar, O. 189, 192, 200, 202, 204, 210,
  213

banking
  development measurement 191
  government ownership and contract
    enforcement 210
  markets 362
  regulation and competition 14,
    358–76
Barber, B.R. 93–4
Barnes, J. 128
Barzel, Y. 91
Baumol, W.J. 381
Bayesian equilibria, judicial
  administrative decisions 318–20
Bayley, J. 131
Beck, T. 187–8, 197, 198, 199, 200, 203,
  209, 210, 211
Benn, A.W. 126
Bentham, J. 61
Berkowitz, D. 199
Berrebi, C. 173
Besen, S.M. 354
bifurcated man 25, 26
Birrell, A. 338
black market, old master paintings
  393–5
Blinder, A. 266
Blomquist, G.C. 149, 162
Boulding, K.E. 44, 46
bounded political rationality 37–43

Bradon, T. 140
Brandeis, Justice 374
Brennan, G. 35, 41, 89
Buchanan, J. 35, 43, 70, 73
Burke, E. 75
Burmese Days 124–5, 130
Burnham, J. 127

Calculus of Consent 73
Calderón, C. 188, 209, 212
Calley, J. 100
Canal affair, France 280
Canon law 298
Canoy, M. 363
Caplan, B. 41
Captive Mind, The 124
car insurance switching costs 374–5
Carson, R.T. 153
casualty number, as measurement of terrorism 144–6
Central and Eastern European countries, judicial independence 260–61
central government, impact of cyberspace 69–75
checks and balances approach, separation of powers 87–8
China, communication systems 109–10
  effect of geography 112
Cho, I.K. 133, 136, 140
Christie, A. 351
citizen-voter 25
citizens, referendum voting 164–5
civic virtue 76
Claessens, S. 200, 205, 209, 212
club good, law enforcement 288–9
Coase, R. 65, 336
cognitive components, public opinion 43–4
cognitive dissonance theory 39
Cold War and George Orwell 125–7
Coles, P. 350, 351
collective decision-making, impact of cyberspace 68–9, 70–75
  Buchanan-Tullock model 73–4
  costs 68, 73–4
commercial laws and enforcement 200–201
communication, influence on innovation 102, 113–18

communication systems, Eurasia 105, 109–12
  impact of geography 111–12
compensating surplus 173
competition
  banking sector 358–76
  car insurance 374–5
  effect of copyright 345–7
  and law enforcement 287–8
Congleton, R.D. 345
Congress of Cultural Freedom 128–9
consensual principle 63
constitution of the state 67–8
contingent valuation surveys, terrorism reduction 152–5
Cook, P.J. 154
cooperation and innovation 117–18
Cooter 294
copyright 13–14, 335–52
  and anti-competitive behaviour 344
  duration 349–50
  interest group lobbying 350–51
  and the market 343–7
  scope 348–9
  structure 347–50
costs
  collective decision-making and cyberspace 68, 73–5
  exit, terrorism avoidance 149–50
  judicial law enforcement 286
  representative government, impact of cyberspace 71
  and separation of agencies 84
  and separation of powers 88–9
creation of the state 65–7
  and cyberspace 66–7
creative activities, effect of market 340–41
credit market
  impact of legal rules 202–203, 205–206
  size 191, 202–203, 216–17
creditor protection 194–5, 201
Cultural Freedom, Congress of 128–9
Culture and Society 127
customer knowledge, switching costs 372
cyberspace
  and collective decision-making 68–9, 70–73, 74–5, 88–9

and creation of the state 66–7
and economic theory of the state 58, 66–95
and exclusion 66
and government roles 69–70
and individuals in society 92–4
and republican view of government 76–8
and representative government 70–73
and separation of powers 80, 81–2, 83–5, 86–7, 88–90
and territorial boundaries 66–7, 68, 91–2

Dahlquist, M. 198, 208
Daily Telegraph 137
David, P. 337
Davison, P. 125
de facto measure for judicial independence 253, 255–64
de jure indicator for judicial independence 247–53, 254–5, 260–64
Debré, M. 279
debt, impact of legal rules 202–203
Deery, P. 139
demand
 restricting competition 368–73
 stimulating competition 366–8
democracy
 and cyberspace 70–71
 as hierarchy of norms 271–2
 and information 2–7
 and judicial power 269–81
 legal constraints 7–13
 theories 22–49
democratic accountability, judiciary 271–3
democratic interactions model, judicial system 273–80
Dewatripoint, M. 310
Diamond, J. 101, 112
Dickens, W.T. 39
direct debits, switching costs 371–2
disinvestment 399–403
Djankov, S. 198
doubts and truth-telling, model 131–8
Downs, A. 21, 26–36, 37–8
 and median voter model 26–36

and political leadership 29
and rational ignorance 31–6
dualism 8, 270
 French legal system 278–9, 295–300
duration of copyright 349–50
dynamic law and finance approach, financial development 187–8

earnings management
 as financial system measurement 193–4
 impact of legal rules 207–208
econometric estimates, judicial independence 263–4
economic analysis and the theory of the state 59–60
economic growth
 and financial institutions 230–34
 and legal institutions 212–15
 impact of legal rules 185–237
 measurement 190
economic impact, terrorism 146–8
economic theory of the state 60–95
 and cyberspace 66–95
 normative sources 60–64
economies of scale, and disinvestment 399–403
Economist Intelligence Unit (EIU) data and judicial independence 261
efficiency of legal system, and enforcement 284–9
embedding effect, contingent valuation 153
employee protection measurement 197
Enders, W, 145
enforcement *see* law enforcement
equity of legal system, role of enforcement 289–91
equity finance, impact of law enforcement 210–11
equity market
 impact of legal rules 203–204, 206–209
 size 191–2, 203–204
Erfurt, property destruction 399–401
Ergungor, O.E. 202, 203, 210
Eurasia
 communication systems 105, 109–12
 per capita income 100, 103–104

Europe
  communication systems 110–11, 112
  innovation 101, 104, 106–108
European Union
  bank competition policy 363–4
  bank merger regulation 365–6
  judicial independence 260–61
evaluative components, public opinion 43–4
exchange-value, cultural products 338–40
exclusion and cyberspace 66
external costs, collective decision-making 73–4
extra-critical courts, Bayesian equilibrium 319–20

Farber, D. 96
Federalist Papers 246
Feld, L. 263
Festinger, L. 39
financial laws and legal origin 187
financial markets
  and economic growth 212–13
  indices 190–94
  and legal origin 209
  and legal rule enforcement 209–12, 214–15
Flores, A.A. 196
Foot, M. 126
foreign investment, impact of terrorism 147
foundation of the state 67–9
Foyer, J. 280
France
  administrative justice system 278–80
  bank merger regulation 365
  republican dualism 295–300
  terrorism and life satisfaction 159–62, 168–70
Freedom House data and judicial independence 261
Frey, B.S. 36, 68, 159
Frickey, P. 96

Gabrius art object data base 383–5
Gardeazabal, J. 147
Garretsen, H. 188, 202, 213
Geertz, C. 353

General Agreement on Tariffs and Trade (GATT) intellectual property rights 351
geography
  influence on communication 105, 109–12
  influence on innovation 101–102
Germany, bank merger regulation 365
Goldstein, P. 343
government expenditure on terrorism avoidance 151
Greece, impact of terrorism on investment 147
Griffiths, P. 354
Guiso, L. 188, 211
Gwartney, J. 267

Habermas, J. 306
Hamilton, A. 246, 265–6
Hamlin, A. 89
Hanemann, W.M. 173
happiness functions, and terrorism policy 157–62
Hardin, R. 38
Harsanyi, J.C. 62
Hausman, J.A. 153
Hayek, F.A. von 44, 243, 244, 294
hedonic market approach
  art market pricing 386–7
  terrorism measurement 148–9
Heilbronner, R.L. 21
Henisz, W. 267
Heritage/*Wall Street Journal* index and judicial independence 261–2
Hirschman, A.O. 38
Hitchens, C. 122, 124, 125, 126, 127, 130
Hobbes, T. 59, 63–4, 65
Holcombe, R.G. 26, 270
Holler, M.J. 102
Holmes, K.R. 197
Holmström, B. 311
Homage to Catalonia 131
Horkheimer, M. 340
Horowitz, J.K. 173
Hovenkamp, H. 374

ICRG *see* International Country Risk Guide
ideas and externalities 338–40

illegal market, old master paintings 393–5
impact studies of terrorism 146–8
incentive
  and copyright 348
  and judicial review of administrative decisions 322–8
  and value, intellectual property 337–41
income
  Eurasia 100, 103–104
  judges, effect on judicial independence 250
independence approach to separation of powers 87–8
independent judiciary *see* judiciary, independence
India, communication systems 105, 109
  effect of geography 111–12
individuals and society, impact of cyberspace 92–4
informal institutions and legal enforcement 188
information
  for creditors, impact of legal rules 205–206
  and democracy 2–7
  transmission *see* communication
Innis, H.A. 102
innovation 100–104, 106–109, 113–18
  and communication system 113–17
  and cooperation 117–18
  game theory 113–18
  influence of geography 101–102
  influence of institutions 101, 102
institutions
  impact on economic development 185–215
  impact on innovation 101, 102
intellectual property, incentives and value 337–41
intellectual property right *see* copyright
interest groups
  and copyright lobbying 350–51
  and cyberspace 71–2
internal costs, collective decision-making 73–4
International Country Risk Guide (ICRG)
  and economic growth 242
  and judicial independence 261
interpretation of legal system 291–5
intuitive criterion, signalling game 136–7
IPOs as measure of equity market 193, 206
irrational behaviour in voting 40–43
issue creation and political entrepreneurs 46–7
Italy
  bank merger regulation 365–6
  black market, art objects 397
  fine-art trading regulation 394
  and terrorism legislation 163

Jappelli, T. 202, 203, 205
Jaspers, K. 123
Johnson, S. 201, 208, 212
Jones, E.L. 101
Josselin, J.-M. 101
judiciary
  accountability 271–3
  and administrative decisions 12, 310–29
  as creative producer 304–306
  and democracy 7–13, 269–81
  independence 9–10, 198, 242–64
  and legal interpretation 291–5
  and republican order 298–9
  role 81, 283–4, 301–307
  tenure, and independence 250, 255
judicial regulation 283–307
  France 11–12, 295–300
  standard model 283–95
judicial review 87, 310–29
judicial system
  and financial markets 209–11
  law enforcement role 284–91
  law interpretation role 291–5

Kahneman, D. 153
Kahnemann, D. 42
Kant, I. 244
Keefer, P. 242
Kelsen, H. 271
King, R.G. 191
Kirestein, R. 311
Kirwan, C. 129
Klapper, L. 205, 209

Klemperer, P. 369
Kliemt, H. 40
Klor, E.F. 173
Knack, S. 242
Knetsch, J.L. 153
Koestler, A. 113, 127–9
Kohlberg, E. 137
Kreps, D. 133, 136, 140
Kuhn, T. 58
Kuran, T. 38, 39, 44, 46, 50
Kuznets, S. 118

La Porta, R. 187, 188, 191, 192, 193, 194, 195, 196–7, 198, 199, 202, 203, 205, 206, 209–10
labour legislation, impact on ownership 208
Lal, D. 101
Landes, D.S. 101
language, Eurasia 105, 109–12
  effect of geography 111–12
Lashmar, P. 126, 129, 130
Lasky, M. 129
law and economics analysis, copyright 336–7
law enforcement, judicial system 284–91
  and financial system 209–12, 214–15
  quality 197–8
laws, and legal origin 199–200
legal constraint, democracy 7–13
legal institutions
  and economic growth 212–3, 214–15
  and financial markets 202–12
legal interpretation 291–5
legal origin 196–7, 199–200
  and financial laws 187
legal rules
  and credit market size 202–203
  and economic growth 185–237
  enforcement mechanisms 194–8
  and financial markets 211–12, 214–15
legislation *see* regulation
Leuz, C. 193, 196, 207
Leviathan 59, 65
Levine, R. 187, 188, 190, 191–2, 193, 194, 197, 199, 202, 203, 204, 205, 206, 212–13

liberal paradigm 58, 95
life satisfaction, impact of terrorist activity 157–62
litigants, seizure strategy 272–3, 277–8
Lochak, D. 280
lock-ins 367
Locke, J. 64, 65
Lomasky, L.E. 41
Lopez-de-Silanes, F. 197, 198, 205
Lowell, A.L. 44
Ludwig, J. 154
Luhmann, N. 46

Maddison, A. 100, 118
Madison, J. 266
majority rule 73–5
Marciano, A. 101, 140
market failures and creation of the state 65–6
market liquidity as measure of stock market 206
market logic and republican logic 299–300
market mobilized capital 192
  and legal rules 204
market standards and judicial regulation 303–304
market structure, effect of copyright 344–7
Mars mapping project 72
Matheson, T. 189, 192, 202, 204, 210, 213
maximisation of utility 62
Mayers, J. 131
McCarthy, M. 132
McNeill, W.H. 101
measuring terrorism 142–71
median voter model 26–36
merger and acquisitions, banks 364–6
Mertens, J.-F. 137
Messick, R. 243
Middle East, communication systems 105
  effect of geography 111
Miller, M. 192
Milosz, C. 124
Mitchell, W.C. 26, 48
model of bounded rationality 42
model of collective decision-making 73–4

model of democratic interactions,
    judicial system 273–80
Modigliani, F. 192
Mokyr, J. 102
monist democracies 7–8, 270
monopoly of state, and separation of
    agencies 82–3
Montesquieu, C.L. de 67, 265
Montgomery, R. 129
Moro, A. 163
Mueller, D.C. 27, 30, 69, 84
Mueller, J.E. 157
My 138–9
Myth of Democratic Failure 21

Nabokov, N. 129
NASA, Mars mapping project 72
Nenova, T. 193, 195, 207
neoclassical economics of democracy 23
Netanel, N.W. 95
Newcomen, T. 100
Nineteen Eighty-Four 123–4, 130,
    138–9
normative principles and theory of the
    state 59–64

Old Master paintings, price formation
    381–96
Oliver, J. 126, 127, 128, 129, 130
opinion falsification and public
    opinion 44–6
Ormrod, R. 9–10
Orwell, G. 5, 121–39
    the List 125–7, 129–30, 132–8
*Orwell: Wintry Conscience of a
    Generation* 131
ownership and copyright 341–3
ownership concentration 193
    impact of legal rules 206–208

Pagano, M. 202, 203, 205
paintings, price formation 381–96
perfectly separating appeals process
    313–14
Pistor, K. 194, 195, 198, 202, 209–10
political behaviour *see* voters
political economy, Schumpeterian
    36–47
political entrepreneurs and issue
    creation 46–7

political irrationality 25–6, 40–43
political leadership and spatial voting
    24–5, 26–31
political preference formation 44–7
political stability and population
    happiness 157–8
Politics and the English Language 131
Pomeranz, K. 101
positivist theory of the state 60–61
Posner, R 62
Powell, A. 131
preference formation
    impact of cyberspace 93–4
    and public opinion 44–6
prestige of judges, effect on judicial
    independence 250
price formation, paintings 381–96
Prisching, M. 26
private benefits of control 207–208
productive function of the state 69,
    79–82
    and cyberspace 80, 81–2
propaganda
    influence on referenda 164–5
    and truth 129–31
property rights dilution, East Germany
    402–403
protection by commercial laws 200
protective function of the state 69,
    79–82
    and cyberspace 80, 81–2
public choice theory and the state 59,
    62–3
public expenditure, terrorism
    prevention 151
public good, law enforcement 288–9
public opinion formation 43–7
public opinion makers, attacks on
    Orwell 132–8
pure separation of powers 87–8

qualitative components, public opinion
    43–4

Rajan, R. 186
rally-round-the-flag effect 157
rational behaviour
    effect of copyright 344–5
    voting 40–43
rational ignorance 31–6

Rawls, J. 64
referenda, terrorism policy 162–5
regulation
   and competition, banking 361–6
   copyright *see* copyright
   fine-art trading, Italy 394
   representative government, impact of cyberspace 70–73
Republic.com 77
republican order, France 295–300
republican view of central government 75–9
retail banking market 362
Reynolds, T.H. 196
rights, definition of, role of judiciary 301–302
risk assessment and terrorism 151
Rodrik, D. 185, 187
Roe, M.J. 197, 208
Rossi, S. 200–201, 211
Rousseau, J.-J. 16, 63, 64
rule formulation through judicial interpretation 294–5
rule of law
   impact on economic growth 185–215
   and judiciary 9–11
   and republican order 298–9

salary, judges', effect on judicial independence 250
Salzberger, E. 279
Samjatin, J.I. 138
Samuels, W.J. 308
Samuelson, P. 15
Sandler, T. 145
Saunders, F.S. 122, 126
Schumpeter, J.A. 2–3, 21–49
scope of copyright 348–9
security expenditures, avoiding terrorism 150
seizure rules
   as democratic control 272–3
   and judicial behaviour 277–8
semiological reduction, and copyright 340
separation of agencies 80–85
separation effects, appeals process 312–22
separation of functions 79–80
separation of persons 85–7

separation of powers 79–90
Shackle, G.L.S. 33
shareholder protection 195–6, 201
Shavell, S. 310, 312–14
Shklar, J. 243
Shleifer, A. 197, 198, 205
Simon, H.A. 42
Smith, A. 61
Smolka, P. (Smollett) 126
social choice theory 62–3
social contract theories 61
social welfare effects, judicial review 311–29
Song, W. 208, 211
Spain, impact of terrorism 146, 147
spatial voting models and political leadership 24–5, 26–31
specialization and decision-making, impact of cyberspace 72
Spiller, M. 310
Splichal, S. 43
stability, banking sector 358–60
start-up costs, banking 372
state
   creation of 65–9
   roles of 69–70, 79–80
Steinbeck, J. 131
Stephen, F. 201, 202, 204, 211–12, 213
Stephenson, M. 243
stock market value
   measurement 193
   and shareholder protection 208
strategic behaviours and judicial discretion 275–7
Strowel, A. 353–4
Sunstein, C. 46, 77–8, 96
switching costs 368–75
   banking 371–3, 374–5
   impact on competition 369–71

Talley, E. 310
Tanenhaus, S. 127
tenure of judges, and judicial independence 250, 255
territorial boundaries, transcended by cyberspace 66–7, 68, 91–2
terrorism, measuring 142–71
Thisse, J.-F 102
Tirole, J. 274, 310
Titanic model of entitlements 303–304

Tollison, R.D. 345
tourism, impact of terrorism 146–7
transaction costs reduction
　cyberspace 66
　through judicial interpretation 293–4
transplant effect and law enforcement 199
TRIPS (Agreement on Trade-Related Aspects of Intellectual Property Rights) 351
truth and propaganda 129–31
truth-telling model 131–8
Tullock, G. 70, 73
Tversky, A. 42

Udehn, L. 21
United Kingdom, bank merger regulation 365
Ulen 294
unanimity principle 63
unequal law enforcement
　and efficiency 285–6
　and equity 290–91
United States, bank competition policy 363
use-value, cultural products 338–40
utilitarianism 61–2, 96
utility-maximisation principle 62

value, intellectual property 337–41
van Hemmen, S. 201, 202, 204, 211–12, 213

Vanberg, V. 43
venture capital, and investor protection 208–209
Viscusi, W.K. 151, 153–4, 166
Voigt, S. 263
Volpin, P. 200–201, 211
vote and popularity functions, and terrorism policy 155–7
voters
　behaviour 26–43
　irrationality 25–6, 40–43
　non-instrumentalistic behaviour 38–41
　rational ignorance 31–6
　rationality 36–8
　and referenda 164–5
voting, impact of cyberspace 70–71

Wealth of Nations 61
Weitzman, M. 113
Williams, R. 127
Williamson, O.E. 293
willingness to accept (WTA) terrorism risk 154
willingness to pay (WTP), terrorism reduction 153–4
wisdom, judicial 12
Wittman, D.A. 21

Zeckhauser, R.J. 151, 153–4
Zingales, L. 186